New Orleans

FOR

DUMMIES®

3RD EDITION

by Julia Kamysz Lane

WILEY

Wiley Publishing, Inc.

New Orleans For Dummies®, 3rd Edition

Published by
Wiley Publishing, Inc.
111 River St.
Hoboken, NJ 07030-5774
www.wiley.com

WILEY

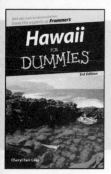
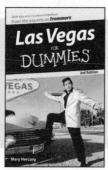

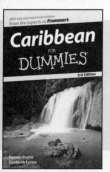
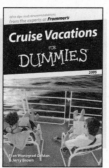

About the Author

Julia Kamysz Lane is a freelance writer and book reviewer whose work has appeared in numerous newspapers and magazines. She also is an editorial consultant at LSU Eye Center. She lives in a 1940s bungalow in Old Lakeview with three dogs, three cats, and one very tolerant husband.

Dedication

This book is dedicated to my parents, Rich and Ellen Kamysz, for supporting my decision at 17 to move 900 miles away to live and study in New Orleans.

Author's Acknowledgments

I would first and foremost like to thank my editor, Caroline Sieg, for her enthusiasm, guidance, and patience and project editor Tim Gallan for coordinating the production of this book. Extra-special thanks should also go to media services coordinator Christine Decuir, and public affairs intern Andrea Polaski, both of the New Orleans Metropolitan Convention and Visitors Bureau, for their invaluable assistance. Special thanks to my friends and colleagues at LSU Eye Center, especially Claude Burgoyne, M.D., and Ed Langlow, M.D., for their support and understanding as the deadline loomed large. I must also thank my former boss and mentor, Clancy Dubos, for hiring me as a *Gambit Weekly* staff writer years ago, which gave me unique insight into the city and local customs.

And grateful thanks to the following for factual and emotional support during the revision of this book: Victoria Cooke, for words of encouragement when I most needed them; Bonnie Suckow, for her compassion and optimism; Golden Richard, for answering some peculiar questions; Paula Gebhardt, for a shared love of books and good writing; Crawford Downs, for being a Mac evangelist (congrats to you and Georgia on baby James!); my father- and mother-in-law Rich and Barb Lane, for taking pride in my work; my sister-in-law Michelle Cochran (congrats to you and Bob on Bobby Jr.!), for reaching out across many miles; and my brother Marty Kamysz (congrats to you and Renee on baby Lauren!), for making me smile and keeping me on my toes.

Lastly, I am greatly indebted to my husband, Brian Lane, who has proven time and time again that marrying him was the smartest thing I have ever done.

Publisher's Acknowledgments

We're proud of this book; please send us your comments through our Dummies online registration form located at www.dummies.com/register/.

Some of the people who helped bring this book to market include the following:

Editorial

Editors: Caroline Sieg, Tim Gallan

Copy Editor: Chad R. Sievers

Cartographer: Roberta Stockwell

Editorial Manager:
Christine Meloy Beck

Editorial Assistants: Nadine Bell,
Melissa S. Bennett

Senior Photo Editor: Richard Fox

Front Cover Photo:
© Brad Rickerby/Getty Images
Description: Woman playing sax
on sidewalk in profile

Back Cover Photo:
© Richard Cummins/Corbis
Description: Display of Cajun
sauces

Cartoons: Rich Tennant,
www.the5thwave.com

Composition

Project Coordinators: Kristie Rees,
Ryan Steffen

Layout and Graphics:
Stephanie D. Jumper,
Michael Kruzil, Lynsey Osborn,
Melanee Prendergast,
Heather Ryan

Proofreaders: Carl William Pierce,
TECHBOOKS Production
Services

Indexer: TECHBOOKS Production
Services

Publishing and Editorial for Consumer Dummies

Diane Graves Steele, Vice President and Publisher, Consumer Dummies

Joyce Pepple, Acquisitions Director, Consumer Dummies

Kristin A. Cocks, Product Development Director, Consumer Dummies

Michael Spring, Vice President and Publisher, Travel

Brice Gosnell, Associate Publisher, Travel

Kelly Regan, Editorial Director, Travel

Publishing for Technology Dummies

Andy Cummings, Vice President and Publisher, Dummies
Technology/General User

Composition Services

Gerry Fahey, Vice President of Production Services

Debbie Stailey, Director of Composition Services

Contents at a Glance

Maps at a Glance

Table of Contents

Introduction

● ●

*1*f you follow the gently winding road that shadows Bayou Barataria in Lafitte, just south of New Orleans, you pass one of my favorite local curiosities. Some proud folks have posted a handmade sign on their front lawn that reads "We weren't born here, but we got here as fast as we could." That captures my feelings exactly about living in New Orleans — I was born and raised in the Chicago area, but from the moment I arrived in New Orleans I felt like I was home.

Most people first hear about New Orleans through Mardi Gras, and I'm no exception. I clearly remember the pretty new girl in my eighth-grade class who passed out brightly colored strands of plastic beads to everyone. As we draped them around our necks, she explained — in an odd, Brooklyn-like accent (that I would later learn *is* the native New Orleans inflection) — that these were "throws" from "krewes" with exotic names like Endymion, Rex, and Zulu.

Years later, I attended Tulane University and thus began my love affair with this peculiar town. It wasn't until I moved away for my first post-graduation job that I realized how much I missed the warm, humid air, the sprawling live oaks, and the sweet scent of Confederate Jasmine, its vines draped over a rusted, wrought-iron fence. I missed the kid doodling on his trumpet at the streetcar stop, the smell and taste of a shrimp po' boy, and the exquisite stone mansion on St. Charles Avenue that I vowed to somehow hide in should a particularly fierce hurricane hit.

I quickly plotted my return and have lived here ever since. If you visit New Orleans, its potent mix of beauty and decay will likely haunt you, too. I hope that you find this book to be both practical and inspirational as you discover New Orleans's many pleasures.

About This Book

New Orleans For Dummies, 3rd Edition is a reference book, not an exhaustive, voluminous guide that requires hours of reading. Although the information is laid out in the logical order of a step-by-step manual, you don't need to read the book in order from front to back. I also don't expect you to remember everything you read — you can just look up and revisit the information as you need it. Each section and chapter is as self-contained as possible so that you can concentrate on what's important to you (and skip the rest).

Dummies Post-it® Flags

As you're reading this book, you'll find information that you'll want to reference as you plan or enjoy your trip — whether it be a new hotel, a must-see attraction, or a must-try walking tour. Mark these pages with the handy Post-it⁽ʳ⁾ Flags included in this book to help make your trip planning easier!

New Orleans For Dummies, 3rd Edition is helpful, authoritative, and interesting without getting mired in unnecessary details. You can find everything from when to visit and where to stay, to how to find the best spots to eat, shop, and *laissez le bon temps rouler* (let the good times roll). To find the information you want, just scan the table of contents or the index at the back of the book.

Remember that travel information can change at any time — especially prices. I therefore suggest that you write or call ahead for confirmation when making your travel plans. The authors, editors, and publisher can't be held responsible for the experiences of readers while traveling. Your safety is important to us, however, so we encourage you to stay alert and be aware of your surroundings. Keep a close eye on cameras, purses, and wallets — all favorite targets of thieves and pickpockets.

Conventions Used in This Book

To fulfill its function as an informative and easy-to-use reference guide, *New Orleans For Dummies,* 3rd Edition employs a few conventions designed to convey critical information in a simple, straightforward manner.

In this book, I include lists of hotels, restaurants, and attractions. As I describe each, I often include abbreviations for the following commonly accepted credit cards:

AE   American Express

CB   Carte Blanche

DC   Diners Club

DISC Discover

MC   MasterCard

V   Visa

I divide hotels into two categories: my personal favorites and those that don't quite make my preferred list but still get my hearty seal of approval. Don't be shy about considering these "runners-up" hotels if you're unable to get a room at one of my favorites — remember, your preferences may differ from mine. The amenities and services that the runners-up offer make these accommodations good choices to consider as you determine where to rest your head at night. (See Chapter 9 for more information.)

I also include some general pricing information to help you as you decide where to unpack your bags or dine on the local cuisine. (See Chapter 10 for more information.) I use a system of dollar signs to show a range of costs for one night in a hotel or a meal at a restaurant (including entree, drinks, and tip). Check out the following table to decipher the dollar signs:

Cost	Hotel	Restaurant
$	Less than $100	Less than $15
$$	$100–$200	$15–$30
$$$	$201–$300	$31–$45
$$$$	$301 and up	$46 or more

For those hotels, restaurants, and attractions that are plotted on a map, a page reference is provided in the listing information. If a hotel, restaurant, or attraction is outside the city limits or in an out-of-the-way area, it may not be mapped.

Foolish Assumptions

In this book I make some of the following assumptions about you and what your needs may be as a traveler:

- ✓ You may be an inexperienced traveler looking for guidance on whether to take a trip to New Orleans and how to plan for it.

- ✓ You may be an experienced traveler who hasn't had much time to explore New Orleans and wants expert advice when you finally do get a chance to enjoy what the city has to offer.

- ✓ You're not looking for a book that provides all the information available about New Orleans or that lists every hotel, restaurant, or attraction. Instead, you're looking for a book that focuses on the best places to give you that uniquely New Orleans experience.

If you fit any of these criteria, then *New Orleans For Dummies,* 3rd Edition gives you the information you need.

How This Book Is Organized

I design and organize *New Orleans For Dummies,* 3rd Edition to serve as two books in one. It's a trip-planning guide to help you figure out (and accomplish) what you need to do to book an interesting vacation that

doesn't break the bank. And it's a savvy reference book, boiling off the
excessive minutiae of other, more conventional travel guides, leaving
you with the essential information you need to enjoy New Orleans
without getting fleeced or disappointed — and without looking like an
obvious tourist.

Part I: Introducing New Orleans

Part I introduces you to New Orleans with a fine-tuned list of the best
the city has to offer and gives you the nitty-gritty lowdown straight from
a local, plus tips on what time of year to visit.

Part II: Planning Your Trip to New Orleans

In this part, you get your hands dirty with the details of planning your
trip, from money matters and how to get to the Crescent City to tips for
travelers with special needs or interests.

Part III: Settling into New Orleans

This part helps you get the lay of the land before you arrive, describes
your lodging options, introduces you to New Orleans's neighborhoods,
and leads you to the best spots to sample the city's culinary delights,
from beignets to jambalaya.

Part IV: Exploring New Orleans

Here I tell you what you need to know to enjoy the many sights and
shopping delights of New Orleans. Plus, I provide you with optional itineraries to manage your time, and finish with a list of day-trips if you wish
to stray from the city for a day or two.

Part V: Living It Up After Dark: New Orleans Nightlife

If you retire to your hotel room after the sun goes down, you may miss
out on at least half of what New Orleans is all about. This part starts
with a rundown of the city's varied and exciting cultural scene and goes
on to the best bars and clubs in the French Quarter and beyond.

Part VI: The Part of Tens

Part V gives you handy information in bite-sized chunks. I take this
opportunity to outline some quintessentially decadent New Orleans
experiences and run down a list of ten places that look like your usual
tourist traps, but aren't.

Icons Used in This Book

In the margins of this book, you find a number of helpful little icons designed to draw your attention to particularly useful bits of information.

 This icon highlights money-saving tips and/or great deals.

 This icon highlights the best the destination has to offer in all categories — hotels, restaurants, attractions, activities, shopping, and nightlife.

 This icon gives you a heads-up on annoying or potentially dangerous situations such as tourist traps, unsafe neighborhoods, rip-offs, and other things to beware of.

 This icon highlights attractions, hotels, restaurants, or activities that are particularly hospitable to children or people traveling with kids.

 This icon points out useful advice on things to do and ways to schedule your time.

Where to Go from Here

Because I break up this book into easily digestible parts and chapters, turn right to the section that interests you. If you already know when you're going to New Orleans and where you're staying, for example, you can skip to Part IV (though you may want to make a pit stop at Chapters 4 and 7). If you've been to New Orleans before and know your way around, you can jump straight to Parts V and VI to look for attractions, sights, and clubs that may be new to you. It's up to you; use the table of contents or the index, zero in on what you're looking for, and *laissez le bon temps rouler!*

Part I
Introducing New Orleans

WHY PILOTS DON'T DRESS FOR MARDI GRAS BEFORE FLIGHTS

"That was a nasty patch of turbulence. I'd better go back and reassure the passengers.

In this part . . .

So you want to visit New Orleans, eh? Well, dust off your passport. You don't actually need it, of course, but because New Orleans is easily the most European city in the United States, doing so can help you get in the proper frame of mind for your visit.

This part of the book helps you get started planning your vacation. First, this part gives you the best the city has to offer, plus a quick insider's lowdown on the Crescent City. Then it helps you decide what time of year to visit.

Chapter 1

Discovering the Best of New Orleans

In This Chapter

▶ Laying your head down at night
▶ Eating some yummy delectibles
▶ Sightseeing in museums
▶ Jamming to tunes
▶ Finding romance

*I*f your vision of New Orleans comes from movies, books, or television, chances are you think it's a fantasy world of nonstop parades and hedonism. Or perhaps you have heard, seen, and read so much about this place that you don't know what to believe. Well, you're not alone. Even the locals have deeply varying views on the Crescent City. The one thing they do agree on is how much they love it. When you arrive in this amazing place, you'll see that New Orleans has a lot more to offer than just its infamous party rep. If you want more information about the hotels, restaurants, clubs, museums, and hot romance spots noted in this chapter, just look for the Best of the Best icon throughout the book.

The Best Hotels

✔ For guaranteed pampering, head to old-line **Hotel Monteleone** and **Le Pavillon. International House** in the Central Business District (built in 1906 to accommodate the world's first trade center) exemplifies New Orleans's talent for adapting older buildings from their original use (or a state of outright neglect) into unique lodging. See Chapter 9.

✔ Pay homage to a former Masonic Temple circa 1926 by checking in at **Hotel Monaco,** also in the Central Business District. In the French Quarter, the **Maison Dupuy** carries the distinction of once being home to the world's first cotton press. See Chapter 9.

✔ Check out **The Ritz-Carlton**'s renovation of a one-time New Orleans institution, Maison Blanche department store, which signifies a return to Canal Street's glory days. See Chapter 9.

✔ On a smaller scale, but with equally impressive results, stay at the recently renovated **Block-Keller House,** which gives a taste of how Mid-City will look as the Canal streetcar works its restoration magic down the line. See Chapter 9.

The Best Restaurants

✔ Savor **Cajun** and **Creole** cuisine. Try Emeril Lagasse's flagship restaurant, **Emeril's,** where you can taste what he calls "*New* New Orleans Cuisine," or if you're a traditionalist, try **Antoine's, Arnaud's,** or Paul Prudhomme's **K-Paul's Louisiana Kitchen.** See Chapter 10.

✔ Dine at one of the Brennan family's restaurants. (The Brennan family is New Orleans's dining dynasty.) Be sure to check out one of their first-rate restaurants such as **Bacco, Brennan's,** or their Garden District jewel, **Commander's Palace.** See Chapter 10.

✔ Eat a greasy, roast-beef po' boy from **Elizabeth's** or the **Central Grocery,** a plateful of shucked oysters from **Acme Oyster House,** a hamburger from **Port of Call** or **Clover Grill,** and a breakfast of *beignets* — a tasty fried doughnut — at **Café du Monde.** For more information, see Chapter 10.

The Best Museums

✔ To discover more about its New Orleans's origins, and the city's storied (and often sordid) past, visit the **Cabildo,** an entertaining museum focusing on life in early Louisiana and the site where the Louisiana Purchase was sold to the United States in 1803. See Chapter 11.

✔ Go to the **Chalmette Battlefield National Park,** which marks the site of the Battle of New Orleans, part of the War of 1812. The park also contains a cemetery for Civil War soldiers. See Chapter 11.

✔ Ride the **Canal Streetcar** to Mid-City's **New Orleans Museum of Art,** now boasting beauty inside and out with its new, extraordinary **Besthoff Sculpture Garden.** See Chapter 11.

The Best Clubs

 ✔ Get a taste of modern-day brass bands getting funky at down-and-dirty hangouts **Donna's** and the **Funky Butt.** See Chapter 16.

 ✔ Catch live jazz at local clubs **Snug Harbor** and **Sweet Lorraine's.** Enjoy R&B at hallowed halls such as **Tipitina's** and the **Maple Leaf.** See Chapter 16.

 ✔ Jam to cajun and *zydeco* tunes (popular music of southern Louisiana combining tunes of French origin with elements of Caribbean music and the blues and that features guitar, washboard, and accordion) at the **Maple Leaf** or at the world's most musical bowling alley and celebrity haunt, **Mid City Lanes Rock 'n' Bowl.** See Chapter 16.

The Best Romantic Experiences

 ✔ Stroll along the lush scenery of the **Garden District** and the rolling expanse of water and parkway at the **Moonwalk.** See Chapter 13.

 ✔ Take your love on a **carriage ride** through the French Quarter or a relaxing **riverboat cruise** along the gently rolling Mississippi.

 ✔ Reserve a dinner for two at always cozy **Bella Luna, Court of Two Sisters,** and **Feelings Café.** For details, see Chapter 13.

Chapter 2

Digging Deeper into New Orleans

Sure, you can come to New Orleans without knowing a thing about it and still have a good time. But you'll get more out of your stay if you get the lowdown before you go. In this chapter, I introduce you to the New Orleans of today in the context of its storied past as well as the books and movies that best evoke its quirky spirit. And before you know it, you'll be well on your way to fitting in with the locals.

History 101: The Main Events

Considering that New Orleans is surrounded by water and was once mainly swamp, it's amazing that anyone found any use for it at all. Its story begins in 1682, when the Sieur de la Salle explored the Mississippi River and claimed all lands drained by the river for the French. He named this territory Louisiana after his king, Louis XIV. Nearly 40 years later, in 1718, Pierre Le Moyne, Sieur d'Iberville, founded New Orleans as a strategic port city. He named it *La Nouvelle Orléans* (New Orleans) after Philippe, Duc d'Orléans.

The French community that settled along this bend in the river — in a town 15 feet below sea level — flourished. So it came as a surprise when in 1762 Louis XIV handed over the Louisiana territory to his Spanish cousin, King Charles III. It didn't last long – only until 1800 — but in that time the French Quarter went up in flames twice and was rebuilt while under Spanish rule. Much of the French architecture was replaced by Spanish styles, leaving permanent reminders (such as courtyards and wrought-iron balconies) of that brief regime. The territory returned to France, but in 1803 Napoleon secretly sold it to the United States, marking the historical Louisiana Purchase. By that time, the Caribbean *gens de couleur libre* (free people of color) were immigrating to New Orleans in droves after the Haitian Revolution, adding to the city's mix of food, music, and architecture.

A New Orleans timeline

1682 Sieur de la Salle stops near what is now New Orleans while traveling down the Mississippi River and claims the territory for Louis XIV.

1699 Pierre Le Moyne, Sieur d'Iberville, rediscovers and secures the mouth of the Mississippi on Mardi Gras day.

1718 The first governor of Louisiana, Iberville's brother, Jean-Baptiste Le Moyne, Sieur de Bienville, founds New Orleans.

1723 New Orleans replaces Biloxi as the capital of Louisiana.

1752 Ursuline Convent completed.

1762 Louis XV secretly cedes Louisiana west of the Mississippi to Spain.

1788 & 1794 Fires destroy much of the city; Spanish-style buildings replace much of the French architecture.

1794 Planter Etienne de Boré granulates sugar from cane for the first time.

1803 France officially takes possession of the Louisiana Territory and sells it to the United States, the famous "Louisiana Purchase".

1805 New Orleans incorporates as a city.

1812 Louisiana admitted as a U.S. state.

1815 Battle of New Orleans resolves the War of 1812.

1832–33 Yellow fever and cholera epidemics kill 10,000 people in two years.

1837 First newspaper covers a Mardi Gras parade.

1840 New Orleans is the fourth-largest city in the United States and is second only to New York as a port.

1850 City becomes largest slave market in the country.

1861–62 Louisiana secedes from the Union.

1865–77 Reconstruction and carpetbaggers flood the city.

1890 Homer Plessy is arrested riding a train recently segregated by Jim Crow laws; he sues the state, leading to the landmark U.S. Supreme Court decision *Plessy v. Ferguson.*

1892 First electric streetcar operates along St. Charles Avenue.

(continued)

(continued)

1900 Louis Armstrong is born.

1928 Huey P. "Kingfish" Long elected governor of Louisiana; four years later, he is elected to the U.S. Senate.

1935 Long is assassinated.

1938 Tennessee Williams arrives in New Orleans.

1956 Lake Pontchartrain Causeway, the world's longest bridge, is completed.

1960 Public schools are integrated.

1964 Canal Streetcar makes last run; riders pelt new buses with tomatoes.

1975 Superdome opens.

1977 Ernest N. "Dutch" Morial becomes the first African American mayor.

1984 Louisiana World Expo spurs redevelopment of riverside area between Canal and Poydras streets.

1988 Anne Rice moves back to New Orleans.

2000 National D-Day Museum opens.

2004 Anne Rice sells her New Orleans properties and moves to the suburbs. Canal streetcar returns with great fanfare.

As the cotton and tobacco industries grew, New Orleans prospered, making it the second-wealthiest city in the nation after New York City. The War of 1812 was resolved in 1815 in the Battle of Orleans. The infamous pirate Jean Lafitte and General Andrew Jackson joined forces at Chalmette Battlefield (see Chapter 11) to claim victory over the British. Success, sophistication, and society reigned, making New Orleans an attractive destination. By the mid-1800s, Louisiana had seceded from the Union and was the fourth-largest city in the United States. After the Civil War ended, a flood of carpetbaggers brought even more cultural influences to the Crescent City.

Those years of prosperity slowly faded away as river transportation became less important and other industries overtook cotton and tobacco in profitability. A century after the War Between the States, New Orleans's leaders actually considered constructing an expressway along the Mississippi River and French Quarter. Fortunately, that never happened, but it reflected the city's desperation to regain what it had lost.

The oil bust of the 1980s negatively impacted the New Orleans economy, and Fortune 500 companies began to flee. Only the hospitality industry continued to thrive, encouraging the talent of musicians, chefs, and other creative entrepreneurs. Today, the local community is enjoying a cultural renaissance, and its citizens show a renewed appreciation for its art, food, language, music, and the many diverse peoples whose long-ago influences remain.

Tracing the Mardi Gras Tradition

It's fitting that Pierre Le Moyne, Sieur d'Iberville, rediscovered and secured the mouth of the Mississippi in 1699 on Mardi Gras day, a holiday cherished by New Orleanians for nearly 175 years. Although Creole societies per European custom already celebrated the holiday, it wasn't until 1837 that a newspaper gave the first official account of a public Mardi Gras parade, complete with masked revelers. Some people deplore the debauchery seen today, but in the mid-1840s, the debauchery was far more extreme and risked being banned.

Thankfully, a group of men formed the first Mardi Gras organization, the Mistick Krewe of Comus, named after the god of mirth and revelry. In 1857, they paraded by torchlight on two mule-drawn floats — so very quaint and quite different compared to today's standards where you see a monstrously large, two-story, tractor-pulled Bacchusaurus float zoom past as part of the superkrewe Bacchus. Comus also invented the "secret society" and issued 3,000 coveted invitations to a ball that would become *the* event for New Orleans's upper class. In time, other krewes joined in on the fun, hosting their own parades and balls.

Most krewes are hierarchies, with one member ruling as king and several others serving as the royal court. (Some krewes, such as Endymion and Bacchus, recruit celebrities from film, television, music, and sports to act as their kings.) Many krewes have roots in private, exclusive organizations, with agendas ranging from the socially aware to purely pleasurable.

Mardi Gras is the culmination of Carnival (please don't confuse the two terms). *Mardi Gras* is French for "Fat Tuesday," though the term generally applies to the final two weeks of *Carnival* (from *carnisvale,* or "farewell to flesh," which begins on January 6, the 12th night of Christmas). The idea of Mardi Gras is to cram as much sin and decadence as you can into this final frenzied fortnight. On Ash Wednesday, the Christian season of Lent begins, preceded by 40 days of fasting and repentance. Of course, not all celebrants on the streets during Mardi Gras are strict religious adherents; most come for the party.

I hope you can come for the next Mardi Gras, which always falls 46 days before Easter. If you're not a math whiz (or just can't find your calendar), don't fret. The dates for the next four years are February 8, 2005, February 28, 2006, February 20, 2007, and February 5, 2008. See the "Mardi Gras Parade Routes" map (see p. 179) in Chapter 11 for the major parades that take place during the last days of Carnival.

All hail Rex (not the dog)

The identity of *Rex* (the King of Carnival) is kept secret until the day before Mardi Gras. To be named King of Carnival is the ultimate honor for a New Orleanian, usually signifying his prominent standing and work in the community. The king is almost always an older man; his queen is usually of college age and always a young debutante as well as the daughter of a prominent member of society. The krewe of Rex parade always ends in an elaborate tradition: The parade stops at Gallier Hall for a toast from the mayor before moving to Canal Street, where Rex gives a speech, toasts his queen, and presents her with a big bouquet of roses.

Building Blocks: Local Architecture

One of the big reasons why I choose to live in New Orleans is the extraordinarily beautiful, old architecture. The delicate gingerbread on an Eastlake Victorian home or the cast-iron railing of an Italianate shotgun house starkly contrast with plain, nearly identical suburban homes across the country. And the sheer number and variety of architectural styles — from the early 1800s Creole cottage to the 1940s bungalow — are breathtaking compared to the cookie-cutter developments found elsewhere.

The most common form of architecture is the classic shotgun. Raised on brick piers, it's a narrow, long structure, where one room lines up behind another. Many natives hated growing up in one because of the lack of privacy; you have to go through the bedrooms before you get to the kitchen, which was typically added on to the back. (Some were lucky and lived in a camelback shotgun, where the bedrooms were on the second floor.) If you open the front and back doors and look down the hall, it gives the appearance of a shotgun barrel. Or, some say it got its name because you could shoot a shotgun through the doors and not hit anything. The breezeway provided a form of air conditioning, as did the brick piers because air flowed underneath the floorboards. You can find this practical yet attractive style throughout New Orleans and especially in what were working-class neighborhoods, such as the Irish Channel (see Chapter 8).

You can find photos of other popular architecture styles — such as the Creole Cottage and the Double Gallery House — at www.prcno.org, the Web site for the nonprofit Preservation Resource Center of New Orleans.

If you want to find out more about New Orleans architecture, page through Lloyd Vogt's illustrated *New Orleans Houses: A House Watcher's Guide* (Pelican Publishing Co.). Or start collecting the *New Orleans Architecture* series (Pelican); each book is devoted to one particular neighborhood, such as the French Quarter, the American Sector, or the

Garden District. My favorite feature of the series is the inclusion of past and present photos of the same house, when possible. Too often, the listing abruptly ends with the word "demolished."

Taste of New Orleans: Local Cuisine

Cajun versus Creole

Much of New Orleans's cuisine rests on two regional foundations: Cajun and Creole cooking. **Cajun cooking** brought New Orleans to national attention in the early 1980s thanks to the popularity of chef Paul Prudhomme. Cajun descends from the households of the Acadian country folk who came from Nova Scotia to settle in rural Louisiana. In their new home, economy often dictated that these folks throw all available foods into a single pot — a tradition that created jambalaya, étouffée, and red beans and rice (which many locals eat every Monday like clockwork).

Most people assume that Cajun food is always prepared spicy and served piping hot. Although Cajun cuisine certainly relies on spice a great deal, its foundation is a combination of regional ingredients. Even though serving Cajun food steaming hot is wise, neither the physical heat nor the spice should overwhelm the flavor.

Creole cooking is more varied and urban than Cajun food. Creole originated in the kitchens of New Orleans proper as a mix of French and Spanish cuisines. It relies heavily on high-quality ingredients smothered in rich, delicate sauces, with African and Caribbean spices providing an extra kick.

Muffuletta versus po' boy

Italian cold cuts and cheese stuffed into round Italian bread and slathered with olive salad dressing: This is a *muffuletta* (say muff-ah-*lot*-ah). That description may not do it justice. Trust me; this savory local fixture is worth every salty bite. Half of a muffuletta makes a great meal, and a quarter makes a nice, filling snack. Few people can eat a whole one. As with many foods in New Orleans, arguments abound as to who makes the best. Check out Chapter 10 to see my picks.

The other signature sandwich of New Orleans, the *po' boy,* proved cheap and filling during the streetcar strike of the late 1920s, with the idea that it's the only food a poor boy or "po' boy" can afford. Though not much different in structure from a hero or a sub, it's fixed in the minds of many locals as *the* premier New Orleans sandwich. The sandwich isn't all that complicated; take a crusty loaf of French bread, slice it open lengthwise, and stuff it with just about anything you can imagine. Roast-beef po' boys are great, especially if you have a little *debris* (gravy) dripping down the sides. Ham and cheese is a standard combo, and hot smoked sausage is also good. Seafood is a reliable standby; fried fish, soft-shell crab, oysters, and shrimp are all popular ingredients. Weird as it may sound, many people enjoy french-fry po' boys; that's right, a sandwich of french fries between two slices of French bread — and hopefully some of that rich, brown gravy. It's in keeping with New Orleans's "anything goes" attitude. (Just skip the french fry po'boy if you're on a low-carb diet!)

Obviously, po' boys aren't exactly health food. The best sandwiches have fried fixings or thick sauces (or both). They are also a *teensy* bit messy; you're just not getting the proper New Orleans experience if your shrimp or roast beef isn't spilling out of the sides of your overstuffed sandwich.

Is your mouth watering yet? See Chapter 10 for restaurant listings and additional places to find snacks, sandwiches, sweets, and more.

Word to the Wise: The Local Lingo

Surprisingly, many native New Orleanians sound like they're from Brooklyn. Perhaps the dialect can be traced back to the enormous influx of Italian and Irish immigrants from New York City in the decades after 1803, when New Orleans became an American city as part of the famous Louisiana Purchase from France. Some locals don't appear to have an accent at all until you hear them pronounce a word like "trout" or "about," which sounds just like a Canadian would say it — must be that Acadian influence. And don't be scared if someone wants to "ax" you a question. For a glossary of New Orleans terms, check out the Cheat Sheet in the front of this book; for terms specific to Mardi Gras, see Chapter 11.

Background Check: Recommended Books and Movies

Turning the pages

Please don't limit your fiction about New Orleans to Anne Rice. As much as many people adore her, I invite you to explore authors whose works also serve as portals to New Orleans. Pulitzer Prize winners John Kennedy Toole's *A Confederacy of Dunces* (Louisiana State University Press) and Shirley Ann Grau's *The Keepers of the House* (Vintage) are classics — as is Walker Percy's *The Moviegoer* (Vintage).

More recent writings that caught my eye include John Biguenet's *Oyster* (Ecco), which is a must-read if you plan a day-trip to bayou country, such as Lafitte (see Chapter 14). Valerie Martin's *The Great Divorce* (Vintage) is about a veterinarian at the New Orleans (read Audubon) Zoo whose marriage is falling apart. Nancy Lemann's *Lives of the Saints* (New American Library) offers frank insight into New Orleans high society. Other authors whose work I admire include Sheila Bosworth, Robert Olen Butler, and Patty Friedmann.

If, after all these suggestions, you still want something by Rice, read *The Feast of All Saints* (Ballantine), a historical novel about *les gens de couleur libre* (free people of color) in 19th-century New Orleans. Christine Wiltz's excellent *Glass House* (Louisiana State University) examines the current state of racial tension.

A short list of nonfiction is near impossible, but forced to pick, I choose *Fabulous New Orleans* (Pelican), by Lyle Saxon; *The Last Madam: A Life in the New Orleans Underworld* (DaCapo Press), by Christine Wiltz; *Frenchmen, Desire, Good Children and Other Streets of New Orleans* (Touchstone), by John Churchill Chase; and any essay collection by the witty, worldly Andrei Codrescu,

Arthur Hardy's Mardi Gras Guide is an annual magazine and my personal Mardi Gras bible come Twelfth Night. It contains the all-important parade schedule, calendar of related events, and informative articles on Carnival history. You can buy one almost anywhere in the city (it usually comes out right after Christmas), order a copy by phone ☎ **504-838-6111,** or purchase one on the Web www.mardigrasneworleans.com/arthur/index.html).

For more reading ideas, I strongly recommend *The Booklover's Guide to New Orleans* (Louisiana State University Press), by *Times-Picayune* book editor Susan Larson.

Screening The Big Easy

Hollywood loves to make movies in and about New Orleans because of its odd combination of eccentricity and timelessness. Tennessee Williams's *A Streetcar Named Desire,* starring Marlon Brando and Vivien Leigh, perfectly captures New Orleans and is a must-see. Another classic is Louis Malle's *Pretty Baby,* which was somewhat scandalous at the time of its release for his portrayal of Brooke Shields as a child prostitute. (Susan Sarandon stars as her mother.) The bordello scenes were shot inside The Columns Hotel on St. Charles Avenue (see Chapter 9). Before you head over to Harrah's New Orleans Casino (see Chapter 11), rent *The Cincinnati Kid,* in which Steve McQueen stars as a New Orleans card shark.

Locals laugh at the put-on accents but still love Dennis Quaid as a semi-corrupt cop and Ellen Barkin as an assistant district attorney in the sexy crime caper *The Big Easy.* Julia Roberts plays a law student in John Grisham's legal drama *The Pelican Brief.* Lastly, if you're planning to go to bayou country for a day-trip (see Chapter 14), try to see *Eve's Bayou* before you go. The scenery is breathtaking, and the actors (including Samuel L. Jackson) are heartbreaking.

Chapter 3

Deciding When to Go

● ●

In This Chapter

▶ Exploring the pros and cons of the different seasons
▶ Perusing a calendar of festivals in and near New Orleans

● ●

*C*ompared to the rest of the country, New Orleans is slow to change. Locals always favor tradition over trends. New Orleans will still be New Orleans whenever you decide to visit, but the timing of your trip should be a crucial consideration. If you don't like hot weather, don't spend too much time here during the summer months, when the humidity sticks to you like cotton candy. If you don't like crowds (especially rowdy, drunken ones), the charms of Mardi Gras or Jazz Fest may be lost on you.

Revealing the Secrets of the Seasons

New Orleans has three seasons: Hot, Cold, and In Between. Except for late spring through early summer (when temperatures are just uniformly hot), the seasons tend to run together. That's because this port city, a natural drop-off point for various cultures, also seems to be a way station for nearly every weather pattern on the North American continent. A butterfly beating its wings in Kansas City seems to affect the weather in New Orleans. As a result, bundling up under layers of clothing in the morning and then stripping down to a tank top and shorts by mid-afternoon isn't uncommon. Unless you're coming in the dog days of summer, prepare for a little bit of everything.

The upcoming sections present each season's advantages and disadvantages. For a summary of average monthly temperatures, see Table 3-1.

Table 3-1			Average Monthly Temperatures for Metropolitan New Orleans									
	Jan	*Feb*	*Mar*	*Apr*	*May*	*June*	*July*	*Aug*	*Sept*	*Oct*	*Nov*	*Dec*
High °F	61	64	72	79	84	89	91	90	87	79	71	64
High °C	16	18	22	26	29	32	33	32	31	26	22	18

	Jan	Feb	Mar	Apr	May	June	July	Aug	Sept	Oct	Nov	Dec
Low °F	42	44	52	58	66	71	74	73	70	60	51	46
Low °C	6	7	11	14	19	22	23	23	21	16	11	8

Spring

Spring is a popular vacation time for many travelers, and New Orleans has more than its share of reasons to visit.

- ✔ The weather is perfect for visiting plantation homes or Audubon Park.

- ✔ Wear shorts: Average highs are in the 70s and 80s.

- ✔ Jazz Fest, held the last weekend of April and the first weekend of May, turns the city into one giant musical mecca.

- ✔ Other events, including the rapidly growing French Quarter Festival, make the spring a "festive" time to visit.

However, visiting in spring does have a few disadvantages:

- ✔ The mercury can climb into the 90s with frightful speed.

- ✔ At the same time, average lows can dip into the 60s and even the 50s. Bring a light sweater or jacket, just in case.

- ✔ In New Orleans, April *and* May bring showers, so bring an umbrella, and be prepared to use it.

Summer

In summer, the living is easy. Shorts and sandals become the standard mode of dress. Here are some valid reasons for visiting New Orleans during the summer:

- ✔ Tourism in New Orleans generally lags in the summer, so it's a great time to beat the crowds and snag a bargain or two.

- ✔ The season brings pleasant breezes, plenty of sunshine, and colorful vegetation.

But keep in mind the following hard facts:

- ✔ It's *hot*. Average highs are in the 80s and 90s, with temperatures often soaring into the 100s. You may want to limit your sightseeing to cooler hours in the early morning and evening; the afternoons can be unbearable. Drink plenty of fluids, seek shade and air-conditioned buildings, and don't skimp on the sunscreen.

✔ It's not just hot; it's humid. In New Orleans, humidity can often be as high as 100 percent, resulting in an atmosphere you can practically drink through a straw. With all that moisture in the air, rain can — and does — fall at the drop of a hat. Keep that umbrella handy, especially if you venture out in the afternoon.

✔ School's out. Teen foot traffic makes for crowded shopping destinations, and attendance at museums, parks, and other kid-friendly attractions rises.

Fall

Fall is a beautiful time of year to visit. Check out the following autumn bonuses for the New Orleans scene:

✔ Fall means a respite from the grisly heat of July and August, making for cool breezes.

✔ The cool breezes also carry romantic properties that shouldn't be discounted. A lazy evening watching the pale sunset over the river is a beautiful experience.

✔ Fall means Halloween, which offers a basketful of revelry options in a city known for playing dress-up. (See "Perusing a Calendar of Events" later in this chapter.)

Some things to look out for, however, include the following:

✔ October and November are the driest months of the year (which isn't necessarily a guarantee against sudden downpours).

✔ It's the tail end (and the most active part) of hurricane season, which begins June 1 and ends in November. Most storms come knocking between August and November, so don't discount the possibility of a sudden and abrupt change of location should a big storm hit.

Winter

To some, winter conjures visions of snowflakes (not to mention slick roads and ice storms) but not in the Crescent City. However, here are some reasons why New Orleans offers its own version of a veritable winter wonderland:

✔ Compared with much of the country, New Orleans gets away easy. The weather is often mild to middling cold, and you'll never get snowed in. Plan to bring a lightweight coat or jacket.

✔ The first three weeks of December are traditionally slow for tourism, so finding a good room at a good rate is much easier.

✔ Crowds aren't a big problem in the early part of December, so waiting in line doesn't take as long.

✔ After December, New Orleans has a lot going on. Don't miss New Year's Eve in the French Quarter, or the Sugar Bowl each January.

✔ You can't forget Mardi Gras. Depending on the year, Carnival can fall almost anywhere in February or early March.

✔ New Orleans is made for romance, making it the perfect spot for a Valentine's Day getaway.

Winter does have its downsides, however. Consider the following:

✔ Although winter is a cakewalk compared to, say, winter in Chicago, cold weather can catch you unawares if you don't plan (and pack) for the possibility. Occasional cold snaps bring the temperature down to freezing and below.

✔ You may want to make room for a larger coat, as well. The wind-chill factor, which can knock another 10 or 20 degrees off the thermometer, exacerbates the cold weather. (You'll still likely experience topsy-turvy weather, so pack lighter wear, too.)

✔ If you don't like large crowds and snarled traffic, you'd do better to avoid New Year's and Mardi Gras.

Perusing a Calendar of Events

New Orleans truly deserves its reputation as a party capital. No matter what time of year you visit, you can find an excuse to *laissez le bon temps rouler* (let the good times roll). The local newspapers' calendars of events are bursting with things to do, from casual celebrations to full-out festivals.

If you're coming to New Orleans for a specific event, especially Mardi Gras or Jazz Fest, you need to do a bit more advance planning than you would otherwise. I can't stress this point enough: Make reservations for these two events (as well as for the Sugar Bowl and the French Quarter Festival) as early as possible. As their dates draw closer, hotel rooms become scarcer than honest politicians (the latter are infamously rare in Louisiana). I recommend that you begin calling 10 to 12 months ahead.

 Don't assume you're off the hook if you come for a smaller event such as, say, the Rayne Frog Festival (hop to the end of this chapter for details). Even during the less popular (and populous) festivals and events, finding a place to stay can become a Herculean exercise if you wait too long. Plan ahead to avoid a headache of scrambling for a room.

The following sections present the city's best festivals and events, listed under the months in which they occur. For more-detailed information, visit the **Times-Picayune** and **Gambit Weekly** Web sites (www.nola.com and www.bestofneworleans.com, respectively), **New Orleans Citysearch**

(www.neworleans.citysearch.com), or **Inside New Orleans** (www.insideneworleans.com). **Huli's Calendar of Louisiana Festivals and Events** is an indispensable, comprehensive resource for festivals throughout the state. You can find this publication at bookstores and newsstands throughout the city; go to www.louisiana-festivals.com or call ☎ 504-488-5993 for a copy or for specific information.

January

The **Nokia Sugar Bowl Football Classic** (☎ 504-525-8573; www.nokiasugarbowl.com). The crowds begin pouring into the city around late December. If you're a football fanatic and can afford to spend the money, the Sugar Bowl is perfect. Getting tickets can be difficult, especially when the Sugar Bowl hosts the national college football championship. If you want to go, check a ticket service such as **Ticketmaster** (www.ticketmaster.com). January 1.

Carnival (☎ 800-672-6124 or 504-566-5011; www.neworleanscvb.com) runs from January 6 to Mardi Gras day, but only the last two weeks leading up to Mardi Gras see a huge increase in tourism. You'll be lucky to find a vacant hotel room within 100 miles of the city if you don't make your reservations well ahead of time. Call for specific dates.

 Mardi Gras (☎ 800-672-6124 or 504-566-5011; www.mardigrasday.com). On this day and most of the two weeks preceding it, life in New Orleans is hectic, to put it mildly. (See Chapters 2 and 11 for more information on Mardi Gras.) Can be as early as February 3 or as late as March 9, but it always falls on the Tuesday 46 days before Easter.

February

The **Black Heritage Festival** (☎ 504-827-0112). This two-day celebration features craft exhibits, soul food (such as jambalaya, fried chicken, and gumbo), and live music in Armstrong Park. You can find related activities along the Riverwalk, in Audubon Park, and at various Louisiana State Museum buildings. Late February or early March.

March

On **St. Patrick's Day,** celebrations and parades overtake the city. The Downtown Irish Club sponsors a parade the Friday before St. Patrick's Day. Call local tavern Molly's on the Market, where the parade kicks off, at ☎ 504-525-5169 for more information. March 17.

St. Joseph's Day. The city's Italians celebrate, often in conjunction with the Irish St. Patrick's Day, with parades and sumptuous food offerings. Call ☎ 800-672-6124 for more information. March 19.

The **Tennessee Williams/New Orleans Literary Festival** (☎ 504-581-1144; www.tennesseewilliams.net) celebrates the life of this famous playwright with performances, lectures, and walking tours. Held over a four-day period in March.

April

The **French Quarter Festival** (☎ 800-673-5725 or 504-522-5730; www.
frenchquarterfestivals.org) serves as the unofficial start of the
city's prime festival season because it leads directly into Jazz Fest.
Hailed as the state's largest free music festival (and the world's largest
jazz brunch), it gets bigger every year, offering plenty of free entertainment (unlike Jazz Fest, which is by ticket only), with an emphasis on
local and regional music and food. Check on room availability well in
advance. Second weekend in April. (*Note:* If it conflicts with Easter, it's
held the first or third weekend in April).

Jazz Fest, the **New Orleans Jazz & Heritage Festival,** (☎ 504-522-4786;
www.nojazzfest.com). A diverse lineup of hundreds of musicians (from
big-ticket names to local acts, representing just about every genre under
the sun) perform on various stages at the New Orleans Fair Grounds,
and many more turn up after hours in the city's music clubs and concert
halls as venues capitalize on the eager, music-hungry traffic. The city is
crowded, prices are higher, and hotel and restaurant reservations are
hard to come by — so plan ahead. Many attendees begin making reservations for the following year's festival even before the current one ends.
Last weekend in April (Friday through Sunday) and first weekend in May
(Thursday through Sunday).

May

The **Greek Festival** (☎ 504-282-0259; www.greekfestnola.com) features Greek food, crafts, music, and dancing. Last weekend in May.

June

The **International Arts Festival** (formerly Reggae Riddums) (☎ 888-
767-1317 or 504-367-1313; http://internationalartsfestival.com)
is another popular music festival, with a decidedly Caribbean feel. The
festival focuses on calypso, reggae, and regional food, and takes place
during the second weekend in June.

July

The popular **Essence Festival** (☎ 800-725-5652 or 504-523-5652; www.
essence.com) is both a music festival and a series of seminars on topics
of importance to the African American community. The festival has featured appearances by Prince, Gladys Knight, Patti LaBelle, Lauryn Hill,
The Isley Brothers, Mary J. Blige, Sinbad, Kenny G, Maya Angelou, Missy
Elliott, Clarence Carter, and Irma Thomas, among many others. Held
during the weekend closest to the Fourth of July.

September

Southern Decadence (☎ 800-876-1484 or 504-522-8047; www.southern
decadence.net), which promises just that — decadence, and lots of it.
Thousands of gays and lesbians converge upon the city during this festival.

They assemble on Sunday in the 1200 block of Royal Street and then head off on a secret parade route known only to the grand marshal. Expect drag queens galore and lots of drinking. The celebration is wild and, like Mardi Gras, not all the street celebrations are appropriate for young children. Labor Day weekend.

September marks the start of football season, with another year of gridiron action for the New Orleans Saints (☎ 504-733-0255; www.new orleanssaints.com). The team struggles, giving credence to a supposed curse. An entire cemetery had to be relocated in order to build the Superdome; some locals suggest the disturbed spirits haunt the team.

October

Louisiana Jazz Awareness Month (☎ 504-834-3632; www.gnofn.org/~jazz), features nightly concerts, lectures, and special radio programs — all sponsored by the Louisiana Jazz Federation. Entire month of October.

Enjoying festivals off the beaten path

Not everything worth doing in Louisiana happens inside the corporate limits of New Orleans. Check out these noteworthy festivals that take place just outside the city.

Festival International de Louisiane (☎ 337-232-8086; www.festivalinternational.com) is a mammoth celebration of the cultural heritage of southern Louisiana (primarily a mix of French, Hispanic, and African-Caribbean cultures). It usually takes place during the last weekend of April in downtown Lafayette, about a two-hour drive from New Orleans.

Lafayette also plays host to **Festivals Acadiens** (☎ 337-233-7060), a celebration of Cajun culture. Cajun food and music are the main attractions, with workshops and other activities sprinkled throughout. Third weekend of September.

The **Original Southwest Louisiana Zydeco Music Festival** (☎ 337-942-2392; www.zydeco.org) in Plaisance (roughly a three-hour drive north of New Orleans) celebrates the unique joys of *zydeco,* the popular accordion-driven music of the Creoles of southern Louisiana. Aside from the event itself, an all-day fair is held on Saturday with music, food, and crafts. The celebration extends to the surrounding areas of Lafayette, Opelousas, and Lake Charles. Labor Day weekend.

I'd be remiss if I didn't at least mention the **Rayne Frog Festival,** in Cajun Country, about a two-hour drive from New Orleans in an area west of Lafayette. Cajuns can turn just about anything into an excuse for a festival, as evidenced by this event's frog races and frog-jumping contests. (Didn't bring a frog? Don't worry; you can rent one. Seriously.) On the culinary side, you can also participate in a lively frog-eating contest. Held every September. For exact dates and full details, contact the **Rayne Chamber of Commerce** (☎ 337-334-2332; www.rayne.org).

The **Gumbo Festival** (☎ 504-436-4712) offers attendees every type of gumbo you can imagine — and many that you can't. The festival features games and carnival rides as well as jazz, blues, and Cajun music to put you in the mood for food — and work off what you eat. Generally held during the second weekend in October — call for specific dates.

With the locals' penchant for masking, it's a given that New Orleans loves Halloween. Children can attend **Boo at the Zoo** (held on and around Halloween; ☎ 866-ITS-AZOO or 504-866-4872; www.auduboninstitute.org) and a yearly program at the **Louisiana Children's Museum** (☎ 504-523-1357; www.lcm.org). Meanwhile, events such as the **French Market Pumpkin Carving and Decorating Contest** (☎ 504-522-2621) and the **Moonlight Witches Run** offer more adult-oriented fun.

Speaking of adult-oriented, the annual **M.O.M.'s Ball,** thrown by a debauched group known as the Krewe of Mystic Orphans and Misfits, is one of the season's hot-ticket events, a notoriously raucous bash. It's an invitation-only event, so you won't find any public ticket information, but keep an eye out for it if you're in town in October.

October is also the start of basketball season, and New Orleanians are thrilled at the long-awaited return of a professional team — the **New Orleans Hornets** — whose new home is the **New Orleans Arena.** This marks the city's second attempt to supplement the Saints with a b-ball franchise (the Utah Jazz originally hailed from here before being wooed away decades ago). Check www.nba.com/hornets or call ☎ 800-HORNETS for more information.

November

The **Bayou Classic** (☎ 225-771-3170) is a college football rivalry between a pair of Louisiana institutions: Grambling University and Southern University. The annual event is one of the major social events of the year, so make your reservations early if you plan to attend — around 75,000 people turn out for the game. Thanksgiving weekend.

The **Celebration in the Oaks** (☎ 504-483-9415). During this festival, sections of City Park's lovely old oaks are draped with lights and holiday-themed figures delight kids of all ages. You can visit the park on foot, by car, or by carriage. Late November to early January.

December

You won't see Dick Clark there, but the **Jackson Square New Year's Eve** celebration is beginning to resemble New York's — right down to the lighted ball dropping from the top of Jackson Brewery. The city also puts on a cool fireworks display over the Mississippi River. Count on revelers crowding the major thoroughfares of the French Quarter.

Part II

Planning Your Trip to New Orleans

The 5th Wave   By Rich Tennant

"I think we should arrange to be there for Cayenne pepper-Garlic-Andouille sausage week, and then shoot over to the Breathmint-Antacid Festival."

In this part . . .

This section takes you through the various steps necessary to reach your ultimate goal — setting foot in New Orleans. It helps you create a workable budget, points out some money-saving tips about cutting costs and avoiding hidden expenses, and lists some invaluable resources for travelers with specific needs — whether you're bringing a large family, needing a wheelchair-accessible hotel, searching for a gay-friendly spot, bringing Fido, or hoping to take advantage of senior-citizen discounts. You uncover the diverse options available to you, including using a travel agent, booking a package tour, and finding a super-secret airfare deal.

You also get the opportunity to tie up a few loose ends, such as the ins and outs of buying travel insurance, renting a car, making reservations, and packing for your trip. After all that, you're ready for the next stop: New Orleans!

Chapter 4

Managing Your Money

- -

In This Chapter

▶ Budgeting your trip
▶ Uncovering hidden costs
▶ Getting the lowdown on cash, credit cards, and traveler's checks
▶ Handling a lost or stolen wallet

- -

*I*n a city as tempting as New Orleans, traveling without a budget is the surest path to financial disaster. Thanks to numerous historical attractions, French Quarter souvenir shops, and fabulous restaurants and bars, you don't need to set foot inside the local casino to break your bank. In fact, you can easily max out your credit card just by sampling the city's many culinary delights.

If the prospect of drawing up a budget makes you weak-kneed in terror or bored to tears, I understand. But don't worry — over the years, I've discovered how to exercise willpower and fiscal responsibility without sacrificing self-indulgences.

Planning Your Budget

The best way to get a handle on your budget is to walk yourself through your trip, starting with transportation to your nearest airport (or, if you're driving, how much gas you expect to use per day). If you're flying, first add up the costs of your transportation to the airport, your flight (see Chapter 5 for tips on saving money here), and the ride to your hotel. Next, add the hotel rate per day, meals (be sure to note if your hotel includes breakfast in its room rate), transportation costs, admission to museums and other attractions, and any other entertainment expenses.

Table 4-1 offers some average costs for you to get started.

Table 4-1	What Things Cost in New Orleans
Expense	**Cost**
Taxi from the airport to the Central Business District or French Quarter	$24–$28; $12 per person for 3 or more passengers
Bus from airport to downtown	$1.50
St. Charles, Canal, or Riverfront streetcar ride for one (one-way)	$1.25
Riverfront streetcar ride for one (one-way)	$1.50
Bus ride for one (one-way)	$1.25
Taxi ride for one in the Quarter (add $1 for each extra passenger)	$5
Inexpensive ($) hotel room for two	under $80
Low to moderate ($$) hotel room for two	$80–$125
Moderate to high ($$$) hotel room for two	$126–$180
Expensive ($$$$) hotel room for two	$181–$250
Very expensive ($$$$$) hotel room for two	more than $250
Moderately priced breakfast for two	$12–$16
Moderately priced lunch for two	$20–$30
Moderately priced dinner for two	$30–$50
Nonalcoholic drink	$1–$1.50
Bottle of beer	$1.50–$4
Cocktail	$3.50–$8
Cup of coffee	75¢–$1.50
Adult admission to New Orleans Museum of Art	$8
Theater ticket at Le Petit Theatre	$21–$26

The costs of some things, such as hotels, are relatively inflexible. Along with airfare or other transportation costs, lodging makes up the largest part of your expenditures. Other factors, such as transportation in the city, are relatively cheap. The incredible number of restaurants and nightlife choices in New Orleans vary as widely in price as they do in style, so it's up to you to go formal or casual and pay accordingly.

Of course, budgeting your vacation isn't so difficult when you're jotting down prices on a piece of paper in the comfort of your own home. Keeping track of your costs after you arrive, however, is another matter altogether. Remember that the key element in budget is "budge," so allow yourself some flexibility — start by tacking a good 10% or even 20% onto the final budget tally. Keep in mind that you can easily go from merely bending your budget to flat-out broke if you don't pay attention.

Transportation

Getting around the most popular parts of the city is a relative bargain. Many hotels and attractions lie within a few miles of one another in the French Quarter or Central Business District. If your destination is farther than you want to walk — or if you're visiting on a particularly hot day — a taxi ride is worth the cost. The average trip in or around the Quarter should be no more than $5.

For public transportation, hop on one of the city's buses or streetcars. Fares are $1.25 each time you get on (transfers cost an additional 25 cents), but a **VisiTour** pass, good for unlimited bus and streetcar rides, costs only $5 for one day and $12 for three days. Check with your hotel's concierge, or check with the **Regional Transit Authority** (☎ **504-248-3900;** www.regionaltransit.org) for information. Many hotels also offer free shuttles to and from the French Quarter or Central Business District. For more information on getting around the city, see Chapter 8.

Lodging

Lodging represents the least elastic part of your budget — after all, you have to stay somewhere. In this book, I share information about *rack rates* and how to save money in this area (details in Chapter 9), but hotels will still comprise a significant portion of your expenses. (*Rack rates* simply mean published rates and tend to be the highest rate paid.) You *can* find inexpensive rooms, though they're usually far from the center of town, or they don't offer much in the way of amenities. (Some guesthouses, for example, wanting to emulate that European feel, offer rooms that share a common bathroom for a cheaper rate, or a backpacker room that more closely resembles your closet at home.) If you want to stay relatively close to the French Quarter or the Central Business District, expect to spend a minimum of $80 to $100 a night. See Chapter 9 for some hotel recommendations and price ranges.

Dining

Dining options in New Orleans range from dirt-cheap to astronomically high. Almost all options are tantalizing; you don't have to spend a lot of money for a great meal. If you want to save a buck or two, get coffee and beignets for breakfast at Café du Monde for about $2.50, a $5 po' boy for lunch at any one of a hundred places, and dinner for under $15 at a place such as Café Maspero in the Quarter.

However, if you feel like you can't come to New Orleans without having breakfast at Brennan's, dinner at Antoine's, or a special night out at one of the fancier restaurants listed in Chapter 10, make sure to put a little money aside and make reservations well in advance.

Sightseeing

Attractions are a somewhat more flexible expense. Of course, your budget for entrance fees and admissions depends on what you want to see. If you're traveling with your entire family, you can expect to shell out more for attractions than if you're backpacking with a buddy. Refer to the attraction listings in Chapter 11 and make a list of your "must-sees," and then figure out your costs from the ticket prices.

Shopping

The amount of money you need for shopping makes up another variable part of your budget. After all, you don't have to buy anything at all if that's your style, though self-restraint can be something of an alien concept in New Orleans. Even a scrupulous penny-counter can succumb to shopping fever when wandering the French Market or some of the souvenir shops in the French Quarter. As an international port city, New Orleans offers as many choices as you can imagine. If you're an antiques buff, you may want to leave your checks and credit cards at the hotel before going anywhere near Magazine or Royal streets.

If you're just looking for souvenirs to take home as proof of your trip, you can find whole colonies of shops selling postcards, posters, sunglasses, and T-shirts in the French Quarter. Being tourist shops, however, they aren't exactly cheap. If you want to save on souvenirs, ask someone to take your picture on Bourbon Street. Voilà! You now have an instant memento of your trip (assuming the person doesn't run away with your camera). See Chapter 12 for the lowdown on shopping in New Orleans.

Nightlife

Your entertainment dollars will likely stretch further in New Orleans than in a place such as New York, where a pair of tickets to the theater can require a second mortgage. Most of the nightlife in New Orleans is relatively inexpensive — but again, your personal preferences determine the final tally. You'll obviously spend more if you go to the opera than if you head to the Maple Leaf or the House of Blues for some local music. Turn to Chapter 16 for nightlife listings, and Chapter 15 for the performing arts scene.

Cutting Costs — but Not the Fun

Want to save money without ruining your vacation? Read on for cost-saving tips for your Crescent City trip:

✔ **Go off-season.** If you can handle hot, humid weather, you can get some great deals from June through August — but remember that when I say hot, I mean blood-boiling, sweat-inducing hot. The first three weeks of December are also a good time for discounts.

✔ **Travel mid-week.** If you can travel on a Tuesday, Wednesday, or Thursday, you may find cheaper flights to your destination. When you ask about airfares, see if you can get a cheaper rate by flying on a different day. For more tips on getting a good fare, see Chapter 5.

✔ **Try a package tour.** For many destinations, you can book airfare, hotel, ground transportation, and even some sightseeing just by making one call to a travel agent or packager for a price much less than if you put the trip together yourself. (See Chapter 5 for more on package tours.)

✔ **Reserve a room with a refrigerator and coffeemaker.** You don't have to slave over a hot stove to cut a few costs; several motels have minifridges and coffeemakers. Buying supplies for breakfast can save you money — and probably calories.

✔ **Always ask for discount rates.** Membership in AAA, frequent-flier plans, trade unions, AARP, or other groups may qualify you for savings on car rentals, plane tickets, hotel rooms, and even meals. Ask about everything; you may be pleasantly surprised.

✔ **Ask if your kids can stay in the room with you.** A room with two double beds usually doesn't cost any more than one with a queen-size bed. And many hotels don't charge you the additional person rate if the additional person is pint-size and related to you. Even if you have to pay $10 or $15 extra for a rollaway bed, you'll save hundreds by not taking two rooms.

✔ **Try expensive restaurants at lunch instead of dinner.** Lunch tabs are usually a fraction of what dinners cost at a top restaurant, and the menu often boasts many of the same specialties.

✔ **Get out of the Quarter.** Really. To many people, the French Quarter *is* New Orleans, and they want to stay where they think all the action happens. Although you'll certainly see plenty of action in the Quarter, New Orleans offers much more for you to see and experience. Plus, hotels outside the Quarter tend to charge less than those inside its borders. So if you don't mind a slightly longer trip to most attractions, book a room in Faubourg Marigny, Uptown, or along the Esplanade Ridge. Thanks to the new Canal streetcar, even Mid-City is convenient to downtown. (See Chapter 8 for detailed neighborhood descriptions and Chapter 9 for more on hotels.)

✔ **Take the streetcar.** What's more romantic than seeing New Orleans from the streetcar? Relax, and ride for only $1.25 (one-way). (See Chapters 8 and 11 for more information.)

✔ **Walk a lot.** You can save money, get some exercise, and see the city the way it was meant to be seen — at a leisurely pace. Stay hydrated and invest in a good pair of walking shoes — the last thing you need on vacation is sore feet. (*Note:* Don't overdo the walking if you're in town during a really hot spell. And wear a hat — the sun is stronger than you may realize!)

✔ **Skip the souvenirs.** Your photographs and your memories could be your trip's best mementos. If you're concerned about money, avoid those Quarter tourist shops with their overpriced T-shirts, key chains, and other useless trinkets. After all, you don't really *need* those riverboat salt-and-pepper shakers, do you?

Handling Money

You're the best judge of how much cash you feel comfortable carrying or what alternative form of currency is your favorite. That's not going to change much on your vacation. True, you'll probably be moving around more and incurring more expenses than you generally do (unless you happen to eat out every meal when you're at home), and you may let your mind slip into vacation gear and not be as vigilant about your safety as when you're in work mode. But, those factors aside, the only type of payment that won't be quite as available to you away from home is your personal checkbook.

Using ATMs and carrying cash

The easiest and best way to get cash away from home is from an automated teller machine (ATM). The **Cirrus** (☎ 800-424-7787; www. mastercard.com) and **PLUS** (☎ 800-843-7587; www.visa.com) networks span the globe; look at the back of your bank card to see which network you're on, and then call or check online for ATM locations at your destination. Be sure you know your personal identification number (PIN) before you leave home, and be sure to find out your daily withdrawal limit before you depart. Also keep in mind that many banks impose a fee every time you use your card at a different bank's ATM, up to $1.50 for domestic transactions. On top of this, the bank from which you withdraw cash may charge its own fee. To compare banks' ATM fees within the United States, use www.bankrate.com.

Charging ahead with credit cards

Credit cards are a safe way to carry money: They also provide a convenient record of all your expenses. You can also withdraw cash advances from your credit cards at banks or ATMs, provided you know your PIN. If you've forgotten yours, or didn't even know you had one, call the number on the back of your credit card and ask the bank to send it to you. It usually takes five to seven business days, though some banks provide the number over the phone if you tell them your mother's maiden name or some other personal information.

Toting traveler's checks

These days, traveler's checks are less necessary because most cities have 24-hour ATMs that allow you to withdraw small amounts of cash as needed. However, keep in mind that you'll likely be charged an ATM withdrawal fee if the bank isn't your own. So if you're withdrawing money every day, you may be better off with traveler's checks — provided that you don't mind showing identification every time you want to cash one.

You can get traveler's checks at almost any bank. **American Express** offers denominations of $20, $50, $100, $500, and (for cardholders only) $1,000. You pay a service charge ranging from 1% to 4%. You can also get American Express traveler's checks over the phone by calling ☎ **800-221-7282;** Amex gold and platinum cardholders who use this number are exempt from the 1% fee.

Visa offers traveler's checks at Citibank locations nationwide, as well as at several other banks. The service charge ranges between 1.5% and 2%; checks come in denominations of $20, $50, $100, $500, and $1,000. Call ☎ **800-732-1322** for information. AAA members can obtain Visa checks without a fee at most AAA offices or by calling ☎ **866-339-3378. MasterCard** also offers traveler's checks. Call ☎ **800-223-9920** for a location near you.

 If you choose to carry traveler's checks, be sure to keep a record of their serial numbers separate from your checks in the event that they're stolen or lost. You'll get a refund faster if you know the numbers.

Dealing with a Lost or Stolen Wallet

Be sure to contact your credit-card companies the minute you discover your wallet has been lost or stolen and file a report at the nearest police precinct (in the French Quarter, go to the **New Orleans Police Department's 8th District** at 334 Royal St.; ☎ **504-565-7530**). Your credit-card company or insurer may require a police report number or record of the loss. Most credit-card companies have an emergency toll-free number to call if your card is lost or stolen; they may be able to wire you a cash advance immediately or deliver an emergency credit card in a day or two. Call the following emergency numbers in the United States:

- ✔ **American Express** ☎ **800-221-7282** (for cardholders and traveler's check holders)
- ✔ **MasterCard** ☎ **800-307-7309** or 636-722-7111
- ✔ **Visa** ☎ **800-847-2911** or 410-581-9994

For other credit cards, call the toll-free number directory at ☎ **800-555-1212.**

Chapter 5

Getting to New Orleans

● ●

In This Chapter

▶ Traveling to New Orleans by airplane, car, or other means
▶ Considering the escorted or package tour options

● ●

So you're ready to come to the Crescent City? Before you pack your bags and throw on those Mardi Gras beads, you have to decide how to get here. Many people rush through this part of the process and end up paying for it later. Even if you know you want to fly, considering your many travel options before you book a flight is worth your time. This chapter covers the pros and cons of using a travel agent and of booking an escorted or package tour. It also mentions some pointers to keep in mind if you choose a more independent route, be it by plane, car, or even train.

Flying to New Orleans

All the major airlines fly to New Orleans's Louis Armstrong International Airport (airline code MSY, for those of you booking on the Web), among them **American Airlines** (☎ 800-433-7300; www.aa.com), **Continental** (☎ 800-525-0280; www.continental.com), **Delta** (☎ 800-221-1212; www.delta.com), **Northwest** (☎ 800-225-2525; www.nwa.com), **Southwest** (☎ 800-435-9792; www.southwest.com), **United** (☎ 800-UNITED; www.united.com) and **US Airways** (☎ 800-428-4322; www.usairways.com). The airport is in Kenner, 15 miles west of the city.

Getting the best deal on your airfare

Competition among the major U.S. airlines is unlike that of any other industry. Every airline offers virtually the same product (basically, a coach seat is a coach seat is a . . .), yet prices can vary by hundreds of dollars.

Business travelers who need the flexibility to buy their tickets at the last minute and change their itineraries at a moment's notice — and who want to get home before the weekend — pay (or at least their companies pay) the premium rate, known as the *full fare.* But if you can book your ticket far in advance, stay over Saturday night, and are willing to travel midweek (Tuesday, Wednesday, or Thursday), you can qualify for the least expensive price — usually a fraction of the full fare. On most flights, even the shortest hops within the United States, the full fare is close to $1,000 or more, but a 7- or 14-day advance purchase ticket might cost less than half of that amount. Obviously, planning ahead pays.

The airlines also periodically hold sales, in which they lower the prices on their most popular routes. These fares have advance purchase require-ments and date-of-travel restrictions, but you can't beat the prices. As you plan your vacation, keep your eyes open for these sales, which tend to take place in seasons of low travel volume — in New Orleans, that would be anytime in the summer and December.

Consolidators, also known as bucket shops, are great sources for inter-national tickets, although they usually can't beat the Internet on fares within North America. Start by looking in Sunday newspaper travel sec-tions; U.S. travelers should focus on the *New York Times, Los Angeles Times,* and *Miami Herald.*

 Bucket-shop tickets are usually nonrefundable or rigged with stiff cancellation penalties, often as high as 50 to 75 percent of the ticket price, and some put you on charter airlines with questionable safety records.

Several reliable consolidators are worldwide and available on the Net. **STA Travel** (☎ 800-781-4040; www.statravel.com), the world's leader in student travel, offers good fares for travelers of all ages. **FlyCheap** (☎ 800-FLY-CHEAP; www.1800flycheap.com) is owned by package-holiday megalith MyTravel and has especially good access to fares for sunny destinations. **Air Tickets Direct** (☎ 800-778-3447; www.air ticketsdirect.com) is based in Montreal and leverages the currently weak Canadian dollar for low fares. Your best bet locally is **Uniglobe Americana Travel** (☎ 504-561-0588 or 504-561-8100).

Booking your flight online

The "big three" online travel agencies, **Expedia** (www.expedia.com), **Travelocity** (www.travelocity.com), and **Orbitz** (www.orbitz.com) sell most of the air tickets bought on the Internet. Each has different business deals with the airlines and may offer different fares on the same flights, so shop around. Expedia and Travelocity also can send you an **e-mail notification** when a cheap fare becomes available to your favorite destination. Of the smaller travel agency Web sites, **SideStep** (www.sidestep.com) receives good reviews from users. It's a browser add-on that purports to "search 140 sites at once," but in reality only beats competitors' fares as often as other sites do.

Great **last-minute deals** are available through free weekly e-mail services provided directly by the airlines. Most of these deals are announced on Tuesday or Wednesday and must be purchased online. Most are only valid for travel that weekend, but some (such as Southwest's) can be booked weeks or months in advance. Sign up for weekly e-mail alerts at airline Web sites or check megasites that compile comprehensive lists of last-minute specials, such as **Smarter Living** (smarterliving.com). For last-minute trips, www.site59.com in the United States often has better deals than the major-label sites.

If you're willing to give up some control over your flight details, use an *opaque fare service* like **Priceline** (www.priceline.com) or **Hotwire** (www.hotwire.com). Both offer rock-bottom prices in exchange for travel on a "mystery airline" at a mysterious time of day, often with a mysterious change of planes en route. The mystery airlines are all major, well-known carriers — and the possibility of being sent from Philadelphia to Chicago via Tampa is remote. But your chances of getting a 6 a.m. or 11 p.m. flight are pretty high. Hotwire tells you flight prices before you buy; Priceline usually has better deals than Hotwire, but you have to play their "name our price" game. *Note:* In 2004, Priceline added nonopaque service to its roster. You now have the option to pick exact flights, times, and airlines from a list of offers — or opt to bid on opaque fares as before.

Great last-minute deals are also available directly from the airlines through a free e-mail service called *E-savers.* Each week, the airline sends you a list of discounted flights, usually leaving the upcoming Friday or Saturday and returning the following Monday or Tuesday. You can sign up for all the major airlines at one time by logging on to **Smarter Living** (www.smarterliving.com), or you can go to each individual airline's Web site. Airline sites also offer schedules, flight booking, and information on late-breaking bargains.

Driving to New Orleans

New Orleans is easily accessible by car. Interstate 10 runs directly through the city from east to west, and just north of the city is Interstate 12, which also travels from east to west. From I-12, you can connect with the Lake Pontchartrain Causeway and drive south to I-10 directly in the metro area or connect with either I-55 to the west of the city or I-59 to the east of the city. Both I-55 and I-59 flow from north to south and connect with I-10. You can also access the city by U.S. highways 11, 51, 61, and 90. For help planning your route into the city, see the "Greater New Orleans" map on the inside front cover of this book.

Before you pack the trunk, however, don't forget this bit of information: As far as sightseeing goes, New Orleans isn't an easy driving city. Getting around the city isn't impossible, but at many tourist destinations, such as restaurants, nightclubs, or antiques shops, you have to fend for yourself for on-street parking. In the French Quarter, on-street parking is as elusive as Shangri-La; even residents have perennial parking woes. In fact, finding free parking near most attractions is something of a crapshoot. Commercial lots are readily available, but they can be expensive, and their locations are sometimes inconvenient.

Again, I don't want to discourage you or scare you off, especially if you have no other option. But be warned: If you drive into New Orleans (especially if you're staying in the French Quarter), you're better served by taking public transportation around the Quarter and saving your car for excursions outside the district.

Arriving by Other Means

Would you prefer to pull in to New Orleans on a train, or perhaps ride in on a cruise? Here are a few options if you want to leave your car at home.

Riding the rails

An increasingly less popular, but scenic, option is to take a train. All trains arrive at New Orleans's **Union Passenger Terminal,** 1001 Loyola Ave. Call **Amtrak** (☎ **800-USA-RAIL** or 504-528-1610; www.amtrak. com) for specific information on train fares and schedules. Ask about senior-citizen discounts and other possible discounts when making a reservation.

Note: The terminal, located at the edge of the Central Business District, serves as both the train station and the Greyhound Bus Terminal.

Cruising into New Orleans

Taking a cruise ship into New Orleans is about as different a travel option as you can think of. The slow, luxurious nature of a sea cruise fits perfectly with the city's "big easy" reputation, and one of the city's most popular party tunes is the 1959 R&B hit "Sea Cruise," by local Frankie Ford.

As a major port, New Orleans is a stop for a number of cruise lines. If you miss a particular attraction during this trip, you can always catch it when your cruise ship stops here on your next major vacation. Or you can get really creative and schedule a Caribbean cruise right in the middle of your New Orleans vacation. **Carnival** (www.carnival.com), **Norwegian** (www.ncl.com), and **Crystal** (www.crystalluxurycruises. com) lines, for example, make stops in or have cruises disembarking from New Orleans. For a unique vessel, try Riverbarge Excursions (www.riverbarge.com).

You usually disembark at the **Julia Street Cruise Ship Terminals 1 and 2;** if you decide to take a cruise from New Orleans — for example, on Carnival's *Holiday* or *Conquest* — you board here, as well. The terminal was originally developed as part of the 1984 Louisiana World Exposition — only about five minutes on foot from the French Quarter. (For port information, call ☎ **504-522-2551.**) Alternatively, many paddlewheel boats for upriver cruises and some southbound cruise ships depart from the **Robin Street Wharf.**

For more information on cruise ships as a vacation option, consider *Cruise Vacations For Dummies* by Fran Wenograd Golden (Wiley), a handy guide to navigating the world of cruise ships. For more information on cruises departing from New Orleans, check out **Cruise Deals for Less (☎ 800-330-1001** or 504-885-7245; www.cruisedealsforless.com).

Joining an Escorted Tour

You may be one of the many people who love escorted tours. The tour company takes care of all the details, and tells you what to expect at each leg of your journey. You know your costs upfront and, in the case of the tame ones, you don't get many surprises. Escorted tours can take you to the maximum number of sights in the minimum amount of time with the least amount of hassle.

If you decide to go with an escorted tour, I strongly recommend purchasing travel insurance, especially if the tour operator asks to you pay upfront. But don't buy insurance from the tour operator! If the tour operator doesn't fulfill its obligation to provide you with the vacation you paid for, why would the tour operator fulfill its insurance obligations? Get travel insurance through an independent agency. (I tell you more about the ins and outs of travel insurance in Chapter 7.)

When choosing an escorted tour, along with finding out whether you have to put down a deposit and when final payment is due, ask a few simple questions before you buy:

- ✔ **What is the cancellation policy?** Can the tour operator cancel the trip if it doesn't get enough people? How late can you cancel if you're unable to go? Do you get a refund if you cancel? If the operator cancels?

- ✔ **How jam-packed is the schedule?** Does the tour schedule try to fit 25 hours into a 24-hour day, or does it give you ample time to relax by the pool or shop? If getting up at 7 a.m. every day and not returning to your hotel until 6 or 7 p.m. sounds like a grind, certain escorted tours may not be for you.

- ✔ **How large is the group?** The smaller the group, the less time you spend waiting for people to get on and off the bus. Tour operators may be evasive about this because they may not know the exact size of the group until everybody has made reservations, but they should be able to give you a rough estimate.

✔ **Is there a minimum group size?** Some tour operators have a minimum group size, and may cancel the tour if they don't book enough people. If a quota exists, find out what it is and how close they are to reaching it. Again, tour operators may be evasive in their answers, but the information may help you select a tour that's sure to happen.

✔ **What exactly is included?** Don't assume anything. You may have to pay to get yourself to and from the airport. A box lunch may be included in an excursion but drinks may be extra. Beer may be included but not wine. How much flexibility do you have? Can you opt out of certain activities, or does the bus leave once a day, with no exceptions? Are all your meals planned in advance? Can you choose your entree at dinner, or does everybody get the same chicken cutlet?

Depending on your recreational passions, I recommend one of the following tour companies:

✔ **Escape Holidays** (☎ 619-448-4489; www.escapeholidays.com) creates custom tours for groups and independent "on your own" vacation packages, featuring the Essence Music Festival, Crescent City Haunts, and Holidays in New Orleans; call or e-mail for a price quote.

✔ **Menopausal Tours** (☎ 866-468-8646; www.menopausaltours.com) caters specifically to women 40 and older. Ladies, get a group of girlfriends together for the "Jazz, Jambalaya & Beignets" tour, a little taste of everything New Orleans has to offer; prices start at $1,075 per person.

✔ **New Orleans Tours** (☎ 888-486-8687 or 504-592-0560; www.notours.com), offers traditional packages, like a Garden District Walking tour ($24 adults, $21 children ages 3–12), or the more adventurous seaplane tour, which flies over the French Quarter, Chalmette Battlefield, Lafitte, and more ($95 adults, $50 children ages 3–12).

Choosing a Package Tour

For many destinations, package tours can be a smart way to go. In several cases, a package tour that includes airfare, hotel, and transportation to and from the airport costs less than the hotel alone on a trip you book yourself. That's because packages are sold in bulk to tour operators, who resell them to the public. It's kind of like buying your vacation at a buy-in-bulk store — except the tour operator is the one who buys the 1,000-count box of garbage bags and resells them 10 at a time at a cost that undercuts the local supermarket.

Package tours can vary as much as those garbage bags, too. Some offer a better class of hotels than others, while some provide the same hotels for lower prices. Some book flights on scheduled airlines; others sell charters. In some packages, your choice of accommodations and travel days may be limited. Some let you choose between escorted vacations and independent vacations; others allow you to add on just a few excursions or escorted day-trips (also at discounted prices) without booking an entirely escorted tour.

To find package tours, check out the travel section of your local Sunday newspaper or the ads in the back of national travel magazines such as *Travel & Leisure, National Geographic Traveler,* and *Condé Nast Traveler.* **Liberty Travel** (call ☎ **888-271-1584** to find the store nearest you; www. libertytravel.com) is one of the biggest packagers in the Northeast and usually boasts a full-page ad in Sunday papers.

Another good source of package deals is the airlines themselves. Most major airlines offer air/land packages, including **American Airlines Vacations** (☎ 800-321-2121; www.aavacations.com), **Delta Vacations** (☎ 800-221-6666; www.deltavacations.com), **Continental Airlines Vacations** (☎ 800-301-3800; www.covacations.com), and **United Vacations** (☎ 888-854-3899; www.unitedvacations.com). Several big **online travel agencies** — Expedia, Travelocity, Orbitz, Site59, Frommer's (www.frommers.com), and www.lastminute.com — also do a brisk business in packages. If you're unsure about the pedigree of a smaller packager, check with the Better Business Bureau in the city where the company is based, or go online at www.bbb.org. If a packager won't tell you where it's based, don't fly with it.

New Orleans is an extremely popular vacation destination. You find no shortage of package tours — and no two are exactly alike (at least in terms of price). Some tours cater to people who want to be left to their own devices, while other tours target people who want a helping hand in searching out the local color. The following are just a few options:

- ✔ **Liberty Travel** (☎ **888-271-1584**; www.libertytravel.com) offers fairly bare-bones packages, which I liken to big-name hotel chains. Its packages are perfectly nice if you're just looking for a room, a cheap airline ticket, and maybe an attraction or two.

- ✔ If you want a package tour with a bit more character, consider **Destination Management, Inc.** (DMI) (☎ **800-471-8222** or 504-592-0500; www.dmineworleans.com). If Liberty Travel is like a generic, nationwide motor lodge, DMI is more like a small, independent hotel — not a mom-and-pop establishment, mind you, but a place that offers better atmosphere and service than the national chains. As a New Orleans–based company, DMI specializes in New Orleans vacation packages. DMI's packages center around different attractions and seasonal events, including Jazz Fest, Mardi Gras, the New Orleans Saints, Halloween — you name it, DMI has a package for it.

✔ **Festival Tours International** (☎ **310-454-4080;** www.gumbopages.
com/festivaltours) offers a Jazz Fest tour. This tour is like the
homey, bed-and-breakfast of New Orleans packages, with five-star
service thrown in for good measure. The brainchild of Nancy Covey,
this tour has atmosphere, character, culture, and slice-of-life authen-
ticity. Unlike other packages for the New Orleans Jazz and Heritage
Festival, the culture and heritage on this trip doesn't stop when
you leave the event site. Covey also takes you on an insider's tour
of Cajun Country, where you experience musicians currently
making the scene.

Chapter 6

Catering to Special Travel Needs or Interests

*I*f your idea of New Orleans comes courtesy of Hollywood, you may imagine a year-round bacchanal. Although you can find plenty of opportunities to party, the Big Easy offers much more. In fact, New Orleans is nothing if not a "one size fits all" vacation spot.

Traveling with the Brood: Advice for Families

Although most people associate New Orleans with hard-core debauchery, the city is also a popular family destination. The farther away you get from Bourbon Street and the strip clubs in the French Quarter, the more family-friendly the city gets. But you don't have to leave the Quarter to find a wealth of kid-centric attractions and activities. New Orleans's unique history and its status as a nexus of different cultures provide for a number of fascinating landmarks, museums, and other sights of interest to children and adults.

In Chapter 11 (and throughout the book), I highlight the attractions that your kids may like with the Kid Friendly icon. To get you started, the following is a list of places and activities guaranteed to keep kids entertained:

- ✔ Aquarium of the Americas

- ✔ Audubon Zoo

- ✔ City Park

- ✔ Louisiana Children's Museum

- ✔ Mimes, jugglers, musicians, and other street performers in the French Quarter, particularly at Jackson Square

- ✔ A ride across the river on the Canal Street Ferry

- ✔ Six Flags New Orleans

You can also call **ACCENT on Children's Arrangements, Inc.** (☎ **504-524-1227;** www.accentoca.com), a company that specializes in tours for children, especially for those whose parents are attending a convention.

Just because something touts itself as fun for kids doesn't necessarily make it fun for *you* and *your family.* Pointing your kids toward a museum that's "good for them" doesn't work and often results in eye rolling or the ubiquitous "Dad, you're a dork." I'm not ignorant of this reality, as many travel guides seem to be; in Chapter 11, I point out which attractions may be more age-appropriate for small fries than for jaded teens (and vice versa). I don't tell you not to bring your kids to a specific attraction. After all, you know your children better than I do, but I hope the guidance helps you plan a daily itinerary that the whole family can enjoy.

Celebrating Mardi Gras with the family

During **Mardi Gras** the French Quarter is no place to bring your kids (see Chapters 2 and 11 for more information). The farther into the Quarter you go, the raunchier the costumes become. You'd be amazed what people get away with. Also, many young women (and some not-so-young) are prone to lift up their shirts and bare their breasts at the slightest provocation. (Increasingly, men are flashing their private parts as well.) Although this practice originated as an incentive to get float riders to throw the best beads, it's evolved (or devolved) beyond that. In recent years, I've witnessed bartering sessions in the middle of the Quarter, whereby women consent to flash their breasts for camera-toting tourists in return for a free drink, a strand of beads, or even just an appreciative hoot.

In past years, the police have announced that they would crack down on this behavior, promising to arrest anyone violating exposure and decency laws. Nevertheless, it would be impossible for the NOPD to address every incident, so this "tradition" isn't going away anytime soon.

Planning with your kids

When on vacation, most kids hate nothing more than a daily itinerary, a history lesson, or anything else crammed down their throats. To help make your trip fun for you and your kids, let them participate in the planning process. Encourage them to read through this book and any tourist brochures you have. Allow them some input in organizing the sightseeing schedule. If they feel like the vacation belongs to them, too, they'll more likely have fun when they get there — and so will you.

Locating kid-friendly accommodations

Because New Orleans is a large tourist destination, you won't have any trouble finding a place to stay that accepts children. Of course, exceptions always exist. You won't likely find many cozy bed-and-breakfast establishments that accommodate children, for instance. But in major hotels, you'll have no problem.

Of course, after you find a hotel that accepts children, your work has just begun. Children are notoriously hard to please, and woe is the weary parent who doesn't take this into account when selecting a place to stay. Sure, most kids are just happy to be away from home and in close proximity to a rooftop swimming pool. But in case that isn't enough, many (if not most) hotels offer kid-friendly amenities, such as pay-per-view movies or in-house video/DVD rental, video games, and even goodies such as chocolate chip cookies upon check-in. Make sure to inquire about nearby restaurants with children's menus (that goes for the in-house restaurant as well).

Keeping the kids entertained

No matter how much planning you do, kids are still prone to fits of boredom and crankiness. Be sure to take along some toys or activities to help them through the rough patches. Depending on their age or tastes, pack coloring books, comics, books, or a portable radio or CD player to keep them occupied.

Be sure to keep your kids' endurance level in mind when planning your itinerary. Long walking tours can tire kids out faster than adults, and long waits can make them restless. This is where a portable radio or CD player can come in handy. Also, stagger events to keep them enjoyable for kids. A day of pounding the pavement may sap your child's enthusiasm for the next day's trip to that aquarium or zoo exhibit she's been dying to see. You also probably don't need me to tell you that a child's energy level fluctuates wildly, and your little munchkin could catch his second or third wind just as you're ready to collapse for the day. Try to keep an eye on such factors as sugar intake and other stimulants to avoid a serious case of child lag in the middle of a long afternoon.

Relying on babysitting services

If you want a night out on your own without the kids, some hotels provide babysitting services; check with your hotel's concierge or with the reservations clerk, or check the listings in Chapter 9. If your hotel doesn't provide such a service, you can contact an agency that watches your children while you wine and dine at Commander's Palace. Employees of these agencies sit with your kids, take them on organized outings, or create a personalized itinerary:

> ✔ **ACCENT on Children's Arrangements, Inc.** (☎ 504-524-1227; www.accentoca.com); licensed, bonded, insured

> ✔ **Dependable Kid Care** (☎ 504-486-4001; www.dependablekidcare.com); licensed, bonded, insured

Making Age Work for You: Tips for Seniors

Mention the fact that you're a senior citizen when you make your travel reservations. Although all the major U.S. airlines except America West have cancelled their senior discount and coupon book programs, many hotels still offer discounts for seniors. In most cities, people older than 60 qualify for reduced admission to theaters, museums, and other attractions, as well as discounted fares on public transportation.

Members of **AARP** (formerly known as the American Association of Retired Persons), 601 E St. NW, Washington, DC 20049 (☎ 888-687-2277 or 202-434-2277; www.aarp.org), get discounts on hotels, airfares, and car rentals. AARP offers members a wide range of benefits, including *AARP: The Magazine* and a monthly newsletter. Anyone older than 50 can join.

 The **U.S. National Park Service** offers a **Golden Age Passport** that gives seniors 62 years or older lifetime entrance to all properties administered by the National Park Service — national parks, monuments, historic sites, recreation areas, and national wildlife refuges — for a one-time processing fee of $10, which must be purchased in person at any NPS facility that charges an entrance fee. (The Jean Lafitte National Historical Park and Preserve headquarters is located in the French Quarter; its satellite sites include the Chalmette Battlefield and National Cemetery six miles southeast of the city. See Chapter 11 for more details.) Besides free entry, a Golden Age Passport also offers a 50% discount on federal-use fees charged for such facilities as camping, swimming, parking, boat launching, and tours. For more information, go to www.nps.gov/fees_passes.htm or call ☎ 888-467-2757.

Many reliable agencies and organizations target the 50-plus market. **Elderhostel** (☎ 877-426-8056; www.elderhostel.org) arranges study programs for those aged 55 and older (and a spouse or companion of any age) around the world. Most courses last five to seven days in the

United States, and many include airfare, accommodations in university dormitories or modest inns, meals, and tuition. One program, "L'Chaim Celebrate New Orleans' Cultural Heritage and Old World Charm," explores the local Jewish community and its contributions to the city since the 18th century.

Recommended publications offering travel resources and discounts for seniors include

- ✔ *The 50+ Traveler's Guidebook* by Anita Williams and Merrimac Dillon (St. Martin's Press)

- ✔ *101 Tips for Mature Travelers,* available from Grand Circle Travel (☎ **800-221-2610** or 617-350-7500; www.gct.com)

- ✔ *Travel 50 & Beyond,* a quarterly magazine (www.travel50and beyond.com)

- ✔ *Travel Unlimited: Uncommon Adventures for the Mature Traveler* by Alison Gardner (Avalon)

- ✔ *Unbelievably Good Deals and Great Adventures That You Absolutely Can't Get Unless You're Over 50* by Joann Rattner Heilman (McGraw-Hill)

Enjoying your stay in New Orleans depends in large part on how you plan for such variables as the distance between your hotel and the attractions you want to see as well as how you deal with the city's crazy weather. The following sections can help you make the best lodging and sightseeing decisions based on your own personal needs.

Lodging

Depending on your health, your hotel's location may be a more important consideration than it is for other travelers. If you plan to do a lot of sightseeing on foot, try to find a hotel that's central to a number of accessible attractions. If you plan to spend most of your time in the French Quarter, you're in good shape; almost everything in this relatively small but eventful area is within walking distance. If walking the Quarter's 13 blocks seems prohibitive for you or a companion, catching a cab is a wise, inexpensive alternative.

If you're outside the Quarter, make sure your hotel is convenient to public transportation and in a safe neighborhood. I recommend the **Pontchartrain Hotel** or the **St. Charles Guest House** (see Chapter 9) for safety and/or convenience to public transportation — both hotels are on St. Charles Avenue, where the streetcar travels. You can enjoy a brief, scenic walk from the streetcar stop to the St. Charles Guest House, located in the increasingly gentrified but still funky Lower Garden District.

No matter where you choose to stay, take a cab if you venture out at night; the extra couple of dollars is worth the security of being delivered right to your door.

Attractions

If you're staying in the French Quarter, you can find plenty of museums, historic landmarks, and other attractions close at hand, and a number of free sightseeing places (for example, **Jackson Square** or the **Moonwalk**) where you can watch the parade of life unfold before you. If you like to gamble, **Harrah's New Orleans Casino** is just across Canal Street from the **Aquarium of the Americas** and **Canal Place.** Check the listings in Chapter 11 for places of particular interest, as well as for information on senior discounts.

Weather

Whether you travel with a group or on your own, some of the best advice I can give you is to be mindful of the weather. In the summer, when tourism is generally down, you won't encounter as many crowds, which makes it a good time to visit. However, the heat and humidity can tire you out faster than normal, especially during the afternoons. If you're visiting in the summer, plan as many indoor activities as possible during the peak afternoon hours. When you do venture outside, carry some bottled water. (Check Chapter 3 for the lowdown on average temperatures during the year in New Orleans.)

If you get lost or separated from your group, have the number of a reliable cab company on hand. I recommend using **United Cab** (☎ **504-522-9771**), the largest and most reliable fleet in the city.

Accessing New Orleans: Advice for Travelers with Disabilities

Most disabilities shouldn't stop anybody from traveling. More options and resources are available than ever before.

The U.S. National Park Service offers a **Golden Access Passport** that gives free lifetime entrance to all properties administered by the National Park Service — national parks, monuments, historic sites, recreation areas, and national wildlife refuges — for persons who are visually impaired or permanently disabled, regardless of age. (The Jean Lafitte National Historical Park and Preserve headquarters is located in the French Quarter; its satellite sites include the Chalmette Battlefield and National Cemetery six miles southeast of the city. See Chapter 11 for more details.) You may pick up a Golden Access Passport at any NPS entrance fee area by showing proof of medically determined disability and eligibility for receiving benefits under federal law. Besides free entry, the Golden Access

Passport also offers a 50% discount on federal-use fees charged for such facilities as camping, swimming, parking, boat launching, and tours. For more information, go to www.nps.gov/fees_passes.htm or call ☎ 888-467-2757.

Many travel agencies offer customized tours and itineraries for travelers with disabilities. **Flying Wheels Travel** (☎ 507-451-5005; www.flying wheelstravel.com) offers escorted tours and cruises that emphasize sports and private tours in minivans with lifts. **Access-Able Travel Source** (☎ 303-232-2979; www.access-able.com) offers extensive access information and advice for traveling around the world with disabilities. **Accessible Journeys** (☎ 800-846-4537 or 610-521-0339) offers trips for wheelchair travelers and their families and friends. **Wheelchair Getaways** (☎ 800-642-2042 or 504-738-2634; www.wheel chairgetaways.com) rents specially equipped vans with wheelchair lifts and other features for the disabled. The Louisiana office is located in Metairie, a suburb of New Orleans.

Avis Rent a Car has an "Avis Access" program that offers such services as a dedicated 24-hour toll-free number (☎ 888-879-4273) for customers with special travel needs. Avis also offers helpful car features such as swivel seats, spinner knobs, and hand controls, and accessible bus service.

Organizations that offer assistance to disabled travelers include the **MossRehab** (www.mossresourcenet.org), which provides a library of accessible-travel resources online; **SATH (Society for Accessible Travel and Hospitality)** (☎ 212-447-7284; www.sath.org; annual membership fees: $45 adults, $30 seniors and students), which offers a wealth of travel resources for all types of disabilities and informed recommendations on destinations, access guides, travel agents, tour operators, vehicle rentals, and companion services; and the **American Foundation for the Blind** (AFB) (☎ 800-232-5463; www.afb.org), a referral resource for the blind or visually impaired that includes information on traveling with Seeing Eye dogs.

For more information specifically targeted to travelers with disabilities, the community Web site **iCan** (www.icanonline.net/channels/ travel/index.cfm) has destination guides and several regular columns on accessible travel. Also check out the quarterly magazine **Emerging Horizons** ($14.95 per year, $19.95 outside the U.S.; www. emerginghorizons.com); **Twin Peaks Press** (☎ 360-694-2462), offering travel-related books for travelers with special needs; and *Open World Magazine,* published by SATH (subscription: $13 per year, $21 outside the United States).

Anticipating building accessibility

Most of the historic sites and a few of the older hotels and restaurants in New Orleans may present problems for people with disabilities because they're exempt from the provisions of the Americans with Disabilities

Act (ADA). I mention problematic places in the relevant chapters of this book, but call ahead and double-check.

All major hotels comply with the ADA, though some of the smaller hotels and most notably B&Bs either aren't in compliance or only partially so. Among hotels, the **Wyndham Canal Place** receives the biggest thumbs-up for accessibility, and the **Dauphine Orleans, Hotel Monteleone,** and **Royal Orleans** are also highly rated. Many major restaurants also comply, as I note in Chapter 10. If a place doesn't have a ramp, however, staffers are usually more than happy to help assist disabled patrons inside their establishments.

Planning for other New Orleans resources

A few resources within New Orleans can make your visit easier after you arrive in the Crescent City. The new Canal Streetcar is wheelchair accessible; contact the **Regional Transit Authority** (☎ 504-248-3900; www. regionaltransit.org) for more information. The RTA also has lift-equipped buses available for individuals as well as for groups. If you're hearing-impaired and have a telecommunications device for the deaf (TTY), the **Louisiana Relay Service** (☎ 800-947-5277) offers a service that can connect you with non-TTY users. Travelers with disabilities can also receive assistance from **Resources for Independent Living** (☎ 504-522-1955).

Following the Rainbow: Resources for Gay and Lesbian Travelers

The **International Gay and Lesbian Travel Association (IGLTA)** (☎ 800-448-8550 or 954-776-2626; www.iglta.org) is the trade association for the gay and lesbian travel industry, and offers an online directory of gay-and lesbian-friendly travel businesses; go to its Web site and click on "Members."

Many agencies offer tours and travel itineraries specifically for gay and lesbian travelers. **Above and Beyond Tours** (☎ 800-397-2681; www.abovebeyondtours.com) is the exclusive gay and lesbian tour operator for United Airlines. **Olivia Cruises & Resorts** (☎ 800-631-6277 or 510-655-0364; www.olivia.com) charters entire resorts and ships for exclusive lesbian vacations and offers smaller group experiences for both gay and lesbian travelers.

New Orleans is one of the most gay- and lesbian-friendly cities in the United States. You won't lack for bars, restaurants, hotels, or other businesses owned by or catering to gays and lesbians, especially in the French Quarter and neighboring Faubourg Marigny — the epicenter of the local gay scene.

New Orleans hosts a number of gay-themed or gay-friendly events year-round. **Southern Decadence** is a major festival for gay and lesbian tourists that takes place on Labor Day weekend. Halloween also has a sizable gay turnout, and, of course, the spectacle of **Mardi Gras** draws even bigger gay crowds (see Chapters 2 and 11). Despite the elitism of some krewes, Mardi Gras is generally an inclusive and unifying event, bringing together the city's disparate populations for one long party. The lower French Quarter even offers a gay-friendly celebration between St. Ann Street (the unofficial boundary that marks the gay section of the Quarter) and Esplanade Avenue, where the Quarter ends. On Mardi Gras day, gays and lesbians converge around noon in front of the **Rawhide 2010 Bar** (see Chapter 16), at St. Ann and Burgundy streets, to see (and be seen in) outrageous costumes and to compete for the much sought-after Bourbon Street Award.

New Orleans's major gay publication is *Ambush* (☎ 800-876-1484 or 504-522-8047; www.ambushmag.com), providing excellent information on what's going on. You can find a copy in most gay-friendly establishments. In the relevant chapters of this book, I note gay-friendly choices for hotels, restaurants, and nightlife. Here are some additional suggestions:

- ✔ Best *hotel* choices for gay and lesbian travelers are the **Lafitte Guest House,** the **New Orleans Guest House,** and the **Ursuline Guest House,** all in the Quarter. If you're willing to travel a bit farther away, the **Macarty Park Guest House** in Bywater is about ten minutes by cab from the Esplanade boundary of the Quarter.

- ✔ Best *restaurant* picks are **Petunia's** and the **Quarter Scene** in the French Quarter and **Feelings Café** and **La Peniche** in the Marigny.

- ✔ Best gay *nightlife* choices are **The Bourbon Pub and Parade, Golden Lantern, Good Friends, Café Lafitte in Exile, MRB (Mississippi River Bottom), Oz,** and **Rawhide 2010,** all in the Quarter, and **The Phoenix** in the Marigny.

New Orleans has a network of services supporting the gay community. The following organizations can connect you with gay-friendly lodgings, help with travel arrangements, and offer food and entertainment recommendations.

- ✔ **Big Easy Lodging** (☎ **800-368-4876** or 504-433-2563; Fax: 504-391-1903; www.crescentcity.com/fql)

- ✔ **French Quarter Reservation Service** (☎ **800-523-9091** or 504-523-1246; www.neworleansreservations.com)

- ✔ **Gay New Orleans Online** (www.gayneworleans.com)

- ✔ **The Lesbian and Gay Community Center,** 2114 Decatur St. (☎ **504-945-1103;** http://lgccno.org)

The following travel guides are available at most travel bookstores and gay and lesbian bookstores, such as New Orleans's own **Faubourg Marigny Bookstore** (600 Frenchmen St.; ☎ **504-943-9875**), or you can order them from **Giovanni's Room** bookstore, 1145 Pine St., Philadelphia, PA 19107 (☎ **215-923-2960**; www.giovannisroom. com; *Out and About* (☎ **800-929-2268** or 415-644-8044; www.outand about.com), which offers guidebooks and a newsletter ($20/yr; 10 issues) packed with solid information on the global gay and lesbian scene; *Spartacus International Gay Guide* (Bruno Gmünder Verlag; www.spartacusworld.com/gayguide) and *Odysseus,* both good, annual English-language guidebooks focused on gay men; the *Damron* guides (www.damron.com), with separate, annual books for gay men and lesbians; and *Gay Travel A to Z: The World of Gay & Lesbian Travel Options at Your Fingertips* by Marianne Ferrari (Ferrari International; Box 35575, Phoenix, AZ 85069), a very good gay and lesbian guidebook series.

Unleashing Fido: Canines in the Crescent City

Dog lovers are increasingly traveling with their well-behaved canine. Not sure if your dog is ready to travel? Contact the **American Kennel Club** (☎ **919-816-3637**; www.akc.org) for information on the Canine Good Citizen test. If your dog passes, you can be assured that he has good manners. Plus, you may be eligible for hotel and insurance discounts.

New Orleans is a prime spot for pooches, featuring dog-friendly hotels, dog bakeries, sidewalk cafes and coffee shops, and parks galore. Before you come, flip through the pages of:

 ✔ *Dogfriendly.com's United States and Canada Dog Travel Guide,* **2nd Edition** (Dogfriendly.com, Inc.) for general travel tips

 ✔ *Fido Friendly* (☎ **888-881-5861**; www.fidofriendly.com), a national travel magazine for dogs

 ✔ *Urban Dog* (☎ **504-897-9577**; www.urbandogmagazine.com) a regional magazine based in New Orleans

If your dog likes to have a good time, join the **Krewe of Barkus** (www. barkus.org) for its annual Mardi Gras party and parade in the Quarter. My dogs especially dig preparade socializing with other krewe members — from Chihuahuas to Rottweilers — in Armstrong Park.

Here are some other places that get my dogs' tails wagging:

 ✔ The best *hotel* choice for dogs in the city is **Hotel Monaco.** My large dog, Desoto, drooled with happiness over the Bone Appetit package and all the attention from staff and guests. If you're planning a day-trip, stay at **Victoria Inn and Gardens** in Jean Lafitte, just 20 minutes south of New Orleans. Innkeepers Roy and Dale Ross are avid dog lovers and their resident Dalmatians welcome two- and four-legged visitors to the pack.

✔ You can find the best *kibbles* at **Three Dog Bakery** in the Quarter and **Bobo's** on Magazine in Uptown.

✔ The best *parks* are **Cabrini** in the Quarter, which is completely fenced, and the **dog levee** at the intersection of Magazine and Leake Avenue on the Mississippi, just a few blocks from **Audubon Park.** The latter is perfect for squirrel-watching and splashing in the large fountain at the main entrance on St. Charles, but your dog *must* be leashed. If you're in the Mid-City area, **City Park** is a puppy playground.

✔ The best *doggie daycare* is **Pooch's Palace** on Magazine.

Before you leave home, make sure your dog is up-to-date on all vaccinations and wears identification tags. I strongly recommend you microchip your dog; ask your vet for more information.

If your dog becomes ill or suffers an injury, contact **Dr. Mike's Animal House** (☎ 504-523-4455) in the Quarter or **Audubon Veterinary Hospital** (☎ 504-891-0685) if you're Uptown. For an after-hours emergency, call **Causeway Animal Hospital** in Metairie at ☎ 504-828-2700; the clinic is open 24/7, and the staff is top-notch.

Chapter 7

Taking Care of the Remaining Details

In This Chapter

▶ Renting a car or not

▶ Purchasing travel and medical insurance

▶ Staying healthy on your trip

▶ Connecting with your phone or computer

▶ Finding out the latest on airline security

*A*fter you book your hotel room and flight (or make other appropriate arrangements), you may assume that the rest of your trip is smooth sailing.

Not so fast! Before you pat yourself on the back and skip ahead to the book's nightlife section (see Chapters 15 and 16), you still need to straighten out a few final details. Taking care of these details now can save you the aggravation of dealing with them later.

Renting a Car — Not!

Should you rent a car in New Orleans? The short answer is no — but a qualified no. If you plan to stay in the French Quarter, a car may be more of a headache than you really need on vacation. Many of the hotels, B&Bs, and guesthouses listed in this book have a limited number of parking spaces. If you stay in an area such as Faubourg Marigny, the Quarter is still just a short walk away.

Accommodations without adequate parking can point you to a nearby garage, but the garages aren't cheap. In some cases, you may have to park on the street, which can present a big problem in the Quarter, where parking spaces are a hot commodity. (Some people swear that they don't actually exist.)

For sightseeing in the Quarter, a car is more of a hindrance than an asset. All the streets are one-way, and on weekdays during daylight hours, Royal and Bourbon streets are closed to automobiles between the 300 and 700 blocks. In the Central Business District, congested traffic at peak hours and limited parking conspire to make a motorist's life difficult. Also, New Orleans meter maids hand out more tickets than box-office attendants. Some signs noting restricted parking spaces are posted so far from the spaces themselves that you may miss them.

Of course, New Orleans offers much more than the very small French Quarter, especially where dining and nightlife are concerned. If you stay in one of the outlying areas, such as Uptown or the Garden District, you're more likely to find off-street parking.

 If you do rent (or bring) a car, steer clear of congested sightseeing areas such as the Quarter and the Central Business District and rely on public transportation instead.

Finding the car you need at the price you want

Car-rental rates vary even more than airline fares. The price depends on the size of the car, the length of time you keep it, where and when you pick it up and drop it off, where you take it, and a host of other factors. Asking a few key questions may save you hundreds of dollars.

- ✔ **Do you charge lower rates for the weekend compared to your weekday rates?** If you're keeping the car five or more days, a weekly rate may be cheaper than the daily rate. Ask if the rate is the same for pickup Friday morning as it is for Thursday night.

- ✔ **Do you assess a drop-off charge if I don't return the car to the same location?** Some do. Others, notably National, don't.

- ✔ **Is the rate cheaper if you pick up the car at a location in town rather than at the airport?** This may be cheaper — and more convenient — if you don't need a car for the trip to and from the airport.

- ✔ **Is age an issue?** Many car rental companies tack on a fee for drivers under 25, while some don't rent to them at all.

- ✔ **May I get the advertised price that I saw in the local newspaper?** If you did in fact see a rate, be sure to ask for it. Otherwise you may be charged the standard (higher) rate. Don't forget to mention membership in AAA, AARP, and trade unions. These memberships usually entitle you to discounts ranging from 5% to 30%.

   Check your frequent-flier accounts. Not only are your favorite (or at least most-used) airlines likely to have sent you discount coupons, but also most car rentals add at least 500 miles to your account.

You'll find desks for the following rental-car companies at the Louis Armstrong New Orleans International Airport:

- ✔ **Alamo** (☎ **800-GO-VALUE;** www.alamo.com)

- ✔ **Avis** (☎ **800-331-1212;** www.avis.com)

- ✔ **Budget** (☎ **800-527-0700;** www.budget.com)

- ✔ **Hertz** (☎ **800-654-3131;** www.hertz.com)

- ✔ **National** (☎ **800-227-7368;** www.nationalcar.com)

Additionally, **Enterprise Rent-A-Car** (☎ **800-736-8222;** www.enterprise.com) maintains an office nearby on Airline Drive, and **Swifty Car Rental,** a local company (☎ **877-469-4007** or 504-733-2277; www.swiftycarrental.com), operates offices throughout the metropolitan area, including one near the airport.

Using the Internet to find deals

As with other aspects of planning your trip, using the Internet can make comparison-shopping for a car rental much easier. You can check rates at most of the major agencies' Web sites. Plus, all the major travel sites — **Travelocity** (www.travelocity.com), **Expedia** (www.expedia.com), **Orbitz** (www.orbitz.com), and **Smarter Living** (www.smarterliving.com), for example — have search engines that can dig up discounted car-rental rates. Just enter the car size you want, the pickup and return dates, and location, and the server returns a price. You can even make the reservation through any of these sites.

Understanding the additional charges

In addition to the standard rental prices, other optional charges apply to most car rentals (and some not-so-optional charges, such as taxes). Many credit-card companies cover the *Collision Damage Waiver* (CDW), which requires you to pay for damage to the car in a collision. Check with your credit-card company before you go so you can avoid paying this hefty fee (as much as $20 a day).

The car-rental companies also offer additional *liability insurance* (if you harm others in an accident), *personal accident insurance* (if you harm yourself or your passengers), and *personal effects insurance* (if your luggage is stolen from your car). Your insurance policy on your car at home probably covers most of these unlikely occurrences. However, if your own insurance doesn't cover you for rentals or if you don't have auto insurance, definitely consider the additional coverage (ask your car-rental agent for more information). Unless you're toting around the Hope diamond, and you don't want to leave that in your car trunk anyway, you can probably skip the personal effects insurance, but driving around without liability or personal accident coverage is never a good idea. Even if you're a good driver, other people may not be, and liability claims can be complicated.

Some companies also offer *refueling packages,* in which you pay for your initial full tank of gas upfront and can return the car with an empty gas tank. The prices can be competitive with local gas prices, but you don't get credit for any gas remaining in the tank. If you reject this option, you pay only for the gas you use, but you have to return the car with a full tank or face charges of $3 to $4 a gallon for any shortfall. If you usually run late and a fueling stop might make you miss your plane, you're a perfect candidate for the fuel-purchase option.

Playing It Safe with Travel and Medical Insurance

Three kinds of travel insurance are available: trip-cancellation insurance, medical insurance, and lost luggage insurance. The cost of travel insurance varies widely, depending on the cost and length of your trip, your age and health, and the type of trip you're taking, but expect to pay between 5% and 8% of the vacation itself. Here is my advice on all three:

✔ **Trip-cancellation insurance** helps you get your money back if you have to back out of a trip, if you have to go home early, or if your travel supplier goes bankrupt. Allowed reasons for cancellation can range from sickness to natural disasters to the U.S. State Department declaring your destination unsafe for travel. (Insurers usually don't cover vague fears, though, as many travelers discovered who tried to cancel their trips in October 2001 because they were wary of flying.)

A good resource is **"Travel Guard Alerts,"** a list of companies considered high-risk by Travel Guard International (www.travel insured.com). Protect yourself further by paying for the insurance with a credit card. By law, consumers can get their money back on goods and services not received if they report the loss within 60 days after the charge is listed on their credit card statement.

Note: Many tour operators, particularly those offering trips to remote or high-risk areas, include insurance in the cost of the trip or can arrange insurance policies through a partnering provider, a convenient and often cost-effective way for the traveler to obtain insurance. Make sure the tour company is a reputable one. Some experts suggest you avoid buying insurance from the tour or cruise company you're traveling with. They say buying from a third-party insurer is better than putting all your money in one place.

✔ For domestic travel, buying **medical insurance** for your trip doesn't make sense for most travelers. Most existing health insurance policies cover you if you get sick away from home — but check before you go, particularly if you're insured by an HMO.

✔ **Lost luggage insurance** isn't necessary for most travelers. On domestic flights, checked baggage is covered up to $2,500 per ticketed passenger. On international flights (including U.S. portions of international trips), baggage coverage is limited to approximately $9.07 per pound, up to approximately $635 per checked bag. If you plan to check items more valuable than the standard liability, see if your homeowner's policy covers your valuables, get baggage insurance as part of your comprehensive travel-insurance package, or buy Travel Guard's "BagTrak" product. Don't buy insurance at the airport because it's usually overpriced. Be sure to take any valuables or irreplaceable items with you in your carry-on luggage because many valuables (including books, money, and electronics) aren't covered by airline policies.

If your luggage is lost, immediately file a lost-luggage claim at the airport, detailing the luggage contents. For most airlines, you must report delayed, damaged, or lost baggage within four hours of arrival. The airlines are required to deliver luggage, once found, directly to your house or destination free of charge.

For more information, contact one of the following recommended insurers:

✔ **Access America** (☎ **866-807-3982;** www.accessamerica.com)

✔ **Travel Guard International** (☎ **800-826-4919;** www.travelguard.com)

✔ **Travel Insured International** (☎ **800-243-3174;** www.travelinsured.com)

✔ **Travelex Insurance Services** (☎ **888-457-4602;** www.travelex-insurance.com)

Staying Healthy When You Travel

Getting sick will ruin your vacation, so I *strongly* advise against it (of course, last time I checked, the bugs weren't listening to me any more than they probably listen to you).

For domestic trips, most reliable healthcare plans provide coverage if you get sick away from home. For travel abroad, you may have to pay all medical costs upfront and be reimbursed later. For information on purchasing additional medical insurance for your trip, see the preceding section.

Avoiding "economy-class syndrome"

Deep vein thrombosis, or as it's known in the world of flying, "economy-class syndrome," is a blood clot that develops in a deep vein. It's a potentially deadly condition that can be caused by sitting in cramped conditions — such as an airplane cabin — for too long. During a flight (especially a long-haul flight), walk around the cabin and stretch your legs every 60 to 90 minutes to keep your blood circulating.

In addition to walking around the cabin and stretching, other preventive measures include

✔ Avoiding alcohol and sleeping pills

✔ Drinking lots of water

✔ Frequently flexing your legs while sitting

If you have a history of deep vein thrombosis, heart disease, or other condition that puts you at high risk, some experts recommend wearing compression stockings or taking anticoagulants when you fly; always ask your physician about the best course for you. Symptoms of deep vein thrombosis include leg pain or swelling, or even shortness of breath.

Talk to your doctor before leaving on a trip if you have a serious and/or chronic illness. For conditions such as epilepsy, diabetes, or heart problems, wear a **MedicAlert identification tag** (☎ 888-633-4298; www.medicalert.org), which immediately alerts doctors to your condition and gives them access to your records through MedicAlert's 24-hour hotline. Contact the **International Association for Medical Assistance to Travelers (IAMAT)** (☎ 716-754-4883 or, in Canada, 416-652-0137; www.iamat.org) for tips on travel and health concerns in the countries you're visiting, and lists of local, English-speaking doctors. The United States **Centers for Disease Control and Prevention** (☎ 800-311-3435; www.cdc.gov) provides up-to-date information on health hazards by region or country and offers tips on food safety.

Using a Cellphone across the United States

Just because your cellphone works at home doesn't mean it'll work elsewhere in the country (thanks to the fragmented cellphone system). It's a good bet that your phone will work in major cities. But take a look at your wireless company's coverage map on its Web site before heading out — T-Mobile, Sprint, and Nextel are particularly weak in rural areas. If you need to stay in touch at a destination where you know your phone won't work, **rent** a phone that does from **InTouch USA** (☎ 800-872-7626; www.intouchglobal.com) or a rental-car location, but beware that you'll pay $1 a minute or more for airtime.

If you're not from the United States, you'll be appalled at the poor reach of the **GSM (Global System for Mobiles) wireless network,** which is used by much of the world. Your phone will probably work in most major U.S. cities, but it definitely won't work in many rural areas. (To see where GSM phones work in the United States, check out www. t-mobile.com/coverage/national_popup.asp.) And you may or may not be able to send text messages home — something Americans tend not to do anyway, for various cultural and technological reasons. (International budget travelers like to send text messages home because it's much cheaper than making international calls.) Assume nothing — call your wireless provider and get the full scoop. In a worst-case scenario, you can always rent a phone; InTouch USA delivers to hotels.

Accessing the Internet Away from Home

Travelers have any number of ways to check their e-mail and access the Internet on the road. Of course, using your own laptop — or even a personal digital assistant (PDA) or electronic organizer with a modem — gives you the most flexibility. But even if you don't have a computer, you can still access your e-mail and even your office computer from cybercafes.

New Orleans has plenty of cybercafes. Although no definitive directory for cybercafes is available — these are independent businesses, after all — but two places to start looking are at www.cybercaptive.com and www. cybercafe.com.

The **Cyber Bar and Café** at the **Contemporary Arts Center** (900 Camp St.; ☎ 504-523-1216) in the Warehouse District is popular with the downtown crowd. In the French Quarter, storm the **Bastille Computer Café** (605-607 Toulouse St.; ☎ 504-581-1150) or plug into **Royal Access** (621 Royal St.; ☎ 504-525-0401).

Aside from formal cybercafes, most **youth hostels** nowadays have at least one computer you can access the Internet. And most **public libraries** offer Internet access free or for a small charge. Avoid **hotel business centers** unless you're willing to pay exorbitant rates.

Most major airports now have **Internet kiosks** scattered throughout their gates. These kiosks, which you also see in shopping malls, hotel lobbies, and tourist information offices, give you basic Web access for a per-minute fee that's usually higher than cybercafe prices. Only use Internet kiosks as a last resort because they're expensive.

To retrieve your e-mail, ask your **Internet Service Provider (ISP)** if it has a Web-based interface tied to your existing e-mail account. If your ISP doesn't have such an interface, you can use the free **mail2web** service (www.mail2web.com) to view and reply to your home e-mail. For more flexibility, you may want to open a free, Web-based e-mail account with

Yahoo! Mail (http://mail.yahoo.com). (Microsoft's Hotmail is another popular option, but Hotmail has severe spam problems.) Your home ISP may be able to forward your e-mail to the Web-based account automatically.

If you need to access files on your office computer, look into a service called **GoToMyPC** (www.gotomypc.com). The service provides a Web-based interface for you to access and manipulate a distant PC from anywhere — even a cybercafe — provided your "target" PC is on and has an always-on connection to the Internet (such as with Road Runner cable). The service offers top-quality security, but if you're worried about hackers, use your own laptop rather than a cybercafe computer to access the GoToMyPC system.

If you're bringing your own computer, the buzzword in computer access to familiarize yourself with is **Wi-Fi** (wireless fidelity), and more and more hotels, cafes, and retailers are signing on as wireless "hotspots" from where you can get high-speed connection without cable wires, networking hardware, or a phone line. You can get Wi-Fi connection one of several ways. Many laptops sold in the last year have built-in Wi-Fi capability (an 802.11b wireless Ethernet connection). Mac owners have their own networking technology, Apple AirPort. If you have an older computer, you can plug in an 802.11b/**Wi-Fi card** (around $50) to your laptop.

You sign up for wireless access service much as you do cellphone service, through a plan offered by one of several commercial companies that have made wireless service available in airports, hotel lobbies, and coffee shops, primarily in the United States (followed by the United Kingdom and Japan). **T-Mobile Hotspot** (www.t-mobile.com/hotspot) serves up wireless connections at more than 1,000 Starbucks coffee shops nationwide. **Boingo** (www.boingo.com) and **Wayport** (www.wayport.com) have set up networks in airports and high-class hotel lobbies. IPass providers also give you access to a few hundred wireless hotel-lobby setups. Best of all, you don't need to be staying at the Four Seasons to use the hotel's network; just set yourself up on a nice couch in the lobby. The companies' pricing policies can be complex, with a variety of monthly, per-connection, and per-minute plans, but in general you pay around $30 a month for limited access — and as more and more companies jump on the wireless bandwagon, prices are likely to get even more competitive.

You can also find places that provide **free wireless networks** in cities around the world. To locate these free hotspots, go to www.personaltelco.net/index.cgi/WirelessCommunities.

If Wi-Fi isn't available at your destination, most business-class hotels throughout the world offer dataports for laptop modems, and a few thousand hotels in the United States and Europe now offer free high-speed Internet access using an Ethernet network cable. You can bring your own cables, but most hotels rent them for around $10. Call your hotel in advance to see what your options are.

In addition, major ISPs have **local access numbers** around the world, allowing you to go online by simply placing a local call. Check your ISP's Web site or call its toll-free number and ask how you can use your current account away from home and how much it costs. If you're traveling outside the reach of your ISP, the **iPass** network has dial-up numbers in most of the world. You have to sign up with an iPass provider, who can then tell you how to set up your computer for your destination(s). For a list of iPass providers, go to www.ipass.com and click on "Individual Purchase." One solid provider is **i2roam** (www.i2roam.com; ☎ **866-811-6209** or 920-235-0475).

Wherever you go, bring a **connection kit** of the right power and phone adapters, a spare phone cord, and a spare Ethernet network cable — or find out whether your hotel supplies them to guests.

Keeping Up with Airline Security Measures

With the federalization of airport security, security procedures at U.S. airports are more stable and consistent than ever. Generally, you'll be fine if you arrive at the airport **one hour** before a domestic flight and **two hours** before an international flight. If you show up late, alert an airline employee and she'll probably whisk you to the front of the line.

Bring a **current, government-issued photo ID** such as a driver's license or passport. Keep your ID ready to show at check-in, the security checkpoint, and sometimes even the gate. (Children under 18 don't need government-issued photo IDs for domestic flights, but they do for international flights to most countries.)

In 2003, the Transportation Security Administration (TSA) phased out **gate check-in** at all U.S. airports. And **e-tickets** have made paper tickets nearly obsolete. Passengers with e-tickets can beat the ticket-counter lines by using airport **electronic kiosks** or even **online check-in** from your home computer. Online check-in involves logging on to your airline's Web site, accessing your reservation, and printing out your boarding pass — and the airline may even offer you bonus miles to do so! If you're using an airport kiosk, bring the credit card you used to book the ticket or your frequent-flier card. Print out your boarding pass from the kiosk and simply proceed to the security checkpoint with your pass and a photo ID. If you're checking bags or looking to snag an exit-row seat, you will be able to do so using most airline kiosks. Even the smaller airlines are employing the kiosk system, but always call your airline to make sure these alternatives are available. **Curbside check-in** is also a good way to avoid lines, although a few airlines still ban curbside check-in; call before you go.

Security checkpoint lines are getting shorter than they were during 2001 and 2002, but some doozies remain. If you have trouble standing for long periods of time, tell an airline employee; the airline can provide a wheelchair. Speed up security by **not wearing metal objects** such as big belt buckles. If you've got metallic body parts, a note from your doctor can prevent a long chat with the security screeners. Keep in mind that only **ticketed passengers** are allowed past security, except for folks escorting disabled passengers or children.

Federalization has stabilized **what you can carry on** and **what you can't.** The general rule is that sharp things are out, nail clippers are okay, and food and beverages must be passed through the X-ray machine — but security screeners can't make you drink from your coffee cup. Bring food in your carryon rather than checking it because explosive-detection machines used on checked luggage have been known to mistake food (especially chocolate, for some reason) for bombs. Travelers in the United States are allowed one carry-on bag, plus a "personal item" such as a purse, briefcase, or laptop bag. Carryon hoarders can stuff all sorts of things into a laptop bag; as long as it has a laptop in it, it's still considered a personal item. The TSA has issued a list of restricted items; check its Web site (www.tsa.gov/public/index.jsp) for details.

Airport screeners may decide that your checked luggage needs to be searched by hand. You can now purchase luggage locks that allow screeners to open and relock a checked bag if they need to hand-search your luggage. Look for Travel Sentry certified locks at luggage or travel shops and Brookstone stores (you can buy them online at www.brookstone.com). Luggage inspectors can open these TSA-approved locks with a special code or key. For more information on the locks, visit www.travelsentry.org. If you use something other than TSA-approved locks, your lock will be cut off your suitcase if a TSA agent needs to hand-search your luggage.

Part III

Settling into New Orleans

"I think I'll have the Cocoa Puffs Etouffee."

In this part . . .

Whew! Congratulations. After you've finished all that planning, you're finally in New Orleans! Or at least, you're finally ready to arrive. You're probably anxious to see the sights, figure out how to pronounce all those strange words, and soak up all the incredible food and music — not to mention savor the experience of sleeping later than usual and ordering room service. Of course, you need a place to stay after you arrive in the Crescent City, so this part also acquaints you with the different neighborhoods and lodging options. It gives you the scoop on booking a hotel room with tips on rack rates and where to find good deals.

Furthermore, this part helps you get the lay of the land with safety tips and the many public-transportation options and other convenient ways of getting around. Plus, this part discusses where you can locate banks and ATMs so you're never without cash.

Now that you're all settled in — or at least settled on when you're going, how you're getting there, and where you're staying — the time has come to get down to the meat and potatoes of your trip. Yep, I'm talking about food. After all, coming to New Orleans without sampling the cuisine is . . . well, unthinkable! A recent America Online and *Travel & Leisure* survey ranked New Orleans No. 1 in the United States for dining out. Soon, you can taste why.

Chapter 8

Arriving and Getting Oriented

● ●

In This Chapter

▶ Finding your way from Point A (the airport) to Point B (your lodging)
▶ Figuring out the lay of the land

● ●

*N*ew Orleans can be a pretty confusing place, geographically speaking. Throw out your compass, because north, south, east, and west are meaningless in a city where the sun rises over the West Bank (which is, strictly speaking, to the east of the city). The Mississippi River replaces the magnetic poles as the focal point for getting your bearings here: Upriver is Uptown, downriver is downtown, and lakeside is toward Lake Pontchartrain.

The city began in the French Quarter, an area that covers 13 blocks between Canal Street and Esplanade Avenue, from the Mississippi River to North Rampart Street. The city's angular layout follows the bend in the river, making directions such as north, south, east, and west relatively useless. Consequently, you'll hear New Orleanians use the terms **riverside, lakeside, uptown,** and **downtown** in place of traditional directions. You'll have no problem if you remember that North Rampart Street is the "lakeside" boundary of the Quarter, Canal Street marks the beginning of "uptown," and the Quarter is "downtown." (These boundaries aren't immutable, however, and some locals may use different reference points. For example, people often refer to the Warehouse District, which is on the other side of Canal Street from the Quarter, as being downtown.)

Building numbers begin at 100 on either side of Canal Street. In the Quarter, however, the numbers start at the river with 400 because the river swallowed four blocks of numbered buildings before the levee was built. Street names change when they cross Canal Street — another reminder of Canal's traditional role as the border between the old, French New Orleans (the Quarter) and the new, American New Orleans. Bourbon Street, for example, becomes Carondelet as it stretches uptown.

This chapter reviews the best ways to enter the city, whether by land or by air. It also gives you the scoop on the different neighborhoods — including where to find them and what makes them unique.

Making Your Way to New Orleans

You know you want to visit New Orleans — but how do you want to get there? Choose the option that best fits your tastes, schedule, and budget.

Arriving by plane

If you fly into New Orleans, you arrive at Louis Armstrong International Airport, located a good 25-minute drive from the corporate limits of New Orleans in the suburb of Kenner. The airport's three-letter airport code, MSY, refers to the airport's former name, Moisant International — named for daredevil aviator John Blevins Moisant. (The SY refers to the fact that the airport sits on the site of a former stockyard.)

Moisant, as most locals still call it, isn't the flashiest, most ultramodern airport in the world. You've probably seen larger bus stations in New York, Chicago, or Atlanta, but Moisant's small size is a blessing in disguise. The whole place is compact; all concourses are attached to a single structure, and clear signage directs you to the baggage-claim area downstairs. Thus, getting around is more or less a snap. Additionally, you can find information booths throughout the airport and in the baggage-claim area. Also in the baggage-claim area is a branch of the **Traveler's Aid Society** (☎ 504-525-8726).

From the airport to the hotel by cab

The easiest way into town if you're traveling in a group of two or more people is to take a taxi. Cabs wait in line just outside the baggage-claim area, so you'll have no trouble finding one. Expect to pay around $28 for a taxi ride to the French Quarter or Central Business District for one or two people, or $12 each if your group includes more than two people. This price is more or less the same as the cost for a shuttle, and even cheaper if you're in a group of more than two or three. Taxis can hold a maximum of five passengers.

United Cab (☎ 504-522-9771) is the largest and arguably most reliable taxi company in the city. Their taxis are usually busy handling radio calls, however, so they don't wait in line with the other taxis at the airport. Two other reputable companies are **A Service** (☎ 504-834-1400) and **Metry Cab** (☎ 504-835-4242). You can also find plenty of mom-and-pop taxi operations hovering around the airport to catch your fare, most of which are reputable and won't rip you off. Still, exceptions always exist, so if you don't trust them, call one of the companies listed here.

Catching a cab safely

How can you tell if an airport taxi service is legitimate? For one thing, unless you're visiting during a heavy tourist season (Jazz Fest, Mardi Gras, or a big business convention) or you're sharing a cab with other travelers, avoid any driver who attempts to negotiate with you on the price. Negotiating is common during the previously mentioned events, but outside of those times I've heard of drivers quoting one price and then demanding another when they pull up to the hotel. Also, look at the car itself. If it looks professionally painted, you're probably safer than if you approach a car that looks as if someone hand-painted the information over the door. Don't enter a cab that doesn't have a phone number on the door, and don't get into a cab if something about the driver rubs you the wrong way; another cab will come along.

A trip into town usually takes about 25 to 30 minutes, though that number varies depending on where you're headed and what traffic is like on Interstate 10 (I-10), the city's main thoroughfare. Generally, tip between 10 and 15 percent.

From the airport to the hotel by shuttle bus

If you don't want to hail a cab, taking an airport shuttle bus is the next easiest option for getting into the city. Depending on your situation, taking a cab may be a more cost-effective and comfortable ride. You can find airport shuttle information desks in the airport, staffed 24 hours a day.

For $1.50, the **Downtown/Airport Express bus** takes you to the corner of Elk's Place and Tulane Avenue — a 30- to 40-minute ride. The bus leaves from the upper level near the down ramp about every 23 minutes from 5:30 a.m. to midnight (every 12 to 15 minutes during rush hours). The **Jefferson Transit Authority** (☎ 504-818-1077) can give you more information.

For $13, the **Airport Shuttle** takes you directly to your hotel from right outside the baggage area. Taking a taxi costs about the same, or less, and is more convenient, particularly if you have two or more passengers. The shuttle leaves every 10 to 15 minutes, but the ride can take up to an hour because you may have to go to several hotels before getting to your own. In comparison, a cab ride takes only about 25 to 30 minutes. Remember to reserve a spot on the shuttle if you intend to ride it back to the airport. To make your reservation, call ☎ 504-522-3500 or make arrangements through your hotel's concierge. The shuttle does offer wheelchair access.

From the airport to the hotel by "cool car" (rental car)

The New Orleans Police Department refers to a rental car as a "cool car" because undercover officers sometimes drive a rental car to make it seem as though they're tourists. You can find car-rental counters near the baggage-claim area of the airport. (See Chapter 7 for a list of car-rental companies that maintain offices in the airport.) To navigate your trip from the airport to your hotel, read the directions in the next section and check out the "Airport Driving Routes" map in this chapter.

Directions for driving from the airport

Follow one of the many signs at the airport to I-10 East. Take I-10 to the I-10/I-610 split, but *don't* take I-610, which branches off to your left. Continue following I-10, which branches right, until you reach the Superdome (you can't miss that). If you want to go to the French Quarter, follow I-10 to the left of the Superdome and take the Vieux Carré (French Quarter) exit. If you're trying to get to the Central Business District, stay to the right of the Superdome and exit at Loyola. If you want to reach the Garden District, stay to the right of the Superdome and take the St. Charles Avenue exit, which drops you squarely in the Lower Garden District, right on the cusp of Lee Circle and the Central Business District. Check with your hotel for exact directions.

Arriving by car

If you drive to New Orleans, you'll probably arrive by way of one of the major thoroughfares: highways 90 or 61 or Interstate 10. To see how your route flows into the Crescent City, see the "Airport Driving Routes" map in this chapter. Both highways 90 and 61 take you right into the city. If you're following I-10, refer to the previous section, "Directions for driving from the airport," for information on specific exits and road construction.

"&@*# this traffic jam"

Please note that the time estimates in this chapter for getting to your destination are under optimum conditions; traffic jams, breakdowns, construction, or other disturbances can stretch your driving time. Be sure to consult your concierge, a desk clerk, or the *Times-Picayune* about any highway construction projects that may be underway during your stay and pad your timetable accordingly. If I-10 is undergoing work or just suffering a nasty traffic jam, consider alternate routes: Of these, the most direct and easiest route is to take Airline Drive (Hwy. 61 South) into or out of New Orleans.

For up-to-date information on highway construction, check out www.dotd.state. la.us. Even if you know of no active construction, always make allowances for traffic problems, especially if you're heading to the airport to catch a flight home.

Airport Driving Routes

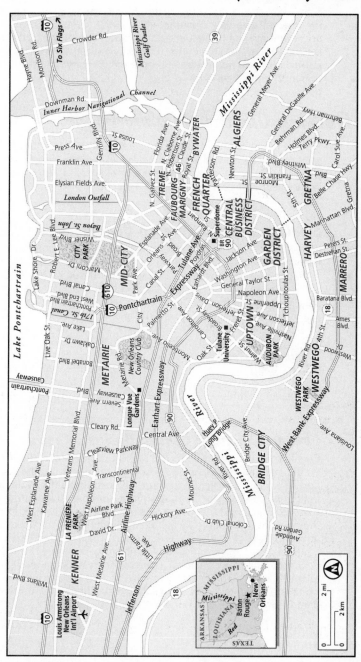

Arriving by train

If you're planning on chugging into New Orleans, your train arrives at
the **Union Passenger Terminal** (☎ **504-528-1610;** www.amtrak.com)
on Loyola Avenue in the Central Business District, just a few blocks
from the French Quarter. After you arrive at the station, taxis are available to take you into town. (If by some fluke they're not, call **United
Cab** at ☎ **504-522-9771.**)

Figuring Out the Neighborhoods

Several towns and unincorporated areas extend along both the east and
west banks of the Mississippi River to make up the New Orleans metropolitan area. This section gives a brief tour of some of the distinct local neighborhoods that make up the city (see the "New Orleans Neighborhoods"
map in this chapter).

Small and famous: French Quarter (Vieux Carré)

Founded in 1718, the Vieux Carré (or Old Square) comprised the original city of New Orleans and is now known as the French Quarter. The
oldest neighborhood in New Orleans is bordered by North Rampart
Street, Esplanade Avenue, Canal Street, and the Mississippi River. Many
people enjoy the French Quarter for the European-style architecture surrounding Jackson Square (the old Ursuline Convent dates back to 1742),
Bourbon Street, and the French Market. Despite its small size, it boasts
more restaurants and bars per square inch than any other city (which is
hyperbole, of course, but not by much). During Mardi Gras, the Quarter
is Party Central. However, you won't find parades here (the narrow, one-
way streets don't even allow buses, much less floats) but rather throngs
of revelers, exhibitionists, and people-watchers. You can best enjoy the
Quarter on foot, by carriage, or as part of an organized tour.

Commercial stuff: Central Business District

Canal Street roughly bounds the district on the north, and the elevated
Pontchartrain Expressway (I-90) bounds the district to the south, between
Loyola Avenue and the Mississippi River. In the midst of the high-rise
buildings, you can see bustling squares and parks, including the newly
restored Piazza d'Italia, which was originally built in 1978 to recognize
the contributions of the local Italian community. You can also find major
attractions, such as the Superdome and World Trade Center, as well as
a burgeoning Museum District, featuring the National D-Day Museum,
Louisiana Children's Museum, Contemporary Arts Center, Ogden Museum
of Southern Art, and the Confederate Museum. Luxury hotels and restaurants and the area's close proximity to the Quarter (without the atten-
dant crowds) make it popular with tourists.

New Orleans Neighborhoods

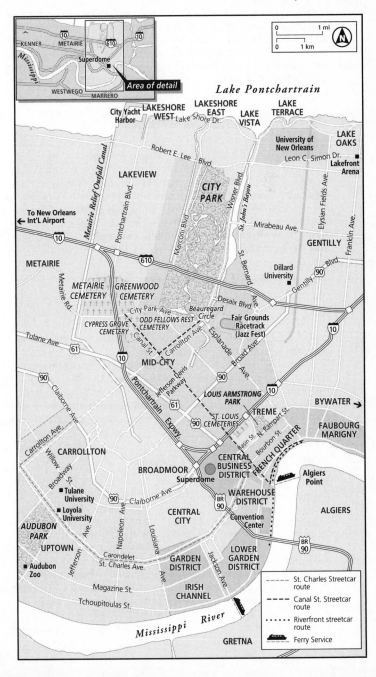

From warehouses to houses: Warehouse District

You can find this area between Julia and St. Joseph's streets within the Central Business District. Once made up almost entirely of warehouses, adaptive reuse and revitalization has turned the neighborhood into an upscale residential neighborhood and Arts District, with most galleries located on what is known as Julia Row. The Convention Center, Riverwalk Shopping Center, music clubs, hotels, restaurants, and museums lure visitors.

Old-world charm: Garden District

Explore the Garden District — bordered by Jackson Avenue, St. Charles Avenue, Louisiana Avenue, and Magazine Street — via the St. Charles Streetcar and on foot. Originally part of the city of Lafayette, it became a fashionable residential area after the United States purchased it and wealthy Americans took up residence there. Visitors come from all over the world to view the beautiful homes and gardens along St. Charles Avenue. Anne Rice's two former homes are located in this neighborhood, as is the world-famous restaurant **Commander's Palace** (see Chapter 14) and the beautifully restored cemetery Lafayette No. 1.

Hip enclave: Lower Garden District

The Lower Garden District houses a number of modest cottages, attractive churches, and some elegant town houses on Coliseum Square. Developed in the early 1800s just downriver from the Garden District, many of its streets are named for Greek Muses — though most have peculiar New Orleans pronunciations. (Ask a local to direct you to Melpomene Street to hear what I mean.) St. Charles Avenue, Jackson Avenue, the Pontchartrain Expressway, and the Mississippi River border this area. Magazine Street is home to many antiques shops, sidewalk cafes, neighborhood bars, coffee shops, and boutiques. Exploring the area on foot is safe during the daytime, although don't stray far from Magazine Street.

Working class: Irish Channel

This area, which originally housed many of New Orleans's Irish immigrants, lies between the Garden District's Magazine Street and the Mississippi River, with its sidewise boundaries at Jackson and Louisiana avenues. If you explore this part of the city on foot, only do so with a large group of people and during the day because it's not the safest neighborhood in town. During the 1800s, the area was a working-class neighborhood, which explains the abundance of double-shotgun cottages. (Shotguns get their name because a person can stand in the front doorway and fire a shotgun out the back door without hitting anything or because they're reminiscent of looking down the barrel of a shotgun.) Walking around the antiques-shop district on Magazine Street and around Felicity Street and Jackson Avenue can give you a real feel for the area.

Churches and cemeteries: Mid-City

Originally called "Back O' Town," swamp covered this area for much of the city's early history. In the early 20th century, however, it was drained and developed. The area, most notable for its churches and cemeteries, stretches along Canal Street between Esplanade Avenue, Perdido Street, City Park, and Derbigny Street (though some claim it starts at Rampart instead of Derbigny). You can experience some parts, notably along Esplanade itself and City Park, on foot; but for safety's sake, stick with a bus or organized tour for other areas, especially the cemeteries.

Students, animals, and more: Uptown

Jackson Avenue, Claiborne Avenue, the Mississippi River, and Carrollton Avenue bound this district, the largest area in the city. You find Tulane and Loyola universities, breathtaking mansions, Audubon Park, Audubon Zoo, and churches and synagogues. Also in this area are the legendary music club **Tipitina's** (see Chapter 16) and several fine restaurants, such as **Pascal's Manale** (see Chapter 10). Magazine Street runs through the district and features antiques shops, boutiques, and art galleries. Take the St. Charles Streetcar or the Magazine bus to explore, though you may want to wander around some areas on foot.

Hip and entertaining: Faubourg Marigny

Faubourg Marigny lies downriver from, and immediately adjacent to, the French Quarter, bordered by Esplanade Avenue, St. Claude Avenue, Press Street, and the Mississippi River. This area, developed during the late 1700s, is one of the earliest suburbs. Today it houses many Creole cottages and bed-and-breakfasts, as well as a range of residents — from bohemian to metrosexual. I hate to give the impression that the area is dangerous because overall it's very quaint and charming, but some areas can be dicey, so only explore the neighborhood on foot during daylight hours. Generally, Frenchmen Street, which is a hip entertainment area, is safe, as is most of the neighborhood close to the river. The farther toward Rampart and St. Claude you get, the riskier it becomes.

Not backwater: Bywater

Bywater, bounded by Press Street, St. Claude Avenue, Poland Avenue, and the Mississippi River, is just downriver from the French Quarter. Some naysayers call this region "backwater" because at first glance it seems like a wasteland of light industry and run-down homes. In fact, Bywater is in the midst of a renaissance. Originally, artisans, free persons of color, and immigrants from Germany, Ireland, and Italy called this area home. Now artists, designers, and residents who simply can't afford the Quarter or Marigny live in its Creole cottages and Victorian shotguns. Within this mix are some funky neighborhood restaurants and bars.

Creole: Algiers Point

One of the city's original Creole suburbs, Algiers Point is the only part of the city on the West Bank, and it has changed little over the decades. Here you find some of the best-preserved small gingerbread and Creole cottages in New Orleans. The neighborhood has begun to attract a lot of attention as a historic landmark, and makes for a nice stroll during the day, though I'd stay in the car rather than walk on foot. (Like parts of Uptown, tranquil areas can give way to less-than-desirable areas at a moment's notice.) It's also becoming a popular neighborhood for locals. A former hole-in-the-wall club called the **Old Point Bar** (see Chapter 16) has established itself as a hip musical destination, adding to the neighborhood's cachet.

Finding Information After You Arrive

You can find a state-run **Tourist Information Center** (☎ 504-568-5661) in the French Quarter at 529 St. Ann St. in the historic Pontalba Buildings on the side of Jackson Square. Other information centers dot the city, many of them owned and operated by tour companies or other businesses. You can find tourist booths at these locations:

- ✔ **Canal and Convention Center Boulevard** (walk-up booth; ☎ 504-587-0739) at the beginning of the 300 block of Canal on the downtown side of the street

- ✔ Just outside the **World Trade Center** (walk-up booth; ☎ 504-587-0734) at 2 Canal St.

- ✔ Near the **Hard Rock Cafe** (walk-up booth; ☎ 504-587-0740) on the 400 block of North Peters Street

- ✔ **Julia and Convention Center Boulevard** (walk-up booth)

- ✔ **Poydras and Convention Center Boulevard** (walk-up booth)

- ✔ **New Orleans Metropolitan Convention & Visitors Bureau** (☎ 504-566-5011; www.nomcvb.com) at 2020 St. Charles Ave.

- ✔ **Vieux Carré Police Station** (small tourist information desk inside the station; ☎ 504-565-7530) at 334 Royal St.

Getting Around New Orleans

You'll probably spend most of your time in the French Quarter, which is only 6 blocks wide and 13 blocks long. Because the area is so small — and the narrow one-way streets, traffic congestion, strict traffic laws, and lack of on-street parking make driving a nightmare — I suggest you walk.

If you're cooped up in a car, you can't see the sights or hear the sounds of the French Quarter in the same way as on your own two feet. If you get tired, you can always hire a carriage and let the mule do the walking.

Use the daylight hours to explore; after dark, stick to well-lit areas with other people around. Watch out for pickpockets on Bourbon Street. Avoid contact with panhandlers, and be wary of people who approach you with a "hard-luck" story — their car broke down, they need money for gas, or their purse was stolen, for example — no matter how well dressed or sincere they seem. I'm not telling you to be rude, but use your judgment. Also avoid people (especially kids) who want to wager with you; a frequent ruse is "I bet I can tell you where you got your shoes." (You got 'em on your feet.) Or, "I bet I can spell your name." (Y-o-u-r-n-a-m-e.) As always, use common sense when exploring any area of the city.

New Orleans features a reliable and thorough public transportation system — streetcars and buses connect all neighborhoods that you may want to visit. Call the **Regional Transit Authority's Ride Line** at ☎ **504-248-3900** for maps, passes, and other information about streetcars or buses. Any of New Orleans's visitor information centers (including the main location at 529 St. Ann St. by Jackson Square) also have information on public transportation.

If you plan to use public transportation frequently during your stay, purchase a **VisiTour pass,** which entitles you to unlimited bus and streetcar rides. You can purchase one at most hotels and banks in the Quarter, Central Business District, and along Canal Street in one-day ($5) or three-day ($12) increments. Two booths also sell them: one outside the Aquarium of the Americas and the other on the 600 block of Decatur Street.

Hopping the St. Charles or Canal streetcars

Since 1835, the St. Charles line (see the "St. Charles Streetcar Route" map in this chapter) has serviced the Central Business District, Garden District, Lower Garden District, Uptown, and Carrollton neighborhoods. The 7-mile ride begins at the corner of Carondelet and Canal streets and takes you from downtown to Uptown (or vice versa) through many historic neighborhoods.

New Orleanians giddily anticipated the April 2004 return of the Canal Streetcar line (see the "Canal Streetcar Route" map in this chapter), 40 years after the last car ran and protesters threw tomatoes at the new buses. (You can see photos of the new Canal Streetcars being built on the **New Orleans RTA** Web site www.norta.com/gallery.) The 5½-mile ride heads up Canal, passing through the Central Business District and Mid-City, and ends at one of two destinations, either north on the Carrollton spur to the 1,500-acre urban oasis of City Park or farther west to the Cypress Grove and Greenwood cemeteries.

Canal Streetcar Route

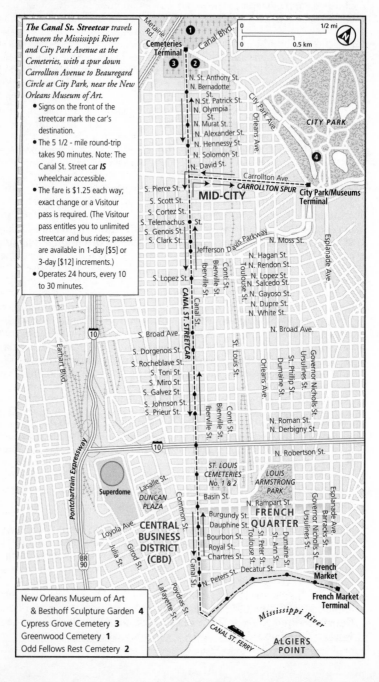

The Canal St. Streetcar travels between the Mississippi River and City Park Avenue at the Cemeteries, with a spur down Carrollton Avenue to Beauregard Circle at City Park, near the New Orleans Museum of Art.

- Signs on the front of the streetcar mark the car's destination.
- The 5 1/2 - mile round-trip takes 90 minutes. Note: The Canal St. Street car **IS** wheelchair accessible.
- The fare is $1.25 each way; exact change or a Visitour pass is required. (The Visitour pass entitles you to unlimited streetcar and bus rides; passes are available in 1-day [$5] or 3-day [$12] increments.)
- Operates 24 hours, every 10 to 30 minutes.

New Orleans Museum of Art
   & Besthoff Sculpture Garden **4**
Cypress Grove Cemetery **3**
Greenwood Cemetery **1**
Odd Fellows Rest Cemetery **2**

A streetcar with a past

Before it was electrified in 1893, the St. Charles Streetcar (which began life as the Carrollton Railroad in 1835) used mule power and steam for propulsion. The St. Charles Streetcar is the oldest railway system in continuous operation in the entire world. The present streetcars date from the 1920s and are listed on the National Register of Historic Places.

Riding either streetcar costs just $1.25 each way (exact change or a VisiTour pass is required). Chapter 11 has a list of sights to see while on the streetcar, which operates 24 hours a day. In order to maintain its distinction as a moving landmark by the National Register of Historic Places, the St. Charles Streetcar doesn't provide modern amenities such as air conditioning or handicap accessibility. However, the Canal Streetcar features air conditioning, wheelchair lifts, and a surprisingly quiet, high-tech braking system. The round-trip for either route takes 90 minutes to two hours.

Generally, you don't have to wait too long for a streetcar — usually no more than half an hour. Downtown, you can board the St. Charles Streetcar at Canal and Carondelet (directly across Canal from Bourbon Street) and the Canal Streetcar at various stops along Canal Street on the eastern edge of the French Quarter. You can also board at a number of designated stops along St. Charles Avenue and Canal Street, respectively. Like taking a bus, you can get on and off the streetcar at will, but you have to pay each time you get back on.

The St. Charles line ends, rather inconveniently, at Palmer Park at Carrollton and Claiborne avenues where you can transfer to a bus for 25¢. Or, take the return trip and stop at one of the many restaurants and shops in the Riverbend (at the corner of St. Charles and Carrollton avenues).

Depending on which destination you choose, the Canal line ends at the cemeteries, which are safe to explore, or City Park. The latter features the New Orleans Museum of Art, the spectacular new Besthoff Sculpture Garden, and the always-blooming New Orleans Botanical Garden. Families will want to head straight to **Children's Storyland,** an amusement park (rated one of the ten best in the country by *Child* magazine), and **Carousel Gardens**, which features a nostalgic, wooden-horse carousel ride.

Because the streetcar is as much a mode of public transportation as a tourist attraction, it gets pretty crowded, especially at rush hour or when school lets out in the midafternoon. Also, the Canal Streetcar is packed during Jazz Fest because it's now the cheapest and most convenient transportation to the Fair Grounds.

Riverfront seating: The Riverfront Streetcar

Established during the 1984 World's Fair, the Riverfront Streetcar line runs along the riverfront from the Convention Center to the far end of the French Quarter at Esplanade. The approximately 2-mile ride, which is a great way to see the river, costs $1.50 (exact change or a VisiTour pass is required). You can board, or get off, along that route at designated stops. The streetcar is wheelchair accessible.

By bus

Buses in New Orleans may generally be more convenient than streetcars, but they don't cover the same routes, and they're not anywhere *near* as picturesque. One or more bus lines connect most neighborhoods, and the fare is $1.25 (exact change or a VisiTour pass is required). Transfers cost 25¢, and buses are wheelchair accessible.

Because you're a visitor to New Orleans, you'll probably need to use only a few of the bus lines, such as **Tulane** (if you happen to stay on Tulane Avenue) or **Magazine** (which runs through the Central Business District, Lower Garden District, and Uptown between the Garden District and the Irish Channel). Buses pick up passengers every other block or so along their routes at designated bus stops. Again, you can get more-specific information from the **Regional Transit Authority's Ride Line** at ☎ **504-248-3900** or by picking up one of the excellent city maps available at the **Visitor Information Center** at 529 St. Ann St.

By taxi

During the day, public transportation is perfectly safe, but I don't recommend taking it at night. You probably won't have any problems if you get on and off at well-lit major intersections, but I suggest a taxi if you're going somewhere not right on the line's route. A good neighborhood can take a turn for the worse in just a few short blocks.

A view from the streetcar

Not only is the $1.25 streetcar ride a bargain, it's also a fun and relaxing way to get an overview of the city. Although the St. Charles route is renowned for its beautiful oak-lined avenue and grand residences, the Canal route is experiencing a commerical and residential renaissance. For a guided tour of the sights, see Chapter 13. You may also want to buy a copy of *St. Charles Avenue Streetcar Line — A Self-Guided Tour* ($5.95), which gives you a wealth of information about the streetcar line and about the buildings along the route. You can find it at the **Historic New Orleans Collection** (at 533 Royal St. in the French Quarter; **504-523-4662**; www.hnoc.org) and elsewhere.

St. Charles Streetcar Route

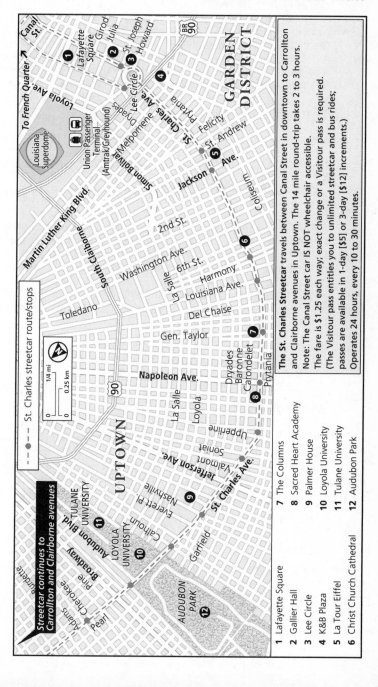

The **St. Charles Streetcar** travels between Canal Street in downtown to Carrollton and Clairborne avenues in Uptown. The 14 mile round-trip takes 2 to 3 hours.

Note: The Canal Street car IS NOT wheelchair accessible.

The fare is $1.25 each way; exact change or a Visitour pass is required. (The Visitour pass entitles you to unlimited streetcar and bus rides; passes are available in 1-day ($5) or 3-day ($12) increments.) Operates 24 hours, every 10 to 30 minutes.

Streetcar continues to Carrollton and Clairborne avenues

- - - - - St. Charles streetcar route/stops

1 Lafayette Square
2 Gallier Hall
3 Lee Circle
4 K&B Plaza
5 La Tour Eiffel
6 Christ Church Cathedral
7 The Columns
8 Sacred Heart Academy
9 Palmer House
10 Loyola University
11 Tulane University
12 Audubon Park

Finding an available cab usually isn't too much trouble, with the exception of busy times such as rush hour or during bad weather. If a cab is empty, driving relatively slowly, and its "On Duty" sign isn't on (if it even has one), chances are it's looking for fares. But as in most major cities, the methods and habits of New Orleans cabbies can be inscrutable. A cab may be on its way to pick up a radio-call fare. Also, the cabbie may be on his lunch break, he may be scrutinizing potential fares for the most lucrative ride (to the airport), or he may just not like the way you look. If you're in a hurry, your best bet is always to call ahead for a cab.

The easiest places to find a taxi include the airport, the French Quarter, and the Central Business District. You can also spot cabs at stands near restaurants, at all the major hotels, and at some smaller hotels as well. If you can't find a cab on the street, call a taxi company. **United Cab** (☎ **504-522-9771**) is the largest and most reliable taxi company in the New Orleans area.

A ride for two people to most major tourist areas doesn't cost more than $10. All taxis cost $2.50 for the first ⅙ of a mile and 20¢ for each additional ⅙ of a mile (or $1.20 per mile). If you travel at a rate less than ⅙ of a mile per 40 seconds, the cabbie charges the additional 20¢ anyway. Add $1 for each additional person. The maximum number of passengers is five. You can also hire taxis for $30 an hour, though taxi companies impose a two-hour minimum and don't take you outside the New Orleans area.

During football and basketball games, Jazz Fest, and other special events, taxi drivers usually expect you to pay $3 per person or the meter rate, whichever is greater. Special events include regularly scheduled sporting events and/or concerts at the Superdome, Saenger Theater, Fair Grounds, and most other stadiums.

In the event that you leave a wallet, piece of luggage, or other important effect in a cab when you exit, call the cab company as soon as possible. Calmly tell the dispatcher your problem, and provide him or her with your route details ("I went from the Canal Place Shopping Center to Commander's Palace"). In case of situations such as this, noting your taxi driver's name (the license should be clearly posted) and the taxi's number (which should be painted on its trunk or on another visible space) is always a good idea.

By car

Though not impossible, driving in New Orleans *is* a big hassle. Parking is an issue (except in the French Quarter, where it's more of a myth). Navigation is confusing because street names change without warning and some streets have more twists and turns than an afternoon's worth of daytime soaps. As for other drivers . . . well, that's another story.

Biking it

If you're feeling especially adventurous, rent a bike and take your own tour around New Orleans, using the information in this book as a guide. **Bicycle Michael's** (☎ 504-945-9505; www.bicyclemichaels.com) and **French Quarter Bicycles** (☎ 504-529-3136; www.fqbikes.com) are two good bets for rentals. Most cyclists in the city ride along the streets with the car traffic or along the popular bike trails in the greater New Orleans vicinity. For a comprehensive list of New Orleans bike shops and maps of bike trails, visit the **New Orleans Bicycle Club** Web site at www.gnofn/~nobc/.

Avoiding the French Quarter

Before I go any further, however, absolutely the best, most essential tip I can give you about driving around New Orleans is to avoid driving in the French Quarter as much as possible. Why? Driving in the Quarter is a headache and a half. Unless you're paid to do it (that is, you're a cab driver), it's not worth the aggravation. The Quarter is small enough, with everything pretty close together, to navigate on foot.

Parking (or not parking) in the Quarter

Driving in the Quarter is a bad idea for a number of reasons, but the biggest is parking, which is practically nonexistent; even residents suffer constant parking woes. Parking spaces are scarce, and the ones that exist always seem to be occupied by people who got there before you — even if you get there at 4 a.m. Even if by fate you do find what seems to be an available spot, chances are it's illegal (of course, the sign pointing out this fact is probably obscured or on the other end of the street).

When choosing your hotel, find out whether your hotel has parking available. If you're staying in a French Quarter hotel that has parking, well, great, but limit your car usage to excursions outside the Quarter. Wait a minute, you're saying. What if I'm staying outside the Quarter, but I want to come in to visit? Good point. My advice is to take the Canal or St. Charles streetcars if possible. Otherwise, park in one of the commercial parking lots on Decatur along the river and walk the rest of the way. You'll also see commercial lots inside the Quarter, notably for some of the bigger hotels, but they're often full, not to mention expensive. Aside from helping you avoid the hassle of finding a parking spot, parking in one of these lots is well worth the security of knowing you won't get towed — or vandalized.

Navigating the Quarter

The streets in the French Quarter are all one-way, which can make a simple right turn an elaborate affair. Additionally, certain tourist-heavy areas — notably Bourbon and Royal streets — are more congested than a Southern gourmand's arteries. Pedestrian traffic is thick, massive, and unrelenting, and no one shows much concern about stopping to let your car cross the street.

To further complicate matters, tourist traffic completely barricades the 300–700 blocks of Bourbon and Royal on weekdays during daylight hours, which turns the merely impractical into the impossible. Chartres Street is also closed on the blocks in front of the St. Louis Cathedral.

Additionally, the streets in the French Quarter are narrow, with no room to pass because on-street parking takes up almost half the available driving space. The lack of space is bad enough when you're stuck in a long line of traffic trying to navigate its way across Bourbon Street, but getting stuck behind a mule-drawn buggy is even worse.

Driving outside the Quarter

Outside the French Quarter, driving is a whole different story. In the Central Business District, getting around in your car is pretty much the same as in your main downtown area back home. Parking spots (at least free ones) can be hard to come by. Traffic can and will be heavy during morning and afternoon rush hour, and probably during lunch as well. You can turn right on red throughout the city unless otherwise specified, but many streets are one-way, and many of those (most notably Tulane Avenue) don't allow left turns.

Enjoying a romantic carriage ride

You'll be hard pressed to resist the mule-drawn carriages at Jackson Square if you have even one romantic bone in your body. The mules sport ribbons, flowers, or even a hat, and each driver fiercely competes with other drivers for the "most unique city story" award. No matter which driver you choose for the 2¼-mile ride through the French Quarter, you'll undoubtedly get a nonstop monologue on historic buildings, fascinating events of the past, and a legend or two. Look for the carriages at the Decatur Street end of Jackson Square from 9 a.m. to midnight in good weather. Most drivers charge around $8 for adults and $5 for children under 12. A private carriage tour, however, costs significantly more. Contact **Good Old Days Buggies** (☎ 504-523-0804) for a private tour, including hotel or restaurant pickup. Chapter 11 has more information on carriage tours.

You can't grab a ride on one, but I recommend you try the gourmet taffy from the Roman Candy mule-drawn cart that is usually parked on St. Charles about a half-mile downriver from Audubon Park. The driver and his mule live Uptown a couple blocks from Whole Foods on Magazine and are beloved by locals and tourists alike. One taste of the taffy (my favorite flavor is chocolate) and you'll always be on the lookout for this old-fashioned treat.

If you park on a parade route, block access to someone's driveway, or break other laws, your car may be towed away and impounded, and getting it back can cost you $100 or more. If you think your car has been towed, call the impounding lot (☎ **504-565-7235**) or the Claiborne Auto Pound, 400 N. Claiborne Ave. (☎ **504-565-7450**).

The driving situation is a little better uptown in the Garden District and other areas. You'll still encounter many one-way streets, however, and as always, free parking is hard to come by. Even if you do find a free spot, it may not be close to the attraction you're looking for. (Of course, no one guarantees that a commercial parking lot is any more convenient.)

Avoiding local hazards: Potholes and drivers

Keep in mind that New Orleans's streets are famous for their potholes, some of which qualify as craters. Local drivers have developed a driving sixth sense; on certain streets, a sort of autopilot takes over that swerves your car this way or that to avoid wrecking your alignment on a nasty bump. Being new to the area, you haven't formed this psychic ability yet, and some potholes aren't so easy to see until after they've jolted you.

Last, but not least, are the New Orleans drivers themselves. Don't get me wrong — this is my home, and I love it — but the people here don't know how to drive. That statement is an overgeneralization, of course, but for the most part, New Orleans drivers are a dangerous mixture of arrogance and cluelessness. Rubbernecking, idling in the passing lane, failure to yield or allow others to merge, and a complete lack of familiarity with turn signals are all trademark characteristics of local drivers. Consider yourself warned.

Chapter 9

Checking in at New Orleans's Best Hotels

. . . .

In This Chapter

▶ Finding the hotel you want
▶ Locating the best price
▶ Turning up in New Orleans sans reservation
▶ Checking into the best hotels in the city
▶ Considering a few more hotel options

. . . .

Most visitors to New Orleans don't plan to spend much time in their hotel room, but there's something to be said for a good night's sleep. Or a sudden storm could encourage you to stick indoors for a little while, in which case, you want to be comfortable. Whether you decide to splurge on a luxurious suite at the Ritz-Carlton or take refuge in a Ramada, this chapter offers a variety of options — and aesthetics — in every price range.

Getting to Know Your Options

When it comes to lodging, many travelers simply look for the cheapest accommodations they can find. Or they choose a hotel that's central to everything (usually right on Bourbon Street) but end up paying twice as much.

To make a hotel choice that best fits your needs, decide what's most important to you. Whatever your preferences, this chapter helps you weigh your options by outlining the advantages and disadvantages of staying in certain neighborhoods. It also gives you an idea of what you can expect to get, value-wise, for your dollar in New Orleans.

Since the 1960s the people of New Orleans have faithfully preserved the Quarter's architectural style. In fact, distinguishing between a new hotel that has been lovingly placed inside the shell of an older building and a hotel built from scratch isn't as easy as it sounds. Even motor hotels (which provide parking spots and have helped alleviate the ever-present problem of on-street parking) maintain a distinctly New Orleans look.

Of course, the city does have some high-rise chain hotels, but you only find them appropriately located in commercial sections, such as the Central Business District. Many of them have been customized to blend in with the scenery. Whatever your preference, New Orleans offers a variety of options.

Watch for the Kid Friendly icon, which points out hotels that are especially good for families.

Listings also note other special considerations, such as which hotels accommodate disabled travelers, which places are the most gay-friendly, which welcome pets, which inspire romance, which are convenient to Mardi Gras parade routes, and so on.

Disabled travelers please take note: Hotels listed as wheelchair accessible may offer only a small number of these rooms, so ask about availability when you make your reservation. Also, "wheelchair accessible" doesn't necessarily mean that the hotel is up to the standards of the Americans with Disabilities Act (ADA) — the hotel may just be accessible from the street and have an elevator and wide doorways. I try to include any special information about steps, bathroom accessibility, or other access concerns.

You won't have any trouble finding atmosphere in this city — even in more modern neighborhoods. Despite the annual influx of hundreds of thousands of visitors, New Orleans has managed to keep historic districts such as the French Quarter free of skyscraper development. Because the city is below sea level, engineers found it to be quite a challenge to create stable, tall buildings. By the time they figured out how to do it, the French Quarter was a protected historic district that didn't allow new development disproportionate in size to its original buildings. In fact, the modest, four-story Pedesclaux-Lemonnier House at 640 Royal St. is still known as the "Skyscraper." It was built between 1795 and 1811 and is believed to be the first four-story building in New Orleans.

The chains: Tried and true

New Orleans has its share of national chain hotels, such as Holiday Inn, Hyatt, Marriott, Sheraton, Ramada, and Radisson. Although these hotels tend to have a homogeneous, seen-one-you've-seen-'em-all quality, the best ones adapt to the color and flavor of New Orleans, both outside and inside. (One good example is the **Holiday Inn-Chateau LeMoyne** in the French Quarter; see its listings later in this chapter.) These chain hotels usually attract business travelers with moderate expense accounts or families with children in tow. Many travelers prefer the consistency assured by a brand name. New Orleans features some fine chain hotels; this chapter lists the best ones.

Boutique hotels: Quiet luxury

Independent hotels — also called boutique hotels — are smaller in scope. They can be family-run, mom-and-pop operations (such as the **Hotel Villa Convento** in the French Quarter), or part of a small group of hotels owned by the same company but not part of a cookie-cutter chain. Boutique hotels may target a specific niche, such as older travelers or budget-minded business travelers. They're also usually cheaper than the bigger chains (though this rule isn't set in stone). Independent hotels are good spots to soak up local character, but they often have fewer amenities than chain hotels.

Motels and motor hotels: No frills

Motels are more or less like hotels, only stripped of the amenities. If you're willing to forego room service, a swimming pool, or atmosphere for a cheaper price, go with a motel. Of course, different types of motels exist — from the ubiquitous Motel 6 to seedy "no-tell motels" — but by and large, they're just places to sleep and shower. I don't recommend any lodging of this ilk in this book, concentrating instead on places with character and (usually) amenities, but you can find toll-free numbers for most of the major motel chains in any metropolitan phone book (and in the Appendix).

B&Bs and guesthouses: The personal touch

Sure, some of your nicer hotels offer fine service. However, *service* and *hospitality* aren't the same. For hospitality, head for a bed-and-breakfast (B&B). Breakfast — be it a full, belt-loosening extravaganza or (more likely) of the continental variety — is only part of the equation. After all, many hotels also offer a complimentary continental breakfast. So what sets a B&B apart? Basically, staying in a room in a B&B is a lot like being a guest in someone's home. In fact, most B&Bs *are* someone's home.

As with hotels, all B&Bs aren't created equal. Some are renovated houses fully dedicated to visitors, with a small living space for the caretaker's family tucked discreetly away, and a communal kitchen where visitors socialize over breakfast. Some are lavish manses, with antique furniture and floor-to-ceiling picture windows. Such picturesque spots may offer an impressive breakfast spread and perhaps a glass of wine in the afternoon as part of the service. Generally, the more you pay, the higher the level of service and hospitality.

Of course, what's in a name and what's offered can sometimes be vastly different. Many places that *call* themselves B&Bs are actually closer to what Europeans call a *home stay* — residences that rent out extra bedrooms, which may sound all well and good, but chances are they're neither licensed nor insured. You may not think the difference sounds like a big deal until you have an accident on the stairs, or you can't find a fire extinguisher or a safe exit during a fire. When inquiring about a B&B, find out whether it belongs to the **Louisiana Bed and Breakfast Association** (☎ 225-346-1857; www.louisianabandb.com). This association's members are licensed, insured, and regularly inspected for fire safety, sanitation, and up-to-date insurance, among other concerns. Be sure to contact the LBBA to verify membership.

I mention a few choice B&Bs in this chapter. If they interest you and you want more choices, calling a B&B reservation service is your best bet. The most reliable (and the most personable as well) is called, appropriately enough, **Bed and Breakfast, Inc. Reservation Service** (☎ **800-729-4640** or 504-488-4640; www.historiclodging.com). Other options are **Bed and Breakfast & Beyond** (☎ **800-886-3709** or 504-896-9977; www.nolabandb.com), **Bed & Breakfast and Accommodations** (☎ **888-240-0070** or 504-838-0071; www.neworleansbandb.com), and **Garden District Bed & Breakfast** (☎ **504-895-4302;** www.bedandbreakfast.com/ppf/inn/626137/Listing.aspx).

Keep in mind that B&Bs are quite popular; regular visitors to Mardi Gras and Jazz Fest can reserve rooms up to a year in advance. So call early!

Similar to B&Bs are guesthouses, which are often closer in size and spirit to hotels, though the atmosphere is closer to a B&B. Like B&Bs, native New Orleanians (or in some cases, visitors who never left) often preside over them and imbue them with a special brand of hospitality. Like B&Bs, they're often furnished with antiques and are heavy on the quaint old-world charm or cozy, homelike atmosphere. Yet again, like B&Bs, guesthouses usually serve some sort of breakfast.

The difference between a B&B and a guesthouse comes down to size and, consequently, the level of service. In a B&B, you may be the only guest, or perhaps one out of six, and in intimate contact with its operators. A guesthouse, on the other hand, is often larger, and in all probability less intimate. Certainly, that may be exactly what you're looking for: more intimacy than a hotel, but without having to actually talk to anyone while you're still waking up at breakfast. (At other times, the differences between a place calling itself a guesthouse and a B&B are indistinguishable; the proprietors probably just thought that the words "guesthouse" sounded better.)

The upper-crust hotels: Top of the line

You know what I'm talking about here: the cream of the crop, the five-star, super-swanky affairs that play host to world leaders, top-level rock stars, and captains of industry. The rooms are spacious and gorgeous, the staff impeccably dressed and unfailingly solicitous, and the restaurants first-rate. Needless to say, the luxurious surroundings and pampering accommodations come with a hefty price tag.

Finding the Best Room Rate

The **rack rate** is the maximum rate a hotel charges for a room. It's the rate you get if you walk in off the street and ask for a room for the night.

You sometimes see these rates printed on the fire/emergency exit diagrams posted on the back of your door.

Hotels are happy to charge you the rack rate, but you can almost always do better. Perhaps the best way to avoid paying the rack rate is surprisingly simple: Just ask for a cheaper or discounted rate. You may be pleasantly surprised.

In all but the smallest accommodations the rate you pay for a room depends on many factors — chief among them being how you make your reservation. A travel agent may be able to negotiate a better price with certain hotels than you can get. (That's because the hotel often gives the agent a discount in exchange for steering his or her business toward that hotel.) One of the benefits of a package tour is a discounted rate (see Chapter 5 for more details).

Reserving a room through the hotel's toll-free number may also result in a lower rate than calling the hotel directly. On the other hand, the central reservations number may not know about discount rates at specific locations. For example, local franchises may offer a special group rate for a wedding or family reunion, but they may neglect to tell the central booking line. Your best bet is to call both the local number and the toll-free number and see which one gives you a better deal.

Room rates (even rack rates) change with the season, as occupancy rates rise and fall. But even within a given season, room prices are subject to change without notice, so the rates quoted in this book may be different from the actual rate you receive when you make your reservation. Be sure to mention membership in the American Automobile Association (AAA), AARP (formerly known as the American Association of Retired Persons), frequent-flier programs, and any other corporate rewards programs you can think of — or your Uncle Joe's Elks lodge in which you're an honorary inductee, for that matter — when you call to book. You never know when the affiliation may be worth a few dollars off your room rate.

The period between Thanksgiving and Christmas is another traditionally slow period. New Orleans can be quite pleasant at this time, especially if you're looking to avoid crowds. For more insight into seasonal and weather considerations, refer to Chapter 3.

Surfing the Web for hotel deals

You can generally shop online for hotels in one of two ways:

- ✔ By booking through the hotel's Web site
- ✔ By booking through an independent booking agency (or a fare-service agency like Priceline)

Internet hotel agencies have multiplied in mind-boggling numbers of late, competing for the business of millions of consumers surfing for accommodations around the world. This competitiveness can be a boon to consumers who have the patience and time to shop and compare the online sites for good deals — but shop they must, for prices can vary considerably from site to site. And keep in mind that hotels at the top of a site's listing may be there for no other reason than that they paid money to get the placement.

Of the "big three" sites, **Expedia** (www.expedia.com) offers a long list of special deals and "virtual tours" or photos of available rooms so you can see what you're paying for (a feature that helps counter the claims that the best rooms are often held back from bargain booking Web sites). **Travelocity** (www.travelocity.com) posts unvarnished customer reviews and ranks its properties according to the AAA rating system. Also reliable are Hotels.com and Quikbook.com. An excellent free program, **TravelAxe** (www.travelaxe.net), can help you search multiple hotel sites at once, even ones you may never have heard of — and conveniently lists the total price of the room, including the taxes and service charges. Another booking site, **Travelweb** (www.travelweb), is partly owned by the hotels it represents (including the Hilton, Hyatt, and Starwood chains) and is therefore plugged directly into the hotels' reservations systems — unlike independent online agencies, which have to fax or e-mail reservation requests to the hotel, a good portion of which get misplaced in the shuffle. More than once, travelers have arrived at the hotel, only to be told that they didn't have a reservation. To be fair, many of the major sites are undergoing improvements in service and ease of use, and Expedia will soon be able to plug directly into the reservations systems of many hotel chains — none of which can be bad news for consumers. In the meantime, **get a confirmation number** and **make a printout** of any online booking transaction.

In the opaque Web site category, **Priceline** (www.priceline.com) and **Hotwire** (www.hotwire.com) are even better for hotels than for airfares. With both sites, you're allowed to pick the neighborhood and quality level of your hotel before offering your money. Priceline's hotel product even covers Europe and Asia, though it's much better at getting five-star lodging for three-star prices than at finding anything at the bottom of the scale. On the down side, many hotels stick Priceline guests in their least desirable rooms. Be sure to go to the BiddingforTravel Web site (www.biddingfortravel.com) before bidding on a hotel room on Priceline; it features a fairly up-to-date list of hotels that Priceline uses in major cities. For both Priceline and Hotwire, you pay upfront, and the fee is nonrefundable. *Note:* Some hotels don't provide loyalty program credits or points or other frequent-stay amenities when you book a room through opaque online services.

Reserving the best room

After you make your reservation, asking one or two more pointed questions can go a long way toward making sure you get the best room. Always ask for a corner room. They're usually larger, quieter, and have more windows and light than standard rooms, and they don't always cost more. If the hotel is under renovation, request a room away from the construction. Inquire, too, about the location of the restaurants, bars, and discos in the hotel — all sources of annoying noise. If you aren't happy with your room when you arrive, talk to the front desk. If another room is available, the front desk staff should be happy to accommodate you, within reason.

Arriving without a Reservation

Assume that through circumstances beyond your control, you're suddenly plopped down in New Orleans without a hotel reservation. Don't panic. Unless Mardi Gras, Jazz Fest, or one of the other larger, room-hogging events is taking place, you'll likely find several hotels with available space. First, look through the listings in this chapter for hotels and call the ones that appeal to your preferences and budget. If that doesn't yield results, you have a few options:

✔ Call Turbotrip.com (☎ 800-473-STAY), the **French Quarter Reservation Service** (☎ 800-523-9091 or 504-523-1246), or one of the B&B agencies listed elsewhere in this chapter.

✔ If you're stranded at one of the major French Quarter hotels and it's full, ask if the front desk staff can check around for you and see what other rooms are available. If the staff can't, check your luggage with the hotel in case someone cancels a reservation while you check around on your own.

New Orleans's Best Hotels

Ashton's Bed & Breakfast
$$ **Esplanade Ridge**

Patrick and Karma Ashton's elegant 1860s Greek revival mansion is a stand out on Esplanade Avenue. The French Quarter is nine blocks away through some iffy areas, so come with a car or cab fare. Be sure to admire the carefully restored original fixtures and woodwork, including a leaded-glass door and black onyx and marble fireplace mantels. If you like a European feel and claw-foot tubs, ask for the Pontalba or Napoleon room in the main house. If you prefer more modern amenities, request the Charpantier room in the former service quarters shaded by a 300-year-old live oak.

See map p. 98. 2023 Esplanade Ave., New Orleans, LA 70116. ☎ *800-725-4131 or 504-942-7048. Fax: 504-947-9382.* www.ashtonsbb.com. *Parking: free. Rack rates: $149–$179 double (includes breakfast). AE, DC, DISC, MC, V. Call regarding wheelchair accessibility.*

French Quarter Accommodations

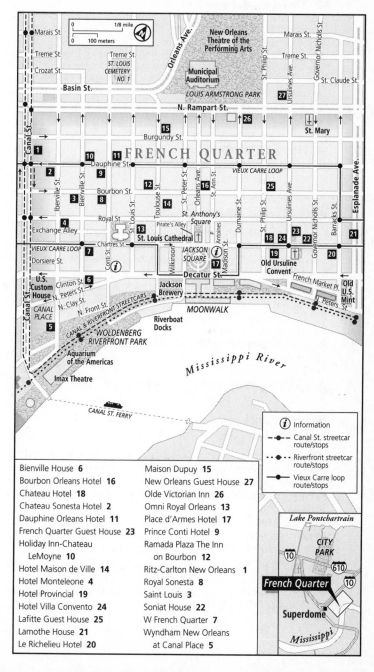

Bienville House **6**
Bourbon Orleans Hotel **16**
Chateau Hotel **18**
Chateau Sonesta Hotel **2**
Dauphine Orleans Hotel **11**
French Quarter Guest House **23**
Holiday Inn-Chateau
  LeMoyne **10**
Hotel Maison de Ville **14**
Hotel Monteleone **4**
Hotel Provincial **19**
Hotel Villa Convento **24**
Lafitte Guest House **25**
Lamothe House **21**
Le Richelieu Hotel **20**

Maison Dupuy **15**
New Orleans Guest House **27**
Olde Victorian Inn **26**
Omni Royal Orleans **13**
Place d'Armes Hotel **17**
Prince Conti Hotel **9**
Ramada Plaza The Inn
  on Bourbon **12**
Ritz-Carlton New Orleans **1**
Royal Sonesta **8**
Saint Louis **3**
Soniat House **22**
W French Quarter **7**
Wyndham New Orleans
  at Canal Place **5**

B&W Courtyards Bed & Breakfast
$$ **Faubourg Marigny**

The coziness of this hospitable B&B may inspire you to forever forgo chain hotels. Owners Rob Boyd and Kevin Wu went to ingenious lengths to convert three 19th-century buildings into appealingly quirky guest rooms. The four rooms and two suites are all completely different (you enter one of them through the bathroom). Though room size varies, the surroundings are uniformly beautiful with two small courtyards, a fountain, a Jacuzzi, and a sundeck. Breakfast is light but beautifully presented. They take good care of you here.

See map p. 98. 2425 Chartres St., New Orleans, LA 70117. ☎ *800-585-5731 or 504-945-9418. Fax: 504-949-3483.* www.bandwcourtyards.com. *Parking: on-street available. Rack rates: $120–$175 double. AE, DISC, MC, V.*

Bienville House
$–$$$ **French Quarter**

This moderately priced hotel has the feel of a more expensive one, thanks to a recent multimillion-dollar renovation. The stately, old-world interior featuring hand-painted wall murals offers a respite from the near-constant bustle of Decatur Street. Rooms are small but comfortable; some include wrought-iron balconies that overlook a flagstone courtyard and pool. Gamay, an upscale bistro featuring contemporary Creole cuisine sits on the premises.

See map p. 95. 320 Decatur St. (4 blocks from Jackson Square), New Orleans, LA 70130. ☎ *800-535-9603 or 504-529-2345. Fax: 504-525-6079.* www.bienvillehouse.com. *Valet parking: $15 cars; $19 sport utility vehicles. Rack rates: $89–$300 double (includes continental breakfast). AE, CB, DC, DISC, MC, V. Building and room entrances are wheelchair accessible; bathrooms aren't.*

Block-Keller House
$–$$ **Mid-City**

When Bryan Block and Jeff Keller heard the Canal Streetcar was coming back, they wasted no time in buying and restoring this classical-revival villa as a magnificent B&B. They were soon rewarded with a visit from Home and Garden Television's "Restore America." The elaborate parlor with its gorgeous stained-glass windows contrasts nicely with the simple Arts and Crafts dining room. Guests enjoy exploring the luxurious accommodations of this historic beauty, not to mention the gentle companionship of resident Labradors Milo and Buster.

See map p. 98. 3620 Canal St. (on the new Canal Streetcar line), New Orleans, LA 70119. ☎ *877-588-3033 or 504-483-3033. Fax: 504-483-3032.* www.blockkellerhouse.com. *Parking: free. Rack rates: $99–$175 double (includes continental breakfast). AE, CB, DC, DISC, MC, V. Wheelchair accessible.*

Bourbon Orleans Hotel

$$-$$$ **French Quarter**

Determining this lavish hotel's best feature is impossible. Is it the central location at the corner of Bourbon and Orleans, the historical pedigree, or the extravagantly decorated public spaces? The extravagance, by the way, extends to the rooms — you find Bath & Body Works shampoos and soaps in your bathroom, and you can order room service through your television. The double rooms are comfortable and bigger than average. The bi-level suites feature living rooms with pullout sofa beds that are good for children, who will also appreciate the hotel's outdoor pool. Be sure to request a room closer to Royal Street and sidestep the clamor of Bourbon. The on-site restaurant offers good meals, and the elegant lobby features a nightly cocktail hour. Other amenities include high-speed Internet access.

See map p. 95. 717 Orleans St. (directly behind St. Louis Cathedral), New Orleans, LA 70116. ☎ *504-523-2222. Fax: 504-525-8166.* www.bourbonorleans.com. *Valet parking: $25. Rack rates: $139–$209 double. Extra person: $20. AE, CB, DC, DISC, MC, V. Wheelchair accessible.*

Chateau Hotel

$–$$ **French Quarter**

One of the best buys in New Orleans, this hotel sits far enough off Bourbon Street to be quiet and intimate but is still within walking distance of virtually everything in the Quarter. Most of the rooms have antiques, giving the place a French provincial look. The rooms are a little on the dark side, but they're actually quite clean. The hotel includes a picturesque pool surrounded by a flagstone courtyard with chaise lounges. With your room fee you get a continental breakfast and newspaper. Seniors, be sure to ask about the 10 percent discount.

See map p. 95. 1001 Chartres St. (3 blocks from Jackson Square), New Orleans, LA 70116. ☎ *504-524-9636. Fax: 504-525-2989.* www.chateauhotel.com. *Parking: free. Rack rates: $89–$159 double. AE, CB, DC, MC, V. Wheelchair accessible but no bars in the bathrooms.*

Chateau Sonesta Hotel

$$-$$$ **French Quarter**

Located in the former D. H. Holmes Department Store building — the 1913 facade has been retained — the Chateau Sonesta is one of the newest hotels in the Quarter. Despite the older exterior, the interior feels modern and luxurious. The rooms are large, if generic, and some feature balconies overlooking Bourbon Street. Among the noteworthy amenities are an outdoor pool, a beauty salon, and a health club. All rooms have minibars, and videos are available for rental. For those who can't escape their computers, the phones have dataports.

New Orleans Accommodations

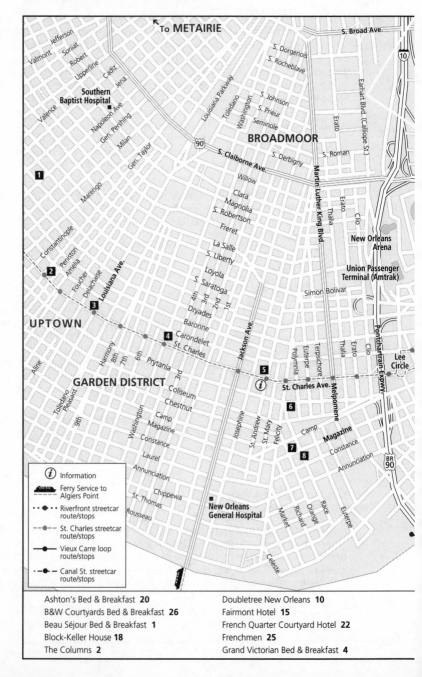

Ashton's Bed & Breakfast **20**	Doubletree New Orleans **10**
B&W Courtyards Bed & Breakfast **26**	Fairmont Hotel **15**
Beau Séjour Bed & Breakfast **1**	French Quarter Courtyard Hotel **22**
Block-Keller House **18**	Frenchmen **25**
The Columns **2**	Grand Victorian Bed & Breakfast **4**

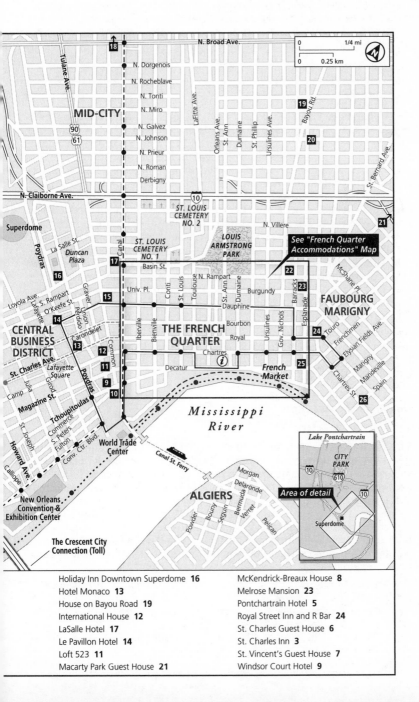

Holiday Inn Downtown Superdome **16**
Hotel Monaco **13**
House on Bayou Road **19**
International House **12**
LaSalle Hotel **17**
Le Pavillon Hotel **14**
Loft 523 **11**
Macarty Park Guest House **21**

McKendrick-Breaux House **8**
Melrose Mansion **23**
Pontchartrain Hotel **5**
Royal Street Inn and R Bar **24**
St. Charles Guest House **6**
St. Charles Inn **3**
St. Vincent's Guest House **7**
Windsor Court Hotel **9**

See map p. 95. 800 Iberville St. (at the corner of Dauphine St.), New Orleans, LA 70112. ☎ 800-SONESTA or 504-586-0800. Fax: 504-586-1987. www.chateausonesta.com. *Parking: $20. Rack rates: $130–$249 double. Extra person: $40. AE, CB, DC, DISC, MC, V. Wheelchair accessible.*

The Columns
$$ Uptown

The Columns is one of the few surviving examples of late-1880s Italianate homes designed by renowned local architect Thomas Sully (see two more Sully beauties at 4010 St. Charles Ave. and 1531 Carrollton Ave.e from the streetcar). In 1915, a hurricane destroyed the original four-story tower but thankfully spared the rest. Its spacious, columned porch is a favorite meeting spot for locals, and hotel guests are encouraged to unwind on the huge second-floor balcony overlooking the avenue. Inside, the sophisticated Victorian Lounge — recognized by *Details Magazine* as one of the "Top Ten Sexiest Places on Earth" — attracts its share of celebrities, including Cameron Diaz, Clint Eastwood, Rod Stewart, and native son Harry Connick, Jr. Jazz bands sometimes serenade happy-hour patrons and always entertain the Sunday champagne brunch crowd. The room size reminds you that this hotel was a 19th-century home; some rooms are cozy in a way that suggests servants' quarters, while others are more expansive. I'm partial to the third-floor Pretty Baby Suite (named for the Brooke Shields movie filmed here), with its lovely Victorian decor.

See map p. 98. 3811 St. Charles Ave. (halfway between Louisiana and Napoleon avenues), New Orleans, LA 70115. ☎ 800-445-9308 or 504-899-9308. Fax: 504-899-8170. www.thecolumns.com. *Parking: on-street available. Rack rates: $110–$180 double (includes southern breakfast). AE, MC, V.*

Dauphine Orleans Hotel
$$–$$$$ French Quarter

This luxurious establishment is just the right blend of charming old-world history (ghosts have been sighted on the premises) and modern elegance, well removed from the madness of Bourbon Street. Lounge in one of the secluded courtyards or read for a spell in the guest library. A recent renovation provided the stately rooms with new furnishings and marble bathrooms. Among the eyebrow-raising amenities are a 24-hour fitness room, Nintendo for the kids, a Jacuzzi, an in-room safe for valuables, and complimentary French Quarter transportation. The staff can also hook you up with a babysitting service. Continental breakfast is served until 11 a.m., and complimentary tea is served every afternoon.

See map p. 95. 415 Dauphine St., New Orleans, LA 70116. ☎ 800-508-5554 or 504-586-1800. Fax: 504-586-1409. www.dauphineorleans.com. *Valet parking: $15. Rack rates: $149–$359 double. Extra person: $15. Children under 17 free in parents' room. AE, CB, DC, DISC, MC, V. Wheelchair accessible.*

Doubletree Hotel New Orleans
$–$$$ Central Business District

Located at the foot of Canal Street, the Doubletree offers great views of the bustling Central Business District and the river. Sure, it's part of a chain, but the atmosphere is pleasant. Rooms are good-sized and comfortable; bathrooms are adequate. The hotel even features a rooftop pool that the kids can enjoy, as well as a fitness center. You also find a nice restaurant and a breakfast cafe on the first floor. The kicker for your small fry: Nintendo in every room and delicious chocolate-chip cookies when you check in. (They're so good, you may not want to share them with the kids.)

See map p. 98. 300 Canal St., New Orleans, LA 70130. ☎ *888-874-9074 or 504-581-1300. Fax: 504-212-3315.* www.doubletreeneworleans.com. *Parking: valet, $22; self-parking next door at Harrah's Casino. Rack rates: $79–$229 double. Extra person: $20. AE, DC, DISC, MC, V. Wheelchair accessible.*

Fairmont Hotel
$–$$$ Central Business District

Hands down, this hotel is one of the city's most elegant. Given such amenities as a high-class restaurant, rooftop pool, workout area, and beauty shop, you may never want (or need) to leave. The hotel offers a lot of local lore: Huey Long used to hold court in the Sazerac bar on the first floor (see Chapter 16 for more information on this respected gathering place). The rooms are as beautiful as you can expect for the price, and each one has its own fax machine for business travelers. A bonus for the tykes: Each room has Nintendo gear.

See map p. 98. 123 Baronne St., New Orleans, LA 70112. ☎ *800-441-1414 or 504-529-7111. Fax: 504-522-2303.* www.fairmont.com/neworleans. *Valet parking: $19. Rack rates: $99–$299 double. Children under 18 free in parents' room. AE, DC, DISC, MC, V. Wheelchair accessible.*

French Quarter Courtyard Hotel
$$–$$$ Central Business District

Despite the name, the courtyard isn't the best thing about this place (though its black fountains and grottolike swimming pool are quite nice). The atmosphere here clinches the deal, from the large staircase that greets you upon entering to the understated look of the rooms. Exposed red-brick walls, antique-reproduction beds, and hardwood floors add up to a pleasant environment and decent approximation of old-style New Orleans charm in a modern hotel setting.

See map p. 98. 1101 N. Rampart St. (a few blocks from the Quarter), New Orleans, LA 70116. Call ☎ *800-290-4233 or 504-522-7333. Fax: 504-522-3908.* www.neworleans.com/fqch. *Valet parking: $12. Rack rates: $119–$289 double. Extra person: $10. Children 18 and under free with parent. AE, DC, DISC, MC, V. Wheelchair accessible.*

Frenchmen
$–$$ Faubourg Marigny

This friendly inn, which occupies two 19th-century buildings that were once grand New Orleans homes, enjoys loyal repeat business from those who've fallen for its slightly funky charms. Rooms vary in size; some are downright tiny (if that's important, ask about size when making a reservation). Some rooms have private balconies; others are loft bedrooms with a sitting area. All are individually decorated and furnished with antiques. A tropical courtyard features a pool and hot tub.

See map p. 98. 417 Frenchmen St. (across the street from the Old U.S. Mint on Esplanade), New Orleans, LA 70116. ☎ 888-365-2877 or 504-948-2166. Fax: 504-948-2258. www.french-quarter.org. *Valet parking: $20. Rack rates: $79–$155 double (includes breakfast). AE, DISC, MC, V.*

Grand Victorian Bed & Breakfast
$$–$$$ Uptown

The name pretty much sums up this elegant B&B; the appointments here are grand, indeed. Famed New Orleans architect Thomas Sully designed the house in 1893, and the proprietors have gone to great lengths to restore the house to its original glory. A bountiful continental breakfast is offered either in the dining room or on the porte-cochere balcony. The rooms vary in size but are uniformly elegant with handsome antique furniture. Business travelers can use available fax and copy machines, as well as dataports for computers.

See map p. 98. 2727 St. Charles Ave., New Orleans, LA 70130. ☎ 800-977-0008 or 504-895-1104. Fax: 504-896-8688. www.gvbb.com. *Parking: some on-street parking. Rack rates: $150–$300 double (includes breakfast; rates higher during special events). Extra person: $25. AE, DISC, MC, V. Wheelchair accessible.*

Holiday Inn-Chateau LeMoyne
$$–$$$ French Quarter

In contrast to its cousin in the Central Business District, this Holiday Inn sports an abundance of New Orleans–style character. Although the buildings are more than a century old (some of the rooms overlooking the courtyard are converted slave quarters), the historic ambience doesn't extend to the guest rooms, which are more or less standard for the chain, although comfortable. It's just around the corner from Bourbon Street but nonetheless removed from the noise of the Quarter and convenient to Canal Street. The restaurant serves breakfast only, but you can order room service until 10 p.m. No video games in the rooms, but an outdoor heated pool and proximity to French Quarter attractions like the Aquarium of the Americas make this a good spot for the small fries.

See map p. 95. 301 Dauphine St. (just around the corner from the Deja Vu Bar & Grill), New Orleans, LA 70112. ☎ 800-747-3279 or 504-581-1303. Fax: 504-523-5709. www.sixcontinentshotels.com/holiday-inn. *Valet parking: $19. Rack rates: $159–$244 double. Extra person: $20. AE, CB, DC, DISC, MC, V. Wheelchair accessible.*

Holiday Inn-Downtown Superdome
$–$$ Central Business District

Accessibility is the key word when describing this hotel. Conveniently close to the Superdome and New Orleans Arena, it's a good bet for sports fans. It's also close to the city's business and financial centers and not too far from the French Quarter (though probably farther than you'd want to walk, especially at night). Each room has a balcony and a city view, but they're standard size for the chain and decorated in typical Holiday Inn style (not that there's anything wrong with that). The hotel also features a heated pool on the roof. In-room Nintendos and movies make this a good bet for kids.

See map p. 98. 330 Loyola Ave. (across from the Louisiana Supreme Court building), New Orleans, LA 70112. ☎ *800-535-7830 or 504-581-1600. Fax: 504-522-0073.* www. holidayinndowntownsuperdome.com. *Parking: $11. Rack rates: $94–$209 double. Extra person: $15. Children 18 and under free in parents' room. AE, CB, DC, DISC, MC, V. Wheelchair accessible.*

Hotel Maison de Ville
$$$ French Quarter

The Maison de Ville blends the charm and size of a B&B with the service and elegance of a five-star hotel. Antiques are abundant, and a beautiful courtyard welcomes you with a fountain and banana trees. The rooms vary in size (some are downright tiny), so ask when you call, as price is no indication of what you get. In-room amenities include bathrobes, hair dryers, and other standard fare; two-bedroom cottages and suites have coffeemakers. Continental breakfast is served on a silver tray in your room, in the parlor, or on the patio. Complimentary sherry and port are served in the afternoon and evening.

See map p. 95. 727 Toulouse St. (½ block from Bourbon St.), New Orleans, LA 70130. ☎ *800-634-1600 or 504-561-5858. Fax: 504-528-9939.* www.maisondeville.com. *Valet parking: $18. Rack rates: $215–$225 double (includes continental breakfast and afternoon service of port and sherry). AE, DC, MC, V.*

Hotel Monaco New Orleans
$$–$$$$ Central Business District

New Orleans does stuffy upscale very well but Hotel Monaco infused a circa-1926, former Masonic Temple with a refreshing, cool elegance. The remarkably inventive renovation, outstanding service, plush room decor, and high-tech amenities have rightfully earned it accolades ranging from the AAA Four Diamond Award to *Condé Nast Traveler*'s "Hot List." The pampering isn't limited to people. My large dog, Desoto, can vouch for how well he was treated; each time a staff member saw him, he was given a biscuit, and fellow guests always inquired as to whether he was enjoying his stay. As a beneficiary of the "Bone Appetit" package, Desoto received a complimentary doggie bed, food and water bowls, leopard-print ball (how fetching!), and a walk by a member of management. If you prefer to leave your pet at home but miss the company, ask about the "Guppy Love" program. Your goldfish — cared for and fed by staff — can give you companionship without the responsibility. The in-house restaurant, Cobalt, is fabulously eclectic in both design and food.

See map p. 98. 333 St. Charles Ave., New Orleans, LA 70130. ☎ *866-561-0010 or 504-561-0010. Fax: 504-561-0036.* www.monaco-neworleans.com. *Valet parking: $20. Rack rates: $150–$400 double. AE, DC, MC, V.*

Hotel Monteleone
$$–$$$ French Quarter

The largest and oldest hotel in the Quarter, the Hotel Monteleone is one of the best big hotels in New Orleans. The rooms come in a variety of styles, from smaller spaces to modern and comfortable family rooms to plush, antiques-filled suites. You can likely find a room here even when the rest of the city is booked. The hotel is famous for its extravagant lobby as well as for the revolving Carousel Bar, with its pleasing view of Royal Street. Laundry, a fitness center, and a babysitting service top a list of amenities that also includes a heated rooftop pool and a hot tub. It's often voted the city's most romantic hotel.

See map p. 95. 214 Royal St. (at the corner of Iberville), New Orleans, LA 70130. ☎ *800-535-9595 or 504-523-3341. Fax: 504-528-1019.* www.hotelmonteleone.com. *Valet parking (space is limited): $15. Rack rates: $189–$230 double. Extra person: $25. Children under 18 are free in their parents' room. AE, CB, DC, DISC, MC, V.*

Hotel Provincial
$$–$$$ French Quarter

Nestled in a series of 19th-century buildings, Hotel Provincial's atmosphere (including flickering gas lamps) makes it feel smaller and more intimate than it really is, more like a guesthouse than a hotel. Rooms have the high ceilings of an earlier age and are decorated with French and Creole antiques. The hotel is located in a quiet stretch of the French Quarter, so you can wind down in peace after a day of sightseeing. Local ghost hunters swear this place is haunted because it was used as a hospital during the Civil War.

See map p. 95. 1024 Chartres St. (4 blocks from Jackson Square), New Orleans, LA 70116. ☎ *800-535-7922 or 504-581-4995. Fax: 504-581-1018.* www.hotelprovincial.com. *Valet parking: $13. Rack rates: $99–$289 double. AE, CB, DC, DISC, MC, V. Wheelchair accessible.*

House on Bayou Road
$$–$$$$ Mid-City

Stepping into the luxurious quiet and elegance of this 18th-century home is like entering a time machine. The rooms and two cottages are individually decorated with antiques. The smaller cottage, which has a queen-size bed, queen sleeper sofa, and hot tub, is a perfect romantic getaway. The staff serves a complimentary full plantation breakfast, and guests can help themselves to beverages in a minifridge throughout the day. The host occasionally offers public cooking classes, for which guests receive a discount.

See map p. 98. 2275 Bayou Rd. (1 mile from the Quarter along Esplanade; turn right at Bayou Road), New Orleans, LA 70119. ☎ *800-882-2968 or 504-945-0992. Fax: 504-945-0993.* www.houseonbayouroad.com. *Parking: Free. Rack rates: $135–$320 double (includes breakfast). AE, MC, V.*

International House
$$–$$$$ Central Business District

Apparently, the youth and vigor of local developer Sean Cummings translates into sensual, state-of-the-art sanctuaries. The extraordinary International House — whose building was constructed in 1906 to house the world's first trade center — now has a soul mate in Cummings' latest vision, Loft 523 (see "Runner-Up Hotels" later in this chapter). *Condé Nast Traveler-London* named International House one of the "Top 10 Boutique Hotels" in the United States, and I expect Loft 523 will soon follow suit. Suave locals savor drinks by candlelight in lovely *loa* (a voodoo word for deity or Holy Spirit). Guests can request any number of pampering packages, from the romantic "Southern Flower Bath" (massage for two is just the beginning) to "Voodoo Chic" (an authentic voodoo priestess transforms your room into a spiritual, personal altar). Busy moms and dads appreciate the "Kid Kit," a special welcome kit of New Orleans coloring books and crayons, a CD with lullabies, a cable movie schedule highlighting children's programming, daily delivery of the *Times-Picayune* turned to the kids' activities page, and surprise gift from local shopkeepers. Licensed, experienced nannies are available to watch little ones or take older kids on tours of local attractions.

See map p. 98. 221 Camp St. (two blocks from the French Quarter), New Orleans, LA 70130. ☎ *800-634-1600 or 504-553-9550. Fax: 504-553-9560.* www.ihhotel.com. *Valet parking: $20. Rack rates: $150–$450 double. AE, DC, MC, V.*

Lafitte Guest House
$$–$$$ French Quarter

This eccentrically charming guesthouse is conveniently located on the quiet end of Bourbon Street, only a quick walk away from the action. Built in 1849, the three-story brick building features wrought-iron balconies on the second and third floors (the outside has been completely restored and looks great). Most rooms have Victorian flair, though some are more modern than others. Rooms vary in size; the penthouse suite (room 40) takes up the entire third floor and accommodates up to six people. Breakfast is brought to your room in the morning, and guests are invited to snack on wine and cheese for a "social" in the parlor in the afternoon. Dry cleaning and babysitting are also available.

See map p. 95. 1003 Bourbon St. (at the corner of St. Philip), New Orleans, LA 70116. ☎ *800-331-7971 or 504-581-2678. Fax: 504-581-2677.* www.lafitteguesthouse. com. *Parking: $12. Rack rates: $159–$219 double (includes breakfast). Extra person: $25. AE, DC, DISC, MC, V.*

Lamothe House
$–$$$ French Quarter

If you don't like the shiny, homogenized feel of a chain hotel, the slightly faded, threadbare ambience of this place may be up your alley. Even the name suggests a Dickensian air of moth-eaten mustiness. A plain Creole-style facade belies the interior, which boasts a mossy, brick-lined court-yard with a fish-filled fountain and banana trees. You also find a swimming pool and hot-tub spa. The rooms, decorated with antiques, are worn in the right places but not shabby. Room sizes vary according to price, so ask when reserving.

See map p. 95. 621 Esplanade Ave., New Orleans, LA 70116. ☎ *800-367-5858 or 504-947-1161. Fax: 504-943-6536.* www.new-orleans.org. *Parking: free. Rack rates: $64–$275 double (includes continental breakfast). AE, DISC, MC, V.*

Le Pavillon Hotel
$$–$$$$ Central Business District

A unique blend of 17th-century grandeur and modern appointments makes this hotel truly elegant. The lobby is a dazzling array of chandeliers, Oriental rugs, and detailed woodwork. Rooms of varying sizes feature original artwork and European and American antiques. Services include 24-hour room service, concierge, babysitting, laundry and dry cleaning, and a complimentary shoeshine. You can indulge yourself in complimentary hors d'oeuvres on weekday afternoons in the Gallery lounge or peanut-butter-and-jelly sandwiches served with milk in the lobby each evening. Other amenities include a heated pool on the roof, a fitness center, and a whirlpool spa.

See map p. 98. 833 Poydras St., New Orleans, LA 70112. ☎ *800-535-9095 or 504-581-3111. Fax: 504-522-5543.* www.lepavillon.com. *Valet parking: $25. Rack rates: $105–$425 double. AE, CB, DC, DISC, MC, V. Wheelchair accessible.*

Le Richelieu Hotel
$–$$ French Quarter

Le Richelieu, located on the Esplanade edge of the Quarter, offers convenience and tranquil old-world charm. Balconies overlooking the street or courtyard and pool accompany many rooms. You can order breakfast and lunch in the courtyard from the small in-house restaurant, or you can eat in the lounge adjacent to the pool. All rooms come with hair dryers, irons and ironing boards, and refrigerators. If you really want to go first class, ask for the VIP suite with its three bedrooms, kitchen, living area, dining area, and steam room. One of the nicest hotels in the Quarter in its price range, it's also the only hotel in the Quarter that offers free self-parking.

See map p. 95. 1234 Chartres St. (6 blocks from Jackson Square or 1 block from Esplanade), New Orleans, LA 70116. ☎ *800-535-9653 or 504-529-2492. Fax: 504-524-8179.* www.lerichelieuhotel.com. *Parking: free. Rack rates: $95–$180 double. Extra adult or child: $15. AE, CB, DC, DISC, MC, V.*

Maison Dupuy
$–$$$ French Quarter

This picturesque hotel, made up of several town houses, has been the site of a cotton press (the first in the United States), a blacksmith shop, and a sheet-metal works. Today, it blends the clockwork efficiency of a large hotel with the attentive service of a B&B. You find desks and comfortable armchairs inside the large rooms, many of which have balconies that overlook the courtyard. On Sundays, the hotel restaurant serves a champagne and jazz brunch buffet. Dominique's Lounge is a nice place to wind down at the end of the day and enjoy award-winning cuisine. The hotel's amenities include a heated outdoor pool and Jacuzzi, an exercise room with treadmill and sauna, twice-daily maid service, and babysitting.

See map p. 95. 1001 Toulouse St. (2 blocks from Bourbon St.), New Orleans, LA 70112. ☎ *800-535-9177 or 504-586-8000. Fax: 504-525-5334.* www.maisondupuy.com. *Valet parking: $18 when available. Rack rates: $99–$229 double. AE, CB, DC, DISC, MC, V. Wheelchair accessible.*

McKendrick-Breaux House
$$ Lower Garden District

One of the city's best B&Bs, it sits in the beautiful Garden District on a street known for its funky atmosphere and abundant dining and shopping options. The antiques-filled rooms are lovely and spacious (some bathrooms are just huge). Many rooms feature artwork by local artists for sale. The public areas are gorgeous and comfortable. Amenities include a hot tub, subtropical garden (fresh flowers may be waiting in your room), and a small pond whose resident turtle comes out for feedings. The owner provides perfect personal service while still giving guests plenty of privacy.

See map p. 98. 1474 Magazine St., New Orleans, LA 70130. ☎ *888-570-1700 or 504-586-1700. Fax: 504-522-7138.* www.mckendrick-breaux.com. *Parking: free. Rack rates: $125–$195 double (includes breakfast). AE, MC, V.*

Melrose Mansion
$$–$$$$ Faubourg Marigny

This restored mansion is intimate, romantic, and elegant — all adjectives that don't come cheap. The spacious accommodations have Victorian-era furnishings. Bed sizes, room sizes, and amenities vary; some have wet bars, Jacuzzi tubs, and separate seating rooms. A breakfast of fresh muffins, fruit, and quiche is served in the parlor or in your room. The hotel also offers a swimming pool and a menu of off-site services (Swedish massage, aromatherapy massage, manicures, and pedicures) that the courteous and friendly staff can arrange for you. Recent renovations added a ten-room annex. This place is popular, so book as far in advance as possible.

See map p. 98. 937 Esplanade Ave. (at the corner of Burgundy), New Orleans, LA 70116. ☎ *800-650-3323 or 504-944-2255. Fax: 504-945-1794.* www.melrosegroup. com. *Parking: street parking available. Rack rates: $200–$450 double (includes champagne breakfast and cocktail hour). AE, DISC, MC, V.*

New Orleans Guest House
$ French Quarter

This gay-friendly establishment, painted bright pink, sits just outside the Quarter, a stone's throw from Armstrong Park, Donna's, and the Funky Butt (see Chapter 16). The old Creole main house has spacious rooms, while the former slave quarters have accommodations that are even larger. Rooms in both locations are tastefully decorated with a different color scheme. The lush courtyard features a tropical garden with plenty of fresh greenery, a banana tree, and intricately carved old fountains (as well as beer and soda machines and a handy ice machine). The surrounding neighborhood is chancy at night the farther you get from Rampart.

See map p. 95. 1118 Ursulines St. (1 block outside the Quarter just across Rampart St.), New Orleans, LA 70116. ☎ *800-562-1177 or 504-566-1177. Fax: 504-566-1179.* www.neworleans.com/nogh. *Parking: Free. Rack rates: $79–$99 double (includes continental breakfast). AE, MC, V.*

Olde Victorian Inn
$$–$$$ French Quarter

Six distinctive Victorian period rooms (each with private bath) are tastefully decorated and whimsically appointed with lace doilies, teddy bears, and the like. The Chantilly Room is a favorite, thanks to a balcony that overlooks busy Rampart Street and Louis Armstrong Park. A cozy courtyard lies out back. Breakfasts change daily, culled from a list of some 30 menus, including Creole pancakes, crepes, and coffeecakes. The owners are happy to help with obtaining dining reservations and offer recommendations on what to see and do, and a friendly "staff" of lovable dogs lends a homey touch. Though the Olde Victorian has no parking spaces, guests are allowed to use the lot of the Best Western Landmark next door (and also avail themselves of its swimming pool).

See map p. 95. 914 N. Rampart St., New Orleans, LA 70116 ☎ *800-725-2446 or 504-522-2446. Fax: 504-522-8646.* www.oldevictorianinn.com. *Parking: available free at Best Western Landmark next door. Rack rates: $135–$225 double. AE, CB, DC, DISC, MC, V.*

Omni Royal Orleans
$$–$$$$ French Quarter

One of the best chain hotels in the city, its richly decorated rooms aren't uniform in size, so communicate your needs when reserving. The downside for families is that only a few rooms have two double beds, but the hotel can supply a rollaway bed. The rooftop swimming pool/observation deck appeals to kids, while parents appreciate the relatively cheap (and bonded) babysitting service. Amenities include terrycloth bathrobes (upon request), umbrellas, makeup mirrors, an extensively equipped fitness center, irons and ironing boards, and emergency mending and pressing services. The hotel's Rib Room is one of the city's premier restaurants (see Chapter 10).

See map p. 95. 621 St. Louis St., New Orleans, LA 70140. ☎ **800-THE-OMNI** *or 504-529-5333. Fax: 504-529-7089.* www.omnihotels.com. *Valet parking: $21. Rack rates: $149–$349 double. Children 18 and under free with parent. AE, CB, DC, DISC, MC, V. Wheelchair accessible.*

Pontchartrain Hotel
$$–$$$$ Garden District

This local landmark is an oasis of tranquility and beauty on sprawling St. Charles Avenue. The unique romantic ambience here is unmatched even in a city known for its atmosphere. Recent renovations have struck a nice balance between a worn, old-world feeling and a freshness of more modern hotels. Antique furnishings (including some Ming vases) contribute immeasurably to the surroundings. Rooms are comfortable and larger than most standard hotel rooms and include cedar-lined closets and pedestal washbasins. The hotel offers 24-hour room service, complimentary shoeshine, and access to a nearby spa with health club and pool.

See map p. 98. 2031 St. Charles Ave., New Orleans, LA 70140. ☎ **800-777-6193** *or 504-524-0581. Fax: 504-529-1165.* www.pontchartrainhotel.com. *Parking: $13. Rack rates: $199–$600 double. Extra person: $10. AE, CB, DC, DISC, MC, V. Wheelchair accessible.*

Prince Conti Hotel
$$ French Quarter

This small but friendly hotel boasts a congenial and helpful staff as well as a prime location just off Bourbon Street that isn't too noisy. The rooms are very comfortable, and many are furnished with antiques, but the bathrooms can be downright microscopic — toilets are practically on top of the sink. Travelers with kids should probably opt for the establishment's sister hotel, the Place d'Armes, which has a swimming pool and is farther removed from Bourbon Street. The Bombay Club, located on the first floor, is famous among locals for its genteel atmosphere and serves some of the best martinis in town (see Chapter 16).

See map p. 95. 830 Conti St. (at the corner of Dauphine St.), New Orleans, LA 70112. ☎ **800-366-2743** *or 504-529-4172. Fax: 504-581-3802.* www.princecontihotel.com. *Valet parking: $16. Rack rates: $159 double (includes breakfast). AE, CB, DC, DISC, MC, V.*

Ramada Plaza The Inn on Bourbon Street
$$$ French Quarter

This elegant hotel is located right on Bourbon Street. As a result, its beauty and amenities are sometimes lost on guests who just want to roll out of bed and into a bar or daiquiri shop. If you plan on sleeping while you're here (as opposed to just passing out), ask for an interior room, somewhat insulated from the street noise. But then you may not get a room with a balcony overlooking the action, which can be especially handy around Mardi Gras. (Decisions, decisions . . .) All rooms are standard in size, yet comfortable, and have king or double beds. Amenities include a fitness room, a business center, a jewelry shop, and a concierge who can put you in touch with babysitting services.

See map p. 95. 541 Bourbon St. (at the corner of Toulouse), New Orleans, LA 70130.
☎ *800-535-7891 or 504-524-7611. Fax: 504-568-9427.* www.innonbourbon.com.
Valet parking: $16. Rack rates: $205–$285 double. AE, CB, DC, DISC, MC, V. Wheelchair accessible.

Ritz-Carlton New Orleans
$$–$$$$ French Quarter

Louisiana's only AAA Five Diamond luxury hotel has quickly rivaled (some say eclipsed) the hallowed Windsor Court. A haven for visiting celebrities, the Ritz-Carlton offers acclaimed dining (Victor's Grill), a comfortable restaurant/bar (the French Quarter Bar), a full-service spa, a mall of shops, and the trademark accommodations for which the Ritz-Carlton chain is known. From the driveway entrance to the beautiful courtyard and rooms, the hotel makes every effort to incorporate the look and feel of the city into its own style. Afternoon tea is served every afternoon from 1:30 to 4 p.m. in the hotel's relaxing Lobby Lounge.

See map p. 95. 921 Canal St., New Orleans, LA 70112. ☎ *800-241-3333 or 504-524-1331. Fax: 504-524-7233.* www.ritzcarlton.com/hotels/new_orleans. *Valet parking: $25. Rack rates: $165–$395 double (penthouse suites are $4,000). AE, DC, DISC, MC, V. Wheelchair accessible.*

Royal Sonesta
$$$–$$$$ French Quarter

The four-star Sonesta offers the best of both worlds: a Bourbon Street location and a gracious, classy hotel. Rooms are a bit more upscale than standard hotel rooms but otherwise pretty typical. Many feature balconies overlooking Bourbon Street, a side street, or a courtyard with a large pool. For a good night's sleep away from the noise of the street, request an inner room. The hotel features an exercise room, business center, excellent concierge service, and room service until 2 a.m. This hotel is the best place in the Quarter to catch a cab — they line up right at the corner.

See map p. 95. 300 Bourbon St. (3 blocks from Canal between Bienville and Conti), New Orleans, LA 70130. ☎ *800-766-3782 or 504-586-0300. Fax: 504-586-0335.* www. royalsonestano.com. *Parking: $20. Rack rates: $249–$389 double. AE, CB, DC, DISC, MC, V. Wheelchair accessible.*

St. Charles Guest House
$–$$ Lower Garden District

Character and economy are the operative words here. The property consists of three separate, connected buildings, the oldest of which dates back about 100 years. Atmospheric touches balance out a general lack of modern conveniences; rooms don't include televisions or phones, though each building has its own pay phone (including one in a fascinating antique phone booth). Owner Dennis Hilton gladly offers use of his office line for individuals with portable computers who want to check their e-mail. Room sizes vary, with backpacker rooms available at the very low end, though these lack air conditioning and private baths. A continental breakfast is served in a cottagelike room that looks out on the swimming pool.

See map p. 98. 1748 Prytania St., New Orleans, LA 70130. ☎ *504-523-6556. Fax: 504-522-6340.* www.stcharlesguesthouse.com. *Parking: on-street available. Rack rates: $55–$105 double. Extra person: $12. AE, MC, V.*

Saint Louis
$$–$$$ French Quarter

You find a splendid courtyard with a fountain at this small hotel right in the middle of the Quarter. Throughout the hotel, antique furniture, original oil paintings, and crystal chandeliers complement a Parisian-style decor. Rooms are standard but comfortable. Most face the courtyard, though some in a new wing don't. The elegant, in-house Louis XVI restaurant serves fine French cuisine.

See map p. 95. 730 Bienville St. (½ block from Bourbon St.), New Orleans, LA 70130. ☎ *888-508-3980 or 504-581-7300. Fax: 504-679-5013.* www.stlouishotel.com. *Valet parking: $16.75. Rack rates: $159–$259 double. Children under 12 free in parents' room. AE, CB, DC, DISC, MC, V. Wheelchair accessible.*

Soniat House
$$–$$$ French Quarter

Located in a creative combination of three early 19th-century homes, Rodney and Frances Smith's tranquil hotel captures all the romance of the plantation era. It's no wonder *Travel & Leisure* once again pronounced Soniat House "one of the best hotels in the world." The rooms are comfortable, though bathrooms are small. Oriental rugs, fine French and English antiques, and beautiful paintings (some on loan from the New Orleans Museum of Art) furnish the rooms. More rooms (some have Jacuzzi bathtubs) are available in the annex of suites across the street. For an additional charge you can get a continental breakfast; the large, fluffy, baked-to-order biscuits and homemade strawberry preserves alone are worth the price.

See map p. 95. 1133 Chartres St. (across the street from the Old Ursuline Convent), New Orleans, LA 70116. ☎ 800-544-8808 or 504-522-0570. Fax: 504-522-7208. www. soniathouse.com. *Valet parking: $22. Rack rates: $195–$285 double. Children under 13 not permitted. AE, MC, V.*

W French Quarter
$$$$ **French Quarter**

Snazzy and upscale in a nouveau-riche kind of way, this link in the too-hip-for-school W chain places as much emphasis on style as it does on service — both, just for the record, are quite good. Lounge in the comfort of your room's patio or balcony, or mingle with other beautiful people in the Living Room, the hotel's lounge. The "Whatever/Whenever" desk goes out of its way to accommodate, and ethernet connections, Internet-access televisions, dataports, and high-tech meeting rooms keep business travelers happy. Bacco, an acclaimed Italian/Creole restaurant, is on the premises (see Chapter 10).

See map p. 95. 316 Chartres St., New Orleans, LA 70130. ☎ 800-448-4927 or 504-581-1200. Fax: 504-523-2910. www.whotels.com/frenchquarter. *Valet parking: $29. Rack rates: $489–$514 double. Children under 16 free in parents' room. AE, CB, DC, DISC, MC, V. Wheelchair accessible.*

Windsor Court
$$$$ **Central Business District**

Once voted by *Condé Nast Traveler* as the best hotel in North America, the Windsor is truly magnificent — from its Italian marble and antique furnishings to its impeccable service — and about as expensive as you'd expect. The hotel is 90 percent suites, though even the smaller guest rooms are spacious. All suites feature balconies or bay windows with views of the city or river. They also have fax machines, minibars, kitchenettes, living rooms, two dressing rooms, and marble bathrooms with plush robes, a hamper, high-end personal care items, and extra hair dryers. (Ask about amenities when you call because they aren't the same in each room.) The 24-hour suite service is much more luxurious than your average room service. Conference rooms are available for business travelers. The hotel also features a resort-size pool, a health club, laundry and dry cleaning, and in-room massage. If you can afford it, this hotel is the place to go for serious pampering. You also find the first-class Grill Room (see Chapter 10) and an afternoon tea with cocktails and sweets in the lobby lounge.

See map p. 98. 300 Gravier St. (1 block from Canal St.), New Orleans, LA 70130. ☎ 888-596-0955 or 504-523-6000. Fax: 504-596-4513. www.windsorcourthotel. com. *Parking: $20. Rack rates: $350–$400 double; suites from $400. Children under 12 free in parents' room. AE, CB, DC, DISC, MC, V. Wheelchair accessible.*

Wyndham New Orleans at Canal Place
$$$$ French Quarter

If you're a shopper, this large, luxurious hotel is the place for you. It's situated above the elegant Canal Place Shopping Center, which you can access directly by a glass elevator from the hotel's 11th floor lobby. The rooms have fine furnishings, including marble foyers and baths. The hotel boasts spectacular views of the Quarter and the Mississippi River. Business travelers are treated to amenities such as office supplies, a coffeemaker, and use of an in-room copier/printer/fax machine.

See map p. 95. 100 Iberville St. (1 block from the Aquarium), New Orleans, LA 70130. ☎ *877-999-3223 or 504-566-7006. Fax: 504-553-5120.* www.wyndham.com/canalplace. *Valet parking: $25. Rack rates: $329–$369 double. AE, CB, DC, DISC, MC, V. Wheelchair accessible.*

Table 9-1   Key to Hotel Dollar Signs

Dollar Sign(s)	Price Range	What to Expect
$	Less than $100	These accommodations are relatively simple and inexpensive. Rooms likely are small, and televisions aren't necessarily provided. Parking isn't provided but rather catch-as-you-can on the street.
$$	$101–$200	A bit classier, these midrange accommodations offer more room, more extras (such as irons, hair dryers, or a microwave), and a more convenient location than the preceding category.
$$$	$201–$300	Higher-class still, these accommodations begin to look plush. Think chocolates on your pillow, a classy restaurant, underground parking garages, maybe even expansive views of the water.
$$$$	$301 and up	These top-rated accommodations come with luxury amenities such as valet parking, on-premise spas, and in-room hot tubs and CD players — but you pay through the nose for 'em.

Runner-Up Hotels

This guide doesn't have enough room to list all the good hotels and B&Bs in New Orleans. If the suggestions in the previous section are all booked up, check out one of the options in this section. Some of these are just as charming and pleasant as the lodgings in the preceding listing, but they may be in a slightly out-of-the-way or dicey location (or I just ran out of space for them all). If you still can't find a room, see the "Finding the Best Room Rate" section earlier in this chapter for strategies on finding a last-minute bunk, listings of room-finding services specializing in hotels or B&Bs, and online-booking sources.

Beau Séjour Bed & Breakfast
$$–$$$ Uptown

See map p. 98. 1930 Napoleon Ave., New Orleans, LA, 70115. ☎ *888-897-9398 or 504-897-3746. Fax: 504-891-3340.* www.beausejourbandb.com. *Parking: limited, on-street parking. Rack rates: $110–$150 double. AE, DISC, MC, V.*

French Quarter Guest House
$$–$$$ French Quarter

See map p. 95. 623 Ursulines St., New Orleans, LA 70116. ☎ *800-887-2817 or 504-522-1793. Fax: 504-524-1902. Parking: $6 within walking distance. Rack rates: $79–$135 double (includes continental breakfast). Extra person: $10. AE, CB, DC, DISC, MC, V.*

Hotel Villa Convento
$$–$$$ French Quarter

See map p. 95. 616 Ursulines St. (around the corner from the Old Ursuline Convent), New Orleans, LA 70116. ☎ *800-887-2817 or 504-522-1793. Fax: 504-524-1902.* www.villaconvento.com. *Parking: $6 within walking distance. Rack rates: $89–$159 double (continental breakfast included). Extra person: $10. AE, CB, DC, DISC, MC, V.*

LaSalle Hotel
$ Central Business District

See map p. 98. 1113 Canal St., New Orleans, LA 70112. ☎ *800-521-9450 or 504-523-5831. Fax: 504-525-2531.* www.lasallehotelneworleans.com. *Parking: $8. Rack rates: $72 double. Children under 12 free in parents' room. AE, DISC, MC, V.*

Loft 523
$$–$$$$ Central Business District

See map p. 98. 523 Gravier St., New Orleans, LA 70112. ☎ *888-813-9373 or 504-200-6523. Fax: 504-200-6522.* www.Loft523.com. *Parking: $20. Rack rates: $199–$349 double; penthouse suites $689 and up. AE, DISC, MC, V.*

Macarty Park Guest House
$–$$ Bywater

See map p. 98. 3820 Burgundy St., New Orleans, LA 70117. ☎ *800-521-2790 or 504-943-4994. Fax: 504-943-4999.* www.macartypark.com. *Parking: limited, free parking. Rack rates: $59–$115 double. Extra person: $15. AE, DISC, MC, V.*

Place d'Armes Hotel
$$–$$$$ French Quarter

See map p. 95. 625 St. Ann St. (just behind the Presbytere), New Orleans, LA 70118. ☎ **800-366-2743** or 504-524-4531. Fax: 504-571-2803. www.placedarmes.com. Parking: $16. Rack rates: $129–$199 double (includes breakfast). AE, CB, DC, DISC, MC, V. Wheelchair accessible.

Royal Street Inn and R Bar
$–$$ Faubourg Marigny

See map p. 98. 1431 Royal St., New Orleans, LA 70116. ☎ **800-449-5535** or 504-948-7499. Fax: 504-943-9880. www.royalstreetinn.com. Parking: free on-street parking with a visitor's permit (available at check-in) and a $50 deposit. Rack rates: $90–$125 double (includes taxes and two drinks).

St. Charles Inn
$ Garden District

See map p. 98. 3636 St. Charles Ave., New Orleans, LA 70115. ☎ **800-489-9908** or 504-899-8888. Fax: 504-899-8892. www.stcharlesinn.com. Parking: free. Rack rates: $75 double (includes breakfast). AE, DC, DISC, MC, V. Wheelchair accessible.

St. Vincent's Guest House
$ Lower Garden District

See map p. 98. 1507 Magazine St., New Orleans, LA 70130. ☎ **504-523-3411**. Fax: 504-566-1518. www.stvincentsguesthouse.com. Parking: limited on-site parking. Rack rates: $59–$99 double (includes breakfast). Extra person: $10. AE, DC, DISC, MC, V. Wheelchair accessible.

Index of Accommodations by Neighborhood

For neighborhood descriptions, see Chapter 8.

Bywater
Macarty Park Guest House ($–$$)

Central Business District
Doubletree Hotel New Orleans ($–$$$)
Fairmont Hotel ($–$$$)
French Quarter Courtyard Hotel ($$–$$$)
Holiday Inn-Downtown Superdome ($–$$)
Hotel Monaco New Orleans ($$–$$$$)
International House ($$–$$$$)
LaSalle Hotel ($)
Le Pavillon Hotel ($$–$$$$)
Loft 523 ($$–$$$$)
Windsor Court ($$$$)

Faubourg Marigny
B&W Courtyards Bed & Breakfast ($$)
Frenchmen ($–$$)
Melrose Mansion ($$–$$$$)
Royal Street Inn and R Bar ($–$$)

French Quarter

Bienville House ($–$$$)
Bourbon Orleans Hotel ($$–$$$)
Chateau Hotel ($–$$)
Chateau Sonesta Hotel ($$–$$$)
Dauphine Orleans Hotel ($$–$$$$)
French Quarter Guest House ($$–$$$)
Holiday Inn-Chateau LeMoyne ($$–$$$)
Hotel Maison de Ville ($$$)
Hotel Monteleone ($$–$$$)
Hotel Provincial ($$–$$$)
Hotel Villa Convento ($$–$$$)
Lafitte Guest House ($$–$$$)
Lamothe House ($–$$$)
Le Richelieu Hotel ($–$$)
Maison Dupuy ($–$$$)
New Orleans Guest House ($)
Olde Victorian Inn ($$–$$$)
Omni Royal Orleans ($$–$$$$)
Place d'Armes Hotel ($$–$$$$)
Prince Conti Hotel ($$)
Ramada Plaza The Inn on Bourbon Street ($$$)
Ritz-Carlton New Orleans ($$–$$$$)
Royal Sonesta ($$$–$$$$)
Saint Louis ($$–$$$)

Soniat House ($$–$$$)
W French Quarter ($$$$)
Wyndham New Orleans at Canal Place ($$$$)

Garden District

Pontchartrain Hotel ($$–$$$$)
St. Charles Inn ($)

Lower Garden District

McKendrick-Breaux House ($$)
St. Charles Guest House ($–$$)
St. Vincent's Guest House ($)

Mid-City

Ashton's Bed & Breakfast ($$)
Block-Keller House ($–$$)
House on Bayou Road ($$–$$$$)

Uptown

Beau Séjour Bed & Breakfast ($$–$$$)
The Columns ($$)
Grand Victorian Bed & Breakfast ($$–$$$$)

Index of Accommodations by Price

$

Bienville House (French Quarter)
Block-Keller House (Mid-City)
Chateau Hotel (French Quarter)
Doubletree Hotel New Orleans (Central Business District)
Fairmont Hotel (Central Business District)
Frenchmen (Faubourg Marigny)
Holiday Inn-Downtown Superdome (Central Business District)
Lamothe House (French Quarter)
LaSalle Hotel (Central Business District)
Le Richelieu Hotel (French Quarter)
Macarty Park Guest House (Bywater)
Maison Dupuy (French Quarter)

New Orleans Guest House (French Quarter)
Royal Street Inn and R Bar (Faubourg Marigny)
St. Charles Guest House (Lower Garden District)
St. Charles Inn (Garden District)
St. Vincent's Guest House (Lower Garden District)

$$

Ashton's Bed & Breakfast (Mid-City)
B&W Courtyards Bed & Breakfast (Faubourg Marigny)
Beau Séjour Bed & Breakfast (Uptown)
Bienville House (French Quarter)
Block-Keller House (Mid-City)

Bourbon Orleans Hotel (French Quarter)

Chateau Hotel (French Quarter)

Chateau Sonesta Hotel (French Quarter)

The Columns (Uptown)

Dauphine Orleans Hotel (French Quarter)

Doubletree Hotel New Orleans (Central Business District)

Fairmont Hotel (Central Business District)

Frenchmen (Faubourg Marigny)

French Quarter Courtyard Hotel (Central Business District)

French Quarter Guest House (French Quarter)

Grand Victorian Bed & Breakfast (Uptown)

Holiday Inn-Chateau LeMoyne (French Quarter)

Holiday Inn-Downtown Superdome (Central Business District)

Hotel Monaco (Central Business District)

Hotel Monteleone (French Quarter)

Hotel Provincial (French Quarter)

Hotel Villa Convento (French Quarter)

House on Bayou Road (Mid-City)

International House (Central Business District)

Lafitte Guest House (French Quarter)

Lamothe House (French Quarter)

Le Pavillon Hotel (Central Business District)

Le Richelieu Hotel (French Quarter)

Loft 523 (Central Business District)

Macarty Park Guest House (Bywater)

Maison Dupuy (French Quarter)

McKendrick-Breaux House (Lower Garden District) Melrose Mansion (Faubourg Marigny)

Olde Victorian Inn (French Quarter)

Omni Royal Orleans (French Quarter)

Place d'Armes Hotel (French Quarter)

Prince Conti Hotel (French Quarter)

Pontchartrain Hotel (Garden District)

Ritz-Carlton New Orleans (French Quarter)

Royal Street Inn and R Bar (Faubourg Marigny)

St. Charles Guest House (Lower Garden District)

Saint Louis (French Quarter)

St. Vincent's Guest House (Lower Garden District)

Soniat House (French Quarter)

$$$

Beau Séjour Bed & Breakfast (Uptown)

Bienville House (French Quarter)

Bourbon Orleans Hotel (French Quarter)

Chateau Sonesta Hotel (French Quarter)

Dauphine Orleans Hotel (French Quarter)

Doubletree Hotel New Orleans (Central Business District)

Fairmont Hotel (Central Business District)

French Quarter Courtyard Hotel (Central Business District)

French Quarter Guest House (French Quarter)

Grand Victorian Bed & Breakfast (Uptown)

Holiday Inn-Chateau LeMoyne (French Quarter)

Hotel Maison de Ville (French Quarter)

Hotel Monaco New Orleans (Central Business District)

Hotel Monteleone (French Quarter)

Hotel Provincial (French Quarter)

Hotel Villa Convento (French Quarter)

House on Bayou Road (Mid-City)

International House (Central Business District)

Lafitte Guest House (French Quarter)

Lamothe House (French Quarter)

Le Pavillon Hotel (Central Business District)

Loft 523 (Central Business District)

Maison Dupuy (French Quarter)

McKendrick-Breaux House (Lower Garden District)

Melrose Mansion (Faubourg Marigny)

Olde Victorian Inn (French Quarter)

Omni Royal Orleans (French Quarter)
Place d'Armes Hotel (French Quarter)
Pontchartrain Hotel (Garden District)
Ramada Plaza The Inn on Bourbon Street (French Quarter)
Ritz-Carlton New Orleans (French Quarter)
Royal Sonesta (French Quarter)
Saint Louis (French Quarter)
Soniat House (French Quarter)

$$$$

Dauphine Orleans Hotel (French Quarter)
Grand Victorian Bed & Breakfast (Uptown)
Hotel Monaco New Orleans (Central Business District)
House on Bayou Road (Mid-City)

International House (Central Business District)
Le Pavillon Hotel (Central Business District)
Loft 523 (Central Business District)
McKendrick-Breaux House (Lower Garden District)
Melrose Mansion (Faubourg Marigny)
Omni Royal Orleans (French Quarter)
Place d'Armes Hotel (French Quarter)
Pontchartrain Hotel (Garden District)
Ritz-Carlton New Orleans (French Quarter)
Royal Sonesta (French Quarter)
W French Quarter (French Quarter)
Windsor Court Hotel (Central Business District)
Wyndham New Orleans at Canal Place (French Quarter)

Chapter 10

Dining and Snacking in New Orleans

. . . .

In This Chapter

▶ Knowing who and what are hot now

▶ Dishing up where the locals eat

▶ Navigating reservation and dress code policies

▶ Discovering the best restaurants in town

▶ Sampling the best places for snacks, sandwiches, and sweets

. . . .

*N*ew Orleans enjoys its reputation as a mecca for great food. The city's port-town status, unique ethnic mix, and proximity to Cajun Country all make it a combustible culinary proving ground. (See Chapter 2 for more information.) A recent survey hosted by America Online and *Travel & Leisure* magazine ranked New Orleans No. 1 in the United States for dining out. That comes as no surprise to locals who are happily spoiled by the rich tradition of good food, from crawfish étouffée to oyster po' boys to shrimp Creole. Almost everything you eat here is fried or served in a rich, buttery sauce — or both. If this horrifies you, you've picked the wrong place to visit. Although the city offers some healthy alternatives, if you skip the decadent pleasures of a New Orleans meal, you're missing the point. Enjoy yourself here; eat responsibly when you get home.

Getting the Dish on the Local Scene

National dining trends eventually show up in New Orleans, but hot chefs here mostly set their own trends, employing ingredients and methods from different cuisines and creating marvelous new combinations. As in Cajun and Creole cooking, fusion is a large part of what food in New Orleans is all about. Influences as varied as Spanish, Italian, West Indian, African, and Native American contribute to a wide range of choices — from eclectic gourmet dishes to down-home Southern cooking. (For additional information on local cuisine, see Chapter 2.)

Thanks to the ubiquitous presence of celebrity chef Emeril Lagasse, Louisiana cooking has a higher profile than ever. His restaurants, **Emeril's, Nola,** and **Emeril's Delmonico,** draw large crowds looking for daring and creative Creole/New American cooking (and maybe a celebrity sighting or two). However, Lagasse is far from the only popular chef in New Orleans. Bayona's Susan Spicer, René Bistrot's René Bajeux, Restaurant August's John Besh, Upperline's Kenneth Smith, and Brigtsen's Frank Brigtsen are just a few of the names you're likely to hear bandied about by local foodies. One name I can almost guarantee you'll hear often in your gastronomic adventures is Brennan — with restaurants such as Bacco, Brennan's, Commander's, Mr. B's Bistro, and Palace Café, this family is the dining scene's answer to the music scene's Neville and Marsalis dynasties.

The French Quarter

Though the Quarter is widely regarded as tourist headquarters, it has an almost unbelievable number of standout restaurants that locals regularly patronize. A list of the best is much too long to run here, but a partial sampling must include classy favorites such as **Antoine's, Arnaud's,** and **Brennan's,** as well as wackier (and much cheaper) options such as **Café Maspero** and **Clover Grill.** Plenty of great spots exist in between those extremes, from the contemporary Italian fare at **Irene's Cuisine,** to the romantic ambience at **Bella Luna** or **Bayona.**

Central Business and Warehouse Districts

Emeril's is one of the biggest names on the local scene — and with good reason. Locals also flock to the **New Orleans Grill** for one of the most elegant dining experiences in the city and **Cobalt** (another winner from Susan Spicer) for hip, experimental cuisine in a space to match. On the other end of the scale, **Mother's** exemplary sandwiches are cheap (and a calorie-counter's nightmare), and **Taqueria Corona's** mouth-watering combination platters (*uno y medio* with a shrimp *flauta* is my favorite) offer plenty of food for little money.

Garden District and Uptown

In the recent past, you could sum up your argument for the Garden District as a gourmet hot spot in just two words: **Commander's Palace.** After all, the James Beard Association voted it best restaurant in the United States a few years back — the food-industry equivalent of receiving an Oscar. But Commander's has some company these days, particularly **Restaurant August** and **René Bistrot.** Uptown, savvy gourmands flock to **Upperline** for chef Kenneth Smith and proprietor JoAnn Clevenger's creative Creole collaborations and **Brigtsen's** in the Riverbend. Farther out, but worth the trip, **Jacques-Imo's** has such an incredible vibe that locals endure as much as an hour-and-a-half wait — the highest praise imaginable in this town.

Mid-City

Mid-City's restaurant reputation is heating up thanks to the reinstated Canal Streetcar. On the Carrollton spur, you find Gérard and Eveline Crozier's welcome return to fine dining with **Chateaubriand Steakhouse** and the newest location of popular Vietnamese chain **Pho Tau Bay.** At the intersection of Canal and Carrollton, you can choose to be serenaded by a jukebox in a cozy booth at **Michael's Mid-City Grill** or servers lip-synching speed metal and hip-hop at **Juan's Flying Burrito.** Locals are still loyal to **Christian's,** which serves French/Creole in a converted church, and **Gabrielle,** for its French cafe ambience and Creole/Cajun menu. Serious steak lovers also herd into the original **Ruth's Chris Steak House** (where the popular chain originated). Personally, I can't decide which place I prefer for a po' boy — cheery, folksy **Katie's** or blue-collar, Mom 'n' Pop **Liuzza's,** home of the giant frozen beer mug.

A word on tourist spots

Aside from the really obvious tourist draws, locals don't go out of their way to avoid too many restaurants. You *will,* however, find a disproportionate ratio of tourists to locals at such Cajun-leaning establishments as **K-Paul's, Michaul's,** and **Mulate's,** which isn't necessarily a reflection on the food itself. A large proportion of tourists usually just means that a restaurant is geared more toward visitor-friendly standby dishes, while locals familiar with the basics seek out more inventive fare. (In all fairness, **K-Paul's** is arguably an exception to this rule; its high tourist count has a lot to do with chef Paul Prudhomme's familiar name and French Quarter location.)

Making reservations

When a review recommends that you reserve a table at a restaurant, it generally means for dinner. You can usually get a table for two at lunch without having to wait too long (if at all). With a couple of exceptions (noted in the reviews), the same goes for breakfast.

Restaurants in New Orleans do a very brisk business except during the hot summer months. Consequently, make reservations before you even leave home if you want to dine at a certain restaurant at a particular time. You may need to reserve a table a month or more in advance, particularly during Mardi Gras and Jazz Fest, if you want to eat at one of the most famous restaurants. If you forgot to make reservations, arrive early — before noon (or even before 11:30 a.m.) for lunch and before 6:30 p.m. for dinner.

Dressing to dine

Legend has it that Antoine's restaurant once turned away Mick Jagger because he wasn't wearing a jacket. Whether that's true or not, top-of-the-line restaurants such as **Antoine's** and **Commander's Palace** obviously require the full jacket-and-tie treatment. Other than that, though, New Orleans, being a tourist-dependent market, is pretty casual about dress codes. Most serious dining spots require the much less stringent "business casual" look (a nice shirt and a jacket or blazer; jeans are usually allowed, but only if they're in good condition — if you're uncertain, call the restaurant ahead of time). Even the best restaurants allow casual wear at lunch. And obviously, no one is going to kick you out of a corner po' boy shop for wearing shorts, flip-flops, and a Hawaiian print shirt. Check the individual restaurant listings that follow for special dress requirements.

Trying some of New Orleans's ethnic eats

As if the roulette wheel of local culinary combinations wasn't enough, New Orleans, like most mid-sized cities, also offers its fair share of ethnic fare. Although I don't go into great detail, check out a few of the best spots with this highly selective and subjective list:

Caribbean: Mango House (8115 Jeannette St., Carrollton, ☎ **504-862-5848**)

Chinese: Five Happiness (3605 S. Carrollton Ave., Carrollton, ☎ **504-482-3935**)

Cuban: Liborio Cuban Restaurant (321 Magazine St., Lower Garden District, ☎ **504-581-9680**)

Japanese: Horinoya (920 Poydras St., Central Business District, ☎ **504-561-8914**) and **Samurai Sushi** (239 Decatur St., French Quarter, ☎ **504-525-9595**)

Mediterranean: Moonlight Café (1921 Sophie Wright Place, Lower Garden District, ☎ **504-522-7313**)

Mexican: Juan's Flying Burrito (2018 Magazine St., Lower Garden District, ☎ **504-569-0000**; 4724 S. Carrollton Ave., Mid-City, ☎ **504-486-9950**) and **Taqueria Corona** (857 Fulton St., Warehouse District, ☎ **504-524-9805**; 5932 Magazine St., Uptown, ☎ **504-897-3974**)

Middle Eastern: Lebanon's Cafe (1500 S. Carrollton Ave., Carrollton, ☎ **504-862-6200**) and **Mona's** (3901 Banks St., Mid-City, ☎ **504-482-7743**; 4126 Magazine St., Uptown, ☎ **504-894-9800**; 3149 Calhoun St., Uptown, ☎ **504-861-2124**).

Thai: Basil Leaf (1438 S. Carrollton Ave., Carrollton, ☎ **504-862-9001**)

Vietnamese: Lemon Grass Restaurant (217 Camp St., Central Business District, ☎ **504-523-1200**) and **Pho Tau Bay** (216 N. Carrollton Ave., Mid-City, ☎ **504-485-SOUP**; 1565 Tulane Ave., Central Business District, ☎ **504-524-4669**)

Ethnic food is fabulous, but sometimes you just want some fried chicken and collard greens. I save a couple of comfort-food bastions (notably **Jacques-Imo's** and **Dooky Chase**) for the listings that appear later in this chapter. But scan over this short list of the best soul-food establishments in town:

Dunbar's Creole Cooking (4927 Freret St., Uptown, ☎ **504-899-0734**)

Henry's Soul Food (2501 S. Claiborne Ave., on the corner of Claiborne and Second Street, Central City, ☎ **504-821-7757**; 209 N. Broad St., Mid-City, ☎ **504-821-8635**)

Lighting up

When it comes to smoking in restaurants, New Orleans is slightly more lenient than the rest of the United States. Although many restaurants prohibit smoking or relegate it to certain sections (notably in the French Quarter, where space and atmosphere are at a premium), many others still tolerate it. If smoking is a priority for you, call ahead to find out the restaurant's policy.

Rewarding good service: Tips on gratuities

The **sales tax** in New Orleans is one of the highest in the United States: 9 percent. Many diners use the following handy guideline when figuring out the tip; they just take the tax and double it to get 18 percent. A general guideline for tipping is 15 to 20 percent, depending upon the level of service and quality of experience you receive.

Keep in mind that some servers must split their tips with the rest of the wait-staff _and_ the kitchen staff. Don't feel obliged to reward poor service, but if the service is excellent, be generous.

Trimming the Fat from Your Budget

 I'm sure you won't be shocked to discover that many tourist places — especially in the French Quarter — charge inflated prices for "signature New Orleans dishes" simply because they can. Keep in mind that many New Orleans specialties, such as jambalaya, étouffée, red beans and rice, muffulettas, and po' boy sandwiches were made with common ingredients out of economic necessity. Any place that charges you a ton of money for any of these is just ripping you off. You can find incredibly tasty versions of these staples very cheaply at any number of places, so go elsewhere.

Another way to save some dough without sacrificing the quality of your New Orleans dining experience is to visit the city's fancier restaurants for lunch rather than dinner. Lunch menus almost always offer more-affordable versions of a particular institution's signature dishes. Eating lunch at the more expensive restaurants frees you up to frequent looser, less-expensive spots, such as Clover Grill or Franky and Johnny's for dinner.

Conversely, you may want to skip lunch altogether, fortifying yourself with a few snacks during your afternoon sightseeing. Of course, granola bars and the odd piece of fruit can only take you so far, in which case you could bend this idea slightly, maybe grabbing a Lucky Dog or a quick po' boy.

New Orleans's Best Restaurants

Grab your fork and get ready to loosen your belt a notch or two because this section explores New Orleans restaurants. I start with my picks of the best and/or most popular restaurants in the city, arranged alphabetically. The price range, neighborhood, and type of cuisine follow the restaurant name. After that, use the indexes to help you identify what best suits your tastes and needs.

The reviews also make note of which restaurants are wheelchair accessible. Call ahead to inquire, however, because some of these places may still be inconvenient — for instance, tables may be too close together.

A note about reservations

Except for the first three weeks of December, restaurants in New Orleans are very busy from September through May. Consequently, if you must eat at a particular restaurant at a certain time, make your reservation at least one week in advance. The earlier you reserve your table the better, especially around Jazz Fest and Mardi Gras, when some restaurants fill up a month or more in advance. Even if you don't make reservations before you leave home, call and see if you can get in. People often cancel reservations at the last minute, or the restaurant may not be booked up in the first place, no matter how popular it is. Some restaurants don't take reservations at all. Long lines out front make up for this informality, however.

One further note: Even if this whole book covered nothing but New Orleans restaurants, it still couldn't do justice to the many fine establishments in the city and its outskirts. These reviews are necessarily brief and to the point. Because space constraints prohibit me from highlighting every worthy establishment, this chapter is merely meant to provide a representative sampling, filled with no-brainers, conventional-wisdom choices, and my personal faves.

What the $ symbols mean

Dining in New Orleans ranges from low-key and friendly to white-gloved formal. To let you know what to expect price-wise, the restaurant listings in this chapter are accompanied by a dollar symbol ($), which gives you an idea of what a complete meal (including appetizer, entree, dessert, one drink, taxes, and tip) costs per person. Most listings contain more than one symbol — for example, $–$$ — to indicate the general price range you're likely to encounter at each restaurant. Aside from price ranges, the difference between one ranking and the next also reflects extras such as location, reputation, type of cuisine, atmosphere, interior, service, and view. Check out Table 10-1 for the lowdown on the dollar symbols.

Table 10-1	Key to Restaurant Dollar Signs
Dollar Sign(s)	*Price Range*
$	Less than $15
$$	$15–$30
$$$	$31–$45
$$$$	$45 or more

New Orleans's Top Restaurants from A to Z

Antoine's
$$–$$$$ French Quarter   FRENCH/CREOLE

Astonishingly, Antoine's is still owned and operated by the family that founded it 150 years ago. Feast on old-world dishes such as *pompano* Pontchartrain (the grilled fillet is topped with tender crabmeat sautéed in butter) and *trout amandine*. The 15 dining rooms run the gamut from plain to opulent, and some sort of caste system governs the seating process. (The front dining room is "reserved" for tourists, and locals are aghast to be mistakenly seated here.) Antoine's gets away with this by virtue of its place in New Orleans culinary history — it's the birthplace of Oysters Rockefeller. Save room for the enormous baked Alaska; after William Faulkner received the Nobel Prize for literature, he was served one inscribed "the Ignoble Prize."

See map p. 126. 713 St. Louis St. (a half block from Bourbon Street). ☎ **504-581-4422.** www.antoines.com. *Make reservations at least a week in advance for the weekend. Main courses: $22–$56 (most under $25). AE, DC, MC, V. Open: Mon–Sat 11:30 a.m–2 p.m. and 5:30–9:30 p.m. Jackets required after 5 p.m., but casual wear is acceptable for lunch. Wheelchair accessible.*

Arnaud's
$$–$$$ French Quarter   CREOLE

Founded in 1918, Arnaud's is a frequently overlooked classic New Orleans restaurant, which bodes well for locals. Unlike some other old-line haunts, the food's quality hasn't diminished with age, and neither has the decor, which features antique ceiling fans, flickering gas lamps, and dark wood paneling. The restaurant consists of 12 buildings connected by stairs and hallways — it sprawls leisurely over an entire city block. Start with the signature shrimp Arnaud marinated in tangy remoulade sauce, followed by Creole bouillabaisse or filet mignon (the latter rivals most local steakhouses). Only the most serious chocoholics can manage to devour every sinful spoonful of the Chocolate Devastation dessert. Before or after your meal, head upstairs to wander the spooky, dimly lit Mardi Gras Museum

French Quarter Dining

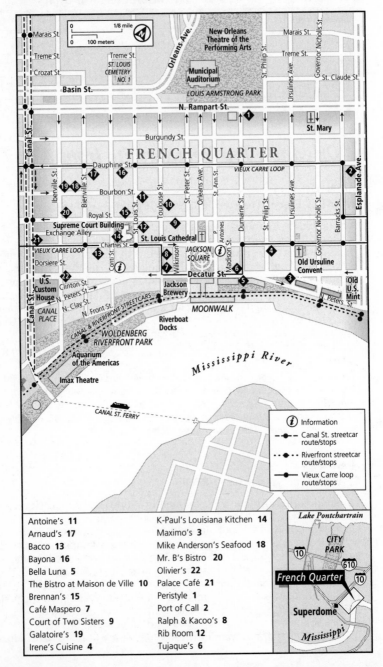

Antoine's **11**

Arnaud's **17**

Bacco **13**

Bayona **16**

Bella Luna **5**

The Bistro at Maison de Ville **10**

Brennan's **15**

Café Maspero **7**

Court of Two Sisters **9**

Galatoire's **19**

Irene's Cuisine **4**

K-Paul's Louisiana Kitchen **14**

Maximo's **3**

Mike Anderson's Seafood **18**

Mr. B's Bistro **20**

Olivier's **22**

Palace Café **21**

Peristyle **1**

Port of Call **2**

Ralph & Kacoo's **8**

Rib Room **12**

Tujague's **6**

featuring costumes and other memorabilia owned by Arnaud's founder, Germaine Wells. For a less formal but no less pleasing experience, try Arnaud's neighboring brasserie, Remoulade.

See map p. 126. 813 Bienville (at the corner of Bourbon Street), an easy walk from anywhere in the French Quarter or Central Business District. ☎ **866-230-8891** *or 504-523-5433.* www.arnauds.com. *Make reservations a week or more in advance for the weekend. Main courses: $19–$38. AE, DC, DISC, MC, V. Open: Lunch Mon–Fri 11:30 a.m.–2:30 p.m.; dinner Sun–Thurs 6–10 p.m., Fri–Sat 6–10:30 p.m.; Sun jazz brunch 10 a.m.–2:30 p.m. Dress code is casual for lunch; dinner requires a jacket for men. Wheelchair accessible.*

Bacco
$–$$ **French Quarter**   ITALIAN/CREOLE

With its Gothic arches and Venetian silk chandeliers, this sumptuously decorated testament to Brennan good taste combines the rich flair of Creole with the hearty comfort of Italian. Executive chef Haley Gabel's signature dishes include crawfish ravioli in a tart, sun-dried tomato pesto butter sauce and sweet Vermouth-steamed mussels flavored with red onions and pancetta. Finish with melt-in-your-mouth tiramisu, topped with a light mascarpone cream, or the local flavor of Mauthe's Creole cream-cheese cheesecake, made by a small dairy farm in Folsom, Louisiana, and served with caramel sauce and toasted hazelnuts.

See map p. 126. 310 Chartres St. (2 blocks from Bourbon Street, 2½ blocks from Canal Street, and 2½ blocks from Jackson Square). ☎ **504-522-2426.** www.bacco.com. *Make reservations a couple of days in advance for the weekend. Main courses: $13.25–$22. AE, DC, MC, V. Open: Daily 11:30 a.m.–2 p.m.; Sun–Thurs 6:30–9:30 p.m., Fri–Sat 6–10:30 p.m. Shorts and T-shirts are allowed. Wheelchair accessible.*

Bayona
$$–$$$ **French Quarter**   INTERCONTINENTAL

Bayona was chef-owner Susan Spicer's first foray into New Orleans dining and remains one of the city's most beloved institutions. Housed in a 200-year-old Creole cottage, the mood is romantic and relaxed, yet invigorating. Tasting the superb cream of garlic soup is worth forfeiting a kiss later, trust me (though I would encourage your dining partner to order the same). Any entree with lamb is heavenly, especially the peppered lamb loin with herbed goat cheese and Zinfandel sauce. Just when you think your taste buds are peaked, one bite of the toasted pecan roulade — with caramel mousse and praline syrup — and you'll reach new heights of ecstasy.

See map p. 126. 430 Dauphine St. (1 block from Bourbon Street). ☎ **504-525-4455.** www.bayona.com. *Reservations required for dinner, recommended for lunch. Main courses: $18–$28. AE, DC, DISC, MC, V. Open: Lunch Mon–Fri 11:30 a.m.–2 p.m.; dinner Mon–Thurs 6–9:30 p.m., Fri–Sat 6–10:30 p.m. Dress is business casual. A low step and small restroom may pose problems for people with disabilities.*

Bella Luna

$$ French Quarter   ECLECTIC/CONTINENTAL

Bella Luna is widely regarded as the most romantic restaurant in the city, thanks to its Italian-villa decor and breathtaking view of the Mississippi River. (When making a reservation, ask for a table closest to the windows.) Chef-owner Horst Pfeifer lovingly oversees an eclectic menu of (among others) Southwestern, German, Italian, and Louisiana cuisines. Dishes are often adorned with unusual herbs grown in Pfeifer's garden at the Ursuline Convent. The menu changes throughout the year, but pasta is a specialty. Look for the salmon tower, with white truffle oil, cucumber and red onion with Louisiana choupique (fish) caviar and capers, and the pork chop with a pecan crust, horseradish mashed potatoes, and a sauce made from Abita Beer (a popular local microbrew). For dessert, try the bananas Foster bread pudding or creamy milk-chocolate-and-cappuccino cheesecake.

See map p. 126. 914 N. Peters St. (1 block from Jackson Square). ☎ *504-529-1583.* www.bellalunarestaurant.com. *Reservations recommended. Main courses: $17.75–$26.50. AE, DC, DISC, MC, V. Open: Mon–Sat 6–10:30 p.m., Sun 6–9:30 p.m. No jeans, shorts, sneakers, or T-shirts. The restaurant is wheelchair accessible thanks to an elevator, but restrooms are down a half-flight of stairs.*

The Bistro at Maison de Ville

$$–$$$ French Quarter   INTERNATIONAL/ECLECTIC

Stepping inside The Bistro is like entering a Parisian bistro, with its red leather banquettes, beveled-glass mirrors, natural wood flooring, and Impressionist-style paintings. One of the city's best-kept secrets, the Bistro is popular among locals for many reasons, from the intimate atmosphere to the inventive dishes and extensive wine list. The leap from "intimate" to "cramped" is short here, however, and the small size can also mean a good wait (especially when the theater crowd pours in). The menu changes every three months, but, depending on the season, you're likely to encounter and enjoy such options as confit of duck, house-smoked duck breast, grilled Italian sausage and cannelini bean cassoulet, or roasted pavé of salmon stuffed with crab, shrimp, and scallops and served with a grilled vegetable polenta cake.

See map p. 126. 733 Toulouse St. (in the Hotel Maison de Ville), ☎ *504-528-9206.* www.maisondeville.com. *Reservations recommended. Main courses: $27.75–$39. AE, DC, DISC, MC, V. Open: Daily 11:30 a.m.–2 p.m. and 6–10 p.m. Dress is cocktail casual. Not accessible for wheelchairs.*

Brennan's

$$–$$$ French Quarter   FRENCH/CREOLE

You've heard of Breakfast at Tiffany's? In New Orleans, the tradition is Breakfast at Brennan's. The morning repasts here have clogged generations of arteries with multicourse feasts featuring such sauce-laden options as Eggs Portuguese (poached and served in a puff pastry ladled with hollandaise), Eggs Benedict, Eggs Hussarde, and Trout Nancy (they're big on proper names here). Such extravagance isn't without its price; spending $50 on breakfast alone is easy (Shoney's all-you-can-eat, this ain't). In spite of the cost, Brennan's is always crowded at breakfast and lunch; expect a bit of a wait, even with a reservation. Dinners are generally calmer, especially if you can snag a table on the gas lamp–lined balcony.

See map p. 126. 417 Royal St. (1 block from Bourbon Street). ☎ *504-525-9711.* www.brennansneworleans.com. *Reservations recommended. Main courses: Breakfast: $15–$20; $36 for 3-course prix-fixe breakfast, Dinner $28.50–$38.50. AE, DC, DISC, MC, V. Open: Daily 8 a.m.–2:30 p.m. and 6–10 p.m. Jacket recommended for men at dinner. Wheelchair accessible.*

Brigtsen's
$$ Uptown CAJUN/CREOLE

The atmosphere in this quaint Victorian cottage is both elegant and homey, thanks to chef-owner Frank Brigtsen's expertise in the kitchen and his wife Marna's warm welcome at the door. The menu changes daily because Brigtsen prefers to use local ingredients whenever possible, but his reputation as one of the city's best chefs remains constant. Brigtsen knows his way around rabbit (a Creole mainstay), and the well-proportioned seafood platter allows you to sample flaky grilled fish, tender baked oyster, spicy deviled crab, and other creative incarnations. Dessert ranges from the familiar comforts of café au lait crème brûlée to the tangy surprise of homemade lemonade ice cream.

See map p. 137. 723 Dante St. (take the St. Charles Streetcar; get off at the corner of St. Charles and S. Carrollton avenues, and walk 3 blocks; take a taxi at night). ☎ *504-861-7610.* www.brigstens.com. *Reservations required. Main courses: $18–$26 (early bird specials available Tues–Thurs 5:30–6:30 p.m. — full meal for less than $20). AE, DC, MC, V. Open: Tues–Sat 5:30–10 p.m. Casual dress. Steps may prove a challenge for people with disabilities.*

Café Maspero
$–$$ French Quarter SANDWICHES/SEAFOOD

With good reason, this place is always packed (its Decatur Street location doesn't hurt either). Café Maspero serves seafood, grilled marinated chicken, and other familiar fare (though you won't find po' boys here), as well as kiddie-friendly items such as burgers and deli sandwiches — almost all served with fries, in impressively large portions, and at ridiculously low prices. That is, low in relation to the rest of the Quarter, anyway. The cafe also offers a huge selection of beers, wines, and cocktails. (Don't confuse this restaurant with Maspero's Slave Exchange a few blocks away.)

See map p. 126. 601 Decatur St. (2 short blocks from Jackson Square and 3 blocks from Bourbon Street). ☎ *504-523-6250. Reservations aren't accepted, and the lines can be long at times, but they usually move fast. Main courses: $9–$16. No credit cards. Open: Sun–Thurs 11 a.m.–11 p.m. (until midnight Fri–Sat). No dress code. Wheelchair accessible, but the crowded tables and narrow doorways make maneuvering a challenge.*

Chateaubriand
$$–$$$ Mid-City   FRENCH/STEAKHOUSE

Chef-owner Gérard Crozier and his wife, renowned sommelier Eveline, named the restaurant — and its signature dish — after French diplomat and author Francois René Auguste Chateaubriand, the founder of romanticism in French literature. The Croziers reinterpret his opulent style with a luxurious, classically masculine space with deep red and mahoghany hues, granite tabletops, and flickering gas lamps. If you go as a pair, order the Chateaubriand for Two, featuring a juicy, 20-ounce certified Angus beef grilled filet accompanied by their famous gratin savoyard (swiss cheese never had it so good). The succulent grilled lobster stuffed with tender lump crabmeat is best paired with the yammy mashed potatoes (sweetened Louisiana yams). The wine cellar, visible from the Viscount Room, holds more than 3,000 bottles; Eveline has created one of the city's finest collections of French wines.

See map p. 132. 310 N. Carrollton Ave. (3 miles from the Quarter — take the Canal Streetcar). ☎ *504-207-0016.* www.chateaubriandsteakhouse.com. *Reservations recommended. Main courses: $19.75–$38. AE, DC, MC, V. Open: Mon–Fri 11:30 a.m.–2:30 p.m.; daily 5:30–10:30 p.m. Wheelchair accessible.*

Christian's
$$–$$$ Mid-City   FRENCH/CREOLE

Your prayers for creative cuisine in an uplifting atmosphere are answered inside this pastel-pink former church. The altar serves as the waiters' station and the sermon board posts the menu offerings. Chef Michel Foucqueteau's menu is a divine blend of classic French and New Orleans Creole. Try the baby veal Christian (sautéed baby veal in a cream sauce with port wine and morel mushrooms) or the shrimp Marigny (plump Gulf shrimp sautéed with pearl onions, mushrooms, sun-dried tomatoes, and garlic, flamed in brandy, and finished with a Dijon butter sauce). The new Canal Streetcar will no doubt heighten its profile in a hurry, so reserve a table as soon as possible.

See map p. 132. 3835 Iberville St. (3 miles from the Quarter — take the Canal Streetcar). ☎ *504-482-4924.* www.christiansrestaurantneworleans.com. *Reservations recommended. Main courses: $25–$35. AE, DC, MC, V. Open: Tues–Fri 11:30 a.m.–2 p.m.; Tues–Sat 5:30–9:30 p.m. Jacket and tie strongly recommended for men. Steps and closely packed tables pose problems for people with wheelchairs.*

Cobalt
$$ Central Business District   REGIONAL AMERICAN

Saints running back Deuce McAllister was recently spotted at this hip enclave adjacent to the equally fab Hotel Monaco. With a little help from celebrity-chef-turned-consultant Susan Spicer, executive chef Brack May offers food as whimsical and delightful as the decor. I especially adore the wrought-iron fence bejeweled in colorful, fake gemstones that separates the dining area from the bar. Start with the playful Louisiana oyster pirogue — a scooped-out, crispy baked-potato skin serves as a boat — floating on a pool of bleu cheese remoulade. Although the entrees are all worthy — from the ancho barbecue rack of lamb to the vegetarian goat-cheese tamale — you may have a hard time choosing from the ecclectic dessert selection. I nearly fainted after one bite of the light, nicely textured milk chocolate–peanut butter mousse, served with a chocolate-covered banana and dripping in sweet, sticky vanilla caramel.

See map p. 137. 333 St. Charles Ave. (3 blocks from the Quarter; take a taxi at night).
☎ *504-482-4924.* www.cobaltrestaurant.com. *Reservations recommended. Main courses: $16–$27. AE, DC, MC, V. Open: Mon–Fri 7:30 a.m.–9:30 a.m. and 11:30 a.m.–2 p.m.; Sat–Sun 8:30–10:30 a.m.; daily 5:30–10 p.m. Jacket and tie strongly recommended for men. Steps and closely packed tables pose problems for people with wheelchairs.*

Commander's Palace
$$–$$$ Garden District   CREOLE

Recently awarded the Lifetime Outstanding Restaurant Award from the James Beard Foundation, Commander's Palace continues to live up to its reputation. Even in a city full of top-notch, elegant restaurants, Commander's Palace maintains a soft spot in locals' hearts with a winning combination of stellar service (you'll be pampered by several attendants throughout your meal), a grand setting (an 1880s Victorian house with a seemingly endless series of dining rooms and a gorgeous courtyard), and outstanding food. The sumptuous turtle soup with sherry is justly famous, and such bright spots as the boned Mississippi roasted quail (stuffed with an awesome Creole crawfish sausage) and the mixed grill (which features lamb and rabbit sausage) light up the menu. Lastly, when the staff suggests the bread pudding soufflé for dessert, you would be wise to do as they say.

See map p. 137 1403 Washington Ave. (take the St. Charles Streetcar to Washington and walk 2 blocks along Washington Ave. toward the river; take a taxi at night).
☎ *504-899-8221.* www.commanderspalace.com. *Reservations required. Main courses: Full brunch $20–$32; main courses $29–$32; prix-fixe $29–$36. AE, DC, DISC, MC, V. Open: Mon–Fri 11:30 a.m.–2 p.m.; jazz brunch Sat 11:30 a.m.–1 p.m., and Sun 10:30 a.m.–1:30 p.m.; daily 6–10 p.m. Men must wear a jacket and tie for dinner. Wheelchairs will need to navigate over one step. Complimentary valet parking.*

Court of Two Sisters
$$–$$$ French Quarter   CREOLE

The bottom line is that the atmosphere here — a historic building with a large, graceful courtyard filled with flowers, soothing fountains, and a wishing well — is better than the food. A strolling jazz band serenades you during the daily jazz brunch, though most locals avoid it (the brunch, not the band) for fear of looking like tourists. The food is often impressive but rarely spectacular. The jazz brunch boasts more than 60 dishes, including meat, fowl, fish, vegetables, fresh fruits, homemade breads, and pastries. For dinner, stick to safe bets such as the chicken Michelle or shrimp remoulade (and keep in mind that the restaurant maintains a $15 minimum

Mid-City Dining

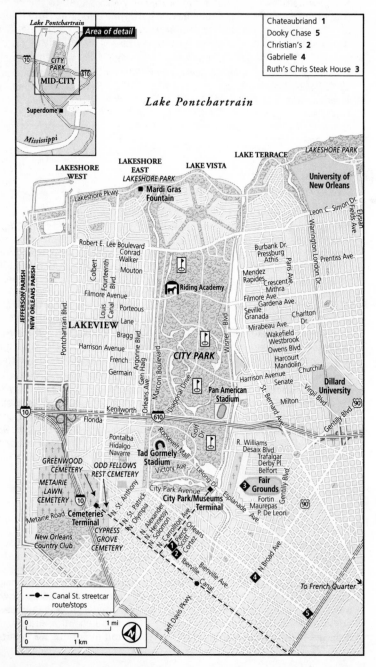

for dinner). Desserts are very good, though; splurge on the pecan pie or crêpes suzette. A children's menu offers shrimp or chicken fingers, with baked potato or fries, a fruit cup or ice cream, and milk. Kids 5 to 12 can also partake of the brunch buffet for $10.

See map p. 126. 613 Royal St. (1 block from Bourbon Street). ☎ *504-522-7261. www.courtoftwosisters.com. Reservations recommended. Main courses: $17–$32 (fixed-price meal available for $38); brunch $22. AE, CB, DC, DISC, MC, V. Open: Jazz brunch buffet daily 9 a.m.–3 p.m.; dinner 5:30–10 p.m. Shorts and T-shirts are allowed. Wheelchair accessible.*

Cuvée
$$ **Central Business District**   CREOLE/NEW AMERICAN

Young chef Bob Iacovone experiments with seasonal ingredients and multicourse tasting menus. The cavernous dining room, lit by gaslight, sets a perfectly intimate mood for such contemporary French creations as lamb shank with a flageolet cassoulet and foie gras crème brûlée with chevre and sour apples. An expansive wine list nicely complements the cuisine.

See map p. 137. 322 Magazine St. ☎ *504-587-9001. www.restaurantcuvee.com. Reservations recommended. Main courses: $18–$28. AE, DC, MC, V. Open: Mon–Fri 11:30 a.m.–2:30 p.m., Mon–Thurs 6–10 p.m.; Fri–Sat 6–11 p.m. Wheelchair accessible.*

Dick & Jenny's
$–$$ **Uptown**   CREOLE/ECLECTIC

The decrepit bargeboard house on an industrial corridor doesn't look that appetizing, but inside you find a young Uptown crowd hungry for contemporary Creole dishes served on plates hand-painted by chef Dick Benz himself. His wife, Jenny, greets patrons, who smile in anticipation of their meal despite long waits. You may want to fast earlier in the day to take advantage of the sumptuous starters like steamed artichoke with warm brie crab dip and an entree-cum-sampler Duck Quatro (duck prepared four ways: confit, foie gras, duck liver cognac flan, and seared breast with white beans). Desserts are deadly; linger over lemon mascarpone crêpes or delight in the crunch of the crispy chocolate fritter.

See map p. 137. 4501 Tchoupitoulas St. (5 miles from the Quarter — take a taxi). ☎ *504-894-9880. No reservations available. Main courses: $12–$19. AE, DISC, MC, V. Open: Tues–Thurs 5:30–10 p.m.; Fri–Sat 5:30–10:30 p.m. Steps and closely packed tables pose problems for people with wheelchairs.*

Dooky Chase
$–$$ **Mid-City**   CREOLE/SOUL FOOD

Chef Leah Chase, a local celebrity and a very sweet lady, oversees the action in this simply decorated establishment that specializes in upscale soul food. The service is always friendly, if not always prompt. The extra wait gives you a chance to wander around and admire the extraordinary collection of African American art. Classic dishes such as gumbo and crispy fried chicken are to die for, though you won't go wrong with more esoteric fare such as Shrimp Clemenceau, a casserole of sautéed shellfish, mushrooms, peas, and potatoes. For dessert, savor the thick, hot bread pudding with shredded coconut and pecans in a praline liqueur sauce (one of the best bread puddings in a city that excels at them).

See map p. 132. 2301 Orleans Ave. (because the neighborhood is a bit dicey, take a cab). ☎ *504-821-2294. Reservations recommended at dinner. Main courses: $10.95–$25; fixed-price 4-course meal for $25 and a "Creole Feast" for $38. AE, DC, DISC, MC, V. Open: Sun–Thurs 11:30 a.m.–10 p.m.; Fri–Sat 11:30 a.m.–11 p.m. Dress is casual, but no shorts or tank tops. Wheelchair accessible.*

Elizabeth's
$ Bywater   CREOLE

As home prices and rents rose in the French Quarter and Faubourg Marigny, artists and other creative types increasingly headed toward Bywater, which in turn re-energized the community and gave new life to the darling little shotguns, Creole cottages, and Italianate center halls. Elizabeth's attracts locals from the farthest reaches of town because very few places offer breakfast period, much less the marvelous, monstrous breakfast po' boy or *pain perdu* (French toast piled high with strawberry-flavored cream cheese). If you're not an early bird, come for lunch instead; the Asian pupu platter (spring rolls, stuffed chicken wings with a piquant sauce, and half a catfish stuffed with oyster cornbread dressing) may sound weird but it tastes so good you don't care. Service is refreshingly attentive.

See map p. 137. 601 Gallier St. (2 miles from the Quarter — take a taxi). ☎ *504-944-9272.* www.elizabeths-restaurant.com. *No reservations necessary. Everything under $10. MC, V. Open: Tues–Sat 7 a.m.–2:30 p.m. A few small steps must be navigated for people with wheelchairs.*

Emeril's
$$–$$$ Warehouse District   CREOLE/NEW AMERICAN

Emeril Lagasse's specialty is what he calls *"New* New Orleans Cuisine," using Creole tradition as a foundation while exploring bold new directions. The desserts outnumber the entrees here, and the menu changes often, but the rack of lamb and fresh duck are favorites, and the grilled, Creole-seasoned chicken is a crowd-pleaser as well. Don't miss the banana cream pie with banana crust and caramel drizzle sauce, which has reduced diners to moaning and pounding on the table to express their pleasure (I'm not kidding). Service can be a little snooty, but when the food is this good, it can be overlooked.

See map p. 137. 800 Tchoupitoulas (8 blocks from Canal — take a taxi). ☎ *504-528-9393.* www.emerils.com. *Reservations required. Main courses: $22–$36; a 7-course degustation menu (which changes nightly) is $75. AE, DC, DISC, MC, V. Open: Lunch Mon–Fri 11:30 a.m.–2 p.m.; dinner Mon–Thurs 6–10 p.m. and Fri–Sat 6–11 p.m. Casual dress. Wheelchair accessible.*

Gabrielle
$$–$$$ Mid-City   FRENCH/CREOLE/CAJUN

Tucked inside this small, dark-purple building is an excellent approximation of a Parisian cafe. The ever-changing menu features crowd-pleasing
gumbos, homemade sausages, rabbit, and seafood dishes. A consistently
tasty (and inventive) entree is the slow-roasted duck with orange sherry
sauce, served with wild mushrooms and red and yellow peppers atop
a bed of shoestring potatoes. As for desserts, the Peppermint Patti — a
concoction made of chocolate cake, peppermint ice cream, and chocolate
sauce — simultaneously soothes and tingles the palate.

See map p. 132. 3201 Esplanade Ave. (2½ miles from the Quarter — take a taxi).
☎ *504-948-6233.* www.gabriellerestaurant.com. *Reservations recommended. Main courses: $18–$32. AE, DC, DISC, MC, V. Open: Tues–Sat 5:30–10 p.m.;
lunch on Fridays only, Oct–May, 11:30 a.m.–2 p.m. Casual dress. The restaurant is
wheelchair accessible, but the restroom isn't.*

Galatoire's
$–$$ French Quarter   FRENCH

One of the classiest restaurants in New Orleans still guided by the same
family who founded it in 1905, generations have stood in line here. Before
the return of the second-floor dining area (closed since World War II),
Galatoire's didn't accept reservations, and even made the Duke and
Duchess of Windsor wait for a table — or so the legend goes. An ongoing
debate rages about this place, however: Is Galatoire's still the best, or is it
coasting on its reputation? Those in the know (including those who have
made Sunday dinner here a tradition) say to order the trout amandine
without sauce, or the red snapper or redfish topped with sautéed crabmeat meunière from the à la carte menu, and you'll be persuaded that this
staunchly traditional spot is still a contender. If you want to snag a coveted table in the mirrored, first-floor dining room — where heeled locals
watch each other preen — prepare to join the long line outside. After
you're in, look for Tennessee Williams's regular table — he always sat at
the table.

*See map p. 126. 209 Bourbon St. (located in the second block of Bourbon Street,
an easy walk from anywhere in the Quarter or the Central Business District).*
☎ *504-525-2021.* www.galatoires.com. *Reservations accepted for second-floor
dining room only. Main courses: $14–$27. AE, DC, DISC, MC, V. Open: Tues–Sun
11:30 a.m.–10 p.m. Men must wear jackets for dinner and on Sunday. The restaurant
is wheelchair accessible, but the restrooms can be a problem.*

Gautreau's
$$–$$$ Uptown   CREOLE

The flickering candlelight and nostalgic photographs set a more romantic mood than the building (an old converted neighborhood drugstore)
might suggest. The upscale menu changes every few weeks; appetizers
have included duck confit and eggplant crisps, and the grilled hanger steak

New Orleans Dining

Brigtsen's **5**	The Grill Room **15**
Cobalt **11**	Herbsaint **10**
Commander's Palace **8**	Jacques-Imo's Café **1**
Cuvée **12**	Lilette **6**
Dick & Jenny's **7**	Mother's **13**
Elizabeth's **16**	Pascal's Manale **4**
Emeril's **9**	Restaurant August **14**
Gautreau's **2**	Upperline **3**

(similar to flank) is a hit, though you may opt for the roasted chicken, served with wild mushrooms, garlic potatoes, and green beans. Try the triple-layer cheesecake (with chocolate, pecan, and almond layers) for dessert, or if it's available, the tarte tatin (apples and sun-dried cherries with a strawberry sorbet).

See map p. 137. 1728 Soniat St. (take the St. Charles Streetcar and walk 2½ blocks down Soniat away from the river; take a taxi at night). ☎ *504-899-7397. Reservations recommended. Main courses: $17.50–$34. DC, DISC, MC, V. Open: Mon–Sat 6–10 p.m. A few steps make the small restrooms inaccessible to wheelchairs.*

The New Orleans Grill
$$–$$$ Central Business District   INTERNATIONAL

An exceptionally high level of service, food quality, and comfort makes The Grill Room (on the second floor of the Windsor Court Hotel) an unforgettable dining experience — at a price you won't soon forget, either. The menu changes frequently and can include such fancy fare as moderately blackened filet of halibut, chilled oysters with frozen champagne ginger granita (champagne seasoned with ginger, which has been frozen into a sorbet), or a rich roasted goose. Though you can indulge your wine-drinking habits and pay upwards of $18,000 for a double magnum (a quadruple-sized bottle) of 1961 Chateau Petrus, wine starts at just $20 a bottle. Eating here is an extravagant experience but not necessarily excessive.

See map p. 137. 300 Gravier St. (1 block from Canal). ☎ *504-522-1992.* www. windsorcourthotel.com. *Make reservations a week or two in advance. Main courses: $28–$39 (3-course lunch specials $25). AE, DC, DISC, MC, V. Open: Daily 7–10:30 a.m., Mon–Sat 11:30 a.m.–2 p.m., Sun–Thurs 6–10 p.m., and Fri–Sat 6–10:30 p.m.; brunch Sun 10:30 a.m.–2 p.m. Jacket required and tie recommended at dinner. Wheelchair accessible.*

Herbsaint
$–$$ Central Business District   FRENCH/NEW AMERICAN

Acclaimed local chef Susan Spicer opened Herbsaint — named for the locally made pastis found in, among other places, the popular local cocktail, the Sazerac — as a French-American outpost. It instantly enhanced her already stellar reputation as the mastermind behind Bayona and Cobalt (see reviews for both earlier in this chapter). The decor is suitably minimal, assuring no distractions from the adventurous cuisine. Offerings such as braised lamb shanks, duck confit, and fried frogs' legs dot a menu that veers between Gallic familiarity and New American experimentation. Try an obscure but pleasant selection from the offbeat wine list, and later, satisfy your sweet tooth with coconut macadamia nut pie or the chocolate beignets with their molten boozy interior.

See map p.137. 701 St. Charles Ave. ☎ *504-524-4114.* www.herbsaint.com. *Reservations recommended. Main courses: $14–$24. AE, DC, DISC, MC, V. Open: Lunch Mon–Fri 11:30 a.m.–2:30 p.m., Mon–Sat 5:30–10:30 p.m. Dress is business casual. Wheelchair accessible.*

Irene's Cuisine
$–$$ French Quarter   ITALIAN/FRENCH PROVENÇAL

Follow the scent of garlic — and locals — to this tiny restaurant located on the corner of a parking garage. Despite a brisk pace, the dark atmosphere (the waiters carry flashlights for a reason) can be really romantic. Start off with an appetizer of grilled shrimp served with just-so crunchy, panéed oysters. Follow that up with rack of lamb (served with a port wine sauce and herb garlic potatoes) or roasted chicken Rosmario, draped in a luxuriant rosemary gravy. If you're into the texture as well as the taste of the food, I recommend the bread pudding with roasted pecans for its alternating crunchy and creamy spoonfuls. Prepare to wait up to 90 minutes for a table; your patience will be amply rewarded.

See map p. 126. 539 St. Philip St. (3 short blocks from Jackson Square and 1 block from Decatur Street). ☎ *504-529-8811. Reservations not accepted (go early to avoid a wait) except for Christmas Eve, New Year's Eve, and Valentine's Day. Main courses: $14–$19. AE, MC, V. Open: Sun–Thurs 5:30–10:30 p.m. and Fri–Sat 5:30–11 p.m. Dress is casual to dressy. Wheelchair accessible.*

Jacques-Imo's Café
$–$$ Uptown   CREOLE/SOUL FOOD

Say it with me: *Jock*-a-moe's. People will gladly wait for more than an hour for some of the tastiest Southern soul food imaginable served in a cozy, low-lit dining room adorned by swamp murals. You can take the easy way out and order tender fried chicken or the stuffed pork chop, and no one would blame you. But the menu has a creative, experimental bent that's well worth pursuing compliments of owner Jack Leonardi (he's the guy in Bermuda shorts, even in winter) and chef Austin Leslie (you'll see him at work when you pass through the bustling kitchen to get to your table). A seafood-stocked Cajun bouillabaisse is an unexpected treat, as is the savory shrimp and alligator cheesecake appetizer in a rich, spicy cream. If you can find the room (and if you can, my hat's off to you), try the coffee bean crème brûlée dessert.

See map p. 137. 8324 Oak St. (2 blocks from Carrollton Avenue). ☎ *504-861-0886.* www.jacquesimoscafe.com. *Reservations accepted for parties of five or more. Main courses: $13.95–$21.50. AE, CB, DC, DISC, MC, V. Open: Mon–Thurs 5:30–10 p.m. and Fri–Sat 5:30–10:30 p.m. Casual attire. Wheelchair accessibility is a problem, though you can roll down a less-than-nice-looking alleyway to the back dining areas.*

K-Paul's Louisiana Kitchen
$$–$$$ French Quarter   CAJUN

The hoopla about Cajun cooking started back in the early '80s with living legend Paul Prudhomme and his renowned restaurant, which offers upscale (and high-priced) takes on traditional Cajun fare. Many of the red-hot chefs and restaurateurs in New Orleans today learned at the stove of Prudhomme. The menu, which changes daily and features a variety of extra-hot interpretations of the Cajun tradition, is known for its blackened redfish and Cajun martini. Also try anything with rabbit, the fiery gumbo, or the Cajun popcorn (fried crawfish tails). If it's available for dessert, order the sweet potato pecan pie with Chantilly cream. You won't find a children's menu per se, but several items are kid-compatible and nonspicy.

See map p. 126. 416 Chartres St. (between Conti and St. Louis streets). ☎ *504-524-7394.* www.kpauls.com. *Reservations suggested for upstairs dining room only; otherwise, you have to wait up to an hour. Main courses: Dinner $25–$35.95. AE, DC, DISC, MC, V. Open: Mon–Sat 5:30–10 p.m. Dress is business casual. Wheelchair accessible.*

Lilette
$$ Uptown   CREOLE/FRENCH

The namesake for chef-owner John Harris's quaint bistro was a French woman with whom he cooked during an extended stay in France. But Harris isn't content to stick to the classics; although he clearly respects tradition, he isn't afraid to experiment. A trademark dish is the spicy *boudin noir* (blood sausage) with cornichons and a house-made mustard sauce. Try the curious dessert goat cheese crème fraîche quenelles — little rounds of goat cheese crème fraîche with poached pears and topped with lavender honey. C'est magnifique!

See map p. 137. 3637 Magazine St. (4 miles from the Quarter — take a taxi). ☎ *504-895-1636. Reservations recommended. Main courses: $18–$30. AE, DISC, MC, V. Open: Tues–Sat 11:30 a.m.–2 p.m.; Tues–Thurs 6–10 p.m. Steps and closely packed tables pose problems for people with wheelchairs.*

Maximo's
$–$$ French Quarter   ITALIAN

If you suffer from a little Creole cooking overload, Maximo's is a fine place to go for Italian food. Jazz or photography buffs appreciate the extraordinarily large collection of Herman Leonard jazz photos (ever see that smoky image of Billie Holiday as she grabs the mike? That's vintage Leonard, who lives in New Orleans, by the way). The solid fare relies heavily on pasta (usually more than a dozen pastas are offered each day). The house specialty is penne Rosa, topped with sun-dried tomatoes, garlic, arugula, and shrimp. Other dependable choices are the veal scallopine or the veal T-bone cattoche, which is served pan-roasted with garlic and fresh herbs. The desserts are serviceable as well, and the wine list is excellent.

See map p. 126. 1117 Decatur St. (4 blocks from Jackson Square). ☎ *504-586-8883.* www.maximositaliangrill.com. *Reservations recommended. Main courses: $9–$28.95. AE, DC, DISC, MC, V. Open: Daily 6 p.m. until the last person leaves. Casual attire. Wheelchair accessible.*

Mike Anderson's Seafood

$–$$ French Quarter   SEAFOOD

This seafood restaurant is strategically located on Bourbon Street to attract tourists, and its comfortable seafood dishes reflect that reality without suffering a plain, lowest-common-denominator quality. You get seafood any way you want it — broiled, fried, baked, or even raw. You also find étouffée, jambalaya, and daily specials from which to choose. Specialties include the crawfish bisque, crawfish étouffée, and the Guitreau (fresh fish filets topped with crawfish tails, shrimp, and mushroom caps sautéed in butter, white wine, and spices). When oysters are in season, you can get them on the half-shell for just 25¢, Monday through Thursday, from 2 until 6 p.m. A reasonably priced kids' menu offers catfish, burgers, shrimp, chicken, and crawfish tails. Pair your meal with a local brew such as Abita Amber, Dixie, Turbodog, or Voodoo.

See map p. 126. 215 Bourbon St. (2 blocks from Canal Street). ☎ *504-524-3884.* www.mikeandersons.com. *Reservations not accepted (expect to wait 15 minutes or longer for a table). Main courses: $10.95–$21.95. AE, DC, DISC, MC, V. Open: Sun–Thurs 11:30 a.m.–10 p.m., Fri–Sat 11:30 a.m.–11 p.m. Casual attire. Not accessible for wheelchairs.*

Mother's

$–$$ Central Business District   SANDWICHES/CREOLE/SHORT ORDER/BREAKFAST

Mother's overstuffed, mountainous po' boys have tipped quite a few scales over the years. The long lines and lack of atmosphere are minor qualms in the face of the Ferdi special — a giant roll stuffed with baked ham, roast beef, gravy, and other bits of beef debris that's just as delightfully, mouth-wateringly sloppy as it sounds. Mother's also offers "the world's best baked ham" as well as seafood platters, serviceable fried chicken, Creole offerings (gumbo, jambalaya), and of course, po' boys. Chicken strips are available for the kids, and most of the sandwiches and breakfast dishes are kid-friendly as well.

See map p. 137. 401 Poydras St. (easy walk from anywhere in the Quarter or Central Business District). ☎ *504-523-9656.* www.mothersrestaurant.net. *Reservations not accepted. Menu selections: $1.75–$20. AE, DISC, MC, V. Open: Mon–Sat 5 a.m.–10 p.m. and Sun 7 a.m.–9 p.m. No dress code. Wheelchair accessible.*

Mr. B's Bistro

$$ French Quarter   CONTEMPORARY CREOLE

This bustling bistro boasts white-glove-level service in a casual atmosphere. Regulars convene here daily for modern, spicy interpretations of Creole classics. The crab cakes are as good as they get, the andouille sausage is superb (order anything it comes with), and the Gumbo Ya-Ya is a hearty, country-style blend of chicken and andouille sausage (my favorite kind; I recommend it gladly). The Cajun barbequed shrimp are large and plump, and served heads on in a rich, thick, buttery sauce. If you come on Sunday, show up early for the jazz brunch and bubbly.

See map p. 126. 201 Royal St. (1 block away from Bourbon or Canal street). ☎ *504-523-2078.* www.mrbsbistro.com. *Reservations recommended. Main courses: $17–$28. AE, DC, DISC, MC, V. Open: Mon–Sat 11:30 a.m.–3 p.m., Sun–Fri 5:30–10 p.m., and Sat 5–10 p.m.; brunch Sun 10:30 a.m.–3 p.m. Dress is business casual. Wheelchair accessible.*

Olivier's
$–$$ French Quarter   CREOLE

Chef Armand Olivier hails from a family famous for its Creole cooking, and the menu is filled with dishes originated by ancestors going back to his great-great-grandmother. The Creole Rabbit is a version of a popular 19th-century Creole staple, braised and simmered in gravy to keep it moist and served with a rich oyster dressing. The beef Bourguignon is also good, with tenderloin tips simmered in a thick roux and served with pasta. The bread pudding dessert is fabulous. The service is highly professional and classy, and the decor is the same without being too fancy.

See map p. 126 204 Decatur St. ☎ *504-525-7734.* www.olivierscreole.com. *Reservations are recommended. Main courses: $12.95–$18.95. Open: Daily 11 a.m.– 10 p.m. AE, DC, DISC, MC, V. Casual attire. Wheelchair accessible.*

Palace Café
$$ French Quarter   CONTEMPORARY CREOLE

Prepare to be pampered at Palace Cafe, another Brennan family creation whose motto seems to be service, service, and more service. At a recent visit, we had no fewer than four different waiters taking care of our every need, one of whom cracked us up with his witty one-liners. Their expertise was invaluable when trying to decide between the traditional dinner menu and seasonal specials, much less choose any one dish. I could eat the signature crabmeat cheesecake, with its crunchy pecan crust, as an appetizer, entree, and dessert — it is *that* good. If it's in season, you must succumb to the garlic-crusted softshell crab, which is flash fried and served on jalapeño corn pudding with fried plantains, green tomato crawfish relish, and avocado lime coulis. In perfect Brennan tradition, Palace Café offers a glorious dessert selection; the Ponchatoula strawberry shortcake topped with sweet double cream melts in your mouth. But if you've never had it, you absolutely must dip your spoon into their famous white-chocolate bread pudding — the best in town.

See map p. 126. 605 Canal St. (an easy walk from anywhere in the Quarter). ☎ *504-523-1661.* www.palacecafe.com. *Reservations recommended. Main courses: $18–$28. AE, DC, DISC, MC, V. Open: Mon–Fri 11:30 a.m.–2:30 p.m.; daily 5:30–11 p.m.; brunch Sat–Sun 10:30 a.m.–2:30 p.m. Dress is business casual. Wheelchair accessible. Complimentary validated parking at neighboring Marriott, Holiday Inn, and garage adjacent to Dickie Brennan's Steakhouse.*

Pascal's Manale
$–$$ Uptown ITALIAN/SEAFOOD/STEAKS

This Uptown favorite bills itself as an Italian–New Orleans steakhouse, but that doesn't quite do justice to the slightly eccentric selection. Pascal's most popular item is its barbecued shrimp (a local favorite that originated here), which is actually marinated in an irresistible, spicy butter sauce, not barbecued. (These plump crustaceans are served with their heads on, so be forewarned if you don't like them that way.) Among other dishes, the combination pan roast features chopped oysters and crabmeat in a blend of shallots, parsley, and seasonings. Even with reservations, you may find a bit of a wait.

See map p. 137. 1838 Napoleon Ave. (take the St. Charles Streetcar to Napoleon and walk 3 blocks away from the river; take a taxi at night). ☎ **504-895-4877.** *Reservations recommended. Main courses: $11–$24. AE, CB, DC, DISC, MC, V. Open: Mon–Fri 11:30 a.m.–10 p.m., Sat 4–10 p.m., and Sun 4–9 p.m. (closed Sun Memorial Day weekend through Labor Day). Dress is business casual. Wheelchair accessible.*

Peristyle
$$ French Quarter FRENCH/ITALIAN/NEW AMERICAN

At press time, the chef and owner of Peristyle, Anne Kearney-Sand, sold the restaurant to longtime friend Tom Wolf of Wolf's of New Orleans. Kearney-Sand had owned the restaurant since 1995, and due to her talent and determination Peristyle flourished despite a devastating fire in 1999 that gutted the place. She excelled at anything, from appetizers (love the caramelized onion tart) to enticing entrees (try the farm-raised quail with roasted shallot applewood–bacon pecan relish) to surprise salads. Although the new owner, Wolfe, will be making menu changes, the restaurant will most likely remain a fabulous dining choice.

See map p. 126. 1041 Dumaine St. (3 blocks from Bourbon Street; take a taxi for safety). ☎ **504-593-9535.** *Reservations recommended. Main courses: $22–$27. AE, DC, MC, V. Open: Tues–Thurs 6–10 p.m. and Fri–Sat 6–11 p.m.; lunch on Fri only 11:30 a.m.–2:30 p.m. Dress is business casual. The front step is a bit steep (about 6 inches), but once inside, navigating via wheelchair is easy.*

Port of Call
$–$$ French Quarter HAMBURGERS

This character-filled, nautical-themed restaurant and bar is famous for its burgers, which locals generally agree are the best in town. They certainly are huge, weighing in at a half-pound without condiments or the accompanying baked potato (sorry, no fries). Steaks are another specialty, though I've found thickness and juiciness levels vary. The place really gets jumping late at night when the restaurant is dark and crowded, and attentive service is at a premium, but it's busy most all the time. For extra atmosphere, sit and eat at the bar. Take-out service is available.

See map p. 126. 838 Esplanade Ave. (take a taxi for safety). ☎ *504-523-0120. Reservations are not accepted. Menu items: $6–$21. AE, MC, V. Open: Sun–Thurs 11 a.m.–1 a.m. and Fri–Sat 11 a.m.–2 a.m. No dress code. Not accessible for wheelchairs.*

Ralph & Kacoo's
$–$$$ French Quarter   CREOLE/SEAFOOD

The New Orleans branch of this restaurant chain is usually crowded at all hours, though you seldom have to wait longer than 15 to 20 minutes, which you can spend at the bar (a full-size replica of a fishing boat) downing drinks and raw oysters and people-watching. The onion rings alone are worth the wait, though the hush puppies and fried crawfish tails also prove popular. This restaurant is a solid, dependable (if not adventuresome) choice for seafood; the portions are large, the prices reasonable, and the fixings fresh. A kids' menu offers burgers and grilled cheese sandwiches and a shrimp boat.

See map p. 126. 519 Toulouse St. (2½ blocks from Bourbon Street and around the corner from Jackson Square). ☎ *504-522-5226.* www.ralphandkacoos.com. *Reservations recommended. Main courses: $14–$40. AE, DC, DISC, MC, V. Open: Mon–Thurs 11:30 a.m.–9 p.m.; Fri–Sat 11:30 a.m.–11 p.m.; Sun 11 a.m.–10 p.m. Casual dress. Wheelchair accessible.*

Restaurant August
$$–$$$ Central Business District   CONTEMPORARY FRENCH

Born on the bayou, executive chef John Besh incorporates his southern Louisiana influences with those found in the South of France, culminating in exciting, experimental cuisine. His risk-taking has gotten August noticed; in 2002, *Condé Nast Traveler* named the restaurant to its "Hot Tables" list, one of the top 50 new establishments worldwide. The playful "BLT" is no diner staple but rather buster crabs, lettuce, and tomatoes on *pain perdu* (French toast). Other inspired entrees include Moroccan spice duck with sweet corn polenta, duck foie gras and dried fruit compote, and pan roast day boat grouper with lobster whipped potatoes and bouillabaisse jus. Executive pastry chef Kelly Fields's dessert list is most intriguing; decide between the goat's milk cheesecake with bee pollen, honey ice cream, and Balsamic sauternes syrup, and the chocolate hazelnut torte with dark chocolate, milk chocolate, and blackpepper raspberry compote.

See map p. 137. 301 Tchoupitoulas St. (4 blocks from the Quarter; take a taxi at night). ☎ *504-299-9777.* www.rest-august.com. *Reservations recommended. Main courses: $17–$37. AE, DC, MC, V. Open: Mon–Fri 11 a.m.–2 p.m.; Mon–Sat 5:30–10 p.m. Dress is smart casual. Steps and closely packed tables make it problematic for people with wheelchairs.*

Rib Room
$$$–$$$$ French Quarter STEAKS/SEAFOOD

The arched windows, high ceilings, and exposed brick remind me of a conservative British men's club, though acting genteel when tackling one of its filets, sirloins, or other meats isn't easy. The chef slow roasts the restaurant's specialty, prime rib, on a rotisserie over an open flame. Spit-roasted lamb, spit-roasted jumbo shrimp, and other satisfying dishes round out the menu. The Rib Room is a good alternative for those individuals tired of seafood or sauce-heavy Creole (though trading those rich creamy sauces for juicy, artery-hardening steak isn't much of a trade-off).

See map p. 126. 621 St. Louis St. (1 block from Bourbon Street in the Omni Royal Orleans Hotel). ☎ *504-529-7045. Reservations recommended. Main courses: $32–$68. AE, DC, DISC, MC, V. Open: Daily 6:30–10:30 a.m., 11:30 a.m.–2:30 p.m., and 6–10 p.m. Dress is business casual. Wheelchair accessible.*

Ruth's Chris Steak House
$$–$$$$ Mid-City STEAKS

This is the original, legendary location of the national upscale steakhouse chain since 1965. The late founder, Ruth Fertel, was a single mother looking for a way to care for her kids when she took over what was then known as Chris Steak House. Local politicians and businessmen and women come here to seal deals over delicious, sizzling platters of prime beef, and reporters come to watch them, conveniently taking the opportunity to partake of the same. Corn-fed, custom-aged beef is prepared a number of ways here, cut into filets, strips, rib-eyes, and porterhouses — none too tough and all beautifully prepared. The restaurant does offer other selections such as lobster, veal, chicken, or fish, but steak is your best bet.

See map p. 132. 711 N. Broad St. (take a taxi). ☎ *504-486-0810.* www.ruthschris. com. *Reservations recommended. Main courses: $18–$65. AE, DC, MC, V. Open: Sun–Fri 11 a.m.–11 p.m. and Sat 4–11 p.m. Dress is business casual. Wheelchair accessible.*

Tujague's
$$$ French Quarter CREOLE

Opened in 1856, Tujague's (pronounced two-*jacks*) is one of the oldest restaurants in New Orleans. It's a favorite institution among New Orleanians, but its simple, traditional charms aren't for everyone. The restaurant features no printed menu; instead, the waiters recite the limited but changing daily selections. Options frequently include the tender beef brisket with horseradish sauce (*very* spicy), shrimp remoulade (with a spicy mustard sauce), and a daily fish special. Ask for the Bonne Femme chicken, a baked garlic number from the original owner's recipe (the restaurant has it every night, but you have to request it). Finish with the classic bread pudding.

See map p. 126. 823 Decatur St. (1 short block from Jackson Square). ☎ *504-525-8676.* www.tujaguesrestaurant.com. *Reservations recommended. Main courses: 6-course meal with choice of 4 entrees (no choice for the other courses) $30–$36 (4-course lunch $6.50–$13.95). AE, DC, DISC, MC, V. Open: Daily 11 a.m.–3 p.m. and 5–11 p.m. Casual attire. Wheelchair accessible.*

Upperline
$$ Uptown ECLECTIC/CREOLE

Nestled in a largely residential section of Uptown, JoAnn Clevenger's fabulous Upperline in a circa 1877 townhouse is every bit as inventive as bigger names such as Commander's Palace or Emeril's with far grander character. What other proprietor compiles lists of her favorite local music clubs, bookstores, artists, and (gasp!) favorite dishes at other restaurants, and shares them (by request) with patrons? No less extraordinary is how she and her head chef, Kenneth Smith, met; they're both vintage menu and out-of-print cookbook buffs and Smith asked a dealer in Michigan where he should find work. She suggested contacting Upperline, Clevenger hired him as an apprentice, and thus, culinary history was made. Speaking of which, Clevenger invented what is now a local staple, fried green tomatoes with shrimp remoulade — pay due homage and order it. I highly recommend the "Taste of New Orleans," a sampler of seven favorites served in three courses. *Note:* Don't come to Upperline if you're in a rush — you absolutely must make a night out of it. Savor the food and atmosphere, ask Clevenger questions (start with an inquiry about her enormous art collection displayed throughout the restaurant), and enjoy her only-in-New Orleans stories.

See map p. 137. 1413 Upperline St. (take the St. Charles Streetcar to the Upperline stop). ☎ *504-891-9822.* www.upperline.com. *Reservations required. Main courses: $18.50–$26.50; sampler $38. AE, CB, DC, MC, V. Open: Sun, Wed–Thurs 5:30–9:30 p.m.; Fri–Sat 5:30–10 p.m. Casual attire. Not accessible for wheelchairs.*

Dining and Snacking on the Go

Snacking is a great American pastime, and New Orleans is nothing if not a city of traditions. So the fact that New Orleans is stuffed to the gills with snack food should come as no surprise — from Lucky Dogs (hot dogs and sausage sold by street vendors in giant hot dog-shaped carts) to the city's twin sandwich staples, the po' boy and the muffuletta. This section suggests the best places to go for these delights as well as bar food, late-night munchies, beignets, and other sugary confections. It also cracks open the subject of oysters and gives you my two cents on the longstanding debate as to the best burger in town.

Savoring the muffuletta experience

What is a muffuletta, you ask? See Chapter 2 to find out more about this savory sandwich. Here are a couple of places to try one:

✔ **Central Grocery** (923 Decatur St., French Quarter, ☎ **504-523-1620**) makes the most likely winner in the great muffuletta debate. The place probably invented the muffuletta, so if you have just one, have it here. You can also buy many New Orleans spices and other deli items here as well.

✔ **Napoleon House** (500 Chartres St., French Quarter, ☎ **504-524-9752**) is the sole seller of *hot* muffulettas. Some locals find the very idea blasphemous, but others swear by it. This European-style cafe also serves other sandwiches, soups, jambalaya, and similar, moderately priced fare. The bar is a popular late-night hangout. Try the Pimm's Cup, a sweet-and-sour mix of lemonade, 7-Up, and Pimm's No. 1 — it's the bar's signature drink. Classical music lends some romantic ambience.

Feasting on po' boys

You can put just about anything — ham, shrimp, oysters, roast beef — between two slices of French bread and you've made yourself a po' boy. See Chapter 2 to find out why these famously simple sandwiches are so important to the local culture. Better yet, taste one by going to one (or more!) of the following establishments:

✔ For the most popular po' boy spot in the Quarter, head to **Johnny's Po-boys** (511 St. Louis St., ☎ **504-524-8129**).

✔ **Mother's** (401 Poydras St., ☎ **504-523-9656**) serves a fine po' boy as does the **Napoleon House** (see the preceding section).

✔ In the Uptown area, **Domilise's** (5240 Annunciation St., ☎ **504-899-9126**) has been serving po' boys, as well as other hot dishes, for more than 75 years. Try the "Peacemaker," a half-shrimp, half-oyster combination.

✔ If you're tired of fried food, go for **Guy's** (5259 Magazine St., ☎ **504-891-5025**) grilled shrimp po' boy (which requires an ice-cold root beer from the self-serve fridge).

When you order a po' boy, you'll be asked if you want it "dressed." Only say yes if you want lettuce, tomato, and mayonnaise on your sandwich.

Hankering for a hamburger

In New Orleans, sports, politics, and current events are popular topics. But those discussions are nothing compared to the amount of discourse spent on who makes the best burger in town. Many places make excellent burgers, but when you get right down it, this is a two-burger race between the **Port of Call** (838 Esplanade Ave., ☎ **504-523-0120**) and the **Clover Grill** (900 Bourbon St., ☎ **504-598-1010**). Both places make big burgers; the Port of Call's is a half-pound, while the Clover Grill's weighs in at a trim third of a pound. Both places keep their burgers juicy (the Clover cooks its burgers under a hubcap, believe it or not, to seal in the juices).

New Orleans Snacks

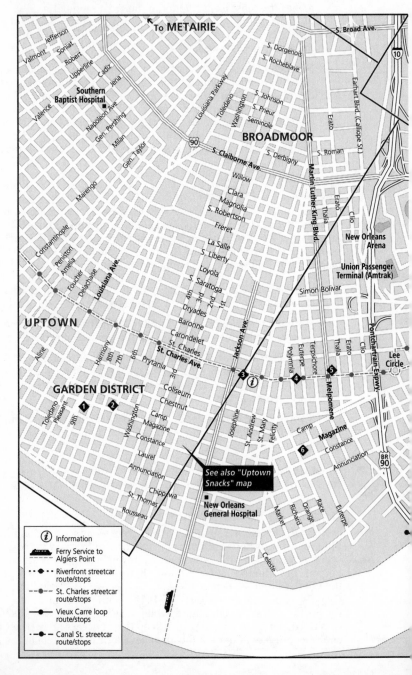

Avenue Pub **4**
Betsy's Pancake House **10**
Bywater Bar-B-Que **11**
CC's Gourmet Coffee House
  (2917 Magazine) **2**
Elizabeth's **12**
Igor's Bar and Grill **3**
Mother's **7**

New Orleans Centre (Café du Monde) **9**
PJ's (644 Camp) **8**
Riverwalk Shopping Center **6**
  Café du Monde
  Häagen-Dazs
Rue de la Course (1500 Magazine) **6**
Rue de la Course (3128 Magazine) **1**
St. Charles Tavern **5**

French Quarter Snacks

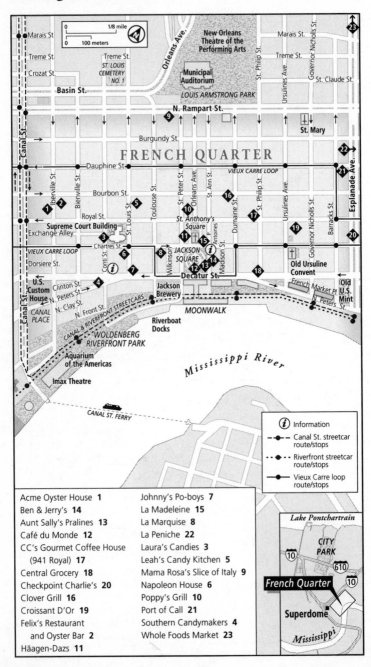

Acme Oyster House **1**
Ben & Jerry's **14**
Aunt Sally's Pralines **13**
Café du Monde **12**
CC's Gourmet Coffee House
   (941 Royal) **17**
Central Grocery **18**
Checkpoint Charlie's **20**
Clover Grill **16**
Croissant D'Or **19**
Felix's Restaurant
   and Oyster Bar **2**
Häagen-Dazs **11**

Johnny's Po-boys **7**
La Madeleine **15**
La Marquise **8**
La Peniche **22**
Laura's Candies **3**
Leah's Candy Kitchen **5**
Mama Rosa's Slice of Italy **9**
Napoleon House **6**
Poppy's Grill **10**
Port of Call **21**
Southern Candymakers **4**
Whole Foods Market **23**

If you have something special to celebrate, **Michael's Mid-City Grill** (4139 Canal St., ☎ 504-486-8200) has the burger for you. For a mere $150, you get a burger topped with mushrooms, sour cream, and caviar — and a free bottle of Dom Perignon. The staff also takes your photo to document the occasion, which is tacked to the collage on the walls (you're not the only one who bought the $150 burger!).

The world is your oyster

In my experience, people new to the art of *oyster shooting* — slurping a raw oyster, often dressed with ketchup and horseradish, right out of its shell and letting it slide, virtually unchewed, right down the gullet — soon curse themselves for not trying the activity sooner. Oyster shooting may *sound* unappetizing, but try it once; it can sometimes be the right alternative to a heavy, sauce-laden meal. The following oyster bars also offer fried oysters, shrimp for peeling and dipping, and, when they're in season, plenty of boiled crawfish:

- ✔ **Acme Oyster House** (724 Iberville St., ☎ 504-522-5973; 7306 Lakeshore Drive, ☎ 504-282-9200) offers some *serious* oysters. Get 'em raw, fried, or in overstuffed po' boys. The Lakeshore location is out of the way, but it's a much shorter wait.

- ✔ **Casamento's** (4330 Magazine St., ☎ 504-895-9761) is so incredibly good it can afford to close for the summer (when oysters aren't at their peak), and locals are back in full force come fall. The home-made gumbo and oyster loaf are always worth the wait.

- ✔ **Felix's Restaurant and Oyster Bar** (739 Iberville St., ☎ 504-522-4440) offers Creole dishes, but specializes in oysters and fried seafood.

Restaurant rescue for vegetarians

If you're a vegetarian traveler, your options in New Orleans are limited. If you can cook a food in animal fat, New Orleanians do. Ham and sausage even lurk in the red beans and rice. Nevertheless, a few places in town cater to the vegetarian market (though none of them are *exclusively* vegetarian, and do a decent job of it, too).

- ✔ **Lebanon's Cafe** (1500 S. Carrollton Ave., Carrollton, ☎ 504-862-6200) is extremely popular with the health- and money-conscious crowd, especially students and parents with little ones. When I need a veggie infusion, I order the sautéed vegetables topped with lightly browned goat cheese over basmati rice.

- ✔ **Mona's** (3901 Banks St., Mid-City, ☎ 504-482-7743; 4126 Magazine St., Uptown, ☎ 504-894-9800; 3149 Calhoun St., Uptown, ☎ 504-861-2124) is an unpretentious spot where people from all walks of life converge for Middle Eastern fare such as gyros, falafel, and the baba ganuj eggplant dip, with much to satisfy vegetarians with international palates.

> ✔ **Slim Goodie's Diner** (3322 Magazine St., Uptown, ☎ 504-891-3447) is a classic diner (check out the red booths) that also happens to serve vegetarian fare. The menu, funky decor, and music ('70s Springsteen when I last went) make it a fun place to eat.
>
> ✔ **Whole Foods Market** (3135 Esplanade Ave., Mid-City, ☎ 504-943-1626; 5600 Magazine St., Uptown, ☎ 504-899-9119), a local favorite for organic produce and vegetarian specialties, offers all items to go.

Aside from these places, call ahead and ask if a particular restaurant that interests you features vegetarian entrees; a good number of them do. (Central Grocery, for example, offers a mean vegetable muffuletta.)

Lucky dogs: Street fare

A tradition in New Orleans since 1948, **Lucky Dog** carts became famous when spoofed in the Pulitzer Prize–winning book *A Confederacy of Dunces.* You can find the carts that sell Lucky Dogs on street corners throughout the French Quarter and Central Business District. (The carts spread out to other locations throughout the city during special events.) Spotting the carts is easy because they look like giant hot dogs.

Lucky Dogs are the perfect food for late-night revelers with a blood-alcohol volume of .05 percent or higher, and the carts are conveniently located throughout the Quarter to accommodate those who stumble out of nearby bars. A regular or foot-long hot dog or sausage dressed with the works (including chili) goes for less than $5.

A slice of pie

If you're in the mood for a familiar pepperoni pizza, or perhaps something a bit more gourmet, stop by one of these places:

> ✔ **Café Roma** (1119 Decatur St., French Quarter, ☎ 504-566-1800; 1901 Sophie Wright Place, Lower Garden District, ☎ 504-524-2419; 3340 Bienville St., Mid-City, ☎ 504-827-2300)
>
> ✔ **Ciro's Coté Sud** (7918 Maple St., Uptown, ☎ 504-866-9551)
>
> ✔ **Mama Rosa's Slice of Italy** (616 N. Rampart St., French Quarter, ☎ 504-523-5546)
>
> ✔ **Reginelli's** (741 State St., Uptown, ☎ 504-899-1414)

Neighborhood watch

For me, nothing quite tops people-watching at a diner or neighborhood joint, observing the ebb and flow of regular Janes and Joes in the tidal pool of the working world. The everyday give-and-take of greasy-spoon waitresses interacting with accountants, mechanics, and eccentrics is as

Uptown Snacks

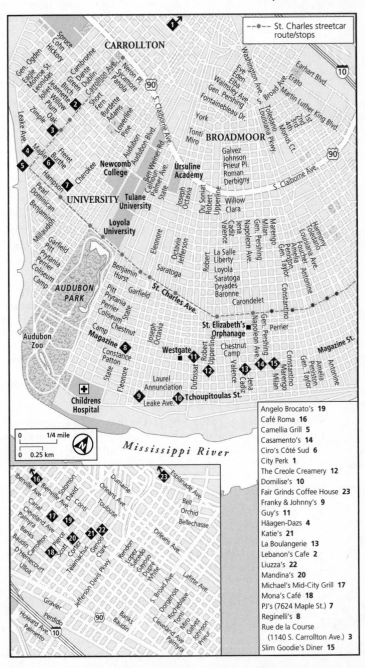

--•-- St. Charles streetcar route/stops

CARROLLTON

BROADMOOR

Newcomb College

Ursuline Academy

UNIVERSITY   Tulane University

Loyola University

AUDUBON PARK

Audubon Zoo

St. Charles Ave.

St. Elizabeth's Orphanage

Westgate

Magazine St.

Childrens Hospital

Tchoupitoulas St.

Mississippi River

0   1/4 mile
0   0.25 km

Angelo Brocato's **19**
Café Roma **16**
Camellia Grill **5**
Casamento's **14**
Ciro's Côté Sud **6**
City Perk **1**
The Creole Creamery **12**
Domilise's **10**
Fair Grinds Coffee House **23**
Franky & Johnny's **9**
Guy's **11**
Häagen-Dazs **4**
Katie's **21**
La Boulangerie **13**
Lebanon's Cafe **2**
Liuzza's **22**
Mandina's **20**
Michael's Mid-City Grill **17**
Mona's Café **18**
PJ's (7624 Maple St.) **7**
Reginelli's **8**
Rue de la Course
   (1140 S. Carrollton Ave.) **3**
Slim Goodie's Diner **15**

fascinating to me as watching native tribal rituals is to an anthropologist. What follows, then, is a short and highly subjective list of neighborhood spots with just as much emphasis on character and atmosphere as on good food:

- ✔ **Betsy's Pancake House** (2542 Canal St., Mid-City, ☎ 504-822-0213) serves breakfast and a filling variety of lunch specials. The waitresses will either annoy or amuse you; I find them to be fun.

- ✔ **Bywater Bar-B-Que** (3162 Dauphine St., Bywater, ☎ 504-944-4445) is the perfect place to harden your arteries with some prime barbecue. It also serves a decent burger and great pizza.

- ✔ **Franky and Johnny's** (321 Arabella St., Uptown, ☎ 504-899-9146) specializes in boiled seafood, but just about any of the sandwiches are rewarding. I love to play Ms Pac Man while waiting for my meal.

- ✔ **Katie's** (3701 Iberville St., Mid-City, ☎ 504-488-6582) is notable both for its purple exterior and for the fine, family-friendly fare served.

- ✔ **Liuzza's** (3636 Bienville St., Mid-City, ☎ 504-482-9120) may be the mother of all neighborhood restaurants. Cool off with a giant frozen mug of beer and indulge in the popular "Frenchuletta," a muffuletta on French bread.

- ✔ **Mandina's** (3800 Canal St., Mid-City, ☎ 504-482-9179) aspires to some odd cross between stuffy upper-crust establishment and regular-Joe hangout. The sandwiches are good, but the real draws are daily specials such as red beans and rice or beef stew, as well as Italian and seafood dishes. Prepare for snobby waiters who can sniff out native New Orleanians from people who moved here from somewhere else; tourists don't stand a chance.

After-hours appetite

Clover Grill is one of the best places in town at which to eat in the predawn hours. Also in the French Quarter, **Poppy's Grill** and **Café du Monde** (800 Decatur St. at Jackson Square, ☎ 504-525-4544) are a couple of other reliable 24-hour snacking destinations. But don't limit your options to them, nor to the French Quarter. You can find some late-night nourishment wherever you happen to be in New Orleans.

- ✔ In the Riverbend, **Camellia Grill** (626 S. Carrollton Ave., Carrollton, ☎ 504-866-9573) is a throwback to the kind of old-style neighborhood diners you occasionally see on television. It's not open around the clock, but it does stay open until the wee hours most nights. On weekend mornings, people line up outside the door for the famous pecan waffles.

- ✔ **Clover Grill** (900 Bourbon St., French Quarter, ☎ 504-598-1010) is a fun 24-hour diner known for its juicy burgers (cooked under a hubcap to seal in the flavors). Breakfast is served around the clock in a cheeky, whimsical atmosphere. This gay-friendly hangout also offers good shakes, malts, a painfully sweet icebox pie, and lots of coffee.

✔ **Igor's Bar and Grill** (2133 St. Charles Ave., Lower Garden District, ☎ 504-522-2145) offers 24-hour food, including the "world-famous" Igor burger, a good jukebox, and plenty of local atmosphere (and, again, self-serve laundry). It's also a good place to shoot pool.

✔ The down-home snacks and meals at **La Peniche** (1940 Dauphine St., Faubourg Marigny, ☎ 504-943-1460) can really hit the spot. This gay-friendly spot has great half-pound hamburgers and homemade desserts; if the Oreo pie doesn't cause you to moan in ecstasy, call a mortician, because you must be dead.

✔ **Poppy's Grill** (717 St. Peter St., French Quarter, ☎ 504-524-3287) is owned by the same folks who run Clover Grill, so the same light-hearted attitude prevails ("dancing in the aisles only"). It serves the same fabulous shakes, burgers, and other diner fare. That's not to say that Poppy's doesn't have its own unique qualities. Check out the scratch 'n' sniff menu or go for the blue plate special — only $5.49 from 11 a.m.– 11 p.m.

✔ **St. Charles Tavern** (1433 St. Charles Ave., Lower Garden District, ☎ 504-523-9823) is also open 24 hours. The fare ranges from burgers to red beans and rice to Creole omelettes (stuffed with shrimp Creole). Don't be surprised if you find a short wait for a table even after 2 a.m.

Sipping a cup of joe

Since the 18th century, when European traders realized New Orleans was the logical importer of coffee from the Caribbean and South America, the Crescent City and coffee have remained inseparable. These are my favorite places to wake up in the morning:

✔ Open 24 hours, the original **Café du Monde** (800 Decatur St., French Quarter, ☎ 504-528-9933) makes a legendary café au lait — strong New Orleans coffee flavored with chicory to make it less bitter and mixed with an equal portion of scalded milk. This prime place for people-watching has been around since 1862. (A handful of Café du Monde satellites are scattered around the city and suburbs.)

✔ **City Perk** (637 N. Carrollton Ave., Mid-City, ☎ 504-482-4847) is now an easy streetcar ride away thanks to the new Canal line. This independent coffeehouse features friendly staff, consistently great drinks, vegan pastries, and yummy panini sandwiches. Grab a seat on the front patio or walk to nearby City Park (about six blocks) for an impromptu picnic. Dogs are welcome on the patio.

✔ **Fair Grinds Coffee House** (333 Ponce de Leon St., Mid-City, ☎ 504-948-3222) boasts rich coffee, homemade gourmet biscotti, an eclectic collection of hand-painted chairs, and for the canine crowd, their own jar of biscuits. Dogs get a lot of attention here, especially if they join their owner on the bench by the front door. You can't beat the people-watching here.

✔ **Rue de la Course** (1500 Magazine St., Lower Garden District, ☎ 504-529-1455; 3128 Magazine St., Uptown, ☎ 504-899-0242; 1140 S. Carrollton Ave., Carrollton, ☎ 504-861-4343) is modeled after 17th-century European coffeehouses, with cool, friendly college kids and locals hanging out and lingering over the morning paper. Chocolate lovers, order the iced cioccolato, which is an improvement on the standard iced mocha. A handful of these exist in the metropolitan area; with its pressed-tin ceiling and odd mix of folks, the original location at 1500 Magazine is best.

Beignets: Sweet treats

Beignets (pronounced ben-*yays*) are basically fried doughnuts generously covered with lots of powdered sugar. Novices may be tempted to shake off some of the sugar. Don't mess with it; the sugar tastes great, especially after the heat of the freshly baked beignet melts it. If anything, you end up adding *more* powdered sugar, courtesy of sugar shakers on the table. **Café du Monde** (800 Decatur St., ☎ 504-528-9933) is Beignet Central. They're a steal at three for about $1, and because the place is open 24 hours (every day but Christmas), you can satisfy your craving at any time. Other non-24-hour Café du Mondes are at the Riverwalk Shopping Center (1 Poydras St., ☎ 504-587-0841) and the New Orleans Centre Shopping Center (1400 Poydras St., ☎ 504-587-0842).

Quick-stop java shops

The presence of two ubiquitous local coffee institutions in New Orleans is akin to that of Starbucks in the rest of the country (New Orleans has those too, by the way). **CC's Gourmet Coffee House** and **PJ's Coffee & Tea Co.** both have multiple locations throughout the metropolitan area. Of the two, I'm partial to homegrown PJ's with its funkier atmosphere.

Some of the more centrally located CC's locations include the following:

✔ 2917 Magazine St., Garden District (☎ 504-891-2115)

✔ 941 Royal St., French Quarter(☎ 504-581-6996)

✔ 2800 Esplanade Ave., Mid-City (☎ 504-482-9865)

Some of the more popular PJ's locations are the following:

✔ 7624 Maple St., Uptown (☎ 504-866-7031)

✔ 644 Camp St., Warehouse District (☎ 504-529-3658)

La patisserie

If you want to pretend that you're grabbing a snack back in French Colonial days, drop by one of these patisseries. Although they all offer seating, you may want to take your pastry to nearby Jackson Square to people-watch.

- ✔ **Croissant D'Or** (617 Ursulines St., ☎ 504-524-4663) provides daily fresh-baked pastries for its sister location, La Marquise, as well, though this location has cheaper prices for the same delectable items. Ask the staff for the history behind the old "Ladies' Entrance" sign on the sidewalk. Opt for a seat beside the decrepit fountain in the courtyard.

- ✔ **La Boulangerie** (625 St. Charles Ave., ☎ 504-569-1925; 3143 Ponce de Leon St., ☎ 504-940-0577; 4526 Magazine St., ☎ 504-269-3777) offerings vary by location. The original spot on Magazine is a full bakery that is worth walking into for the smell alone. The Mid-City location bakes select pastries and breads, and the downtown location on St. Charles serves coffee, breakfast, and lunch.

- ✔ **La Madeleine** (547 St. Ann St. ☎ 504-568-0073) serves delectable French pastries and other light menu items. It also maintains locations in the Garden District and in the Riverbend.

- ✔ The lush courtyard at **La Marquise** (625 Chartres St., ☎ 504-524-0420) makes a great place to take a leisurely breakfast or an afternoon break. Croissant D'Or's sister shop offers all sorts of delicious pastries, soups, salads, and sandwiches.

For your sweet tooth

The one word you need to know when discussing homegrown New Orleans–style sugary snacks is *pralines* (pronounced *praw*-leens, not *pray*-leens). Give these tasty confections (made with brown sugar and pecans) a try and you may become addicted. At **Aunt Sally's Pralines** (810 Decatur St., ☎ 800-642-7257 or 504-944-6090) or **Southern Candymakers** (334 Decatur St., ☎ 800-344-9773 or 504-523-5544) you can watch the staff making the famous local candy. **Laura's Candies** (331 Chartres St., ☎ 800-992-9699 or 504-525-3880) offers pralines, fudge, and golf-ball-size truffles. Some people cast their vote for best praline to **Leah's Candy Kitchen** (714 St. Louis St., ☎ 504-523-5662), and because it stays open until 10 p.m., it wins the late-night candy-craving vote by default.

Screaming for ice cream

You can find ice-cream carts throughout the French Quarter, especially around Jackson Square. **Häagen-Dazs Ice Cream Parlors** are located at 621 St. Peter St. (☎ 504-523-4001), the Riverwalk Shopping Center (1 Poydras St., ☎ 504-523-3566), and the Riverbend (8108 Hampson St.,

☎ 504-861-2500). Outposts of **Ben & Jerry's** are located on Jackson Square (537 St. Ann St., ☎ **504-525-5950**) and in City Park (☎ **504-486-7113**).

For a really special treat, head to **The Creole Creamery** (4924 Prytania St., ☎ **504-894-8680**) for unusual gourmet flavors like bananas Foster and lemon garlic. Or take the Canal Streetcar to an old favorite, **Angelo Brocato's** (214 N. Carrollton Ave., ☎ **504-486-0078**). Its creamy and rich gelato will make you an instant fan of Italian ice cream.

Technically, it's not ice cream, but if you're here during the summer, cool off with a New Orleans tradition: the sno ball. It's basically shaved ice dowsed in one or more flavored syrups. Locals also like to top their sno ball with condensed cream or whipped cream. You'll find sno ball stands throughout the city, but **Hansen's Sno Blitz** (4801 Tchoupitoulas St.; ☎ **504-891-9788**) and **Plum Street Sno Balls** (1300 Plum St., ☎ **504-866-7996**) are my favorites. (*Note:* Sno balls are seasonal, so only look for them April through September.)

Index of Establishments by Neighborhood

Clover Grill (Breakfast/Sandwiches/Hamburgers/Short Order, $)

Court of Two Sisters (Creole, $$–$$$)

Croissant D'Or (French/Sweets, $)

Felix's Restaurant and Oyster Bar (Sandwiches/Seafood, $–$$)

Galatoire's (French, $–$$)

Häagen-Dazs Ice Cream Parlor (Ice Cream, $)

Irene's Cuisine (Italian/French Provençal, $–$$)

Johnny's Po-boys (Sandwiches/Seafood, $–$$)

K-Paul's Louisiana Kitchen (Cajun, $$–$$$)

La Madeleine (French/Sandwiches/Sweets, $)

La Marquise (Coffee/Sandwiches/Sweets, $)

Laura's Candies (Sweets, $)

Leah's Candy Kitchen (Sweets, $)

Mama Rosa's Slice of Italy (Sandwiches/Pizza, $)

Maximo's (Italian, $–$$)

Mike Anderson's Seafood (Seafood, $–$$)

Mr. B's Bistro (Creole, $$)

Olivier's (Creole, $–$$)

Palace Café (Creole, $$)

Peristyle (French/Italian/New American, $$)

Poppy's Grill (Breakfast/Sandwiches/Hamburgers/Short Order, $)

Port of Call (Hamburgers, $–$$)

Ralph & Kacoo's (Creole/Seafood, $–$$$)

Rib Room (Steaks/Seafood, $$$–$$$$)

Samurai Sushi (Japanese/Seafood, $–$$)

Southern Candymakers (Sweets/Ice Cream, $)

Tujaque's (Creole, $$–$$$)

Garden District/Uptown

Basil Leaf (Thai, $–$$)

Brigtsen's (Cajun/Creole, $$)

Café Roma (Pizza/Sandwiches, $)

Camellia Grill (Breakfast/Sandwiches/Short Order, $)

Casamento's (Sandwiches/Seafood, $–$$)

CC's Gourmet Coffee House (Coffee/Sweets, $)

Ciro's Coté Sud (French/Italian/Pizza, $)

Commander's Palace (Creole, $$–$$$)

The Creole Creamery (Ice Cream, $)

Dick & Jenny's (Creole/Eclectic, $–$$)

Domilise's (Sandwiches/Seafood, $)

Dunbar's Creole Cooking (Creole/Soul, $)

Five Happiness (Chinese, $–$$)

Franky & Johnny's (Sandwiches/Seafood, $)

Gautreau's (Contemporary Louisiana, $$–$$$)

Guy's (Sandwiches/Seafood, $)

Häagen-Dazs Ice Cream Parlor (Ice Cream, $)

Hansen's Sno Blitz (Sno Balls, $)

Igor's Bar & Grill (Sandwiches/Seafood/Short Order, $)

Jacques-Imo's (Creole/Soul Food, $–$$)

Juan's Flying Burrito (Mexican, $)

La Boulangerie (French/Sweets, $)

La Madeleine (French/Sandwiches/Sweets, $)

Lebanon's Café (Middle Eastern, Sandwiches, $)

Liborio's Cuban Restaurant (Cuban, $)

Lilette (Creole/French, $$)

Mango House (Caribbean/Seafood, $–$$)

Mona's (Middle Eastern/Sandwiches, $)

Moonlight Café (Mediterranean/Sandwiches, $)

Pascal's Manale (Italian/Seafood/Steaks, $–$$)

PJ's Coffee & Tea Co. (Coffee/Sandwiches/Sweets, $)

Plum Street Sno Balls (Sno Balls, $)

Reginelli's (Pizza, Sandwiches, $)

Rue de la Course (Coffee/Sweets, $)

St. Charles Tavern (Sandwiches/
Seafood/Short Order, $)
Slim Goodie's Diner
(Breakfast/Sandwiches/Short Order/
Vegetarian, $)
Taqueria Corona (Mexican, $)
Upperline (Eclectic/Creole, $$)
Whole Foods
(International/Sandwiches/
Vegetarian, $)

Mid-City

Angelo Brocato's (Sweets/
Ice Cream, $)
Ben & Jerry's (Ice Cream, $)
Betsy's Pancake House
(American/Breakfast/Sandwiches/
Short Order, $)
Café Roma (Pizza/Sandwiches, $)
CC's Gourmet Coffee House (Coffee/
Sweets, $)
Chateaubriand (French/Steakhouse,
$$–$$$)

Christian's (French/Creole, $$–$$$)
City Perk (Coffee/Sandwiches/
Sweets, $)
Dooky Chase (Creole/Soul Food,
$–$$$)
Fair Grinds Coffee House (Coffee/
Sweets, $)
Gabrielle (French/Creole/Cajun,
$$–$$$)
Henry's Soul Food (Soul, $)
Juan's Flying Burrito (Mexican, $)
Katie's (Sandwiches/Seafood, $)
La Boulangerie (French/Sweets, $)
Liuzza's (Sandwiches/Seafood, $)
Mandina's (Sandwiches/Seafood,
$–$$)
Mona's (Middle Eastern/
Sandwiches, $)
Pho Tau Bay (Vietnamese, $)
Ruth's Chris Steak House (Steaks,
$$–$$$$)
Whole Foods
(International/Sandwiches/
Vegetarian, $)

Index of Establishments by Cuisine

American/New American

Betsy's Pancake House (Mid-City, $)
Cobalt (Central Business District, $$)
Cuvée (Central Business District, $$)
Emeril's (Warehouse District,
$$–$$$$)
Herbsaint (Central Business District,
$–$$)
Peristyle (French Quarter, $$)

Breakfast

Bacco (French Quarter, $–$$)
Betsy's Pancake House (Mid-City, $)
Brennan's (French Quarter, $$–$$$)
Camellia Grill (Uptown, $)
Clover Grill (French Quarter, $)
Court of Two Sisters (French Quarter,
$$–$$$)
Elizabeth's (Bywater, $)

The New Orleans Grill (Central
Business District, $$–$$$)
Mother's (Central Business District,
$–$$)
Poppy's Grill (French Quarter, $)
Rib Room (French Quarter, $$$–$$$$)
Slim Goodie's Diner (Uptown, $)

Cajun

Brigtsen's (Uptown, $$)
Gabrielle (Mid-City, $$–$$$)
K-Paul's Louisiana Kitchen (French
Quarter, $$–$$$)

Caribbean

Mango House (Uptown, $–$$)

Chinese

Five Happiness (Uptown, $–$$)

Coffee

CC's Gourmet Coffee House (French Quarter/Garden District/Mid-City, $)
City Perk (Mid-City, $)
Fair Grinds Coffee House (Mid-City, $)
La Marquise (French Quarter, $)
PJ's Coffee & Tea Co.
(Uptown/Warehouse District, $)
Rue de la Course (Uptown, $)

Contemporary Louisiana/French Provençal

Cobalt (Central Business District, $$)
Gautreau's (Uptown, $$–$$$)
Herbsaint (Central Business District, $–$$)
Irene's Cuisine (French Quarter, $–$$)
Restaurant August (Central Business District, $$–$$$)

Creole

Antoine's (French Quarter, $$–$$$$)
Arnaud's (French Quarter, $$–$$$)
Bacco (French Quarter, $–$$)
Brennan's (French Quarter, $$–$$$)
Brigtsen's (Uptown, $$)
Christian's (Mid-City, $$–$$$)
Commander's Palace (Garden District, $$–$$$)
Court of Two Sisters (French Quarter, $$–$$$)
Cuvée (Central Business District, $$)
Dick & Jenny's (Uptown, $–$$)
Dooky Chase (Mid-City, $–$$$)
Dunbar's Creole Cooking (Uptown, $)
Elizabeth's (Bywater, $)
Emeril's (Warehouse District, $$–$$$$)
Felix's Restaurant and Oyster Bar (French Quarter, $–$$)
Gabrielle (Mid-City, $$–$$$)
Jacques-Imo's (Uptown, $–$$)
Lilette (Uptown, $$)
Mother's (Central Business District, $–$$)
Mr. B's Bistro (French Quarter, $$)
Olivier's (French Quarter, $–$$)
Palace Café (French Quarter, $$)

Ralph & Kacoo's (French Quarter, $–$$$)
St. Charles Tavern (Garden District, $)
Tujague's (French Quarter, $$–$$$)
Upperline (Uptown, $$)

Cuban

Liborio's Cuban Restaurant (Garden District, $)

French

Antoine's (French Quarter, $$–$$$$)
Brennan's (French Quarter, $$–$$$)
Chateaubriand (Central Business District, $$–$$$)
Christian's (Mid-City, $$–$$$)
Ciro's Coté Sud (Uptown, $)
Croissant D'Or (French Quarter, $)
Gabrielle (Mid-City, $$–$$$)
Galatoire's (French Quarter, $–$$)
Herbsaint (Central Business District, $–$$)
La Boulangerie (Mid-City/Uptown, $)
La Madeleine (French/Sandwiches/Sweets, $)
Lilette (Uptown, $$)
Olivier's (French Quarter, $–$$)
Peristyle (French Quarter, $$)
Restaurant August (Central Business District, $$–$$$)

International/Eclectic

Bayona (French Quarter, $$)
Bella Luna (French Quarter, $$)
The Bistro at Maison de Ville (French Quarter, $$–$$$)
Cobalt (Central Business District, $$)
Cuvée (Central Business District, $$)
Dick & Jenny's (Uptown, $–$$)
The Grill Room (Central Business District, $$–$$$)
Upperline (Uptown, $$)
Whole Foods (Mid-City/Uptown, $)

Italian

Bacco (French Quarter, $–$$)
Ciro's Coté Sud (Uptown, $)
Irene's Cuisine (French Quarter, $–$$)

Maximo's (French Quarter, $–$$)
Pascal's Manale (Uptown, $–$$)
Peristyle (French Quarter, $$)

Japanese

Horinoya (Central Business District, $–$$)
Samurai Sushi (French Quarter, $–$$)

Mediterranean

Moonlight Café (Garden District, $)

Mexican

Juan's Flying Burrito (Garden District/Mid-City, $)
Taqueria Corona (Uptown/Warehouse District, $)

Middle Eastern

Lebanon's Café (Uptown, $)
Mona's (Mid-City/Uptown, $)

Pizza

Café Roma (French Quarter/Mid-City/Uptown, $)
Ciro's Coté Sud (Uptown, $)
Mama Rosa's Slice of Italy (French Quarter, $)
Reginelli's (Sandwiches/Pizza, $)

Sandwiches/Hamburgers

Acme Oyster House (French Quarter, $–$$)
Betsy's Pancake House (Mid-City, $)
Café Maspero (French Quarter, $–$$)
Café Roma (French Quarter/Mid-City/Uptown, $)
Camellia Grill (Uptown, $)
Casamento's (Uptown, $–$$)
Central Grocery (French Quarter, $)
City Perk (Mid-City, $)
Clover Grill (French Quarter, $)
Domilise's (Uptown, $)
Elizabeth's (Bywater, $)
Felix's Restaurant and Oyster Bar (French Quarter, $–$$)
Franky & Johnny's (Uptown, $)

Guy's (Uptown, $)
Igor's Bar & Grill (Garden District, $)
Johnny's Po-boys (French Quarter, $–$$)
Katie's (Mid-City, $)
La Madeleine (French Quarter, $)
La Marquise (French Quarter, $)
La Peniche (Faubourg Marigny, $)
Lebanon's Café (Uptown, $)
Liuzza's (Mid-City, $)
Mama Rosa's Slice of Italy (French Quarter, $)
Mandina's (Mid-City, $–$$)
Mona's (Mid-City/Uptown, $)
Mother's (Central Business District, $–$$)
PJ's Coffee & Tea Co. (Uptown/Warehouse District, $)
Poppy's Grill (French Quarter, $)
Port of Call (French Quarter, $–$$)
Reginelli's (Sandwiches/Pizza, $)
Slim Goodie's Diner (Uptown, $)
Moonlight Café (Garden District, $)
St. Charles Tavern (Garden District, $)
Whole Foods (Mid-City/Uptown, $)

Seafood

Acme Oyster House (Sandwiches/Seafood, $–$$)
Café Maspero (French Quarter, $–$$)
Casamento's (Uptown, $–$$)
Horinoya (Central Business District, $–$$)
Domilise's (Uptown, $)
Felix's Restaurant and Oyster Bar (French Quarter, $–$$)
Franky & Johnny's (Uptown, $)
Gabrielle (Mid-City, $$–$$$)
Guy's (Uptown, $)
Igor's Bar & Grill (Garden District, $)
Johnny's Po-boys (French Quarter, $–$$)
Katie's (Mid-City, $)
Liuzza's (Mid-City, $)
Mandina's (Mid-City, $–$$)
Mango House (Uptown, $–$$)
Mike Anderson's Seafood (French Quarter, $–$$)
Mother's (Central Business District, $–$$)

Olivier's (French Quarter, $–$$)
Pascal's Manale (Uptown, $–$$)
Ralph & Kacoo's (French Quarter, $–$$$)
Rib Room (French Quarter, $$$–$$$$)
Samurai Sushi (French Quarter, $–$$)
St. Charles Tavern (Garden District, $)

Short Order

Betsy's Pancake House (Mid-City, $)
Camellia Grill (Uptown, $)
Clover Grill (French Quarter, $)
Igor's Bar & Grill (Garden District, $)
La Peniche (Faubourg Marigny, $)
Mother's (Central Business District, $–$$)
Poppy's Grill (French Quarter, $)
Slim Goodie's Diner (Uptown, $)
St. Charles Tavern (Garden District, $)

Soul Food

Dooky Chase (Mid-City, $–$$$)
Dunbar's Creole Cooking (Uptown, $)
Henry's Soul Food (Central City/Mid-City, $)
Jacques-Imo's Café (Uptown, $–$$)

Steaks

Chateaubriand (Central Business District, $$–$$$)
Pascal's Manale (Uptown, $–$$)
Rib Room (French Quarter, $$$–$$$$)
Ruth's Chris Steak House (Mid-City, $$–$$$$)

Sweets/Ice Cream/Sno Balls

Angelo Brocato's (Mid-City, $)

Aunt Sally's Pralines (French Quarter, $)
Ben & Jerry's (French Quarter/Mid-City, $)
CC's Gourmet Coffee House (French Quarter/Garden District/Mid-City, $)
City Perk (Mid-City, $)
The Creole Creamery (Uptown, $)
Croissant D'Or (French Quarter, $)
Fair Grinds Coffee House (Mid-City, $)
Häagen-Dazs Ice Cream Parlor (Ice Cream, $)
Hansen's Sno Blitz (Sno Balls, $)
La Boulangerie (Mid-City/Uptown, $)
La Madeleine (French Quarter, $)
La Marquise (French Quarter, $)
Laura's Candies (French Quarter, $)
Leah's Candy Kitchen (Sweets, $)
PJ's Coffee & Tea Co. (Uptown/Warehouse District, $)
Plum Street Sno Balls (Uptown, $)
Rue de la Course (Uptown, $)
Southern Candymakers (French Quarter, $)

Thai

Basil Leaf (Uptown, $–$$)

Vegetarian

Lebanon's Café (Uptown, $)
Mona's (Mid-City/Uptown, $)
Slim Goodie's Diner (Uptown, $)
Whole Foods (Mid-City/Uptown, $)

Vietnamese

Lemon Grass Restaurant (Central Business District, $–$$)
Pho Tau Bay (Mid-City, $)

Index of Establishments by Price

$

Acme Oyster House (Sandwiches/Seafood,French Quarter)
Angelo Brocato's (Sweets/Ice Cream, Mid-City)

Aunt Sally's Pralines (Sweets, French Quarter)
Bacco (Italian/Creole, French Quarter)
Basil Leaf (Thai, Uptown)
Ben & Jerry's (Ice Cream, French Quarter/Mid-City)

Betsy's Pancake House (American/Breakfast/Sandwiches/Short Order, Mid-City)

Bywater Bar-B-Q (American/Sandwiches, Bywater)

Café Maspero (Sandwiches/Seafood, French Quarter)

Café Roma (Pizza/Sandwiches, French Quarter/Garden District/Mid-City)

Camellia Grill (Breakfast/Sandwiches/Short Order, Uptown)

Casamento's (Sandwiches/Seafood, Uptown)

CC's Gourmet Coffee House (Coffee/Sweets, French Quarter/Garden District/Mid-City)

Central Grocery (Sandwich, French Quarter)

Ciro's Coté Sud (French/Italian/Pizza, Uptown)

City Perk (Coffee/Sandwiches/Sweets, Mid-City)

Clover Grill (Breakfast/Sandwiches/Hamburgers/Short Order, French Quarter)

Croissant D'Or (French/Sweets, French Quarter)

Dick & Jenny's (Creole/Eclectic, Uptown)

Domilise's (Sandwiches/Seafood, Uptown)

Dooky Chase (Creole/Soul Food, Mid-City)

Dunbar's Creole Cooking (Creole/Soul, Uptown)

Elizabeth's (Creole, Bywater)

Fair Grinds Coffee House (Coffee/Sweets, Mid-City)

Felix's Restaurant and Oyster Bar (Sandwiches/Seafood, French Quarter)

Five Happiness (Chinese, Uptown)

Franky & Johnny's (Sandwiches/Seafood, Uptown)

Galatoire's (French, French Quarter)

Guy's (Sandwiches/Seafood, Uptown)

Häagen-Dazs Ice Cream Parlor (Ice Cream, French Quarter/Mid-City)

Hansen's Sno Blitz (Sno Balls, Uptown)

Henry's Soul Food (Soul, Central City/Mid-City)

Herbsaint (French/New American, Central Business District)

Horinoya (Japanese/Seafood, Central Business District)

Igor's Bar & Grill (Sandwiches/Seafood/Short Order, Garden District)

Irene's Cuisine (Italian/French Provençal, French Quarter)

Jacques-Imo's (Creole/Soul Food, Uptown)

Johnny's Po-boys (Sandwiches/Seafood, French Quarter)

Juan's Flying Burrito (Mexican, Mid-City/Garden District)

Katie's (Sandwiches/Seafood, Mid-City)

La Boulangerie (French/Sweets, Mid-City/Uptown)

La Madeleine (French/Sandwiches/Sweets, French Quarter/Uptown)

La Marquise (Coffee/Sandwiches/Sweets, French Quarter)

La Peniche (Sandwiches/Hamburgers/Short Order, Faubourg Marigny)

Laura's Candies (Sweets, French Quarter)

Leah's Candy Kitchen (Sweets, French Quarter)

Lebanon's Café (Middle Eastern, Sandwiches, Mid-City)

Lemon Grass Restaurant (Vietnamese, Central Business District)

Liborio's Cuban Restaurant (Cuban, Garden District)

Liuzza's (Sandwiches/Seafood, Mid-City)

Mama Rosa's Slice of Italy (Sandwiches/Pizza, French Quarter)

Mandina's (Sandwiches/Seafood, Mid-City)

Mango House (Caribbean/Seafood, Uptown)

Maximo's (Italian, French Quarter)

Mike Anderson's Seafood (Seafood, French Quarter)

Mona's (Middle Eastern/Sandwiches, Mid-City/Uptown)

Mother's (Sandwiches/Creole/Short Order/Breakfast, Central Business District)

Olivier's (Creole, French Quarter)

Pascal's Manale (Italian/Seafood/Steaks, Uptown)

Pho Tau Bay (Vietnamese, Mid-City)

PJ's Coffee & Tea Co. (Coffee/Sandwiches, Uptown/Warehouse District)

Plum Street Sno Balls (Sno Balls, Uptown)

Poppy's Grill (Breakfast/Sandwiches/Hamburgers/Short Order, French Quarter)

Port of Call (Hamburgers, French Quarter)

Ralph & Kacoo's (Creole/Seafood, French Quarter)

Reginelli's (Pizza, Sandwiches, Uptown)

Rue de la Course (Coffee/Sweets, Garden District/Uptown)

St. Charles Tavern (Sandwiches/Seafood/Short Order, Garden District)

Samurai Sushi (Japanese/Seafood, French Quarter)

Slim Goodie's Diner (Breakfast/Sandwiches/Short Order/Vegetarian, Uptown)

Southern Candymakers (Sweets/Ice Cream, French Quarter)

Taqueria Corona (Mexican, Uptown/Warehouse District)

Upperline (Eclectic/Creole, Uptown)

Whole Foods (International/Sandwiches/Vegetarian, Mid-City/Uptown)

$$

Acme Oyster House (Sandwiches/Seafood, French Quarter)

Antoine's (Creole/French, French Quarter)

Arnaud's (Creole, French Quarter)

Bacco (Italian/Creole, French Quarter)

Basil Leaf (Thai, Uptown)

Bayona (International, French Quarter)

Bella Luna (Eclectic/Continental, French Quarter)

The Bistro at Maison de Ville (International/Eclectic, French Quarter)

Brennan's (French/Creole, French Quarter)

Brigtsen's (Cajun/Creole, Uptown)

Café Maspero (Sandwiches/Seafood, French Quarter)

Casamento's (Sandwiches/Seafood, Uptown)

Chateaubriand (French/Steakhouse, Central Business District)

Christian's (French/Creole, Mid-City)

Cobalt (Regional American, Central Business District)

Commander's Palace (Creole, Garden District)

Court of Two Sisters (Creole, French Quarter)

Cuvée (Creole/New American, Central Business District)

Dick & Jenny's (Creole/Eclectic, Uptown)

Dooky Chase (Creole/Soul Food, Mid-City)

Emeril's (Creole/New American, Warehouse District)

Five Happiness (Chinese, Uptown)

Gabrielle (French/Creole/Cajun, Mid-City)

Galatoire's (French, French Quarter)

Gautreau's (Contemporary Louisiana, Uptown)

The Grill Room (Central Business District)

Herbsaint (French/New American, Central Business District)

Horinoya (Japanese/Seafood, Central Business District)

Irene's Cuisine (Italian/French Provençal, French Quarter)

Jacques-Imo's (Creole/Soul Food, Uptown)

K-Paul's Louisiana Kitchen (Cajun, French Quarter)

Lemon Grass Restaurant (Vietnamese, Central Business District)

Lilette (Creole/French, Uptown)

Mandina's (Sandwiches/Seafood, Mid-City)

Mango House (Caribbean/Seafood, Uptown)

Maximo's (Italian, French Quarter)

Mike Anderson's Seafood (Seafood, French Quarter)

Mother's (Sandwiches/Creole/Short Order/Breakfast, Central Business District)

Mr. B's Bistro (Creole, French Quarter)

Olivier's (Creole, French Quarter)

Palace Café (Creole, French Quarter)

Pascal's Manale (Italian/Seafood/Steaks, Uptown)

Peristyle (French/Italian/New American, French Quarter)

Port of Call (Hamburgers, French Quarter)

Ralph & Kacoo's (Creole/Seafood, French Quarter)

Restaurant August (Contemporary French, Central Business District)

Ruth's Chris Steak House (Steaks, Mid-City)

Samurai Sushi (Japanese/Seafood, French Quarter)

Tujaque's (Creole, French Quarter)

Upperline (Eclectic/Creole, Uptown)

$$$

Antoine's (Creole/French, French Quarter)

Arnaud's (Creole, French Quarter)

The Bistro at Maison de Ville (International/Eclectic, French Quarter)

Brennan's (French/Creole, French Quarter)

Chateaubriand (French/Steakhouse, Central Business District)

Christian's (French/Creole, Mid-City)

Commander's Palace (Creole, Garden District)

Court of Two Sisters (Creole, French Quarter)

Dooky Chase (Creole/Soul Food, Mid-City)

Emeril's (Creole/New American, Warehouse District)

Gabrielle (French/Creole/Cajun, Mid-City)

Gautreau's (Contemporary Louisiana, Uptown)

The New Orleans Grill (International, Central Business District)

K-Paul's Louisiana Kitchen (Cajun, French Quarter)

Ralph & Kacoo's (Creole/Seafood, French Quarter)

Restaurant August (Contemporary French, Central Business District)

Rib Room (Steaks/Seafood, French Quarter)

Ruth's Chris Steak House (Steaks, Mid-City)

Tujaque's (Creole, French Quarter)

$$$$

Antoine's (Creole/French, French Quarter)

Chateaubriand (French/Steakhouse, Central Business District)

Emeril's (Creole/New American, Warehouse District)

Rib Room (Steaks/Seafood, French Quarter)

Ruth's Chris Steak House (Steaks, Mid-City)

Part IV
Exploring
New Orleans

"Honey, come on – that's part of the charm of New Orleans. Where else would they put a voodoo doll on your pillow instead of a mint at turndown?"

In this part . . .

You have at least one foolproof way to work off all the sinful food you savor in New Orleans — sightseeing! Nothing helps the digestion like a vigorous workout, and you'll get more than that simply deciding which of New Orleans's many sights and attractions you want to see — to say nothing of actually *visiting* them! Chapter 11 covers the absolute, must-see attractions, followed by a comprehensive list of other worthwhile places. Next, you find information on one way of seeing the sights you've picked — the guided tour.

Then comes the shopping. New Orleans is a city of excess, especially for shopping. Whether you want to browse the familiar brand-name department stores or comb through funky boutiques, Chapter 12 familiarizes you with the city's diverse shopping areas.

Lastly, you find some helpful suggestions on how to structure your time, in case you're still having trouble figuring out what to see first and how to go about it. Chapter 13 suggests some great itineraries for taking in the sights, and Chapter 14 throws in a couple of day-trips you may enjoy, if you have the time and energy. Just make sure you get back to town by sundown; New Orleans always offers plenty to do at night (which is, incidentally, covered in Part V).

Chapter 11

Discovering New Orleans's Best Attractions

- -

In This Chapter
▶ Reviewing the top attractions in town
▶ Introducing additional sights by location and type
▶ Taking a guided tour

- -

*T*hanks to great food and music, New Orleans has an embarrassment of riches. However, the thing about New Orleans that charms many people is its unique sense of character and identity. This chapter presents a selective, alphabetical list of the top places where you can soak up the best of the Crescent City, while also having a good time and maybe discovering something new along the way.

New Orleans's Top Sights

No matter how you want to spend your time, New Orleans offers a multitude of choices. Read the following to get an idea.

Aquarium of the Americas
French Quarter

This stylish, entertaining, and winningly educational aquarium — one of the top ten in the United States — features breathtaking exhibits that make you feel as if you're walking under water or exploring a tropical rain forest. The aquarium features an interactive, hands-on activity area for kids, along with popular exhibits of penguins (fed daily at 11 a.m. and 4 p.m.) and sharks (fed on Tuesdays, Thursdays, and Saturdays at 1 p.m.). Aquarium volunteers in blue or green shirts can answer your questions and steer you in the right direction if you're lost. Give yourself 1½ to 2 hours to see the aquarium.

See map p. 174. One Canal St. (at the Mississippi River). ☎ *800-774-7394 or 504-581-4629.* www.auduboninstitute.org. *Open: Sun–Thurs 9:30 a.m.–6 p.m., Fri–Sat 9:30 a.m.–7 p.m. Admission: $18 adults, $15 seniors, $11 children 2–12,*

New Orleans Attractions

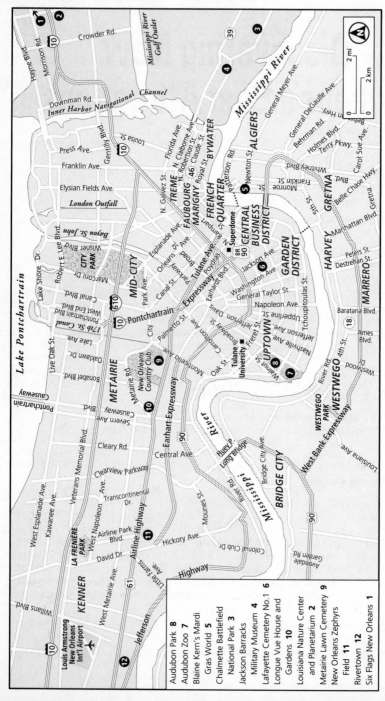

Audubon Park **8**
Audubon Zoo **7**
Blaine Kern's Mardi
    Gras World **5**
Chalmette Battlefield
    National Park **3**
Jackson Barracks
    Military Museum **4**
Lafayette Cemetery No. 1 **6**
Longue Vue House and
    Gardens **10**
Louisiana Nature Center
    and Planetarium **2**
Metairie Lawn Cemetery **9**
New Orleans Zephyrs
    Field **11**
Rivertown **12**
Six Flags New Orleans **1**

A New Orleans IMAX experience

Next door to the Aquarium of the Americas is the IMAX Theatre (☎ **800-774-7394** or 504-581-4629), with large-screen 3-D documentaries (past shows have featured everything from dinosaurs to the Rolling Stones) that are sure to delight the kids. You can purchase tickets separately for $8 for adults and $5 for children 2–12 years old ($7 for seniors 65 and up), or save a couple of bucks with the aquarium/IMAX combination admission. Shows run hourly from 10 a.m.–8 p.m. The theater is wheelchair accessible.

children 2 and under get in free. Parking: 3-hour complimentary parking in the Hilton New Orleans Riverside parking lot with ticket stub. Wheelchair accessible.

Armstrong Park
French Quarter

This spot, once the only place where slaves could congregate, used to be called Congo Square. (Congo Square still exists inside the park.) Transformed into a public park and dedicated to jazz legend Louis Armstrong, the park offers visitors stately sycamores, peaceful lagoons, and rolling grassy knolls. You can also find the **Municipal Auditorium** and the **Mahalia Jackson Theater for the Performing Arts** (see Chapter 15), and soon it will be the site of the much-anticipated **New Orleans Jazz National Historical Park**. During Mardi Gras, the all-canine **Krewe of Barkus** and its two- and four-legged fans gather here prior to the parade. You can see every possible breed — from All-Americans (also known as mutts) to Louisiana Catahoula Leopard Dogs to Wheaten Terriers — most dressed according to the parade theme. Some lucky dogs even have their own minifloat. The park entrance is just outside the Quarter in the Faubourg Tremé neighborhood at St. Ann and Rampart streets. The area is safe during the day, but I don't recommend venturing there at night unless you go as part of a large group or during an event. Give yourself 30 to 60 minutes to visit the park.

See map p. 174. On N. Rampart Street, between Toulouse and St. Phillip streets, facing the French Quarter. Open: seasonal hours. Admission: free. Wheelchair accessible.

Audubon Park
Uptown

This 340-acre public park is one of the most beautiful and tranquil spots in the city. A refuge for nature lovers, it's also a busy social thoroughfare; bicyclists, joggers, dog walkers, and horseback riders (call Cascade Stables at ☎ 504-891-2246 for details) come to enjoy the atmosphere and the scenery. Tucked into this sprawling expanse of land are tennis courts, riding and jogging paths, a public golf course, resident populations of squirrels and birds (keep an eye out for wood ducks and egrets), and hundreds of

---

Cruising from A(quarium) to Z(oo)

You can purchase a combination ticket for admission to both the Aquarium of the Americas and the Audubon Zoo, with a riverboat ride on the sternwheeler *John James Audubon* taking you between the two. Combination admissions for all three (cruise, aquarium, and zoo) are $34 (adults) and $16.50 (children 2–12). Other combination admissions are also available. Trips depart from the Riverwalk (in front of the aquarium) at 10 a.m., noon, 2 p.m., and 4 p.m., and from the zoo at 11 a.m., 1 p.m., 3 p.m., and 5 p.m. (Call ☎ 800-774-7394 or 504-581-4629 for more information or to confirm schedule.)

---

centuries-old live oaks. Come here to have a picnic, exercise, or just relax by the fountain at the St. Charles Avenue entrance — but don't stay after dark. Allow 30 to 60 minutes for an appreciative stroll.

See map p. 170. 6500 St. Charles Ave. (across from Tulane and Loyola universities, nestled between St. Charles Avenue and Magazine Street). Take the St. Charles Streetcar and get off in front of the park. ☎ *504-581-4629. Open: Daily 6 a.m.–10 p.m. Admission: free. Wheelchair accessible.*

Audubon Zoo
Uptown

More than 1,800 animals, including some rare and endangered species, live in this sprawling maze of carefully constructed lagoons, waterfalls, and vegetation. Situated inside Audubon Park on the bank of the Mississippi River, the zoo features an array of exhibits, including a replica of a Louisiana swamp and the Dragon's Lair exhibit featuring spectacular 6- to 9-foot-long Komodo dragons from Indonesia. The zoo boasts a white alligator, two white Bengal tigers, and a host of other exotic animals. The **Jaguar Jungle** exhibit is a stunning acre-and-a-half replica of an ancient Mayan city filled with spider monkeys, macaws, iguanas, and other creatures; low-lying fog adds an air of mystery. Give yourself two to four hours to thoroughly enjoy the zoo.

See map p. 170. 6500 Magazine St. ☎ *800-774-7394 or 504-581-4629.* www.audubon institute.org. *Take the St. Charles Streetcar and get off at the park entrance. A free shuttle through the park runs every 20 minutes. If you prefer, take the Magazine Street bus and get off at the zoo. Admission: $11 adults, $7 seniors (older than 65), and $6 children 2–12. Parking: free. Wheelchair accessible. Open: Daily 9:30 a.m.– 5 p.m.; open till 6 p.m. weekends in the summer. Last ticket sold one hour before closing. Closed Mardi Gras day, the first Friday in May, Thanksgiving, and Christmas.*

Bourbon Street
French Quarter

As you walk along Bourbon Street, between the 100 and 1000 blocks, you may feel like you've just crashed the world's largest ongoing, open-air fraternity party. This is New Orleans Party Central, for better or for worse, and at night it's definitely not a kids' attraction — unless you're a kid between the ages of 21 and 100. Bourbon Street is an odd mix of the authentic and the contrived, with its carnival-style barkers trying to lure you into strip clubs, its buggy drivers ferrying tourists, and its requisite street performers and scam artists competing for your attention (and your money). Most, if not all, bars on Bourbon Street (which is blocked off for pedestrians only) stay open until the wee, wee hours — some well into the morning. You can even take an alcoholic drink with you for a stroll — as long as you carry it in a plastic "go-cup." During the daylight hours, Bourbon Street becomes more relaxed and can almost look deserted. Only restaurants, T-shirt and souvenir shops, and a few bars stay open during the day. Depending on the ages of your children and your definition of family values, you may want your kids to see Bourbon Street only in daylight — or not at all. With the kids during the day, allow about an hour for a visit. If you're a bigger kid looking to cut loose at night, well, take your time.

Cabildo
French Quarter

The Cabildo, where the French government turned over the Louisiana Purchase to the United States in 1803, was built in 1795 as the Spanish seat of government. Worthwhile exhibits cover all aspects of life in early Louisiana, including antebellum music, mourning and burial customs, and the changing roles of women in the South. Each room seems more interesting than the one before. Allow at least an hour for your visit.

See map p. 174. 701 Chartres St. (at St. Ann Street on Jackson Square; 2 blocks from Bourbon Street). ☎ **800-568-6968** *or 504-568-6968.* http://lsm.crt.state.la.us/site/cabex.htm. *Admission: $5 adults, $4 students and seniors, free for children under 12. Wheelchair accessible, though the elevator is small. Open: Tues–Sun 9 a.m.–5 p.m.*

City Park
Mid-City

The new Canal Streetcar takes you directly to the lovely urban oasis that is City Park. At 1,500 acres, it's the fifth largest urban park in the United States and shelters the largest collection of mature live oaks in the world. Give yourself at least an hour to explore the park, two to three if you have children or want to linger at two or more of the spots listed here. (Much longer, of course, if you're going to play 18 holes of golf.) If you plan to visit the **New Orleans Museum of Art** (☎ 504-488-2631; see listing later in this chapter), which is located on the park grounds, allow another hour to an hour and a half. For additional details on the following activities inside the park, go to the **City Park Web site** at www.neworleanscitypark.com.

The **Carousel Gardens** (☎ 504-483-9381) in City Park house one of the country's few remaining carved wooden carousels. Two miniature trains take riders on a 2½-mile trip through the park. Also check out the small Ferris wheel and wading pool. Admission is $2, single-ride tickets are $1,

French Quarter Attractions

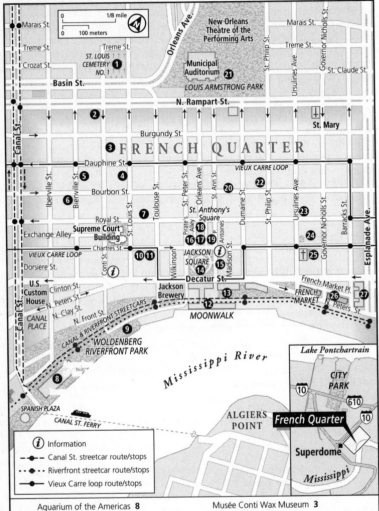

and $10 buys you unlimited rides. The **Botanical Gardens** (☎ 504-483-9386) offers visitors 12 acres of gardens, fountains, ponds, and sculptures, plus a horticultural library and a gift shop. Open Tuesday through Sunday from 10 a.m. to 4:30 p.m., admission is $5 adults, $2 children 5 to 12, and children under 4 can get in free with a parent. Offering 26 larger-than-life storybook-themed play areas. **Storyland** (☎ 504-483-9381) is great for children. Admission is $2, free for kids under 2. Other features of the park include the following:

✔ Four 18-hole public golf courses with lessons by PGA pros, electric carts, rentals, pro shop, and restaurant (☎ **504-483-9397**), plus a 100-tee driving range (☎ **504-483-9394**)

✔ Softball center (☎ **504-483-9422**)

✔ Pedal boats (☎ **504-483-9371**) for the 8 miles of lagoons

✔ Thirty-six tennis courts (☎ **504-483-9383**)

✔ Fishing (☎ **504-483-9371**) in the park's lagoons for bass, catfish, and perch. Permits are required and may be purchsed on-site — call or visit the city park Web site for details.

✔ Horseback rides, lessons, and pony rides (☎ **504-483-9398**)

See map p. 183. City Park is located all the way up Esplanade Avenue out of the French Quarter. ☎ *504-482-4888.* www.neworleanscitypark.com. *Take the Esplanade bus from the French Quarter and get off at the park. Open: sunrise til sunset. Parking: free. Wheelchair accessible.*

French Market
French Quarter

This nexus of local trade, located right next to the river (from St. Phillip Street to the edge of the Quarter at Esplanade Avenue), has been a fixture since the early 1700s. Its shops, flea market, and farmer's market are still neat places to shop for souvenirs, gifts, T-shirts, jewelry, arts and crafts, and fresh produce. Finish your shopping spree by indulging in some beignets at **Café du Monde,** located right along the market. Give yourself at least 30 to 60 minutes to wander the market.

See map p. 174 The French Market stretches along Decatur and N. Peters streets from St. Ann to Barracks. Admission: free. Wheelchair accessible. Open: most shops from 10 a.m.–6 p.m. daily. The Farmer's Market and Café du Monde are open 24 hours.

Jackson Square
French Quarter

Historically, Jackson Square served New Orleans as the place of execution, military parade ground, and town square. Today, beautiful landscaping, trees, benches, and a tranquil fountain make this square one of the more popular public places in the city. Just outside the iron fence, artists set up shop on the sidewalk while mules stand along Decatur Street, patiently waiting to take tourists for a trip around the Quarter. Consult a tarot card reader or a psychic while watching clowns, street musicians, and mimes vie for your tips. You can grab some ice cream, a soft drink, or another snack from a street vendor, or head for one of the restaurants located on each corner of the square. Allot 30 to 60 minutes to look around — considerably more if you decide to run away and join the street mimes.

See map p. 174. The square fronts the 700 block of Decatur Street and is bounded by Chartres, St. Ann, and St. Peter streets. www.jackson-square.com. Admission: free. Open: seasonal hours, but usually from dawn to dusk.

Louisiana Children's Museum
Warehouse District

This spacious, two-story interactive museum is really a playground in disguise. The hands-on exhibits open up the worlds of science and nature and role playing. Kids can be chefs, tugboat captains, or even TV anchors in a simulated television studio. Activities and exhibits include everything from a pint-sized grocery store to a "challenges" exhibit where they shoot hoops from a wheelchair and a math and physics lab. Allow 90 minutes to 2 hours.

See map p. 177. 420 Julia St. (4 blocks from the Convention Center). ☎ *504-523-1357. www.lcm.org. (Mon 9:30 a.m.–4:30 p.m. in Jun–Aug), Sun noon to 4:30 p.m. Admission: $6, children under 1 free. Parking: Hourly lots nearby. Wheelchair accessible. Open: Tues–Sat 9:30 a.m.–4:30 p.m.*

Louisiana Nature Center and Planetarium
New Orleans East

The Nature Center is nestled in Joe Brown Park, an 85-acre stretch of Louisiana forest. Guided walks are given every day except Monday; a nature film runs on weekdays; and the weekends offer special activities such as canoeing, bird-watching, and arts-and-crafts workshops. The "Turtle Pond" exhibit is home to native Louisiana reptiles, including baby alligators, Southern painted turtles, and Gulf Coast box turtles. The surrounding wetlands support native plants such as blue flag iris and lizardtail. Binoculars help kids locate animals, and signs identify what they see. The center features 3 miles of trails available for public use and a wheelchair-accessible wooden walkway. The planetarium offers shows on Saturday and Sunday.

See map p. 170. Nature Center Drive in the Joe Brown Memorial Park. ☎ *800-774-7394 or 504-246-5672. www.auduboninstitute.org. Take 1-10 to Exit 244. Pass Plaza Shopping Center and turn left onto Nature Center Drive. Or catch the Lake Forest Express bus at Canal and Basin (2 blocks from French Quarter), get off at Lake Forest Boulevard and Nature Center Drive, walk 3 to 4 blocks. Admission: $5 adults, $4 seniors, $3 children (2–12). Parking: free. Wheelchair accessible. Open: Tues–Fri 9 a.m.–5 p.m., Sat 10 a.m.–5 p.m., Sun noon to 5 p.m.*

Central Business District/Warehouse District Attractions

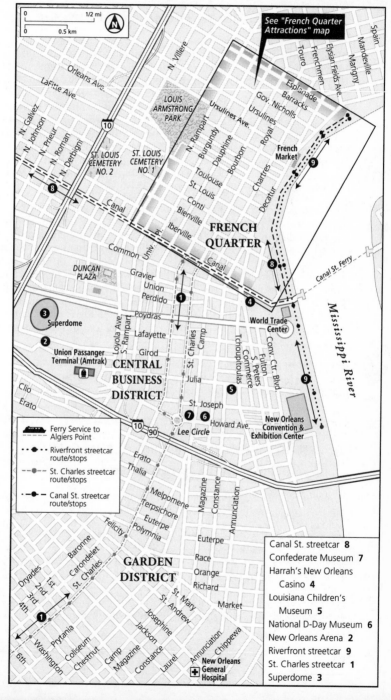

See "French Quarter Attractions" map

Canal St. streetcar **8**
Confederate Museum **7**
Harrah's New Orleans
 Casino **4**
Louisiana Children's
 Museum **5**
National D-Day Museum **6**
New Orleans Arena **2**
Riverfront streetcar **9**
St. Charles streetcar **1**
Superdome **3**

Mardi Gras
Central Business District/French Quarter/Garden District/ Mid-City/Uptown

Although it's not confined to one physical location, Mardi Gras — the biggest free party thrown on the North American continent — is by far New Orleans's most popular attraction. You could write volumes about its rich and colorful history (and many people have; see Chapter 2). Revelers flock to the city from all over the United States — and the world — while some locals, who don't feel like fighting the crowds, hightail it out of town for the final few days. If you like crowds, you'll love joining the raucous street party in the French Quarter, especially on Bourbon Street between the 500 block and 1000 block. For these who prefer a little elbow room, I suggest you head as far Uptown as possible (think Napoleon Avenue).

For a family-friendly Mardi Gras experience, check out the parades in other parts of the city, most notably the parade route along **St. Charles Avenue** uptown. Also, the suburbs are increasingly becoming a haven for families. Although it's a bit of a drive, you can find a much more G-rated experience (okay, maybe PG-13) if you decamp along one of the major suburban parade routes. **Veterans Highway** in Metairie (on the East Bank of Jefferson Parish), the **Westbank Expressway** (one of the main thoroughfares across the river, on the West Bank of Jefferson Parish), or **St. Bernard Parish** (just north of the city proper) make good spots. Compared to the bacchanalia on Bourbon Street, these suburban areas offer a whole other world. Sure, some drinking and partying goes on, but for the most part, they're good for a family outing.

If you drive a car to New Orleans, *never* park along a parade route for at least two hours before or after a parade. You'll see signs telling you the parade dates and times all over the place. If you choose to ignore these

---

An impressive Mardi Gras sight: Mardi Gras Indians

Groups (or "tribes") of African American men who dress in elaborate Native American costumes are called "Mardi Gras Indians." The costumes are their pride and joy, and they put serious work into them, usually taking a whole year to put one together. Feathers, sequins, headdresses — the costumes are unbelievable. Some people say that the tradition originally developed as a way of showing thanks to Native Americans who helped escaped slaves. The Indian parades never follow an organized route, but roam at will. Fights used to break out when two different tribes met on the street, but today the tribes just engage in an elaborate call-and-response ceremony instead. (Some Mardi Gras Indian tribes are also musical groups. The most popular these days is the Wild Magnolias, who have played and recorded albums with such luminaries as Dr. John, Bruce Hornsby, and Robbie Robertson.)

Mardi Gras Parade Routes

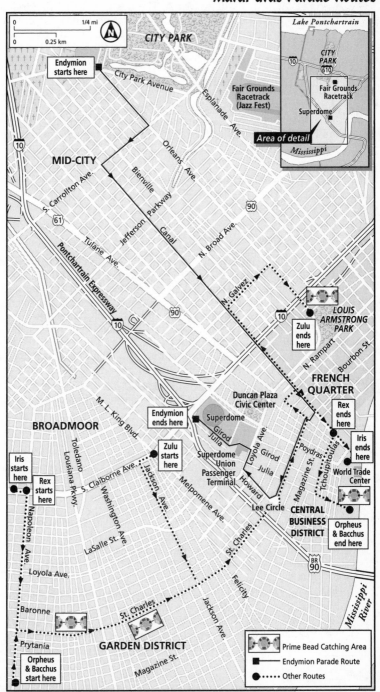

warnings, your car will be towed. The best bet for getting to Mardi Gras parades is to walk or take public transportation. Even for people who know how to get around, traffic is impossible, so if you must drive, give yourself plenty of time. Or call a cab; the number for **United Cab,** the city's largest and most well-known cab fleet, is ☎ **504-522-9771.**

Your kids are sure to enjoy the Mardi Gras experience; costumes, crowds, and parades are quite a stimulant. Make sure your kids get plenty of sleep the night before so they don't tire out early. Mardi Gras certainly won't bore them, but it can make for a long day. Avoid spending the kids' college fund on overpriced Mardi Gras food by bringing snacks and drinks with you. Also, decide on a meeting place in advance in case someone gets lost or separated.

Citywide parades roll nearly every day in the two weeks prior to Mardi Gras day. Admission: free. Wheelchair accessible.

Moonwalk
French Quarter

Although the name conjures up that '80s dance move, the Moonwalk is a riverside path whose view of the Mississippi River and the Crescent City Connection (a twin-span bridge to Algiers Point, an established New Orleans neighborhood) makes for a romantic stroll. From the Moonwalk, you can watch river traffic coming into and going out of the second busiest port in the world. Named for Mayor Moon Landrieu, during whose administration it was built, the Moonwalk is directly across the street from Jackson Square. Allow 10 to 15 minutes for general sightseeing, or more if you're looking for *amore.*

See map p. 174. Jackson Square. ☎ *504-587-0738. Admission: free. Wheelchair accessible. Open: 24 hours a day, but go before midnight for safety's sake.*

National D-Day Museum
Central Business District

This one-of-a-kind museum features quietly poignant and thought-provoking exhibits relating to D-Day, June 6, 1944, when the Allies stormed the beaches of Normandy and changed the course of World War II. The museum includes a 110-seat theater playing the Oscar-nominated documentary *D-Day Remembered.* The museum also features exhibits devoted to other beach landings and amphibious invasions during the war, often told through the personal stories and artifacts of the soldiers themselves. Allow one to two hours for the curious, at least half a day for serious history buffs.

See map p. 177. 945 Magazine St. (at Howard Avenue) ☎ *504-527-6012.* www.dday museum.org. *In the Warehouse District; enter on the Howard Avenue side. Admission: $10 adults, $6 seniors, $5 children under 18, children under 5 free. Parking: On-street and hourly lots available nearby. Wheelchair accessible. Open: Daily 9 a.m.–5 p.m. (excluding Thanksgiving, Christmas, New Year's, and Mardi Gras day).*

Mardi huh? What those strange words mean

Talking the talk and walking the walk are crucial if you plan to go to New Orleans during Mardi Gras. With these terms, you can talk the talk like a pro. Walking the walk, on the other hand, is entirely up to you.

- ✔ **Ball** or **Tableau Ball:** Krewes host these themed, masked balls. Themes change from year to year.

- ✔ **Boeuf Gras** (fattened calf): The calf represents ritual sacrifice, as well as the last meal eaten before Lent. It's also the symbol of Mardi Gras and the first float of the Rex parade.

- ✔ **Carnival:** A celebration beginning January 6 (the 12th night after Christmas) and ending Mardi Gras day.

- ✔ **Court:** A krewe's king, queen, and attendants.

- ✔ **Doubloon:** Krewes throw these metal coins during parades. They feature the logo of the krewe on one side and its theme for a particular year on the other.

- ✔ **Fat Tuesday:** Otherwise known as Mardi Gras, the last day before Ash Wednesday, which is the first day of Lent.

- ✔ **Favor:** Krewe members give these souvenirs, which feature the krewe's logo and date, to people who attend their ball.

- ✔ **Flambeaux:** Flaming torches carried by parade participants on foot; they aren't members of the krewe.

- ✔ **King Cake:** An oval, sugared pastry decorated with purple, gold, and green (Mardi Gras colors) that contains a small doll representing the baby Jesus.

- ✔ **Krewe:** The traditional word for a Carnival organization.

- ✔ **Lagniappe** (pronounced lan-*yap*): Loosely means "a little extra," and refers to any small gift or token — even a scrap of food or a free drink.

- ✔ **Mardi Gras:** French for "Fat Tuesday." Technically, if you say "Mardi Gras day," you're really saying "Fat Tuesday day."

- ✔ **Rex:** Latin for "king." The King of Carnival is Rex.

- ✔ **Second Line:** A group of people that follows a parade, dancing to the music. Also, a musical term that specifies a particular shuffling tempo popularized in much New Orleans music.

- ✔ **Throws:** Inexpensive trinkets thrown from floats to parade watchers, including doubloons, minifootballs, plastic swords, and spears and all sorts of knick-knacks. The most coveted throws are the gilded coconuts of the Zulu Social Aid and Pleasure Club.

New Orleans Museum of Art
Mid-City

Take the new Canal Streetcar to City Park, where a stately, oak-lined avenue leads you to New Orleans's premier fine arts museum, nicknamed "NOMA" by the locals. You can find a magnificent 40,000-piece permanent collection of African American, Asian, European, and pre-Columbian works, including paintings, sculpture, and a decorative glass collection, plus ever-changing art exhibits from around the world. Past exhibits have featured works by Degas, Fabergé, and Monet, as well as Egyptian treasures and a commemoration of the Louisiana Purchase. The spectacular new Besthoff Sculpture Garden is a study in contrasts with its natural backdrop of moss-draped oak trees and the clean lines of modern and contemporary sculpture. NOMA always has special exhibits and tours for kids. Allow two to three hours for your visit.

See map p. 183. 1 Collins Diboll Circle. ☎ *504-488-2631.* www.noma.org. *Admission: $8 adults, $7 seniors, $4 children 3–17; free to Louisiana residents Thurs after 5 p.m.; sculpture garden free, same hours as museum. Parking: free. Wheelchair accessible. Open: Tues, Wed, Fri–Sun 10 a.m.–5 p.m., Thurs 12:30–8:30 p.m.*

Old U.S. Mint
French Quarter

Built in 1835, this huge Greek Revival building now belongs to the Louisiana State Museum, but it used to mint money for both the United States and the Confederacy. These days, it plays host to a large exhibit showcasing New Orleans jazz. The museum features a comprehensive collection of pictures, musical instruments (including Louis Armstrong's first trumpet), and other artifacts that trace the development of jazz. Joint tours of the Mint and two or more of the other Louisiana State Museum properties, such as the Presbytere and the Cabildo, are available. Allow an hour, maybe more for serious jazz buffs.

See map p. 174. 400 Esplanade Ave. ☎ *800-568-6968 or 504-568-6968.* http://lsm.crt.state.la.us/site/mintex.htm. *Admission: $5 adults, $4 seniors and students, free for children under 12. Wheelchair accessible. Open: Tues–Sun 9 a.m.–5 p.m.*

Presbytere
French Quarter

This building was intended as a home for the Spanish clergy, but it took many years to finish and wound up being used as a courthouse instead. Today, it's a branch of the Louisiana State Museum and home of a Mardi Gras exhibit, featuring colorful costumes and interactive displays on the festival's history. Allow about an hour.

See map p. 174. 751 Chartres St. (at Jackson Square). ☎ *800-568-6968 or 504-568-6968.* http://lsm.crt.state.la.us/site/presbex.htm. *Admission: $5 adults, $4 seniors and students, free for children under 12. Wheelchair accessible. Open: Tues–Sun 9 a.m.–5 p.m.*

Mid-City Attractions

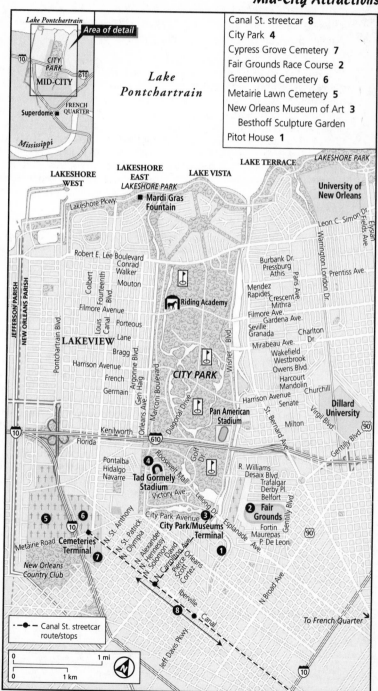

Canal St. streetcar **8**
City Park **4**
Cypress Grove Cemetery **7**
Fair Grounds Race Course **2**
Greenwood Cemetery **6**
Metairie Lawn Cemetery **5**
New Orleans Museum of Art **3**
   Besthoff Sculpture Garden
Pitot House **1**

St. Charles Streetcar and Canal Streetcar
Central Business District/Garden District/Uptown/Carrollton and Riverfront/Central Business District/Mid-City

The oldest continually operating streetcar system in the world, the St. Charles Streetcar began in 1835 as a mule-drawn railway and was electrified in 1893. In one of those quirky convergences of tradition and modernity that New Orleans is so famous for, the streetcar is both a national historic attraction *and* a functioning arm of the New Orleans public transit system. The Canal Streetcar began running again in April 2004 after 40 years of being out of service, proving that modern doesn't always mean better. Get in line with the locals who are thrilled to see it literally back on track. Flip to Chapters 8 and 18 for information on the streetcar routes and attractions along the way. The St. Charles round-trip is about 14 miles and takes two to three hours; the Canal round-trip is nearly 11 miles and takes one to two hours.

☎ **504-248-3900.** www.norta.org. *Admission: $1.25 each way (exact change required); a VisiTour pass provides unlimited rides on streetcars or buses at a cost of $5 for 1 day or $12 for 3 days. Ask at your hotel or a tourist office for the nearest VisiTour pass vendor.*

St. Louis Cathedral
French Quarter

The oldest continuously operating cathedral in the United States, the St. Louis Cathedral dates from 1794, though the church was largely rebuilt in the 1850s. It has quite an interesting history and is the third building to stand on this spot. The first church was destroyed by a hurricane in 1722, and the second by the great fire of 1788. Supposedly the cathedral's bells were kept silent for religious reasons (it was Good Friday), so they didn't ring out to alarm folks of the fire, which went on to destroy more than 800 buildings. Be sure to check out the beautiful stained-glass windows and mural depicting the life of King Louis IX, the cathedral's patron saint. Located directly behind the cathedral, St. Anthony's Garden is named for Pere Antoine, a popular rector who served New Orleans in the late 18th and early 19th centuries. Legend claims that many duels were fought here in the past. Now, however, the main attraction comes at night, when a huge shadow of Christ appears against the back of the church — thanks to a statue and a carefully placed spotlight. The garden isn't open for tours, but it is worth peeking into it from Royal Street, Pirates' Alley, or Pere Antoine's Alley.

See map p. 174. 615 Pere Antoine Alley (at Jackson Square). ☎ **504-525-9583.** *Admission: Entry and tours are free, but donations are requested. Wheelchair accessible. Open: Tours are given Mon–Sat 9 a.m.–5 p.m. and Sun 2–5 p.m.*

Six Flags New Orleans
New Orleans East

This 140-acre theme park opened in 2000 as Jazzland Theme Park and was purchased by Six Flags soon thereafter. Jazz and Louisiana are still the dominant motifs, with rides and attractions such as Lafitte's Pirate Ship, Voodoo Volcano, the Big Easy (a giant, 90-foot Ferris wheel), and the Mardi Gras Menagerie carousel. The park boasts four thrill-packed roller coasters, including the Zydeco Scream (a boomerang coaster that drops into reverse toward the end) and the Mega Zeph (a 4,000-foot-long coaster — the park's signature ride). The park also includes a bayou-themed section with alligators and Cajun crafts and dancing. A definite family attraction, Six Flags presents enough history and New Orleans themes to almost qualify as informative. Thrill-junkies of all ages should allow between four hours and a full day, depending on your level of addiction.

See map p. 170 12301 Lake Forest Boulevard ☎ **504-253-8100**. www.sixflags. com/parks/neworleans. *Located at the intersection of I-10 and I-510, approximately 12 miles from the Central Business District; off I-10, take exit 246A South onto I-510, then Lake Forest Boulevard East. Admission: $35.99 adults and children taller than 4 feet, $24.99 children under 4-feet tall, $24.99 online special, free for children 2 and under. Parking: $7. Wheelchair accessible. Open: Daily Memorial Day–mid-August, weekends only in spring and fall.*

Finding More Cool Things to See and Do

Need to find an activity to keep the kids smiling and the teenager happy? Care to enlighten the historian inside you, or perhaps catch a game? The following suggestions should keep your diverse tastes and needs satisfied.

Especially for kids

Touring New Orleans with your small fry in tow will obviously be a drastically different experience from the one you'd have coming alone or with your significant other. But that doesn't mean you have to sacrifice for the sake of the kids. Finding attractions that appeal to all age groups is easier than you think. For example, a romantic riverboat ride (see "Dinner on the water: Riverboat cruises" later in this chapter for more information) also appeals to the young 'uns — just in a different way. Here are some kid-tested sights that you'll likely find interesting as well.

Blaine Kern's Mardi Gras World
Algiers

If your visit doesn't coincide with Mardi Gras season, this place gives you a taste of what it's all about. You see people building and/or decorating a Mardi Gras float (this is where most of the floats in the city are made). You can watch a Mardi Gras film and even get your picture taken in a Mardi Gras costume. Furthermore, you get complimentary king cake and coffee. Budget around two hours to get here; take the tour and find your way back to the Quarter.

See map p. 170. 223 Newton St., Algiers Point. ☎ **800-362-8213** *or 504-361-7821.* www. mardigrasworld.com. *Take the Canal St. Ferry — free for pedestrians — and a van will meet you, take you to the site, and bring you back. (Van reservations only* *needed for parties of 15 or more.) Admission: $13.50 adults, $10 seniors (older than 62), $6.50 children 3–12, free for children under 3. Parking: free. Wheelchair accessible. Open: Daily 9:30 a.m.–4:30 p.m. (closed some holidays)*

Chalmette Battlefield National Park
Chalmette

This park is the site of the historic Battle of New Orleans, where General Andrew Jackson and a ragtag band staged a desperate defense of the city against the British. This last major battle of the War of 1812 actually took place *after* the war was officially over — the participants just hadn't yet received word. Replica cannons, a reconstructed bunker, and the Chalmette Monument, which honors the battle's fallen soldiers, create a sense of history underscored by the collection of battlefield memorabilia housed in the visitor center. Also on the grounds is the Chalmette National Cemetery, which holds the bodies of 14,000 Union soldiers who died during the Civil War (as well as the bodies of American soldiers from every subsequent American war). Oddly enough, only one combatant from the Battle of New Orleans rests here. To see the park, give yourself at least an hour, plus 30 to 60 minutes to get to and from the park.

See map p. 170. 8606 W. Saint Bernard Hwy., Chalmette (about 7 miles down river from New Orleans). ☎ 504-281-0510. No public transportation available. A taxi from the French Quarter costs about $15 each way for 1 or 2 people (add $1 for each additional person). Admission: free. Parking: free. Open: Daily 9 a.m.–5 p.m.

Musée Conti Wax Museum
French Quarter

The climate control here makes this a good place to escape from the heat. As you'd expect, you see the requisite Haunted Dungeon with its monsters and scenes from well-known horror tales. You also find a large section devoted to Louisiana legends such as Andrew Jackson, Marie Laveau, Napoleon Bonaparte, Huey Long, Pete Fountain, Louis Armstrong, and even a Mardi Gras Indian. Allow 30 to 60 minutes, unless you're procrastinating to beat the heat.

See map p. 174. 917 Conti St., near the corner of Burgundy. ☎ 800-233-5405 or 504-581-1993. http://get-waxed.com. Admission: $6.75 adults, $6.25 seniors (older than 62), $5.75 children 4–17, free for children under 4. Parking: On-street and hourly lots within one block. Wheelchair accessible. Open: Mon–Sat 10 a.m.–5 p.m, Sun noon to 5 p.m.

Rivertown
Kenner

Offering a nice little tourist area along the banks of the Mississippi River, the city of Kenner sits about 10 miles northwest of the French Quarter. A sort of town within a city, Rivertown is a great family spot for visitors, with a multitude of kid-friendly attractions. (*Note:* All the following Rivertown attractions share the same telephone number: ☎ **504-468-7231.**)

✔ Kids love the six working train layouts at the **Louisiana Toy Train Museum** at 519 Williams Blvd.

✔ The planetarium and observatory at the **Freeport McMoRan Daily Living Science Center** (409 Williams Blvd.) is also worth a visit. Shows run at 2 p.m. Tuesday through Friday, with three shows on weekends. On Thursday through Saturday, 7:30 to 10:30 p.m., you can view the night sky.

✔ If your child likes magic, puppet shows, mimes, and stories, visit the **Children's Castle** at 503 Williams Blvd.

✔ Kids, as well as sports fans of all ages, get a kick out of seeing memorabilia and film clips of the New Orleans Saints NFL franchise at the **Saints Hall of Fame** at 415 Williams Blvd.

✔ You can see many animals, as well as a small aquarium, at the **Louisiana Wildlife Museum,** 303 Williams Blvd. The museum also features tales of everyday life from 1750 to 1850 told by people in period costume.

✔ Finally, the **Mardi Gras Museum of Jefferson Parish** (415 Williams Blvd.) caters to those people who didn't come during Mardi Gras, didn't visit Mardi Gras World, or just can't get enough Mardi Gras fun.

☎ *504-468-7231.* www.rivertownkenner.com. *All museums are within a 3-block area and an easy walk from each other. Admission to each: $3 for adults, $2.50 for seniors and children under 12. A multiticket pass is also available at $15 for adults, $11 for seniors, $9 kids (pass doesn't include the Children's Castle). Parking: free. All museums are wheelchair accessible. Open: Tues–Sat 9 a.m.–5 p.m.*

Especially for teens

Most teenagers admit to a fondness for hanging out in that great social organism, the mall. If your teen fits in this category, the **Riverwalk, The Shops at Canal Place,** and **Jax Brewery** shopping centers (see Chapter 12) are good bets for shopping or just hangin' around.

If your kid likes vampires, that ultimate Goth magnet — the cemetery — is almost certainly to attract him or her. The cemeteries of New Orleans are attractions in their own right, filled with elegant statuary, crypts, and tombs, but youngsters find them especially appealing. (For information on guided cemetery tours, see "Fun with the dead: Cemetery tours " at the end of this chapter.) This section lists some popular local haunts.

Lafayette Cemetery No. 1
Garden District

This place may not be as old as St. Louis Cemetery No. 1, but the Lafayette Cemetery No. 1 still features its share of large above-ground tombs. Anne ce fans take note: This cemetery is also the family burial place of the fictional vampire Lestat. The cemetery has figured into many books and films, including the movie version of *Interview with the Vampire*. The famous **Commander's Palace** restaurant sits right across the street from the cemetery. Touring the cemetery alone is unsafe. Only visit here on a guided tour (see the end of this chapter) or in a large group. Allow 30 to 60 minutes.

See map p. 170. 1400 block of Washington Avenue. Admission: free. Wheelchair accessible. Open: Mon–Fri 7:30 a.m.–2:30 p.m., Sat 7:30 a.m. to noon.

Metairie Lawn Cemetery
Metairie

The largest of all New Orleans cemeteries, Metairie is also the youngest (built after the Civil War). You find some of the most amazing tombs in the city here. Pick up a free cassette-tape tour (with player) at the office. Unlike most of the other cemeteries in New Orleans, you can tour the cemetery from your car or walk safely through it. Give yourself an hour.

See map p. 170. 5100 Pontchartrain Blvd. ☎ *504-486-6331. The Canal Streetcar takes you from the French Quarter to the cemeteries at the end of Canal Street. From there, the Metairie Cemetery is only a block or two (ask the driver), but you have to walk several more blocks from the street to the office. Admission: free. Wheelchair accessible. Open daily 8 a.m.–5 p.m.*

New Orleans Pharmacy Museum
French Quarter

Louis Dufilho, the first licensed pharmacist in the United States, opened an apothecary shop here in 1823. The Creole-style town home also served as his residence, and he supposedly grew herbs for his medicines in the courtyard. The museum opened in 1950, and it features lots of voodoo potions, giant syringes, bone saws, leeches, and other medical instruments, as well as a cosmetics counter (old-time pharmacists also manufactured makeup and perfumes). You'll quickly develop an appreciation for modern medicine. Allow 20 to 30 minutes.

See map p. 174. 514 Chartres St. (2 blocks from Bourbon Street). ☎ *504-565-8027.* www.pharmacymuseum.org. *Admission: $5 adults, $4 seniors and students, children under 12 free. Wheelchair accessible. Open: Tues–Sun 10 a.m.–5 p.m.*

St. Louis Cemetery No. 1
French Quarter

Founded in the late 1700s, this "city of the dead" is the oldest extant cemetery in the city and features large tombs, monuments, and smaller, unmarked niches that resemble baker's ovens. People still leave gifts at the tomb of legendary voodoo queen Marie Laveau to pay their respects and perhaps to ask for supernatural aid. Louis the vampire from Anne

Rice's *Vampire Chronicles* has an empty tomb here, and the acid-dropping scene from *Easy Rider* was shot here. Only visit here in a large group or on an organized tour because the neighborhood is in a high-crime district. For this reason (and to avoid the errant ghoul or vampire), come only during daylight. Allow 30 to 60 minutes.

See map p. 174. 400 block of Basin Street (4 blocks from Bourbon Street). ☎ *504-482-5065. Admission: free, but organized tours aren't. Call Save Our Cemeteries at* ☎ *504-525-3377 for information on taking a tour. Wheelchair accessible for the most part, but some spots might pose problems. Open: Mon–Sat 9 a.m.–3 p.m., Sun 9 a.m. to noon.*

Especially for history buffs

Almost all the sights in this chapter have historic value, but here are a few that die-hard History Channel buffs don't want to miss.

1850 House, Lower Pontalba Building
French Quarter

The beautifully restored Pontalba Apartments (as they're locally known) were built in 1849, originally as individual town houses. The Baroness Pontalba built them in an effort to combat the deterioration of the older part of the city. Take a look at the private courtyard, servants' quarters, and huge rooms with their high ceilings, marble fireplaces, and authentic period furniture to get a fascinating look at the lifestyles of the rich and famous, 19th-century style. Allow 15 to 30 minutes.

See map p. 174. 523 St. Ann St. (on Jackson Square). ☎ *800-568-6968 or 504-568-6968.* http://lsm.crt.state.la.us/site/1850ex.htm. *Admission: $3 adults, $2 seniors and students, free for children under 12. Not accessible for wheelchairs. Open: Tues–Sun 9 a.m.–5 p.m. Closed state holidays.*

Beauregard-Keyes House
French Quarter

This lovely house, built in 1826, is named for two of its most famous tenants: Confederate General Pierre Gustave Toutant Beauregard, who resided here after the Civil War, and author Frances Parkinson Keyes, who wrote many of her novels here, including the most famous, *Dinner at Antoine's*. Take a gander at the twin staircases, the Doric columns, and the "raised cottage" architecture, and try to imagine what life was like when this place was a boardinghouse during the Civil War. The house itself isn't wheelchair accessible, but the beautiful garden adjoining the house is. Allot 45 to 75 minutes to peruse the house.

See map p. 174. 1113 Chartres St. (2 blocks from Bourbon Street). ☎ *504-523-7257. Admission: $5 adults, $4 seniors, students, and AAA members, $1.50 children under 13. Open: hourly tours depart Mon–Sat 10 a.m.–3 p.m.*

Confederate Museum
Warehouse District

Billed as the oldest museum in Louisiana, this place has displayed Civil War artifacts since 1891. The memorabilia includes uniforms, photographs, guns, battle flags, swords, and personal belongings of Gen. Robert E. Lee, Gen. P. G. T. Beauregard, and Confederate president Jefferson Davis. The museum houses the second-largest collection of Confederate memorabilia in the United States. A visit to the museum takes about 30 to 60 minutes.

See map p. 177. 929 Camp St. ☎ 504-523-4522. www.confederatemuseum.com. *Take the St. Charles Streetcar to Lee Circle and walk one block to Camp Street. Admission: $5 adults, $4 students and seniors, $2 children under 12. Parking: On-street and hourly lot nearby. Not accessible for wheelchairs. Open: Mon–Sat 10 a.m.–4 p.m.*

Gallier House Museum
French Quarter

Noted architect James Gallier once resided in this house, which people say served as the model for vampires Lestat and Louis's home in Anne Rice's *Vampire Chronicles.* The house was thoroughly modern back in 1857 — it has hot and cold running water and a bathroom. The guided tour gives you insight into mid-19th-century New Orleans life. Allow an hour to explore this modern miracle.

See map p. 174. 1132 Royal St. (1 block from Bourbon Street). ☎ 504-525-5661. Admission: $5 adults, $3 children, free for children under 8. Not accessible for wheelchairs. Open: Mon–Sat 10 a.m.–4 p.m.

Germaine Wells Mardi Gras Museum
French Quarter

This museum, which houses the Mardi Gras gowns worn between 1910 and 1960 by former Arnaud's owner Germaine Wells, sits atop Arnaud's restaurant (see Chapter 10). Give yourself 15 to 20 minutes to peruse the costumes.

See map p. 174. 813 Bienville St. (½ block from Bourbon Street). ☎ 866-230-8892 or 504-523-5433. www.arnauds.com/museum.html. *Admission: free. Not accessible for wheelchairs. Open during restaurant hours.*

Hermann-Grima House
French Quarter

Cooking demonstrations are held in the period kitchen of this 1832 house every Thursday from May through October. The house's interior depicts funeral customs of the time, except during December, when the house gets decorated for a "Creole style" Christmas. Tours cover both the house and the stable. Joint tours of this property and the Gallier House museum are available; call for details. Allow 30 to 60 minutes, or two hours or more for the combined tour.

See map p. 174. 820 St. Louis St. (½ block from Bourbon Street). ☎ *504-525-5661. Admission: $6, $5 seniors and children 8 and older, free for children under 8. Wheelchair accessible, but call ahead so that workers can put out the portable ramp. Open: Mon–Fri 10 a.m.–4 p.m.*

Historic New Orleans Collection
French Quarter

If you want the lowdown on the evolution of New Orleans, visit this complex of buildings (one of which dates from 1792) where you can see art, maps, and original documents from Louisiana's past. The collection's research center provides a treasure trove of research materials. You find the research center in a beautifully restored courthouse and police station at 410 Charles St. The exhibits change periodically. Allow 30 to 60 minutes.

See map p. 174. 533 Royal St. (1 block from Bourbon Street). ☎ *504-523-4662.* www. hnoc.org. *Admission: free. Guided tours cost $4 and are given at 10 a.m., 11 a.m., 2 p.m., and 3 p.m. Wheelchair accessible. Open: Tues–Sat 10 a.m.–4:30 p.m.*

Jackson Barracks Military Museum
Holy Cross

Generals Robert E. Lee and Ulysses S. Grant served here prior to the Civil War; now it serves as headquarters for the Louisiana National Guard. The reason to visit is the military museum, where a chronological history traces the involvement of Louisiana soldiers in major wars and skirmishes from the American Revolution to today. You also see flags, guns, artillery pieces, uniforms, and other military hardware on display among the museum's artifacts. Allot 60 to 90 minutes to see the museum and to get there from the Quarter. *Note:* On April 30, 2004, Jackson Barracks was struck by lightning and the subsequent fire, although limited to the attic, forced the staff to move all historical artifacts to a safe location. Call ahead to ensure the museum has re-opened.

See map p. 170. 6400 St. Claude Ave. ☎ *504-278-8242. Take the St. Claude bus and get off in front of the museum. Admission: free. Parking: free. Wheelchair accessible. Open: Mon–Fri 8 a.m.–4 p.m.*

Lafitte's Blacksmith Shop and Bar
French Quarter

Records verify this building's existence since 1772 though many insist that it's much older and is, in fact, the oldest building in the Mississippi Valley. According to legend, the pirate Jean Lafitte and his brother Pierre used it as a front for their illegal activities, posing as blacksmiths while selling ill-gotten pirate booty (and, some say, slaves). Since 1944, it's been a bar, and was the preferred haunt of Tennessee Williams. Kids can't go inside, but you can get an excellent view of the dark interior through the open doorway. Only budget a couple of minutes here, unless you plan to have a drink or two.

See map p. 174. 941 Bourbon St. ☎ 504-522-9377. Admission: no cover charge. Part of it is not accessible to wheelchairs. Open: daily 11 a.m.–close (no set closing time).

Napoleon House
French Quarter

People claim that Mayor Nicholas Girod's home was offered to the exiled Napoleon Bonaparte as a refuge, but Napoleon died before the scheme got off the ground. Some doubt this tale's veracity, claiming that the building was built after Napoleon's death. Whatever the truth, the building's been trading on this near brush with glory ever since, and it's become a favorite spot of bohemian locals in recent decades. Today, the Napolean House bar and cafe provides patrons with a dark and quiet atmosphere. Unless you want to grab a drink or a bite to eat, only allow yourself a few minutes here. Kids are also welcome.

See map p. 174. 500 Chartres St. (at the corner of Chartres and St. Louis streets, 2 blocks from Bourbon Street and Jackson Square). ☎ 504-524-9752. Admission: no cover. Wheelchair accessible. Open: Daily 11 a.m.–1 a.m.

Old Absinthe House
French Quarter

According to legend, Andrew Jackson and the Lafitte brothers (pirates Jean and Pierre) met in this 1806 building to plan the Battle of New Orleans. The drink for which the bar is named is illegal these days, so the bar serves anisette instead — which tastes like absinthe but, thankfully, doesn't cause brain damage. Stop here for a few minutes to look around, or longer if you're going to drink. Because it's a bar, kids aren't allowed inside.

See map p. 174. 240 Bourbon St. ☎ 504-523-3181. www.oldabsinthehouse.com. *Admission: no cover. Wheelchair accessible. Open: Daily from 9 a.m. till whenever they decide to close!*

Old Ursuline Convent
French Quarter

Some people say this structure is the oldest building in New Orleans and the entire Mississippi Valley, as well as the only surviving building from the French colonial period in what is now the United States. Erected between 1745 and 1752, it was once run by the Sisters of Ursula, who had the first girls-only school in the United States. In 1831, the state assembly met here. Today, it houses a Catholic archive with documents that go back to 1718. Give yourself 60 to 75 minutes to see it all.

See map p. 174. 1100 Chartres St. (2 blocks from Bourbon Street). ☎ **504-529-3040.** *Admission: $5 adults, $4 seniors, $2 students, children under 8 free. Not accessible for wheelchairs. Open: tours run Tues–Fri 10 a.m.–3 p.m. on the hour (closed for lunch at noon); Sat–Sun 11:15 a.m., 1 p.m., and 2 p.m.*

Our Lady of Guadalupe Chapel and International Shrine of St. Jude
French Quarter

Erected in 1826 across the street from St. Louis Cemetery No. 1, Our Lady served as a convenient place to hold funerals for victims of yellow fever and other diseases. Our Lady serves as a shrine to both St. Jude (saint of impossible causes) and a guy called St. Expedite. Legend claims that this saint's statue showed up at the church in a crate, marked only with the word "expedite" stamped on the outside. The name stuck, and today people know him as the saint to whom you pray when you want things in a hurry (I'm not making this up). Allow 15 minutes.

See map p. 174. 411 N. Rampart St. (3 blocks from Bourbon St.). ☎ **504-525-1551.** www.saintjudeshrine.com. *Admission: free. Wheelchair accessible. Open: Daily 7 a.m.–7 p.m.*

Pitot House
Mid-City

James Pitot, the first mayor of incorporated New Orleans, moved this beautiful house in 1810, which was originally built on a different spot in the late 1700s. This excellent example of an 18th-century, West Indies–style plantation home features wide galleries and large columns. Seeing the house takes one to two hours plus transportation time.

See map p. 183. 1440 Moss St. (near City Park). ☎ **504-482-0312.** *Admission: $5 adults, $4 seniors and students, $2 children under 12. Parking: free. The first floor is wheelchair accessible, but the second floor isn't. Open: Wed–Sat 10 a.m.–3 p.m.*

Enjoying the outdoors: Parks and gardens

New Orleans boasts a number of areas of interest to fans of the outdoors. Whether you're looking for spacious parks or impressive gardens, check out these choice selections.

Longue Vue House and Gardens
New Orleans

Natural and formal gardens, gorgeous fountains, and tranquil ponds form the backdrop for this beautiful Greek Revival mansion, which sits at the end of an oak-lined drive just minutes from downtown New Orleans. Inside, savor the beautiful antiques, rice-paper wall coverings, Oriental carpets, and other lovely touches. Families will want to check out the Discovery Garden, a half-acre, interactive garden for children of all ages. A visit here takes one to two hours plus transportation time.

See map p. 170. 7 Bamboo Rd. ☎ 504-488-5488. www.longuevue.com. *Catch the Canal Streetcar at any stop on Canal and get off at the cemeteries; take the Metairie Road bus, get off at Bamboo Road, and walk ½ block. Admission: $10 adults, $9 seniors, $5 children and students; children under 5 free. Parking: free. Wheelchair accessible, though parts of the garden are wild and may be rough going. Open: Mon–Sat 10 a.m.–4:30 p.m., Sun 1 p.m.–5 p.m. Closed most holidays.*

Washington Artillery Park
French Quarter

This spot and Jackson Square have long been two of the most popular places for tourists and young people. Street performers often run through their routines for tips in front of the steps leading to the top of the levee (which double as seats for a small amphitheater). This place had fallen into disrepair for awhile, but the Audubon Institute prettied it up a few years ago by relandscaping the area, reopening the public restrooms, and providing a tourist information center.

Just west of the French Market, along the riverfront. ☎ 504-587-0738. Admission: free. Wheelchair accessible. Open: 9a.m. to dusk.

Woldenberg Riverfront Park
French Quarter

This park, which features almost 20 acres of green grass, open space, and hundreds of trees and shrubs, makes for a nice break along the Mississippi River. This area has historically been the city's promenade; nowadays it stretches from the Moonwalk to the Aquarium of the Americas and features works by popular local artists. At night, or even during the day, take a romantic stroll and watch the many ships sail by.

Riverfront behind the 500 block of Decatur Street. ☎ 504-587-0738. Admission: free. Wheelchair accessible. Open: dawn to 10 p.m.

If you're the sporting (or betting) type

Granted, the Crescent City isn't a sports mecca on the order of, say, Chicago or New York, but it does offer some areas of interest for gamers and fans of major- and minor-league franchises, including the NFL's New Orleans Saints, of course, the city's long-suffering football team, as well as the family favorite New Orleans Zephyrs minor-league baseball club. In 2002, New Orleans officially became the NBA home of the former Charlotte Hornets, salving the deep wound left in the local hoops consciousness when the New Orleans Jazz packed up for Utah back in 1979.

Fair Grounds Race Course
Mid-City

One of the oldest racetracks in the country, this course has hosted Pat Garrett, Frank James (brother of Jesse and a betting commissioner), and

Generals Ulysses S. Grant and George Custer, among others. The racing season runs from Thanksgiving Day to late March. The New Orleans Jazz and Heritage Festival (also known as Jazz Fest) is also held here every year during the last weekend of April and the first weekend of May.

See map p. 183. 1751 Gentilly Blvd., Mid-City (approximately 10 minutes by car from the Central Business District and the French Quarter). ☎ 504-944-5515. www.fgno. com. *Parking: free; valet $4. Admission: during racing season, $4 for the clubhouse, $1 for the grandstand; during the off-season (off-track betting only), $1. Wheelchair accessible. Open: first post time is 12:30 p.m. and last race around 4:37 p.m.*

Harrah's New Orleans Casino
Central Business District

Because gambling is a hot-button issue around here, I'm neither advocating nor condemning it as an attraction, family or otherwise. Nevertheless, this place is *huge,* both in terms of its size and its impact (for good or ill) on the local community. You may want to take a look at it for those reasons alone.

See map p. 177. 512 S. Peters St. ☎ 800-VIP-JAZZ or 504-533-6000. www.harrahs. com/our_casinos/nor. *Parking: Valet and garage parking are available; call the information number for prices and other details. The casino is wheelchair accessible. Open: 24 hours.*

New Orleans Arena
Central Business District

This arena shares many facilities with its neighbor and older sibling, the Superdome, including parking spaces, power, water, and staff. Smaller than the Superdome but larger than other area venues, it hosts sporting events (including some Tulane University basketball home games), concerts, and other touring events. The arena is also home to the New Orleans Hornets NBA team, which relocated from Charlotte at the end of the 2001–02 basketball season.

See map p. 177. 1501 Girod St. (next to the Superdome, even though the street names are different). ☎ 504-587-3663. www.neworleansarena.com. *Wheelchair accessible.*

New Orleans Zephyrs Field
East Jefferson

Although New Orleans doesn't host a major league baseball team, it does have the Zephyrs — the AAA farm team of the Houston Astros. Since their arrival in New Orleans in the 1990s, the Zephyrs have become a popular team among jaded local sports fans.

See map p. 170. 6000 Airline Dr., East Jefferson. ☎ 504-734-5155. www.zephyrs baseball.com *for game times and admission. Located approximately 9 miles from the French Quarter, on the way to the airport. Take the Airline bus and get off by the stadium.*

Mississippi gaming: Riverboat casinos

Harrah's isn't the only craps game in town. You may also want to look into a couple of riverboat casinos in the area:

✔ **Bally's Casino** (1 Stars and Stripes Blvd., about 9 miles northeast of the French Quarter; ☎ **800-57-BALLY** or 504-248-3200; www.ballysno.com). A taxi costs about $18.

✔ **The Boomtown Belle Casino** resides in Harvey (4132 Peters Rd., located about 15 miles due south of the French Quarter; ☎ **504-366-7711**; www.boomtownneworleans.com). The taxi ride costs about $24.

✔ In Kenner, you find the **Treasure Chest Casino** (5050 Williams Blvd., 15 miles northwest of the French Quarter; ☎ **504-443-8000**; www.treasurechestcasino.com). Many locals give this casino the highest marks of the casinos mentioned here. A taxi runs about $24.

Superdome
Central Business District

One of the largest buildings in the world in terms of diameter (680 feet), the Superdome provides a climate-contolled environment for 76,000 New Orleans Saints fans or more than 100,000 concert-goers. The Superdome also hosts trade shows and conventions. As of this writing, tours of the Superdome facility had been suspended as a security measure following the terrorist attacks of September 11, 2001; there are no immediate plans to reinstate them.

See map p. 177. 1500 Poydras. ☎ 504-587-3663; www.superdome.com. Take the Poydras bus and get off in front of the Superdome.

Seeing New Orleans by Guided Tour

To tour or not to tour? That is the question. The answer depends on your idea of a vacation. If you prefer to be independent and take a spontaneous approach, you'll probably be happier doing your own thing. If you enjoy socializing and knowing what to expect, a tour could be exactly what you want. You can get an entertaining overview of the city (or of a specific part of it, such as the French Quarter or the Garden District) by taking a guided tour. Depending on the tour operator you choose, you'll definitely see some good sights, (hopefully) be entertained by your guide, and discover a thing or two.

Bear in mind, that as often as not your tour will offer more entertainment value than historical significance. I mention some exceptions in this chapter, but most tours here are Show Biz, baby. They all mean well, and most of them even have their facts right, but you'll also get plenty of drama, intrigue, history, and innuendo — New Orleans's rich history more than holds its own with daytime soaps.

Nevertheless, tours are still a lot of fun and a nice way to meet other people. They can also provide the perfect compromise for those days when you're trying to balance your aching feet against the urge to get out and see some sights. General orientation tours and specialty tours make up the two main types of guided tours. You find information on both types in this section.

Time versus info: General orientation tours

If you only have limited time but still want to experience as much as possible, consider a general orientation tour. Riding around the city on a half-hour carriage tour, you get a condensed New Orleans history lesson, find out about the local architecture, locate the good clubs, and see the attractions. However, general information is all that you'll get. Walking tours and bus tours may take a little longer, but with a thorough guide, you can walk away feeling like you're in the know.

Cooling off with a bus tour

If you can't take the heat, a bus tour — where you can see the sights without leaving the air conditioning — is just your cup of iced tea. Aside from seeing the whole city, you can also take a tour that goes outside of town to plantations or swamps. Licensed guides narrate these tours, and buses come variously equipped with TVs, VCRs, and DVDs, stereo sound, bathrooms, cellphones, and equipment for travelers with disabilities. (If a particular amenity is important to you, make sure to ask for the appropriate bus ahead of time.)

Help! I've been de-toured

If you're interested in taking a tour, keep your eyes open. Some hotel concierges have been known to take kickbacks from certain tour operators to steer business exclusively to them. Obviously, not every concierge is on the take, but your best bet would be to book any tours directly through the operator; no reputable operator will force you to go through a third party.

If you can't find sufficient tour information at your hotel, call or visit the **State Office of Tourism** (529 St. Ann St., right on Jackson Square; ☎ **504-568-5661**). Aside from offering a multitude of booklets, brochures, and other such material, the staff also has someone from the New Orleans Convention and Visitor's Bureau on hand to give you the straight dope on tours and attractions, and to steer you toward a reputable tour that's right for your budget, needs, or time frame. For more information on tourist offices, see Chapter 8.

One of the oldest and most reliable tour companies, **New Orleans Tours** (☎ 504-592-0560) offers city and neighborhood tours by bus, as well as riverboat cruises, swamp tours, plantation tours, walking tours, nightlife tours, jazz tours, and combination tours. For more options, check out these other tour companies as well:

- ✔ **Dixieland Tours** (☎ 800-489-8747)
- ✔ **Gray Line** (☎ 800-535-7786 or 504-569-1401)
- ✔ **Hotard Coaches** (☎ 504-944-0253)

Strolling the Quarter

Because the French Quarter is the oldest and arguably most interesting part of New Orleans, most tourists focus on this area. No large buses are allowed in the Quarter (though you will see smaller buses and vans), so walking is your best option for getting around.

Strolling around the French Quarter on your own is the best way to see the area. Traveling on your own gives you the freedom to linger in a pastry shop or park, stop to watch street entertainers, poke your head in all the cute stores you find, admire the local architecture, or follow your nose into off-the-beaten-path nooks and crannies. Chapter 13 lists several itineraries for walking tours that you can take on your own. If you still feel like you want to bring someone along to tell you what you're seeing, contact **Friends of the Cabildo** (☎ 504-523-3939), a nonprofit group that gives two-hour walking tours of the French Quarter. Cost is $10 for adults, $8 for seniors and students, and free for kids 12 and under.

Because the French Quarter is part of the Jean Lafitte National Park, you can also get a free tour from the **National Park Service.** The service offers only one tour each day at 9:30 a.m., and each person must pick up his or her own ticket. The tickets are given out starting at 9 a.m. on a first-come, first-served basis. For more information, stop by the **Visitor's Information Center** at 419 Decatur St. or call ☎ 504-589-2133.

University of New Orleans professor emeritus W. Kenneth Holditch (who really knows his stuff) leads the **Heritage Literary Tours** (732 Frenchmen St., ☎ 504-949-9805). He gives a general tour centered on the literary legacy of the French Quarter (which has played host to a considerable number of famous and colorful writers over the years) as well as a more specialized tour about Tennessee Williams. If you arrange it in advance, he can (probably) design a tour for you around a specific author. He's a character in his own right, and his tours are fun, informative, and loaded with anecdotes. Tours are $20 for adults and $10 for students; call ahead if you have something specific in mind.

Riding in style: Carriage tours

Like bus tours, a carriage tour may or may not be up your alley. Riding through the French Quarter in a mule-drawn carriage certainly gives you a more intimate experience than riding around in a bus with 50 or 60 other name-tag-wearing passengers. It can also be quite romantic with the hypnotic clip-clop of the mules' hooves. A good carriage driver can show you the highlights of the Quarter in just 30 minutes; spend an hour touring, and you'll feel like a native.

 Carriage rides stay in the Quarter, and no one guarantees the veracity of the information you receive. Some drivers are licensed tour guides, though most aren't. Nevertheless, each one has his or her area of expertise. Some have eaten their way through the city, some are historians, and others pride themselves on knowing the location of every bar. One driver may regale you with ghost stories, another may tell you jokes, and a third may not say much. Talk to the driver for a minute and try to gauge his or her personality before hopping in.

Most of the carriages in the Quarter line up along Decatur Street at Jackson Square and at carriage stands at the corners of Royal and St. Louis, Bourbon and Conti, or Bourbon and Toulouse. Also keep your eyes open for carriages cruising throughout the Quarter or parked on a corner waiting for a fare.

You see two types of carriages: the large hard-topped, bus-like models that you share with anybody else that comes along, and the smaller convertible models that you hire individually for your party. Generally, carriages have abandoned the per-person rates, charging $50 for a half-hour ride and $105 for an hour (the latter price includes picking you up from your hotel).

 If your tour lasts less than 30 minutes, your driver is giving you a "zip tour." If this is the case, confront the driver and find out if the tour can be extended. If the driver doesn't comply, complain to the driver's boss. If the driver refuses to give you the boss's name, write down the driver's name (if you know it), the company name, and the carriage number (on its side or back), and call the city's **Taxicab Bureau** (☎ **504-565-6272**) to complain.

If you want a carriage to pick you up, call one of the following licensed carriage companies:

- ✔ **Good Old Days Buggies** (☎ **504-523-0804**)
- ✔ **Mid-City Carriages** (☎ **504-581-4415**)
- ✔ **Old Quarter Tours** (☎ **504-944-0446**)
- ✔ **Royal Carriages** (☎ **504-943-8820**)

Filling a niche: Specialty tours

Specialty tours are good bets if you're deeply interested in a particular subject. Although anyone can parrot the touristy info you'll get on a basic orientation tour, you'll more likely sound like an expert to family and friends back home if you take a specialty tour.

Gay New Orleans

The Bienville Foundation's **Gay Heritage Tour** (☎ 504-945-6789) is a 2½-hour tour that shows you the city from a gay-friendly perspective. You explore the Quarter and hear about such figures as Tennessee Williams, Clay Shaw, and Ellen DeGeneres. Robert Batson, the knowledgeable and personable tour guide, also explains the importance of various gay landmarks. The $20 tour leaves from Alternatives (a gay-targeted gift shop at 909 Bourbon St.); days and times vary seasonally (the tour doesn't run during August or December), so be sure to call for information.

Discovering New Orleans's African American heritage

If you want to delve into New Orleans's history of Africans and African Americans, contact **African American Heritage Tours** (☎ 504-288-3478). Tours include trips to plantations, Xavier University (the first Black Catholic university in the United States), and a narrative on historic sites such as Liberty Bank, which was founded by African Americans.

Hepcats unite: Jazz tours

Photographer for the *Times-Picayune* and well-known local jazz historian John McCusker leads **John McCusker's Cradle of Jazz Tour** (☎ 504-282-3583). He takes visitors on a bargain-priced ($25), 2½-hour van tour every Saturday morning that traces the history of New Orleans jazz. He points out the spots where jazz was born, where it matured, and where performers such as Louis Armstrong were born or played their music. You must make reservations in advance.

Fun with the dead: Cemetery, vampire, and ghost tours

Many cemeteries simply aren't safe unless you're with an organized group. I strongly advise against wandering through any cemetery (especially St. Louis No. 2) alone or without an official tour.

The members of **Save Our Cemeteries** (☎ 504-525-3377), a nonprofit organization, do more to restore and maintain New Orleans's cemeteries than anyone else. Their tours are a good crash course for newcomers to the subject.

Fred Hatfield (☎ 504-891-4862), a semiretired native New Orleanian, has spent his whole life in the neighborhood of **Lafayette Cemetery No. 1.** Consequently, he's done extensive research on the people buried there, as any good neighbor would do. His combination walking tours of the Garden District and Lafayette No. 1 take about two hours and cost $14 per person; he also gives individual tours of the cemetery for $9. All tours require a minimum of four people. He's usually home, so give him a call.

Many visitors have raved about the wealth and quality of information they receive from **Historic New Orleans Walking Tours** (☎ **504-947-2120;** www.tourneworleans.com). Here you can find a number of French Quarter tours, including tours for history and "mystique," as well as the following cemetery tours:

✔ The **Cemetery/Voodoo Tour** takes you to the tomb of Marie Laveau and to an actual voodoo temple. You get the straight facts about voodoo's West African religious roots and its modern-day practitioners. In short, it's long on the authentic and short on the wink-wink-nudge-nudge sensationalism you may get elsewhere. You also see other famous burial sites and hear the stories of some legendary locals.

✔ The **Garden District/Cemetery Tour** tours this historic neighborhood pointing out rocker Trent Reznor's castle, Indianapolis Colts quarterback Peyton Manning's boyhood home, and Anne Rice's former home.

✔ **Haunted History Tours** (☎ **504-861-2727;** www.hauntedhistory tours.com) offers vampire tours and tours of the cemeteries. You can also opt for the Haunted History Tour itself, which details various ghost stories and legends in the Quarter. The tour is entertaining, but don't put too much stock in the "facts."

✔ **Magic Walking Tours** (☎ **504-588-9693**) even let's you go on a vampire hunt. If you're really lucky, your guide may even let you carry the wooden stake and mallet.

No petting the gators: Swamp tours

Swamp tours can be a great deal of fun. You see some incredible scenery and wildlife, you're out on the water, and you get a feel for what it's like to live out on the bayous. Your guide may call alligators up to the boat for a little snack of chicken, but be careful to keep your hands inside the boat because gators can't always tell the difference.

You can find plenty of swampland within the metro area worth exploring, but the really isolated swamp areas lie three hours outside the city.

✔ **Cypress Swamp Tours** (☎ **504-581-4501**) tour the Bayou Segnette area (near Westwego, on the West Bank across the Crescent City Connection) for $22 per adult and $12 for children under 12.

✔ **Dr. Paul Wagner,** a well-known swamp ecologist and a national conservationist, gives excellent tours of the Honey Island Swamp area. His **Honey Island Swamp Tours** (☎ **504-242-5877** or 985-641-1769) cost $20 per person.

✔ **Gator Swamp Tours** (☎ **800-875-4287** or 504-484-6100) also have good tours of the Honey Island Swamp, approximately 40 minutes east of New Orleans; they charge $20 per adult and $10 for children under 12.

 ✔ **Jean Lafitte Swamp Tours** (☎ **800-445-4109** or 504-587-1719) tour
  the Bayou aux Carpes, a patch of private land flush with all sorts
  of wildlife near the intercoastal canal, just 20 minutes from the
  Crescent City Connection; cost is $24 for adults and $13 for children under 12.

Ask when calling about the length of each tour, whether the tours are
private or public, and how many people are allowed on one tour. You
don't want one that's too crowded.

Other tour companies operate in the Atchafalaya Basin, a vast swamp
about 2½ hours west of New Orleans, between Baton Rouge and Lafayette.
These include **McGee's Landing** (☎ **800-445-6681** or 318-228-2384) and
bilingual (English/French) tours with **Angelle's Atchafalaya Basin Swamp
Tours** (☎ **337-228-8567**). The basin is pretty big, so the good tours take
more time; you may want to budget your afternoon around it.

Shopping for old stuff: Antique tours

Macon Riddle's Antique Tours (☎ **504-899-3027;** www.neworleans
antiquing.com) provides an enthusiastic and educational way to see
New Orleans's antique districts. Macon Riddle picks you up at your
hotel, takes you on a customized antique shopping tour, and even makes
lunch reservations for you. She even takes care of shipping your antique
finds home.

Dinner on the water: Riverboat cruises

Riverboat cruises are extremely popular in New Orleans, as you may
expect. Gambling cruises, however, are a thing of the past (riverboat
casinos rarely leave the dock, because most gamblers want to be able to
come and go at will). You can still find harbor cruises, dinner and dancing cruises, river cruises, and combination cruises where you also visit
the Audubon Zoo or Chalmette Battlefield. The riverboats come in several different forms: steam- or diesel-powered, with their paddle wheels
on the side or on the stern, and so forth. From personal experience, I
can tell you that standing at the railing of a riverboat at night, watching
the water flow, is a very romantic experience. Companies and boats
offering riverboat tours include the following:

 ✔ **Creole Queen Paddle Wheel Tours** (☎ **800-445-4109** or 504-524-
  0814)

 ✔ **John James Audubon** (☎ **800-233-BOAT** or 504-586-8777)

 ✔ **New Orleans Steamboat Co.** (☎ **800-233-BOAT** or 504-586-8777)

Chapter 12

Shopping the Local Stores

In This Chapter

▶ Getting the lowdown on major shopping areas

▶ Perusing the big-name stores

▶ Browsing at the market

▶ Venturing into the different neighborhoods

*V*acation shopping is an odd thing. You'd think that spending yet *more* money is the last thing a vacationer would want to do. But for whatever reason, whether trying to find that perfect memento of their trip or suddenly deciding to redecorate their home with antiques, vacationers *shop* — a *lot*.

This chapter explores shopping in New Orleans from a couple different angles. It runs through the big-name stores, neighborhood markets, and the major shopping areas, some of which feature antiques shops and art galleries.

Surveying the Scene

New Orleans has a nice advantage over other American cities for the shopping vacationer: As an international port, the city has access to a variety of imported items. If you can name it, you can probably find it in New Orleans. Selection isn't limited to things such as home furnishings, pottery, and designer clothing — also on hand is quite a bit of imported fine jewelry. Don't neglect the locally crafted jewelry, however. Some local designers, such as Mignon Faget, work with such innovation and creativity that their shops seem more like art galleries.

If you're shopping for antiques or contemporary art, you can find plenty on Royal and Magazine streets. Royal Street boasts the finest, most expensive goods; Magazine Street promises more bargain-basement finds. Also in that area, and on Julia Street, are the city's art galleries. (I cover these areas individually later in this chapter.)

New Orleans Shopping

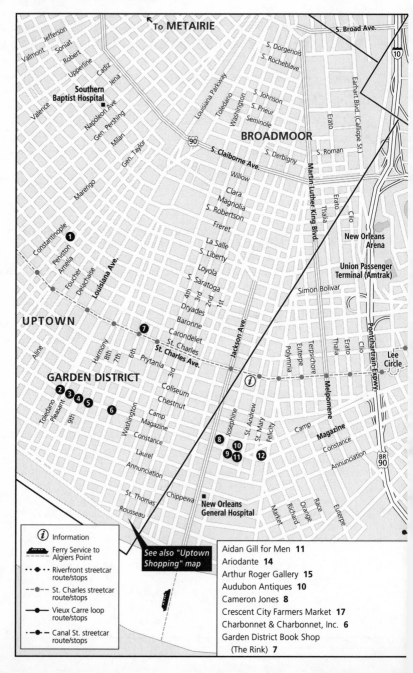

See also "Uptown Shopping" map

ⓘ Information

Ferry Service to Algiers Point

Riverfront streetcar route/stops

St. Charles streetcar route/stops

Vieux Carre loop route/stops

Canal St. streetcar route/stops

Aidan Gill for Men **11**
Ariodante **14**
Arthur Roger Gallery **15**
Audubon Antiques **10**
Cameron Jones **8**
Crescent City Farmers Market **17**
Charbonnet & Charbonnet, Inc. **6**
Garden District Book Shop
　(The Rink) **7**

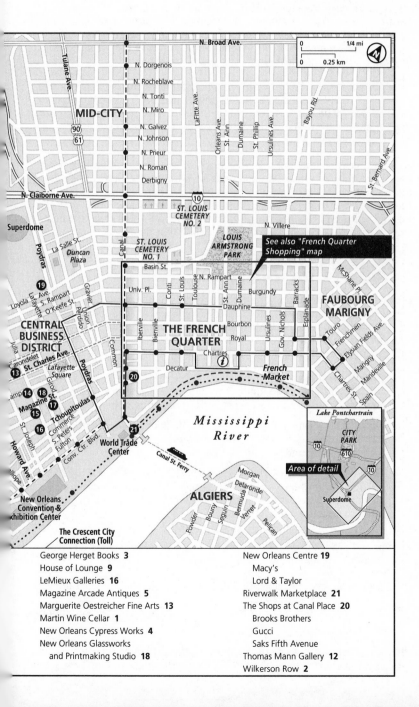

Shop hours vary, but, on average, most are open Monday through Saturday from 10 a.m. to 5 p.m., with quite a few shops open later on Saturday night and Sunday afternoon. The French Quarter's souvenir shops, not missing a trick, often remain open until 11 p.m. every day. If you have a particular store in mind, call ahead for hours.

A word on sales tax: Weigh your options carefully if buying a large, expensive item. Because sales tax in New Orleans is 9 percent, you may save money by having the item shipped to you at home. Of course you pay for shipping and handling instead of the sales tax, but the difference may be in your favor.

A program called **Louisiana Tax-Free Shopping** benefits shoppers who hail from other countries. If you aren't from the United States, look for store windows with this program's logo; these merchants give you a tax-refund voucher that you can cash in, either at the airport or by mail. To take advantage of this program, you need a valid foreign passport and round-trip airline ticket. Call ☎ 504-568-5323 for details.

Checking Out the Big Names

Because corporate America has made inroads here during the last half-century, local homegrown institutions have found it difficult to compete with the deep pockets of the big-name corporations. As a result, New Orleans is now almost exclusively the province of the big-name corporate chains. Here's a list of the big players:

- ✔ **Brooks Brothers:** The Shops at Canal Place, 300 block of Canal Street (☎ 504-522-4200; www.brooksbrothers.com); open Monday to Saturday from 10 a.m. to 7 p.m., and Sunday from noon to 6 p.m.

- ✔ **Gucci:** The Shops at Canal Place, 300 block of Canal Street (☎ 504-524-5544; www.gucci.com); open Monday to Saturday from 10 a.m. to 7 p.m., and Sunday from noon to 6 p.m.

- ✔ **Lord & Taylor:** New Orleans Centre, 1400 Poydras St. (☎ 504-581-5673; www.lordandtaylor.com); open Monday to Friday from 10 a.m. to 8 p.m., Saturday from 9 a.m. to 6 p.m., and Sunday from noon to 6 p.m.

- ✔ **Macy's:** New Orleans Centre, 1400 Poydras St. (☎ 800-456-2297 or 504-592-5985; www.macys.com); open Monday to Saturday from 10 a.m. to 9:30 p.m., and Sunday from 11 a.m. to 7 p.m.

- ✔ **Saks Fifth Avenue:** The Shops at Canal Place, 300 block of Canal Street (☎ 504-524-2200; www.saksfifthavenue.com); open Monday to Saturday from 10 a.m. to 7 p.m., and Sunday from noon to 6 p.m.

These big-name stores, of course, need a place to house their wares, and New Orleans offers plenty of alternatives for shoppers hoping to meet all their shopping needs under one roof. In addition to the Canal Place Shopping Center (see the "Canal Street" section, later in this chapter), the following shopping areas are good choices for a little mall-browsing:

- ✔ **Jackson Brewery:** Just across from Jackson Square (600 Decatur St.; ☎ 504-566-7245; www.jacksonbrewery.com), the old **Jax Brewery** is now a complex of shops, cafes, restaurants, and entertainment spots. Look for gourmet and Cajun and Creole foodstuffs, fashions, toys, hats, crafts, pipes, posters, and souvenirs. You also find a huge **Virgin Megastore** (☎ 504-671-8988) and for pet lovers, **Woof & Whiskers** (☎ 504-568-0065). The Brewery hours are Sunday to Thursday from 10 a.m. to 9 p.m., and Friday to Saturday from 10 a.m. to 10 p.m. Note that many shops in the Brewery close at 5:30 or 6 p.m.

- ✔ **New Orleans Centre:** This place (1400 Poydras St.; ☎ 504-568-0000; www.neworleanscentre.com) offers upscale department stores, such as **Lord & Taylor** and **Macy's,** plus three levels of specialty shops, restaurants, and a huge food court. Add on the fancy office tower and you get plenty of foot traffic in this spacious environment. Hours are Monday to Saturday from 10 a.m. to 8 p.m., and Sunday from noon to 6 p.m.

- ✔ **Riverwalk Marketplace:** Actually a covered mall running along the river from Poydras Street to the Convention Center (1 Poydras St.; ☎ 504-522-1555; www.riverwalkmarketplace.com), this is a popular venue that's also quite atmospheric. Take a break from shopping and just watch the river roll by or the occasional free entertainment. Among the more than 100 specialty shops are such big hitters as **Eddie Bauer, The Sharper Image,** and **Banana Republic**, plus several eateries.

Going to Market

New Orleans's premier street market is the French Market (☎ 504-522-2621), a complex of shops that begins on Decatur Street across from Jackson Square. In the market, you can find candy, cookware, fashions, crafts, toys, New Orleans memorabilia, candles — all manner of goodies. Also in the complex are **Café du Monde** (☎ 504-581-2914) and the **Farmer's Market** and **Flea Market** (☎ 504-596-3420), which are located in the 1200 block of North Peters. Hours are from 10 a.m. to 6 p.m. (Café du Monde is open 24 hours.)

The original **Crescent City Farmers Market** (700 Magazine St.; ☎ 504-861-5898; www.crescentcityfarmersmarket.org) is held every Saturday from 8 a.m. to noon in a parking lot at the corner of Magazine and Girod streets in the Warehouse District. It offers fresh local produce, flowers, cooking demonstrations, and more. Plenty of free, off-street parking is available because it's a Saturday and the meter maids aren't out and about. Depending on where you're staying, you may be able to walk here. Come early for the best selection, or wait for the cooking demonstration at 10 a.m.

Discovering the Best Shopping Neighborhoods

The trick to shopping in New Orleans is knowing where to go. The major shopping areas you want to visit are the French Quarter, the Central Business District, the Warehouse District, and along Magazine Street, both in the Garden District and the Uptown area. The best strategy for shopping in these neighborhoods is to just wander around and see which shops catch your eye. Here is a rundown of the city's best shopping areas and the scoop on what you can find inside.

French Quarter

This section breaks down some of the Quarter's more prominent shopping streets — Bourbon, Decatur, and Royal. But first, I take a quick look at some of the noteworthy shops found elsewhere in the Quarter.

- ✔ **Animal Art** (617 Chartres St.; ☎ 504-529-4407) is for animal lovers because it features fine furniture, paintings, ceramics, and more, all depicting its namesake.

- ✔ **Chi-Wa-Wa Ga-Ga** (37 French Market Place; ☎ 504-581-4242) is the small store for small dogs, offering off-the-rack clothes, costumes, and accessories for your (or your friend's) well-dressed pooch.

- ✔ **Faulkner House Books** (624 Pirates Alley; ☎ 504-524-2940) is in the one-time home of Nobel Prize–winner William Faulkner, who wrote his early works *Mosquitoes* and *Soldiers' Pay* here. The one room (and hallway) of this private home may be small in comparison to chain bookstores, but it boasts possibly the finest selection per square foot of any bookstore on the planet. The stock tends to be highly collectible and literary, including a large collection of first-edition Faulkners and rare and first-edition classics by other authors.

- ✔ **Kaboom** (901 Barracks St.; ☎ 504-529-5780) is a used-book store that primarily stocks fiction, but with a little digging, you can turn up some real gems.

- ✔ **Latin's Hand** (1025 N. Peters St.; ☎ 504-529-5254) features hammocks, dresses, jackets, sandals, and leather goods, all imported from places such as Brazil, El Salvador, Guatemala, Bolivia, and Mexico.

- ✔ **Tower Records** (408 N. Peters St.; ☎ 504-529-4411) is part of the well-known national chain, but this location distinguishes itself with an extensive collection of local and regional music.

French Quarter Shopping

A Gallery for Fine
  Photography **4**
Animal Art **12**
Beckham's Bookshop **6**
Bergen Galleries **14**
Body Hangings **22**
The Bottom of the Cup
  Tearoom **18**
Bryant Galleries **3**
Café du Monde **20**
Chi-na-wa Ga-Ga **25**
Diane Genre Oriental Art
  and Antiques **1**
Farmer's Market
  & Flea Market **26**
Faulkner House Books **19**
Importicos **16**
Jackson Brewery **21**
Kaboom **29**

Kiel's Antiques **9**
Latin's Hand **24**
Le Petit Soldier Shop **11**
The Little Toy Shoppe **23**
Louisiana Music Factory **5**
Manheim Galleries **10**
Marie Laveau's House
  of Voodoo **15**
Rock and Roll Records
  & Collectibles **27**
Rodrigue Studios **13**
Rothschild's Antiques
  (241 Royal) **2**
  (321 Royal) **8**
Sigle's Antiques
  & Metalcraft **28**
Three Dog Bakery **17**
Tower Records **7**

ⓘ Information
—●— Canal St. streetcar
  route/stops
●—●—● Riverfront streetcar
  route/stops
—●— Vieux Carre loop
  route/stops

Bourbon Street

If you're looking for silly slogan T-shirts or the usual trinkets and souvenirs, check out Bourbon Street. Of course, most of the stuff is of the "My Grandma Went to Bourbon Street and All I Got Was This Stupid T-Shirt" variety, and if you're seen buying that kind of stuff, forget about trying to blend in: You've just slapped the scarlet "T" (for tourist) on your shirt, and it ain't coming off. (On the plus side, it's one of the few places in the world you can window-shop while carrying a large plastic cup full of booze.)

If you're looking for something a little different, **Marie Laveau's House of Voodoo** (739 Bourbon St., ☎ **504-581-3751**), a popular attraction in the French Quarter, is a good place to find a voodoo doll (though hopefully you don't need one). The resident psychic and palm reader can give you a reading as well.

Canal Street

Longtime fans of and visitors to New Orleans may remember when Canal Street was *the* place to shop. With the return of the Canal Streetcar, look for increased commercial ventures, shops, and restaurants along the route. For now, **The Shops at Canal Place,** located at the foot of Canal Street (365 Canal St.; ☎ **504-522-9200** or 504-581-5400), represents the extent of the Canal Street shopping experience — but it's a plush one, with polished marble floors, a landscaped atrium, fountains, and pools. This mall features more than 50 shops. It's open Monday to Wednesday from 10 a.m. to 6 p.m., Thursday from 10 a.m. to 8 p.m., Friday and Saturday from 10 a.m. to 7 p.m., and Sunday from noon to 6 p.m.

Decatur Street

One of the French Quarter's main drags, Decatur Street runs along the river and gets a lot of foot traffic. Although the main attraction is the **Jax Brewery** (which I mention more in depth in "Checking Out the Big Names" section earlier in this chapter), you also find a number of worthwhile shops for serious collectors and enthusiasts. Among the best are the following:

- ✔ **Beckham's Bookshop** (228 Decatur St.; ☎ **504-522-9875**) is a real treasure trove for book and music lovers alike, with two levels of old editions, rare secondhand books, and thousands of classical LPs. You may get lost wandering the musty, Byzantine aisles.

- ✔ **Body Hangings** (835 Decatur St.; ☎ **800-574-1823** or 504-524-9856), in case you're wondering, refers to cloaks, which are this store's specialty. A selection of capes and scarves is also available.

- ✔ **The Little Toy Shoppe** (900 Decatur St.; ☎ **504-522-6588**) presents strikingly beautiful dolls as well as wooden toys from Germany, stuffed animals, tea sets, and miniature cars and trucks.

✔ **Louisiana Music Factory** (210 Decatur St.; ☎ **504-586-1094;** www. louisianamusicfactory.com) offers a large selection of regional music, including Cajun, zydeco, R&B, jazz, blues, and gospel. The Factory also sells reference books, posters, and T-shirts, and occasionally provides live in-store performances and beer bashes. More than just a record store, it's an integral part of the city's music community.

✔ **Rock and Roll Records & Collectibles** (1214 Decatur St.; ☎ **504-561-5683**), despite its name, has a lot more than just rock-and-roll on sale. The owners claim to have the biggest and best collection of vinyl anywhere, and that includes 45s and 78s. Indeed, the collection even takes up floor space. There's no telling what you can find here.

Royal Street

Along Royal Street you can find many fine-art galleries and shops selling antiques, jewelry, perfume, and candy as well as shops for coin and stamp collectors.

First, check out these general-interest sites:

✔ **The Bottom of the Cup Tearoom** (732 Royal St.; ☎ **504-523-1204**) is supposedly the oldest tearoom in the United States. You can have someone read your tarot cards or tea leaves or build your astrological chart; you can also get a reading from "pure clairvoyant psychics." I can't vouch for their accuracy, but they're sure a lot cheaper than those 1-900 psychic lines. The store offers books, jewelry, crystal balls, tarot cards, crystals, and healing wands.

✔ **Importicos** (736 Royal St.; ☎ **504-523-3100**) features an international selection of hand-crafted silver jewelry; pottery; textiles; leather, wood, stone, and metal items; and teak, mahogany, and wrought-iron furniture.

✔ **Le Petit Soldier Shop** (528 Royal St.; ☎ **504-523-7741**), as its name implies, sells miniature soldiers made by local artists. Armies represent a span from ancient Greece up to Desert Storm, and you can find quite a few miniatures that resemble major figures in military history, such as Eisenhower, Grant, Lee, Hitler, and Napoleon. Also available is a good-size collection of medals and decorations.

✔ **Three Dog Bakery** (827 Royal St.; ☎ **504-525-2253**) makes pastries and other treats for pooches. My dogs love this place; Desoto drools over the Big Scary Kitty cookie, Darby begs for Jump 'n' Sit Bits, and Shelby just comes for the belly rubs from the friendly staff.

For antiques, check out these places:

✔ **Diane Genre Oriental Art and Antiques** (431 Royal St.; ☎ **504-595-8945**) is a nice change of pace if you've looked at too many European antiques. It offers East Asian porcelains, 18th-century Japanese woodblock prints, and Chinese and Japanese textiles, scrolls, screens, engravings, and lacquers.

- ✔ **Kiel's Antiques** (325 Royal St.; ☎ 504-522-4552) was established in 1899 and is still a family business. It houses a considerable collection of 18th- and 19th-century French and English furniture, chandeliers, jewelry, and other items.

- ✔ **Manheim Galleries** (403–409 Royal St.; ☎ 504-568-1901) showcases a huge collection of Continental, English, and Oriental furnishings, along with porcelain, jade, silver, and fine paintings.

- ✔ **Rothschild's Antiques** (241 and 321 Royal St.; ☎ 504-523-5816 or 504-523-2281) isn't only an antiques store but also a full-service jeweler. Look for antique and custom-made jewelry among the more standard offerings of antique silver, marble mantels, porcelain, and English and French furnishings.

- ✔ **Sigle's Antiques & Metalcraft** (935 Royal St.; ☎ 504-522-7647) is the place if you're a big fan of the lacy ironwork that distinguishes French Quarter balconies. Sigle's offers some of its antique ironwork already converted into more-packable household items such as planters.

If you're in the mood for fine art, visit these galleries:

- ✔ **A Gallery for Fine Photography** (241 Chartres St.; ☎ 504-568-1313; www.agallery.com) offers rare photographs and books from the 19th and 20th centuries, with an emphasis on New Orleans and Southern history and contemporary culture. The owner calls it "the only museum in the world that's for sale"; I agree.

- ✔ **Bergen Galleries** (730 Royal St.; ☎ 800-621-6179 or 504-523-7882; www.bergenputmangallery.com) boasts the South's largest selection of posters and prints. It also specializes in New Orleans, Louisiana Cajun, and African American fine art. The service here is extremely personable.

- ✔ **Bryant Galleries** (316 Royal St.; ☎ 800-844-1994 or 504-525-5584; www.bryantgalleries.com) represents a number of American and European artists. Look for glasswork, graphic art, and bronzes depicting jazz themes. The staff is quite friendly here.

- ✔ **Rodrigue Studios** (721 Royal St.; ☎ 504-581-4244) features the famous Blue Dog by Cajun artist George Rodrigue, who began painting blue portraits of his late dog for a children's book in 1984. Now his work has achieved international renown, hanging in galleries in Munich and Yokohama. Take a trip here to see this canine pop icon in home territory.

Warehouse District

Julia Street, from Camp Street down to the river and along some of its side streets, is your best bet for contemporary art galleries in New

Orleans (an area known as the Arts District). Of course, some of the works are a bit pricey, but collectors can get some good deals and casual viewers can take in lots of fine art. While on Julia Street be sure to check out these places:

- ✔ **Ariodante Contemporary Craft Gallery** (535 Julia St.; ☎ 504-524-3233) features hand-crafted furniture, glass, ceramics, jewelry, and decorative accessories.

- ✔ **Arthur Roger Gallery** (432 Julia St.; ☎ 504-522-1999) has played a large role in nurturing the local art community and developing ties to the New York art scene. Regional exhibits have shared this space with more far-flung shows, and the gallery represents a number of prominent artists.

- ✔ **LeMieux Galleries** (332 Julia St.; ☎ 504-522-5988) showcases the work of local and regional craftspeople as well as contemporary artists from Louisiana and the Gulf Coast.

- ✔ **Marguerite Oestreicher Fine Arts** (726 Julia St.; ☎ 504-581-9253) has consistently been a showcase for emerging artists, with a focus on contemporary painting, sculpture, and photography.

Magazine Street, Garden District, and Uptown

Running from Canal Street to Audubon Park, Magazine Street offers 6 miles of almost 150 shops, some in 19th-century brick storefronts, others in quaint, cottage-like buildings. Overall, it's a very unique, funky stretch; the 5400 and 5500 blocks (between Jefferson Avenue and Joseph Street) are my favorite stretch. Because it's a less ritzy area of the city, you can usually find some bargains here. Look for antiques, art galleries, boutiques, crafts, fashion, and custom-designed furniture.

 I'm not pointing a finger at any of the antiques dealers or shops here, but in general, it helps to be discerning when looking at antiques. You never know; someone may have passed off an everyday household item as a priceless family heirloom. As the song says, you better shop around. Some places ask entirely too much money for their wares when a little digging can find you something very similar at a much more reasonable price.

Following are some noteworthy shops on Magazine Street, from art galleries to antiques stores and more:

- ✔ **Aidan Gill for Men** (2026 Magazine St.; ☎ 504-587-9090) carries everything to maintain a man's good looks, from handmade shaving gear to luxurious creams and soaps as well as timeless fashion accessories. Owner Aidan Gill and his staff also provide hairstyling and old-fashioned hot-towel shaves.

- ✔ **Audubon Antiques** (2025 Magazine St.; ☎ 504-581-5704) stocks everything from curios to authentic antique treasures spread out over two floors.

Uptown Shopping

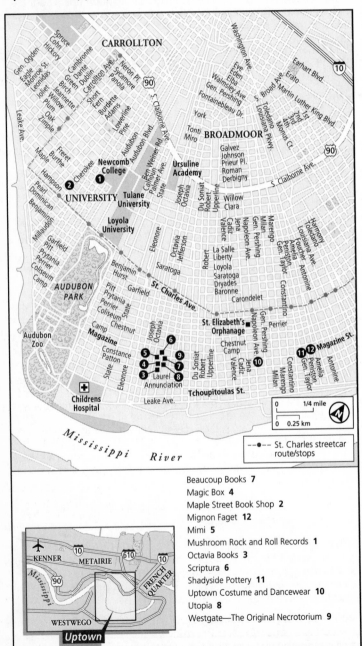

Beaucoup Books **7**
Magic Box **4**
Maple Street Book Shop **2**
Mignon Faget **12**
Mimi **5**
Mushroom Rock and Roll Records **1**
Octavia Books **3**
Scriptura **6**
Shadyside Pottery **11**
Uptown Costume and Dancewear **10**
Utopia **8**
Westgate—The Original Necrotorium **9**

- **Beaucoup Books** (5414 Magazine St.; ☎ 504-895-2663) is another popular independent bookseller with a strong emphasis on local and regional reference books plus a children's room. Ask owner Mary Price Dunbar for her picks.

- **Cameron Jones** (2127 Magazine St.; ☎ 504-524-3119) is a surprise respite from heavy old antiques, with its eclectic, contemporary collection of home accent pieces, furniture, custom-designed rugs, original art works, unusual lighting fixtures, and soothing wall fountains.

- **Charbonnet & Charbonnet, Inc.** (2728 Magazine St.; ☎ 504-891-9948) is the place to go for country pine; they have beautiful English and Irish pieces on display, and custom furnishings are also built on site.

- **Garden District Book Shop** (2727 Prytania St.; ☎ 504-895-2266) is a popular independent bookstore beloved by local fans. Anne Rice has used it as a starting point for a number of her book-signing tours; the store usually keeps a number of signed Rice books on hand. However, you can find much more.

- **George Herget Books** (3109 Magazine St.; ☎ 504-891-5595) has more than 20,000 rare and used books on any subject you can think of.

- **House of Lounge** (2044 Magazine St.; ☎ 504-671-8300) offers a sexy, sophisticated collection of designer lingerie and loungewear for women and smoking jackets and more for men. Erin Brockovich couldn't resist spending hundreds of dollars when she stopped by.

- **Magazine Arcade Antiques** (3017 Magazine St.; ☎ 504-895-5451) carries an excellent selection of 18th- and 19th-century furnishings as well as music boxes, dollhouse miniatures, porcelain, antique toys, and a host of other treasures. Budget a fair amount of time for this place.

- **Magic Box** (5508 Magazine St.; ☎ 504-899-0117) is a treasure trove of toys for kids of all ages.

- **Maple Street Book Shop** (7523 Maple St.; ☎ 504-866-4916) is quintessentially New Orleans, from its curled and yellowed photo murals to its shotgun home. Founded by her mother more than 40 years ago, daughter Rhoda Faust carries on Maple Street's promise to "Fight the Stupids!" The Walker Percy and Ellen Gilchrist collections are literary eye candy.

- **Martin Wine Cellar** (3827 Baronne St.; ☎ 504-899-7411) carries an expansive selection of wines, spirits, and champagnes for unexpectedly reasonable prices. Also on hand are preserves, coffees, teas, crackers, biscotti, cookies, and cheeses.

- **Mignon Faget** (3801 Magazine St.; ☎ 504-891-2005) features fine jewelry designed by local artist Mignon Faget, whose muses are nature and Louisiana motifs. (I adore the sterling-silver Creole

Cottage Key Ring and the unique Red Bean Tie Tack.) Her gallery also offers home accessories, signature fragrances, stationery, baby clothing, and more.

✔ **Mimi** (5500 Magazine St.; ☎ 504-269-6464) is an upscale women's boutique (in a marvelously restored Arts and Crafts brick building) featuring clothing and accessories designed by Donna Karan, Michael Kors, and other fashion trendsetters.

✔ **Mushroom Rock and Roll Records** (1037 Broadway St.; ☎ 504-866-6065), located on Fraternity Row in the university area in the heart of Uptown, is a hip little place that is good for alternative music. As if that weren't enough, frugal students enjoy the comprehensive collection of used CDs (though they're not arranged in any particular order, so happy digging) and a large selection of T-shirts and other paraphernalia.

✔ **New Orleans Cypress Works** (3105 Magazine St.; ☎ 504-891-0001) designs custom furniture using antique cypress and heart of pine.

✔ **New Orleans Glassworks and Printmaking Studio** (727 Magazine St.; ☎ 504-529-7277) displays blown-glass sculptures, lampworking, bronze pours, printmaking, and bookbinding. The heart of the activity here is a state-of-the-art, 800-pound furnace. Visitors can commission glass, hand-bound books, or prints, as well as watch daily demonstrations of glassblowing, glass painting, metal sculpture, and other arts.

✔ **Octavia Books** (513 Octavia St.; ☎ 504-899-READ). Husband-and-wife proprietors Tom Lowenburg and Judith Lafitte handpick books of regional and national interest stocked in a spacious, modern setting complete with outdoor patio and waterfall. Their renovation of a 100-year-old former grocery earned them Best of New Orleans Architecture honors from *New Orleans Magazine* and a Golden Hammer award from the City of New Orleans.

✔ **Scriptura** (5423 Magazine St.; ☎ 504-897-5555) carries a unique assortment of paper products from around the world, including fine stationery, leather journals, and greeting cards plus writing instruments and custom wax seals.

✔ At **Shadyside Pottery** (3823 Magazine St.; ☎ 504-897-1710) you can witness the creation of *raku,* a particular type of pottery that has a cracked look.

✔ **Thomas Mann Gallery** (1804 Magazine St.; ☎ 504-581-2113) features "techno-romantic" jewelry designer Thomas Mann, who claims a lot of the credit for bringing contemporary jewelry and sculpture to New Orleans. This store/gallery seeks to "redefine contemporary living" via its eclectic collection of jewelry, lighting, and home furnishings.

✔ **Uptown Costume & Dancewear** (4326 Magazine St.; ☎ **504-895-7969**) is the place to go for spooky monster masks, hats, wigs, makeup, and all kinds of mischievous mask wear.

✔ **Utopia** (5408 Magazine St.; ☎ **504-899-8488**) has a unique collection of contemporary clothing, jewelry, accessories, and gifts as well as playful, fun furniture designed by David Marsh.

✔ **Westgate — The Original Necrotorium** (5219 Magazine St.; ☎ **504-899-3077**; www.westgatenecromantic.com) celebrates the inner Goth, a one-stop shop for death-related items including "necromantic" art and jewelry (featuring plenty of skeletons and other death images). The book section offers related titles. Although some people may find the artwork disturbing, open-minded visitors with a healthy dose of curiosity will appreciate its unique offerings.

✔ **Wilkerson Row** (3137 Magazine St.; ☎ **504-899-3311**) is an award-winning furniture shop whose custom designs are influenced by 19th-century New Orleans architecture.

Chapter 13

Following an Itinerary: Six Great Options

● ●

In This Chapter

▶ Spending one, three, or five days in New Orleans

▶ Enjoying New Orleans with the kids

▶ Experiencing the historical, spooky, and romantic highlights of the French Quarter

▶ Taking Fido on the town

● ●

*A*lthough I give a lot of lip service to exploring New Orleans on your own, the truth is, you do need some structure. However, that doesn't preclude fun. Why not arrange your day around spooky, supernatural sights or romantic hot spots? This chapter presents suggestions for themed itineraries, as well as suggestions on what to do if your time is limited or if you're bringing your family or man's best friend. It covers where to go, what to look for, and how much time to budget for each stop. It also tips you off to some good places for meals and snacks along the way.

New Orleans in One Day

If you're only in New Orleans for one day, you're not going to be able to see and do everything. So how do you solve this dilemma? Spend the whole day in the French Quarter (see Chapters 2, 8, and 11). As much as I stress throughout this book that New Orleans is more than this historic district, I'd never advise you not to take in the Quarter's sights. It *is* the single most popular attraction in the city for good reason, with a lot of culture, history, and lore in its small (6 blocks wide by 13 blocks long) confines.

To get into the spirit of the city, take your time getting started in the morning with a visit to **Café du Monde** (see Chapter 10) for **beignets** (fried doughnuts covered in powdered sugar) washed down with a **café au lait.** After lingering for a bit at Café du Monde, begin the day's touring with a 30- to 60-minute stop at historic **Jackson Square** (see

New Orleans in One Day

1 Jackson Square
2 Cabildo
3 Presbytere
4 St. Louis Cathedral
5 Faulkner House Books
6 1850 House/Lower Pontalba Building
7 Moonwalk
8 Old Ursuline Convent
9 Beauregard-Keyes House
10 Royal Street
11 Historic New Orleans Collection
12 Bourbon Street
13 Lafitte's Blacksmith Shop
14 Old Absinthe House
15 Preservation Hall

Chapter 11). While in the neighborhood, check out the **Cabildo** and the **Presbytere** (see Chapter 11), allowing roughly an hour for each. Then wander over to the **St. Louis Cathedral,** on the north side of the square at 721 Chartres (see Chapter 11), for a short 15-minute go-through. Afterward, pop in at **Faulkner House Books** (see Chapter 12) for a little bit of literary history and maybe to buy a rare first-edition hardback or two. You may also want to gander at the beautifully restored **Pontalba Apartments** (formally known as **1850 House, Lower Pontalba Building;** see Chapter 11) at 523 St. Ann St.; allow about one hour.

Right about now, you may realize that all you had for breakfast was the rough equivalent of three very sugary donuts. My suggestion is to forego an actual sit-down restaurant and roll some sightseeing into your lunch. Stroll down to Decatur Street and sample a **muffuletta** (one of New Orleans's premier sandwiches) at **Central Grocery** (see Chapter 10). Take your sandwich across the street, wander along the **Moonwalk** (see Chapter 11), and eat by the banks of the Mississippi.

After lunch, a little walking helps the digestive process. Wind your way up Ursulines to the **Old Ursuline Convent** and tour the oldest surviving building in the Mississippi Valley (see Chapter 11). Allow about an hour before wandering over to the **Beauregard-Keyes House** across the street; plan to spend about 45 minutes to an hour at this literary landmark (see Chapter 11).

Next, walk westward down **Royal Street,** checking out the shops and galleries along the way (see Chapter 12). Save enough energy for the insightful exhibits on New Orleans history at the **Historic New Orleans Collection** (see Chapter 11) for a nice overview.

Steel yourself for a predinner stroll down **Bourbon Street.** Stop in at **Lafitte's Blacksmith Shop and Bar** (Chapters 11 and 16) for a drink, and darned if you won't absorb some more history in the process. To continue the historical theme, you can hang out at the **Old Absinthe House** (Chapters 11 and 16), sipping an anisette, and imagine what it must have been like back in the days of Andrew Jackson and Jean Lafitte.

For dinner, only one place is worth considering if you only have one day in town. **Commander's Palace** (see Chapter 10) is widely considered one of the best restaurants in the United States. Visiting celebrities regularly stop to relax in the luxurious dining rooms (all decorated in New Orleans flair). The restaurant is a bit pricey, but the pampering, food, and luxurious surroundings are well worth the cost.

Make a pit stop at your hotel to recharge your batteries because you haven't had the complete New Orleans experience until you've heard some music. Start out in the Quarter, first heading to **Preservation Hall** (see Chapter 15) for authentic, traditional jazz. Then head back to **Bourbon Street,** which by now should be in full, raunchy swing.

New Orleans in Three Days

Say you have more than just one day to spend in New Orleans. Great! Whether you have one or two extra days, this itinerary maps out where to go and what to do. (If you're in town for more than three days, consider taking a day to get away from it all with one of the day-trips in Chapter 14.)

For **day one** of this itinerary, see the preceding section to get the most out of the famous French Quarter. Start **day two** by adhering to my New Orleans Golden Rule: Get out of the Quarter!

If you're staying in the French Quarter, have breakfast at the breezy and friendly **Clover Grill** (see Chapter 10). From there, head down to Decatur Street for a glimpse of the Mississippi River and to look for souvenirs at **Jax Brewery** (see Chapter 12). Allow about an hour to an hour and a half. Next, cross Canal Street and head into the **Warehouse District** (see Chapter 8), specifically toward **Julia Street,** a bustling corridor of art galleries (see Chapter 12).

From there make your way by streetcar, auto, or other propulsive means (*not* by foot) to the **Garden District** (see Chapter 8). You can take a walking tour (see Chapter 11) or stroll around on your own to admire the stately elegance of the gorgeous manses, especially those along St. Charles Avenue and Prytania Street. Closer to the river, along **Magazine Street,** the elegance gives way to a loose and funky vibe. Here you find smaller shotguns and cottages (see Chapter 2), and more art galleries and antiques shops (see Chapter 12). Allow at least two hours to explore the district.

For lunch, Uptown offers several great options. I recommend **Franky & Johnny's** (just off Magazine at Arabella Street; see Chapter 10) for filling sandwiches and New Orleans staples. Afterward, take a cab to **City Park** (see Chapter 11) and spend a little time enjoying its tranquil charms. While you're there, you simply must wander the halls of the **New Orleans Museum of Art** and reflect on its marvelous new **Besthoff Sculpture Garden** (see Chapter 11). Allow two to three hours for the park, museum, and garden.

If you're feeling hungry, cross the bridge at Bayou St. John to Esplanade Avenue and grab a healthy snack at **Whole Foods Market** (see Chapter 10) or caffeine and homemade, gourmet biscotti at **Fair Grinds Coffee House** (see Chapter 10). Take a cab from the park along grand old Esplanade Avenue and gaze at the funky neighborhood that's home to the Fair Grounds Race Course. Esplanade takes you right up to the border of the French Quarter.

New Orleans in Three Days

To METAIRIE

S. Broad Ave.

Jefferson
Valmont
Soniat
Robert
Upperline
Cadiz
Jena

S. Dorgenois
S. Rocheblave

S. Johnson

Louisiana Parkway
Toledano
Washington
S. Prieur
Seminole

Southern
Baptist Hospital

Napoleon Ave.
Gen. Pershing
Milan

BROADMOOR

S. Derbigny
S. Roman

Valence

Gen. Taylor

90 S. Claiborne Ave.

Earhart Blvd. (Calliope St.)
Erato

10

Marengo

Willow
Clara
Magnolia
S. Robertson

Erato
Thalia
Clio

New Orleans
Arena

Constantinople

Freret

La Salle
S. Liberty

Martin Luther King Blvd.

Union Passenger
Terminal (Amtrak)

16

Peniston
Amelia
Foucher
Delachaise

Louisiana Ave.

Loyola
S. Saratoga
4th 3rd 2nd 1st
Dryades
Baronne

Simon Bolivar

UPTOWN

Carondelet
St. Charles

Jackson Ave.

Euterpe
Terpsichore
Polymnia

Clio
Erato
Thalia

Lee
Circl

Pontchartrain Expwy.

Aline
Harmony
8th
7th
6th
Prytania
3rd

4

St. Charles Ave.

Melpomene

Coliseum

i

GARDEN DISTRICT

Chestnut
Camp
Magazine
Constance

Washington
Josephine
St. Andrew
St. Mary
Felicity

Camp

Magazine
Constance
Annunciation

BR
90

Toledano
Pleasant
9th

Laurel
Annunciation

5

Chippewa

Orange
Richard
Race
Euterpe

15

St. Thomas
Rousseau

New Orleans
General Hospital

Market

Celeste

(i) Information

"Take a Break" stop

Ferry Service to
Algiers Point

Riverfront streetcar
route/stops

St. Charles streetcar
route/stops

Vieux Carre loop
route/stops

Canal St. streetcar
route/stops

Lake Pontchartrain

CITY
PARK

10
610

Area of detail

10

Superdome

1

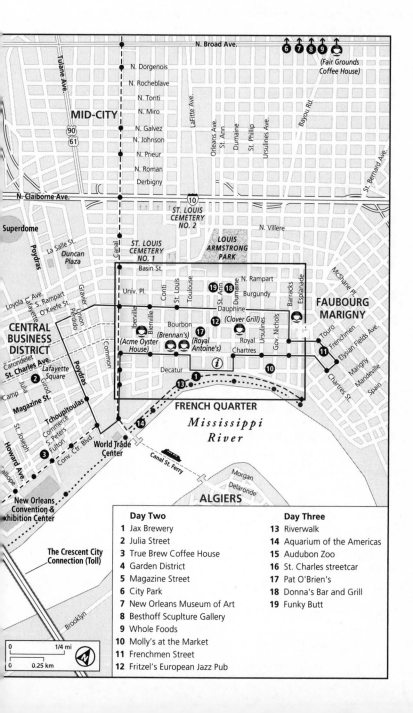

Day Two
1 Jax Brewery
2 Julia Street
3 True Brew Coffee House
4 Garden District
5 Magazine Street
6 City Park
7 New Orleans Museum of Art
8 Besthoff Scuplture Gallery
9 Whole Foods
10 Molly's at the Market
11 Frenchmen Street
12 Fritzel's European Jazz Pub

Day Three
13 Riverwalk
14 Aquarium of the Americas
15 Audubon Zoo
16 St. Charles streetcar
17 Pat O'Brien's
18 Donna's Bar and Grill
19 Funky Butt

Streetcar highlights

Taking the St. Charles Streetcar? Watch for these sights along the way. (For a map of the streetcar route, see Chapter 8.) When traveling from the French Quarter through the Garden District toward Audubon Park, note that odd-numbered addresses are on the right, even-numbered addresses on the left.

✔ After passing Julia and St. Joseph streets, you go around Lee Circle. That's General Robert E. Lee atop the massive column. Note that he's facing north so that his back won't be to the Yankees. The statue was erected in 1884.

✔ At 2040 St. Charles is La Tour Eiffel. If it looks like the Eiffel Tower in Paris, that's because it actually *was* a part of the tower, built in Paris as an upper-level restaurant and then moved to New Orleans and reassembled in 1936.

✔ The Columns Hotel (1883), located at 3811 St. Charles, was the location of a Storyville bordello in the movie *Pretty Baby.*

✔ Does the Palmer House at 5705 St. Charles look familiar? If you've seen *Gone With the Wind,* it should, It's a replica of Tara.

✔ Audubon Park (extending all the way from St. Charles to the Mississippi River) was the site of the 1884 World's Industrial and Cotton Centennial Exposition. The renowned Audubon Zoo is on the far side of the park.

✔ After passing Tulane University and the old St. Mary's Dominican College (now Loyola's Broadway campus), you enter what used to be the town of Carrollton, named for General William Carroll, a commander at the Battle of New Orleans. Carrollton was founded in 1833 and incorporated in 1845. New Orleans annexed the city in 1874.

✔ After the streetcar turns right onto Carondelet, look ahead and a little to the left. The tall building with the cupola at 325 Carondelet is the Hibernia Bank Building (1921), the tallest building in the city until 1962. The cupola is lit at night in colors that change with the seasons.

Taking the Canal Streetcar? (For a map of the streetcar route, see Chapter 8.) New Orleans's former main street is undergoing a well-received revival. Keep an eye out for:

✔ Block-Keller House (3620 Canal St.), a magnificently restored classical-revival villa now serving as a B&B. Hosts Bryan Block and Jeff Keller received a well-deserved 2003 Renaissance Award from *New Orleans Magazine.*

✔ City Park, the New Orleans Museum of Art, and the Besthoff Sculpture Garden at the end of the Carrollton spur.

✔ The former upscale brothel at 4332 Canal St. infamously busted by the FBI.

✔ The Cypress Grove and Greenwood cemeteries at the end of the line (no pun intended).

After a little downtime at your hotel — or additional French Quarter touring for the truly hearty — treat yourself to a quintessential (and fairly cheap) French Quarter dining experience slurping down raw oysters at **Acme Oyster House** (see Chapter 10). If seafood isn't your thing, head to the Quarter's edge and grab a burger at **Port of Call** (see Chapter 10). Either way, you dine relatively cheaply and rub elbows with some down-to-earth locals.

Now, get ready for some music. Digest and unwind with a drink at a local watering hole. I recommend **Molly's at the Market** (see Chapter 16), a homey hangout that won me over with its charming atmosphere and friendliness. Next, hop across Esplanade to **Frenchmen Street** (see Chapter 16) for a whirlwind tour of jazz, funk, and world music. You can easily spend an evening at just one of these clubs, but I recommend that you stroll from place to place. After a couple hours, head over to **Fritzel's European Jazz Pub** (Chapter 15) to catch a late-night jam session before collapsing into bed.

After using day two to sample the city's charms beyond the French Quarter (though you've really only scratched the surface), treat **day three** as a reward, indulging in some of the more touristy but no less entertaining sights, including the hedonistic pleasures of a breakfast at **Brennan's** (see Chapter 10). Allow about an hour to savor the experience. From there, head over to **Riverwalk Marketplace** (Chapter 12) to finish up any last-minute shopping, followed by a tour of the amazing **Aquarium of the Americas** (Chapter 11). Allow one to two hours to take it all in (closer to two to include a film at the **IMAX Theater**).

Next, take a riverboat cruise aboard the stern-wheeler *John James Audubon,* which deposits you at the world-renowned **Audubon Zoo** (see Chapter 11). If your plentiful Brennan's breakfast has begun to wear off, grab lunch (or at least a snack) at the zoo. Allow about two hours. Next, travel back to the French Quarter by riverboat or by the **St. Charles Streetcar** (see Chapter 11), which provides a scenic glimpse of the city's grandest boulevard. (See the sidebar "Streetcar highlights" in this chapter for a list of sights to see along the way.)

Return to your hotel to rest up for another signature New Orleans dining experience — dinner at **Antoine's** (see Chapter 10). After dinner, take a leisurely last stroll through the Quarter, making sure to stop at **Pat O'Brien's** (see Chapter 16), where the expansive courtyard, complete with flaming fountain, is touristy but cool in a kitschy way. Then wind your way to the Rampart Street border of the Quarter, where you can finish the night with some eclectic New Orleans music — and more than a little atmosphere — at **Donna's Bar and Grill** and the **Funky Butt** (Chapter 16).

New Orleans in Five Days

If you're in town for more than three days, see the preceding section to get the most out of your first three days. For **day four** of this itinerary get out of the city completely. I recommend you choose from one of the three day-trip suggestions in Chapter 14.

If you like regional music, start driving to Lafayette and make a day of touring **Atchafalaya Basin,** shopping at **Cajun Village,** and a night of Cajun dining and dancing at **Randol's Restaurant and Cajun Dance Hall.** If you're too tired to drive back to the city, check in at **Bois des Chenes Inn,** a former cattle and sugar cane plantation, for a good night's sleep.

If you like the outdoors, head south to Lafitte. Spend the morning at **Barataria Preserve** followed by lunch at **Restaurant des Familles** in nearby Crown Point or an English tea at **Victoria Inn & Gardens.** Then spend the afternoon communing with alligators on a swamp tour, courtesy of **L'il Cajun Swamp Tours,** before dining at **Voleo's.** Again, if you're too tired to return to the city, stay overnight at Victoria Inn & Gardens. If you like to fish, you're welcome to fish off the pier or ask hosts Roy and Dale Ross if they can set up a fishing charter for you with **Captain Phil Robichaux.** Prepare to get up super early the next day to catch some reds (tasty red fish) and maybe a crab or two.

For **day five,** you have your pick of lovely plantation homes along River Road. My personal favorites are **Laura,** for including the slave community in its tours and maintaining the slave cabins (instead of having destroyed them as some plantations did); **Oak Alley,** for its beautiful oak-lined avenue and fantasy of Southern plantation living; and the 54,000-square-foot **Nottoway,** known locally as the White Castle for its formidable presence. Along the way you can feast on fresh seafood at **B & C Seafood Market & Cajun Deli** (about a mile from Laura). For details on the establishments I recommend visiting on days four and five, see Chapter 14.

New Orleans for Families with Kids

The dynamics of your visit will be very different if you're bringing the family along than if you come alone or with an adult friend. Happily, more than enough diversions are available that appeal to grown-ups and little ones alike.

On **day one,** start with a breakfast at **Café du Monde** (see Chapter 10) followed by a brief walk through the French Quarter, taking in **Jackson Square** (see Chapter 11) and maybe a historic home or two. But spend the majority of the morning enjoying the many delights of the **Aquarium of the Americas** (see Chapter 11), allowing one to two hours before a brief lunch either on-site or at one of many nearby restaurants. After lunch, take the *John James Audubon* stern-wheeler to the **Audubon Zoo** (see Chapter 11), where you can while away the afternoon (allow at least two hours) ooh-ing and aah-ing the wildlife on display. Take the **St. Charles**

Streetcar (see Chapter 8) to wind your way back toward downtown, disembarking near Lee Circle, the Quarter a short hop away by cab. Grab a bite at **Café Maspero** (see Chapter 10) and retire to your hotel to rest up for the next day. If you or the kids get restless, a **carriage ride** (see Chapter 8) is a pleasant way to enjoy the sights of the French Quarter.

On **day two,** after breakfast at **Mother's** or **Clover Grill,** a cheerful gay-friendly establishment (see Chapter 11), take the Canal Street Ferry (it's free, and departs from the foot of Canal Street every quarter hour; a pedestrian-only commuter boat also runs at 15-minute intervals) to **Blaine Kern's Mardi Gras World** (see Chapter 11), where you'll spend the morning (about two hours round-trip) looking at floats-in-progress and finding out some interesting tidbits about Carnival. Afterward, the ferry takes you back to the Quarter (it costs a dollar this way), where you can do a bit more walking around, taking in the **Moonwalk** and the Mississippi and perhaps even the open-air **French Market** (see Chapter 11). Take your time, but budget about 20 minutes to have a quintessential New Orleans lunch courtesy of **Central Grocery** (see Chapter 10) before taking the Canal Streetcar to **City Park** (see Chapter 11). Here you can enjoy the **New Orleans Museum of Art,** the **Besthoff Sculpture Garden,** and the park's **Carousel Gardens** (see Chapter 11), allowing about two and a half to four hours, depending on your stamina, before hopping a cab back to your hotel and dinner at **Remoulade** (309 Bourbon St., ☎ 504-523-0377), a kid- and budget-friendly cousin to the legendary **Arnaud's** (see Chapter 10). Squeeze in a bit more strolling in the evening, but be sure to rest up for the following day.

Day three starts with a leisurely jazz brunch at **Court of Two Sisters** (see Chapter 10) before stopping by the **Presbytere** (see Chapter 11) for an entertaining look at Mardi Gras memorabilia. Then take a short hop to the Warehouse District for the fun, interactive exhibits at the **Louisiana Children's Museum** (see Chapter 11). Allow about an hour at each museum.

Follow it up with some shopping and a quick lunch at **Jax Brewery** (see Chapter 12) or the **Riverwalk Marketplace** (see Chapter 12) if you went to the Children's Museum. Then, assuming you've come during the right time of year, reward your brood for putting up with all the historical stuff with a fun-filled afternoon at **Six Flags New Orleans** (see Chapter 11). If Six Flags is closed when you visit, a jaunt out to the **Louisiana Nature Center and Planetarium** (see Chapter 11) is a good substitute.

If you gorged on goodies at Six Flags, go easy on dinner and walk off some of those calories, enjoying one last look at the French Quarter by night, perhaps enjoying a final, lingering gaze out over the Mississippi by **Washington Artillery Park** (see Chapter 11). Then take time for souvenir packing and sleep before heading back home.

New Orleans for Families with Kids

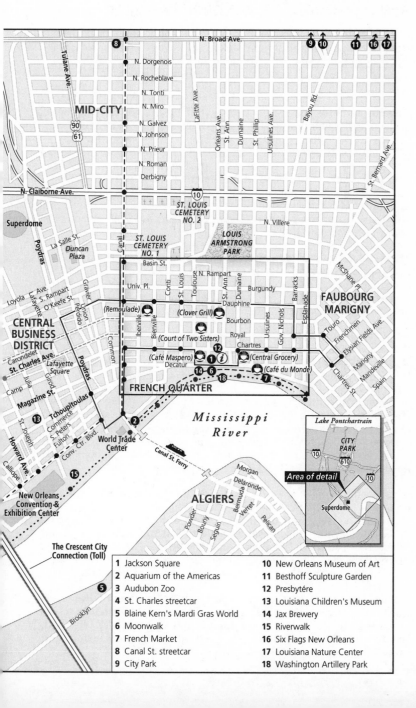

1	Jackson Square	**10**	New Orleans Museum of Art
2	Aquarium of the Americas	**11**	Besthoff Sculpture Garden
3	Audubon Zoo	**12**	Presbytére
4	St. Charles streetcar	**13**	Louisiana Children's Museum
5	Blaine Kern's Mardi Gras World	**14**	Jax Brewery
6	Moonwalk	**15**	Riverwalk
7	French Market	**16**	Six Flags New Orleans
8	Canal St. streetcar	**17**	Louisiana Nature Center
9	City Park	**18**	Washington Artillery Park

Supernatural and Scary New Orleans

In addition to its great indigenous music and food, New Orleans boasts atmosphere galore. This itinerary explores the city's darker side, inasmuch as you *can* explore it during the day. Voodoo, graveyards, psychics — they're all here. And they're all easily squeezed into a single day (and night) of sightseeing.

As befits a tour of things associated with the night, you have the option of sleeping in (a natural New Orleans pastime in its own right). When you do roll out of bed, make your first stop a quick one at **Our Lady of Guadalupe Chapel and International Shrine of St. Jude** (see Chapter 11). Say a quick prayer to St. Expedite, in preparation for your next stop, an organized tour of **St. Louis Cemetery No. 1** (see the listing in Chapter 11 for the lowdown on a tour by **Save Our Cemeteries** as well as Chapter 11 for more detailed cemetery-tour information). You'll probably find a tour getting underway around 10 a.m. or 10:30 a.m., so plan your time accordingly.

Afterward, head over to the **New Orleans Pharmacy Museum** at 514 Chartres St., between St. Louis and Toulouse streets (see Chapter 11; note that it's closed Mondays). If you don't think a pharmacy can be spooky and supernatural, take a look at the leeches and the drill once used to relieve headaches. Allow 15 to 30 minutes.

With all that morbidity, you probably built up a good appetite, right? If so, you can find a number of good restaurants in the area, including **Napoleon House, Café Maspero,** and the **Court of Two Sisters** (see Chapter 10), which evoke a suitably spooky atmosphere.

Sufficiently refreshed, you can take a brief pause and head over to **Body Hangings** on Decatur Street (see Chapter 12). Peruse the selection of cloaks and capes before making your way to **Marie Laveau's House of Voodoo** (see Chapter 12). Have your palm read, talk to a psychic, and buy a voodoo doll to give to (or take care of) a friend back home; allow half an hour.

Next, head one block riverward to the **Bottom of the Cup Tearoom** (see Chapter 12; note that it's closed Sundays) to have your fortune told. Then, take a taxi or walk down Royal Street to Canal Street and hop the **St. Charles Streetcar** (see Chapter 8). Get off at Washington Street and go one block south to **Lafayette Cemetery No. 1** (see Chapter 11). This cemetery is generally safe as long as you're with a few people. If you want to take an organized tour, contact the organizations in Chapter 11.

Finally, if you're up for it, go to Magazine Street for a jaunt down to this tour's souvenir shop, **Westgate — The Original Necrotorium** (see Chapter 12; note that it's closed Sundays and Mondays). It's filled with "necromantic" art and jewelry, peppered with images of skeletons and other things associated with death.

Supernatural and Scary New Orleans

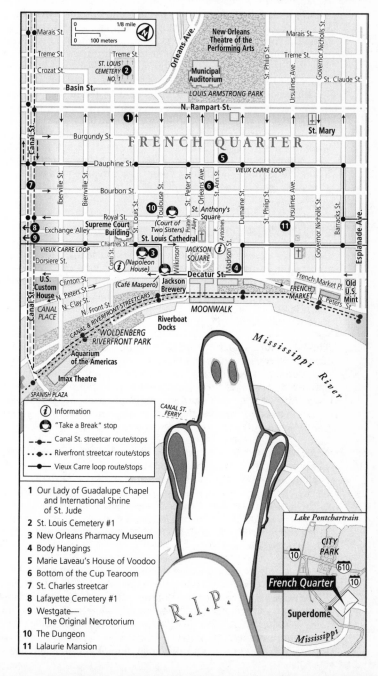

1 Our Lady of Guadalupe Chapel and International Shrine of St. Jude

2 St. Louis Cemetery #1

3 New Orleans Pharmacy Museum

4 Body Hangings

5 Marie Laveau's House of Voodoo

6 Bottom of the Cup Tearoom

7 St. Charles streetcar

8 Lafayette Cemetery #1

9 Westgate— The Original Necrotorium

10 The Dungeon

11 Lalaurie Mansion

Regarding nightlife, though it doesn't open until midnight, the **Dungeon** (Chapter 16) is an essential stop. If you enjoyed Westgate and/or have an affinity for the Goth subculture, you can find plenty of friends here. While you're waiting for the Dungeon to open, walk by what is believed to be the most haunted house in the Quarter, the stunning though infamous **Lalaurie Mansion** at 1140 Royal St. In the early 1800s, a well-to-do Creole couple, Dr. Louis and Delphine Lalaurie, resided there with a houseful of slaves. To the horror of high society, when a fire broke out in 1834, it was discovered that Madame Lalaurie had been slowly torturing to death some of her slaves, hidden away in secret rooms. Supposedly the cook, who was chained to her stove, started the fire, choosing death over her hell-on-earth existence. The Lalauries fled an angry mob and were never seen again. Subsequent occupants didn't stay long because they reported chilling screams and moans, strange occurrences, and for a lucky few, ghost sightings. (*Note:* Currently, the mansion is a private residence, so please be respectful.)

New Orleans for Honeymooners

Of course, almost anything you do in New Orleans, from antiques shopping to binge drinking on Bourbon Street, can be romantic — if you're with the right person. However, this itinerary is specifically designed to enhance, or maybe induce, some *amore.* I forego the must-see sights and historic attractions in favor of a leisurely day in the French Quarter, with plenty of time to stop and smell the roses.

This itinerary assumes a late start (especially if you're on your honeymoon). When you do get moving, start your day with a jazz brunch at **The Court of Two Sisters** (see Chapter 10); allow about an hour. Next, saunter down **Royal Street** and browse the antiques shops and art galleries (see Chapter 12), keeping an eye out for that special piece of furniture you need for the new house. Spend as much time as you want. You're in no hurry to rush from place to place.

Next, head down toward the river and browse the **French Market** (see Chapters 11 and 12) for some souvenirs and tokens of your affection for each other; allow at least a half hour, more if you're really interested in all the cheap jewelry displays. You can follow that, if you like, by taking in the action at **Jackson Square** (see Chapter 11). Depending on how early or late you ate breakfast, you can grab an optional lunch (or a quick romantic snack) at **Café du Monde** or **La Marquise** just off the square (see Chapter 10).

Ease into the afternoon with a leisurely **carriage tour** of the French Quarter (see Chapter 8); allow about 30 minutes. Then stroll to the **Riverwalk Marketplace** (see Chapter 12) for a bit of exploring before boarding the 2 p.m. *Creole Queen* paddle-wheeler for a riverboat cruise (see Chapter 11). It takes you 7 miles downriver to **Chalmette Battlefield National Park** (see Chapter 11), where you can enjoy a brief walking tour before the return trip upriver, arriving back at 4:30 p.m.

New Orleans for Honeymooners

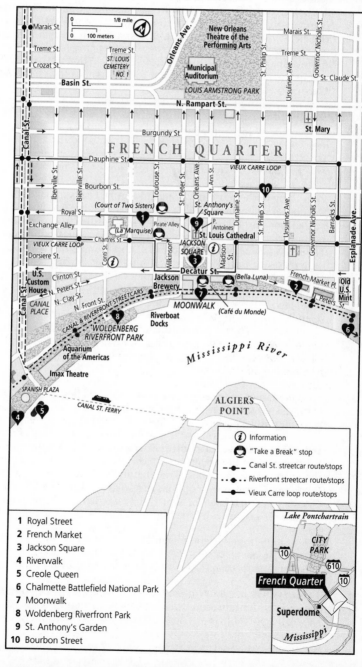

1 Royal Street
2 French Market
3 Jackson Square
4 Riverwalk
5 Creole Queen
6 Chalmette Battlefield National Park
7 Moonwalk
8 Woldenberg Riverfront Park
9 St. Anthony's Garden
10 Bourbon Street

Continue your river motif with a relaxed stroll along the **Moonwalk** and **Woldenberg Riverfront Park** (see Chapter 11 for both). Watch the sun set before making your way to **Bella Luna** (see Chapter 10), whose commanding river view makes this one of the most romantic restaurants in the city; wedding proposals are almost as common as appetizers here.

After dinner, feel free to stroll through any section of the Quarter that catches your fancy; you may want to take a quick look at **St. Anthony's Garden** (see Chapter 11). After that, stroll to your heart's content. Enjoy a bit more of the Mississippi River, or saunter down **Bourbon Street** for a taste of the city's naughtier pleasures, before calling it a night and retiring to the pleasure of one another's company.

New Orleans for Dog Lovers

First thing in the morning, bring Fido and a Frisbee to **Cabrini Park** (at the corner of Barracks and Dauphine streets; see Chapter 6) for exercise, socializing, and taking care of business (be sure to scoop!). You'll have both worked up an appetite, so let your pooch pick out pastries at **Three Dog Bakery** (see Chapter 12) and then head for a patio table at **Café du Monde** (see Chapter 10). Afterwards, stroll along the **Moonwalk** (see Chapter 11) before heading back to the Quarter. Your pooch will want to pass by **Pug Place** (look for the sign), a private residence at 736 Dumaine Street, which is presided over by the pug you'll likely see in the open floor-to-ceiling window. Reach through the wrought-iron gate and be sure to give him a pat on the head — he adores the attention. Do some window-shopping at **Animal Art** (see Chapter 12) and **Chi-Wa-Wa Ga-Ga** (see Chapter 12), where dinky dogs dig the Krewe of Barkus-worthy costumes.

You know what they say – a tired dog is a good dog. In the afternoon, head over to **Audubon Park** or **City Park** to do some people-, dog-, and bird-watching while strolling along lagoons shaded by sprawling live oaks (see Chapters 6 and 11 for both). If you choose to go Uptown, after your walk, grab a bite to eat at **PJ's Coffee & Tea Co.** at 7624 Maple St. and relax on the dog-friendly, fenced-in patio (see Chapter 10). For something more filling, sit down at a sidewalk (dog-friendly) table at **Lebanon's Café** (see Chapter 10). Your snack options in Mid-City include **City Perk** and **Fair Grinds Coffee House.** For something more hearty, **Whole Foods** — and its outdoor, dog-friendly seating — is close by (see Chapter 10 for all).

If your four-legged friend becomes ill or suffers an injury, call **Dr. Mike's Animal House** at ☎ 504-523-4455 or go directly to 1120 N. Rampart St. (See Chapter 6 for additional veterinarian contact information.)

Before you leave your hotel, make sure your dog is wearing a collar with up-to-date identification tags. Also, pack bottled water (enough for both of you), a portable bowl, dog treats, and poop bags.

Chapter 14

Going Beyond New Orleans: Three Day Trips

In This Chapter

▶ Spending a day in Cajun Country
▶ Taking a sightseeing tour of remarkable plantation homes
▶ Getting back to nature — without driving all day to do it

*Y*ou could probably spend your next three or four vacations in the Crescent City and still not get to everything on your list. But sometimes you just need to get away from it all. This chapter offers three relaxing day-trips to help clear your head. Each requires a bit of a drive from the French Quarter and the New Orleans city limits. So gas up the car, get out your maps, and hit the road.

Day-Trip No. 1: Discovering Cajun Country

This day-trip takes you to Lafayette, the heart of Cajun Country, where you discover this unique region's food, culture, and music.

The **Lafayette Parish Convention and Visitors Commission** (P.O. Box 52066, Lafayette, LA 70505, ☎ **800-346-1958** in the United States, 800-543-5340 in Canada, or 337-232-3737; fax: 337-232-0161; www.lafayette travel.com) can give you the scoop on all Lafayette has to offer. If you plan to come out this way, call for a brochure. They may even persuade you to extend your stay.

Creoles, *zydeco* (popular music of southern Louisiana combining tunes of French origin with elements of Caribbean music and the blues and that features guitar, washboard, and accordion) musicians, and non-Cajun residents don't much care for the "Cajun Country" label. Also, many citizens of Acadian descent aren't too wild about it either, especially in large urban centers such as Lafayette. Although the people here are proud of their heritage, some of them bristle at the rather touristy simplification of the term. If you drive through Lafayette, you can find that it's a city like any other. You don't have

---

Where in the world is Cajun Country?

Cajuns are the descendants of Acadians, settlers who were forced out of their established colony in Nova Scotia in the mid-18th century. Arriving in the French colony of Louisiana, they found themselves in relative isolation, farming in the low-lying wetlands and developing their own distinct culture. To experience some true Cajun culture, you need to drive two to three hours from New Orleans to Lafayette. There, you can find the food, music, and lifestyle that developed as the Acadians mingled with their neighbors and became an integral part of Louisiana life and lore.

---

to abandon your car and paddle through dense swamp to get to a hotel or restaurant, nor do you encounter fiddle-playing *Deliverance* extras on every street corner and front porch.

Getting to Lafayette

Lafayette (167 miles — give or take a few — west of New Orleans) is a straight shot from New Orleans on Interstate 10. Drive in mid- to late morning so that you don't get caught in rush-hour traffic in Baton Rouge or Lafayette — or New Orleans, for that matter.

Taking a tour of Cajun Country

The New Orleans area offers some authentic swamp tours, but the Atchafalaya Basin holds the distinction of being the third-largest swamp in the United States. A boat tour is a great way to experience this mystical region. **Angelle's Atchafalaya Basin Swamp Tours** (See map p. 237. Whiskey River Landing, P.O. Box 111, Cecilia, LA 70521; ☎ **337-228-8567**) operates tours in glass-bottomed boats or smaller, open boats. To get to the swamp from I-10, take Exit 115 to Henderson, go through Henderson to the levee, and turn right. The landing is the fourth exit on the left. Fares are $12 for adults, $10 for seniors (55 and up), and $6 for children. Departures are at 10 a.m., 1 p.m., and 3 p.m. daily (weather permitting).

Seeing the sights of Cajun Country

The sights in this day-trip wet your feet in the bayous of the Cajun experience. What's a bayou, exactly? Coming from the Choctaw word meaning "small stream," a *bayou* is a sluggish offshoot of a lake or river that flows through swampland — and an integral part of swampland culture.

Acadian Village

Acadian Village is a reconstructed (actually, reassembled) Cajun bayou community in which houses have been transported from their original location to this site beside a sleepy bayou. If you're the exploring type, take the footpath and venture along the bayou's banks. Peek inside the

Day-Trip No. 1: Discovering Cajun Country

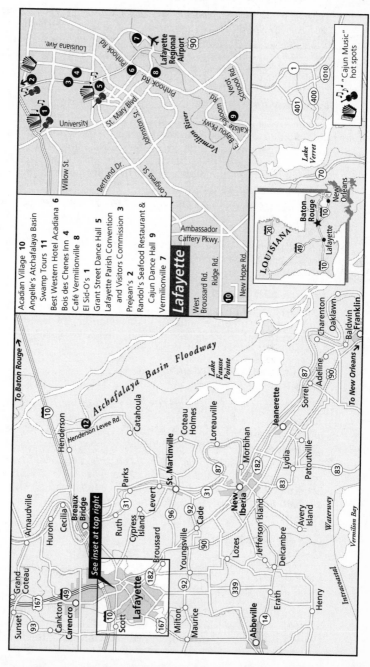

"Cajun Music" hot spots

Acadian Village **10**
Angelle's Atchafalaya Basin Swamp Tours **11**
Best Western Hotel Acadiana **6**
Bois des Chenes Inn **4**
Café Vermilionville **8**
El Sid-O's **1**
Grant Street Dance Hall **5**
Lafayette Parish Convention and Visitors Commission **3**
Prejean's **2**
Randol's Seafood Restaurant & Cajun Dance Hall **9**
Vermilionville **7**

Lafayette

LOUISIANA

houses to glimpse the Cajun furniture. The gift shop sells Cajun handicrafts and books. Allow one to two hours.

See map p. 237. 200 Greenleaf Dr., Lafayette, LA 70506; ☎ *800-962-9133 or 337-981-2364. Fax: 337-988-4554.* www.acadianvillage.org. *Take I-10 from Lafayette to Exit 97. Go south on Highway 93 to Ridge Road and then take a right on Ridge Road followed by a left on West Broussard. Admission: $7 adults, $6 seniors, $4 children 6–14; free for children under 6. Open: daily 10 a.m.–5 p.m.*

Vermilionville

Vermilionville is a small village on Bayou Vermilion that attempts to recreate Cajun life as it existed in the 18th and 19th centuries. Costumed staff members demonstrate crafts from the period. Shows feature Cajun music and dancing, and the restaurant serves authentic Cajun fare. Although it's a bit contrived, Vermilionville is fun and informative nonetheless. Allow one to two hours.

See map p. 237. 300 Fisher Rd, Lafayette, LA 70508. ☎ *866-99-BAYOU or 337-233-4077. Fax: 337-233-1694.* www.vermilionville.org. *Take I-10 from Lafayette to Exit 103A. Get on the Evangeline Thruway going south until you get to Surrey Street and then follow the signs. Closed most major holidays. Admission: $8 adults, $6.50 seniors, $5 students; free for children under 6. Open: Tues–Sun 10 a.m.–4 p.m.*

Where to stay in Cajun Country

If you want to enjoy the area's nightlife (see the "Passing a good time: Cajun Country nightlife" sidebar in this chapter), plan to spend the night in Lafayette rather than make the two-hour drive back to New Orleans.

Best Western Hotel Acadiana
$$–$$$$

The Hotel Acadiana offers great value for your vacation dollar, providing all the conveniences you'd expect in a large chain hotel, including a complimentary airport shuttle. The hotel's restaurant, Bayou Bistro, serves great Cajun food, and the hotel itself is located close to local sights.

See map p. 237. 1801 W. Pinhook Rd., Lafayette, LA 70508. ☎ *800-874-4664 in Louisiana, 800-826-8386 in the United States and Canada, or 337-233-8120. Fax: 337-234-9667.* www.bestwestern.com/hotelacadiana. *Parking: free. Rates: $79–$210 double. AE, DC, DISC, MC, V.*

Bois des Chenes Inn
$$–$$$

Once the center of a 3,000-acre cattle and sugar cane plantation, this plantation home is now a small but lovely bed-and-breakfast. With only five accommodations — two suites in the main plantation home and three rooms in the carriage house — each room has been lovingly restored and furnished with Louisiana French antiques. Room rates include not only a Louisiana-style breakfast but a bottle of wine and a tour of the house as well. Also available are nature and bird-watching trips into Atchafalaya Swamp, as well as guided fishing and hunting trips. These adventures are conducted by the inn's owner, a retired geologist.

See map p. 237. 338 N. Sterling St., Lafayette, LA 70501. ☎ *337-233-7816.* www. members.aol.com/boisdchene/bois.htm. *Parking: free. Rates: $100–$150 double. Rates include breakfast. Extra person $30. AE, MC, V.*

Where to dine in Cajun Country

Although all these restaurants have their merits — and very strong ones at that — if you have time for only one, I recommend Prejean's.

Café Vermilionville
$$–$$$

Want atmosphere? Café Vermilionville is located in a meticulously restored Acadian cypress house dating back to 1799. With plenty of fresh seafood on the menu, specialties include Creole bronze shrimp and the unique Louisiana Crawfish Madness, which is crawfish tails prepared according to the chef's mood: au gratin, étouffée, fried, or in crawfish beignets (oh yes, crawfish beignets).

See map p. 237. 1304 W. Pinhook Rd., Lafayette, LA 70508. ☎ *337-237-0100.* www.cafev.com. *Reservations and appropriate attire recommended. Main courses: $17–$26. AE, DC, DISC, MC, V. Open: Mon–Fri 11 a.m.–2 p.m. and Mon–Sat 5:30–10 p.m.*

Prejean's
$–$$

While in the heart of Cajun Country, treat yourself to a night at Prejean's, *the* spot for nouvelle Cajun cooking. Although it gives the appearance of being simply another family restaurant, the bill of fare reveals this place to be one of the finest restaurants in Acadiana, with some of the best ingredients and recipes you'll find in Cajun cuisine. Highlights include crawfish enchiladas, crawfish étouffée, grilled or fried oysters, gumbo, shrimp, and alligator. Kids can dine on burgers or chicken fingers. Live Cajun music plays nightly at 7 p.m.

See map p. 237. 3480 I-49 North, Lafayette, LA 70507 (next to the Evangeline Downs Racetrack). ☎ *337-896-3247.* www.prejeans.com. *Reservations strongly recommended. Main courses: $15–$26; children's menu $3.50–$8.95. AE, DC, DISC, MC, V. Open: Sun–Thurs 7 a.m.–10 p.m. and Fri–Sat 7 a.m.–11 p.m.*

Randol's Restaurant and Cajun Dance Hall
$–$$

For the full Cajun experience, go to Randol's and enjoy live Cajun music with your cuisine. Randol's serves up seafood fresh from the bayou, prepared any way you want it: fried, steamed, blackened, or grilled. The house

Passing a good time: Cajun Country nightlife

While in Lafayette, check out some of the local nightlife. A visit to **El Sid-O's** (see map p. 237. 1523 Martin Luther King Dr. in Lafayette), a hot spot for zydeco music, is an essential stop. The place is run by Sid Williams, whose brother Nathan is an acclaimed zydeco musician and leader of the popular group Nathan and the Zydeco Cha-Chas. The decor may not be very fancy, but that just adds to its appeal. A lot of zydeco history has gone down between these walls. Call ☎ **337-235-0647** to find out who's playing.

Grant Street Dance Hall (See map p. 237. 113 W. Grant St. in Lafayette) is the place where out-of-town rock bands are most apt to play when they pass through town (unless they're stadium-sized acts filling the nearby Cajundome). Local bands also call this place home, from alternative-rock outfits to Cajun and brass bands. Call ☎ **337-237-8513** or visit www.grantstreetdancehall.com for information.

specialty seafood platter guarantees to fill you up. It includes a cup of seafood gumbo, fried shrimp, fried oysters, fried catfish, stuffed crab, crawfish étouffée, deviled crab, and coleslaw. With live music every night at 7 p.m., you can take in a few dances before, during, and after your meal.

See map p. 237. 2320 Kaliste Saloom Rd., Lafayette, LA 70508. ☎ *800-962-2586 or 337-981-7080. Fax: 318-981-7083.* www.randols.com. *Reservations for 20 or more only. Main courses: $7.95–$18. MC, V. Open: Sun–Thurs 5 p.m.–10 p.m. and Fri–Sat 5 p.m.–11 p.m.*

Day-Trip No. 2: Plantations along the Great River Road

Once the focal point of a self-sustaining community, plantation homes flourished in Louisiana from the 1820s to the beginning of the Civil War. Although dozens of grand, beautiful homes once dotted the landscape (particularly around the Mississippi River because the homes were generally built near riverfronts), today the number has dwindled to a relative few. This trip meanders along the river between New Orleans and Baton Rouge, stopping at a number of stately plantation homes along the way.

Getting to the plantations

This trip follows Interstate 10 west of New Orleans. Each plantation listing includes driving times and directions. The plantations are listed in the order in which they appear on the "Day-Trip No. 2: Plantations along the Great River Road" map, running north from New Orleans along the Mississippi River. Keep in mind that the river winds a bit, so some distances may be deceiving.

Taking a plantation tour

All plantations listed in this section offer guided tours. Most present engaging historical details about the homes and their owners; I especially recommend you visit Laura and Destrehan Manor. Except where otherwise noted, tours generally last between 30 to 45 minutes. Some plantations schedule tours continuously (that is, a tour begins whenever a group arrives asking for one) or every 15 minutes or so. The Oak Alley and Houmas House tours begin on the half-hour. See the individual listings for admission prices.

Seeing the sights

Houses are spread apart and individual visits can take some time — seeing all the homes in a single day is unlikely. My advice is to pace yourself and find out how far you get by midday (or even midmorning). With a home or two under your belt, go through the list and concentrate on the ones that appeal to you the most. If you only have time for two or three, you can check out Laura, Oak Alley, and Madewood in one day at a comfortable pace. Allow one to one and a half hours for each visit, two and a half hours if you're a serious enthusiast.

With the exception of Destrehan Manor, with an elevator to the second floor, these plantation homes are rough going for those traveling in wheelchairs.

Destrehan Manor

The oldest plantation open to the public in the Lower Mississippi Valley, and the site of some of the largest live oaks in the country, Destrehan Manor was built in 1787 by a free person of color and restored using some of the earliest methods of construction. (In a nice touch, one room has been deliberately spared the renovation process, allowing a glimpse of the true ravages of age.) A cameo in the film *Interview with a Vampire*, along with its proximity to New Orleans, has made this a popular attraction. Guided tours start every 20 minutes.

See map p. 242. 13034 River Rd., Destrehan, LA 70047. ☎ **985-764-9315.** *Fax 985-725-1929.* www.destrehanplantation.org. *Located approximately 25 miles from New Orleans. Take I-10 West to Exit 220 (I-310 South), stay on I-310 for about 6 miles, exit onto River Road, and turn left at the light. Admission: $10 adults, $5 teenagers, $3 children 6–12; free for children under 6. Open: daily 9 a.m.–4 p.m.*

Houmas House Plantation & Gardens

The grand live oaks, magnolias, and formal gardens alone are worth the trip. The structure is actually two houses joined together; the original was built in 1790, and in 1840 a larger, Greek Revival–style house was built next to it (some time in the intervening years, a roof was built over both, joining them together). This bit of architectural jury-rigging adds to the intrigue.

Day-Trip No. 2: Plantations along the Great River Road

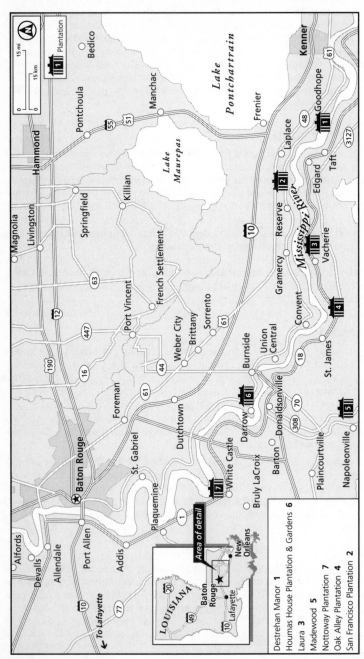

See map p. 242. 40136 Highway 942 Burnside, LA 70725 (58 miles from New Orleans). ☎ *888-323-8314 or 225-473-7841. Fax: 225-474-0480.* www.houmashouse.com. *Take I-10 from New Orleans or Baton Rouge, exit onto Highway 44 to Burnside, turn right on Highway 942. Admission: $10 adults, $6 children 13–17, $3 children 6–12; free for children under 6. Open: daily Feb–Oct 10 a.m.–5 p.m. and Nov–Jan 10 a.m.–4 p.m. Closed holidays.*

Laura: A Creole Plantation

This is the belle of the ball, the one plantation home you should definitely see. You'll find a refreshing, educational atmosphere rather than the touristy patronization you might get from other homes. General manager Normal Marmillion and his outstanding staff share what daily life on a sugar plantation was like for both the masters and the slaves (a disappointingly rare insight on most plantation tours) in the 18th and 19th centuries. This cultural history of Louisiana Creoles is astoundingly detailed thanks to former occupant Laura Locoul's diary. The house is a brightly painted, classic Creole home — perhaps plain compared to neighboring Oak Alley — sheltering more than 375 original artifacts spanning a 200-year period in the lives of one family. Basic tours last about an hour. If you want a longer tour, you can schedule in advance a special 90-minute tour; topics include "Women on the Creole Plantation" and "Plantation Slaves, Artisans, and Folklore." The famous Br'er Rabbit stories were first collected here by a folklorist in the 1870s. Be sure to walk the grounds afterward to view the slave cabins, overseer cottages, barns, and the 1829 Maison de Reprise.

See map p. 242. 2247 Highway 18, Vacherie, LA 70090. ☎ *888-799-7690 or 225-265-7690.* www.lauraplantation.com. *Located about 60 miles from New Orleans. Take I-10 West about 28 miles from New Orleans to Exit 194 (Gramercy). Cross the bridge and turn left onto Highway 18 (River Road); travel about 4 more miles. Admission: $10 adults, $5 students and children 6–17; free for children under 6. Open: daily 9:30 a.m.–5 p.m. Closed major holidays.*

Madewood

Another must-see stop on this route, Madewood is an imposing two-story Greek Revival mansion with a bit of history behind it (surprise, surprise!). The owner commissioned it solely for the purpose of outdoing his brother, who had a grand house of his own. The construction took eight years, including four just to cut the lumber and make the bricks. In a cruel twist of fate, the owner died of yellow fever just before the house's completion. Current owner Keith Marshall's parents bought and saved it from disrepair in 1964, and photos of the laborious restoration process are a revelation. Marshall and his wife, Millie Ball (travel editor for *The Times-Picayune*), are gracious hosts who tell delightful stories. You can stay overnight, either in the main house for $225, or in a more secluded raised cottage. (A bronze plaque notes that Brad Pitt slept here while filming *Interview with the Vampire*.)

See map p. 242. 4250 Highway 308, Napoleonville, LA 70390. ☎ *800-375-7151 or 985-369-7151. Fax: 985-369-9848.* www.madewood.com. *Located approximately 72 miles from New Orleans. Take I-10 West from New Orleans to Exit 182 (Donaldsonville). Cross the Sunshine Bridge onto Highway 70; follow it to Spur 70. Follow signs that say "Bayou Plantations," turn left onto Highway 308, and then travel south about 6 miles. Admission: $8 adults, $4 children and students. Open: daily 10 a.m.–4 p.m. Closed holidays.*

Nottoway Plantation

The last stop on this tour is a comparative stone's throw (about 25 miles) from Baton Rouge. The house has a formidable presence, with 22 enormous columns and its original slate roof. Sixty-four rooms cover more than 54,000 square feet, including a grand ballroom, beautiful archways, and original crystal chandeliers. It was saved from Civil War destruction by a Northern gunboat officer who had once been a guest here. You can have lunch or dinner in the restaurant, and stay overnight in one of the restored bedrooms for between $125 and $250 a night. The rate includes a full plantation breakfast, a wake-up tray of muffins, juice, and coffee, and a house tour.

See map p. 242. 30970 Mississippi River Rd. (P.O. Box 160), White Castle, LA 70788. ☎ *866-LASOUTH or 225-545-2730. Fax: 225-545-8632.* www.nottoway.com. *Located 69 miles from New Orleans. From New Orleans, follow I-10 West to the Highway 22 exit, and then turn left on Highway 70 across Sunshine Bridge; exit onto Highway 1 and drive 14 miles north through Donaldsonville. From Baton Rouge, take I-10 West to the Plaquemine exit and then Highway 1 south for 18 miles. Admission: $10 adults, $4 children 5 to 12; free for children under 5. Open: daily 9 a.m.–5 p.m. Last tour begins at 4:30 p.m. Closed Dec 25.*

Oak Alley Plantation

Originally named Bon Sejour, the most popular plantation home in Louisiana gets its current name from a quarter-mile alleyway of live oaks. Along with Laura and Madewood, this is the best bet for those wishing to abridge this trip into a "best of" tour, offering exactly what the word "plantation" conjures up. A nonprofit foundation runs the place, and authentically costumed guides lead tours. The mansion has been lovingly restored, though its furnishings range from antiques to modern. You can stay the night (it also serves as a bed-and-breakfast), with rates from $105 to $135. On-site is a restaurant open for breakfast and lunch.

See map p. 242. 3645 Highway 18, Vacherie, LA 70090. ☎ *800-44-ALLEY or 225-265-2151. Fax: 225-265-7035.* www.oakalleyplantation.com. *Located 60 miles from New Orleans. Take I-10 West to Exit 194 (Gramercy). Turn left on Highway 641 (South), and follow the highway, which turns into Highway 3213. Continue over the Veteran's Memorial Bridge. Turn left onto Highway 18 and drive 7½ miles to the plantation. Admission: $10 adults, $5 students, $3 children 6–12; free for children under 6. No credit cards accepted. Open: daily Mar–Oct 9 a.m.–5:30 p.m. and Nov–Feb 9 a.m.– 5 p.m. Closed in the a.m. on New Year's Day (call for details), Thanksgiving, Christmas.*

San Francisco Plantation

This fanciful home's broad galleries resemble a ship's double decks, and atop two sets of stairs is a broad main portal much like a steamboat's grand salon. English and French 18th-century furniture and paintings are featured as part of the restoration. The contrast between the plantation and its neighbor, a huge oil refinery practically in its backyard, is a bit jarring but oddly enough adds some poignant perspective on how much the times have changed.

See map p. 242. 2646 Highway 44 (P.O. 950), Garyville, LA 70051. ☎ *888-322-1756 or 985-535-2341. Fax: 985-535-5450.* www.sanfranciscoplantation.org. *Located approximately 35 miles from New Orleans. Take I-10 West to U.S. 51 (23 miles). Turn south and continue for 3 miles to Highway 44 and then go west for 5 miles. Admission: $10 adults, $5 students 13–18, $3 children 6–12; free for children under 6. Open: daily 9:30 a.m.–5 p.m. Closed major holidays and Mardi Gras.*

Where to stay and dine

For accommodations at a plantation, see the preceding listings for Oak Alley Plantation, Madewood, and Nottoway Plantation.

For dining, see the preceding listings for Oak Alley Plantation (lunch) and Nottoway Plantation (lunch and dinner). Two noteworthy eateries near Houmas House are **The Cabin** (5405 Hwy. 44 at the intersection of Highway 22, in Burnside, approximately 3 miles from Houmas House; ☎ **225-473-3007;** www.thecabinrestaurant.com) and **Hymel's** (8740 Hwy. 44 in Convent, approximately 8 miles south of Burnside; ☎ **225-562-7031**). Near Laura and Oak Alley, I like the family operation **B & C Seafood Market & Cajun Deli** (2155 Hwy. 18 in Vacherie, about 1 mile from Laura; ☎ 225-265-8356).

Day-Trip No. 3: New Orleans Nature Getaway

This trip takes you a world away from the other experiences in this book and gets you back to New Orleans in time for an evening out. Grab breakfast at one of your favorite local morning spots before driving across the Mississippi River on the Crescent City Connection to the West Bank. Spend the morning at **Barataria Preserve** followed by lunch at **Restaurant des Familles** in nearby Crown Point or an English tea at **Victoria Inn & Gardens** in Lafitte. Then spend the afternoon communing with alligators on a swamp tour before dining at **Voleo's.**

Getting back to nature

In New Orleans, get on Interstate 10 East heading toward the Mississippi River and the West Bank. (Yes, it's the West Bank, though it's directly *east* of New Orleans. Go figure.) Cross the Crescent City Connection; after you're over it becomes the West Bank Expressway, an elevated thoroughfare that connects a good deal of the West Bank. Go to Exit 4B,

Day-Trip No. 3: New Orleans Nature Getaway

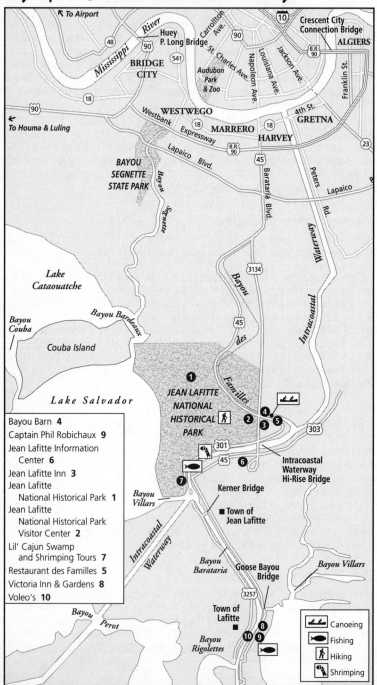

Bayou Barn **4**
Captain Phil Robichaux **9**
Jean Lafitte Information
    Center **6**
Jean Lafitte Inn **3**
Jean Lafitte
    National Historical Park **1**
Jean Lafitte
    National Historical Park
    Visitor Center **2**
Lil' Cajun Swamp
    and Shrimping Tours **7**
Restaurant des Familles **5**
Victoria Inn & Gardens **8**
Voleo's **10**

Barataria Boulevard, and get off, turning left at the second stoplight onto Barataria Boulevard. Then drive about 9 miles to Barataria Preserve.

Taking a swamp tour

 L'il Cajun Swamp and Shrimping Tours (See map p. 246. Hwy. 301, just outside Jean Lafitte National Park, next to Frank's Boat Launch; ☎ **800-725-3213** or 504-689-3213; www.lilcajunswamptours.com) are led by Captain Cyrus Blanchard, one character of a tour guide who isn't afraid to give his opinion on anything. (Be sure to ask about his pet alligator, Julie.) His tour includes Bayou Barataria and is roughly two hours long. Admission is $17 adults, $15 seniors, $13 children 4–12, and free for children under 4. Tour times are 10 a.m. and 2 p.m. The boat is wheelchair accessible, but the bathrooms aren't.

Seeing the sights

The **Barataria Preserve** is a branch of the **Jean Lafitte National Historical Park and Preserve,** which encompasses several locations around the state. The preserve sprawls over approximately 20,000 acres of hardwood forest, cypress swampland, and freshwater marshlands, with 8 miles of hiking trails (including 2½ miles of boardwalk) and waterways, preserving a representative sample of the environment of the delta, including bayous, swamps, marshes, and natural levee forests.

The wildlife preserve was once home to prehistoric human settlements (archaeologists have unearthed village sites along the bayous dating back some 2,000 years). The trails and waterways make it a natural spot for hiking and exploration, and for getting some perspective on the peoples who settled this area, which was a delta formed by the Mississippi River some 2,500 years ago. You can easily lose yourself here, either taking a "natural history walk," striking out on your own along the pathways, or exploring the 9 miles of canoe trails (closed to motorized boats and accessible by three canoe launch docks; see canoe rental information later in this section), as well as 20 miles of waterways accessible to all types of craft. Picnic tables are scattered throughout, and fishing (with a valid Louisiana fishing license) and hunting and trapping (by permit only) are allowed; the marshes are dotted with recreational hunting and fishing camps. Hunting permits and fishing licenses can be purchased online at www.wlf.state.la.us or at a nearby marina — the closest is 2 miles away at Cochiara's Marina, 4477 Jean Lafitte Blvd. in Lafitte, ☎ **504-689-3701.** *Note:* Bring mosquito repellent!

Head to the **Visitor Center** (See map p. 246. 6488 Barataria Blvd. in Marrero; ☎ **504-589-2330;** www.nps.gov/jela/Barataria Preserve.htm) for maps, exhibits, and films. Trails in the preserve are open daily from 7 a.m. to 7 p.m. (during daylight savings hours) and 7 a.m. to 5 p.m. (standard time), and the visitor center is open daily from 9 a.m. to 5 p.m. (closed on Christmas Day). No admission fee is required, though donations are welcome. The visitor center, restrooms, and the Bayou Coquille Trail are all wheelchair accessible.

Canoe rentals are available at **Bayou Barn** (See map p. 246. 7145 Barataria Blvd. in Crown Point; ☎ **504-689-2663**), next door to Restaurant des Familles (mentioned in the following paragraph) and **Jean Lafitte Inn** (See map p. 246. ☎ **504-689-3271**), located next to the park just off Barataria Boulevard (before you get to the Lafitte/LaRose Highway, which you cross on your way to Restaurant des Familles). The last time I canoed the bayou, I accidentally bopped an alligator on its head with my paddle (they sleep just below the surface). The adventure continued when a heavy thunderstorm (complete with lightning bolts) hit just after the halfway point. Scary stuff, but it was still a refreshing change of pace from the city. Rentals must be returned by dark at either location.

Where to dine

For lunch, select from seafood, Cajun, or Creole dishes (I can't resist the spicy shrimp balls) while overlooking a picturesque bayou at **Restaurant des Familles** (See map p. 246. 7163 Barataria Blvd. in Crown Point; ☎ **504-689-7834**). The restaurant is open Tuesday through Saturday for lunch and dinner (as well as Sunday for brunch).

Alternatively, treat yourself to a feast for all the senses with an afternoon tea and garden tour at **Victoria Inn & Gardens** (See map p. 246. 4707 Jean Lafitte Blvd. in Lafitte; ☎ **800-689-4797** or 504-689-3399; www. victoriainn.com). The teas — specially blended for the inn — are served in delicate, antique china cups with a mouth-watering assortment of tea breads, scones, finger sandwiches, and sweets. I recommend you sit on the gallery overlooking the Shakespeare Herb Garden. Tea is served daily between 2 p.m.–5 p.m. Reservations are required; adults cost $15, children 10 and under $8 (garden tours are free). Dinner is available nightly at **The Restaurant at Victoria Inn**, featuring Creole cuisine by candlelight.

You may like what you see during the tour — that lakeside pool is as refreshing as it looks — and decide to stay. Hosts Roy and Dale Ross see to your every need, whether its reserving a saltwater fishing excursion with **Captain Phil Robichaux** (☎ **504-689-2006**) or giving you frank recommendations on local attractions. Single rooms cost $95, doubles and queens $110, luxury suites with Jacuzzi from $140. Well-behaved dogs are welcome; call ahead for details.

For dinner, go to **Voleo's** (See map p. 246. 5134 Nunez St. in Lafitte; ☎ **504-689-2482**), where former Paul Prudhomme apprentice David Volion presides over award-winning Cajun, Creole, and German dishes at cheap bayou prices. This is one of my favorite places to eat in all of Greater New Orleans. Try the sinfully rich seafood gumbo or signature flounder Lafitte and taste why.

Part V

Living It Up After Dark: New Orleans Nightlife

JAZZ GROUPS TO AVOID

The Modern Saw Quartet

Jazz fusion group: Return to Whatever

The Balloon Jazz Orchestra

In this part . . .

*N*ew Orleans after dark is nothing like New Orleans during the day. The experience is completely different — with its own landmarks, history, and etiquette. Chapter 15 delves into the local theater and performing arts scenes, while Chapter 16 focuses on the city's best clubs and bars, whether you want the quickie tourist experience or something more authentic. Chapter 16 also ferrets out the best spots for real-deal Cajun and zydeco music.

Chapter 15

Applauding the Cultural Scene

● ●

In This Chapter

▶ Finding out what's playing and where to get tickets

▶ Getting the lowdown on the New Orleans theater scene

▶ Making the New Orleans opera, ballet, and orchestra scenes

● ●

*T*he performing arts likely aren't the first thing you think of when coming to New Orleans. After all, in terms of size, scale, and importance, the scene here is a far cry from, say, New York City's. No one comes to New Orleans on vacation with the express purpose of seeing the ballet or some edgy, off-Broadway fare. What New Orleans *is* known for is its food, music, and rich history (in no particular order). But you can make a strong argument in favor of its performing arts taking a respectable fourth place.

Historically, New Orleans has enjoyed status as a small but thriving center for the performing arts; at one time, it boasted what was the continent's first opera house. The city hasn't seen the likes of that heady heyday in decades, but the theater and performing arts thrive in a city as creative and multicultural as this one.

Finding Out What's Playing and Getting Tickets

The *Times-Picayune* (in its weekly **Lagniappe** entertainment section) and *Gambit Weekly* are good places to look for listings, reviews, and previews of major arts events. If you're looking for information before you arrive, try their Web sites: www.nola.com and www.bestofnew orleans.com, respectively. Another good source is the local CitySearch site (http://neworleans.citysearch.com).

A great way to find out what's happening is www.culturefinder.com, a site with information on arts venues in a variety of cities. You can search for arts events by date and a list of featured organizations and venues, with upcoming or ongoing events for that locale, along with contact information.

New Orleans doesn't have a local ticket broker such as New York's TKTS. Tickets to most local productions are easily available through the venue's box office, and most of the larger spaces (such as the Saenger, the Orpheum, and the Contemporary Arts Center) take credit cards; they also usually offer tickets via **Ticketmaster** (☎ **504-522-5555**). Smaller theaters accept cash only (though Southern Rep and NORD accept local checks) at the door the night of the show. For a popular event, such as an opera production or a Broadway touring company, reserve as far in advance as possible, or ask your hotel concierge (assuming your hotel has one) to find out about acquiring tickets for you.

Raising the Curtain on the Performing Arts

Do you have a free evening and want to take in a show, catch the symphony, or enjoy an opera? If so, the following section can give you all the details.

Theater

New Orleans actually boasts a good theater scene, a tight community that makes up in passion, creativity, and quality what it lacks in size. Though no heir apparent to Tennessee Williams is waiting in the wings to usher the city into a glorious new age, theater in New Orleans is much more than touring companies of national productions and amateur dinner theater (though you find plenty of both). New Orleans boasts a handful of inventive local companies staging intriguing original works or creative reinterpretations of classics (and usually drawing pretty good crowds). Of course, tried-and-true standby fare such as *The Fantasticks* is always being produced somewhere, by someone, at any time.

So what's hot right now? As you would expect, national tours of big-name productions are always popular. Whenever you come, the Saenger Theatre on Canal Street will most likely offer that season's hot ticket, whether it be *Proof* or *The Producers*. Local classics, such as anything written by Williams, are a good bet.

Without further ado, the following lists the more prominent theater spaces in the city:

✔ One of the city's major hubs for the arts, **Contemporary Arts Center** (900 Camp St. in the Warehouse District; ☎ **504-528-3800**; www.cacno.org) features exhibits of contemporary art (of course), and also hosts some small productions in its intimate performance spaces. You find experimental works by local playwrights as well as the occasional comedy and musical (concerts, dance productions, and film screenings also take place here). The rooms are small enough that no seat is really bad. A cybercafe is also on the premises: Cybercafe @ the CAC. The CAC itself has no dress code, though the promoters/producers of specific shows or events may impose one.

✔ **le chat noir** (715 St. Charles Ave. in the Central Business District; ☎ 504-581-5812; www.cabaretlechatnoir.com) is one of the hippest, hottest spots in the city. The intimate (135-seat) space lends itself to give-and-take exchanges between audience and performers. Typical fare may include a one-woman (or -man) show of the life and songs of French chanteuse Edith Piaf, a performance art piece with audience participation, or a set by a singer or local jazz band. Stick around after the show; the piano bar on Saturday nights has been compared favorably to the edgy, unpredictable vibe of Parisian cabaret. Attire is semiformal.

✔ A long-running kid-friendly theater, **Le Petit Theatre du Vieux Carre** (616 St. Peter St. in the French Quarter; ☎ 504-522-2081) produces three children's shows every season and is home to one of the oldest nonprofessional theater troupes in the United States. The main performance stage, open from September to June, generally presents well-chosen plays and musicals. A smaller performance space sports edgier, experimental fare from local writers.

✔ **NORD Theater** (705 Lafayette St. in Gallier Hall, one block from Poydras Street in the Central Business District; ☎ 504-565-7860), a long-running arm of the New Orleans Recreation Department, is primarily a vehicle for local children, though the productions and target audience aren't limited to children. The summer production is usually kid-oriented, while the fall one is a better bet for adults. The theater stages four productions a year, mostly musicals — Broadway, off-Broadway, or original. This comfortable, intimate theater (seating capacity is 120) has plenty of legroom, and no dress code.

✔ The venerable **Saenger Theatre** (143 N. Rampart St; ☎ 504-525-1052; www.saengertheatre.com) opened in 1927, and restoration efforts have managed to retain some of its original elegance. The decor is Florentine Renaissance, with Greek and Roman sculpture, fine marble statues, and cut-glass chandeliers. The ceiling looks like a night sky, with realistic clouds and stars. Against this backdrop, locals enjoy touring theater productions (some are Best Musical Tony Award winners) and popular performances by everyone from David Bowie to Neil Young and comedians like *The Daily Show*'s Lewis Black.

✔ **Southern Rep Theatre** (Canal Place Shopping Center; ☎ 504-522-6545; www.southernrep.com) focuses on Southern playwrights and actors, and benefits from a convenient location on the lip of the Quarter at Canal Street; plenty of validated parking is in the shopping center's spacious, multilevel garage. The pace slows down in summer, but it does have children's programs. Performance space is intimate, but comfortable, as befits its high-rise digs; the atmosphere (and dress code) is casual.

✔ **True Brew Coffee House and Theater** (200 Julia St. in the Warehouse District; ☎ 504-524-8440) seats around 100 people in relative comfort, with the added benefit of coffees, teas, and pastries. Productions include one-act plays, some filled with local references and in jokes that don't mean much to visitors. Comedy and live music are also regular offerings.

✔ **Zeitgeist Multi-Disciplinary Arts Center** (1724 Oretha Castle Haley Blvd.; ☎ 504-525-2767; www.zeitgeistinc.org) complements the Contemporary Arts Center. The bill of fare is left of center all the way, from performance art to edgy original plays and independent films — everything from Andy Warhol to Leni Riefenstahl to original works on growing up gay in New Orleans.

Dining before (and after) the show

You'll have no trouble making an evening of dining and theater in New Orleans. If you're lucky, you can find a restaurant that matches the mood and feel of the play, musical, or piece you're going to see. A playbill for a touring show at the Saenger Theatre, for example, will likely include ads placed by the **Palace Café** (see Chapter 10) and **Dominique's** (in the **Maison Dupuy** hotel, 1001 Toulouse St.; ☎ 504-522-8800). If you want to mingle, head to the **Sazerac** bar in the Fairmont Hotel (see Chapter 16) to see and be seen by some of the city's elite. These establishments are a fine start (or finish) to an evening at the elegant Saenger.

On your way to or from Southern Rep, a host of French Quarter choices are nearby, although I prefer the bistro elegance of **Mr. B's Bistro** (see Chapter 10). If you're looking for something more casual, try an overstuffed oyster po' boy at **Acme Oyster House** (see Chapter 10). For a performance at Le Petit, the nearby **The Bistro at Maison de Ville** is a favorite of theater patrons and performers; the elegant **Court of Two Sisters** is also a good spot (see Chapter 10 for both). To satisfy your post-theater munchies, head down St. Peter to Dumaine and plop yourself down at the **Clover Grill**, the "happiest grill on earth" (see Chapter 10).

In the Central Business District, the family-friendly **Bon Ton Café** (401 Magazine St.; ☎ 504-524-3386) is the perfect complement to an evening at NORD Theater. Nothing nearby mirrors the unique Parisian cabaret experience at le chat noir, though **Mother's** provides some amusing contrast (see Chapter 10). Closer in spirit, the **Veranda** (inside the **Hotel Inter-Continental**, 444 St. Charles Ave.; ☎ 504-585-4383) and **Palace Café** (see Chapter 10) are a straight shot down St. Charles Avenue.

Performing arts venues

Unless otherwise noted, most of the events put on by the arts organizations in this chapter occur at one of the places listed here (all of which are wheelchair accessible). You can generally purchase tickets for these venues at their box office or through Ticketmaster (☎ 504-522-5555). Keep in mind that unless you receive specific information to the contrary, appropriate dress for these venues is business dress or black-tie formal:

✔ **The Orpheum Theater** (129 University Place. in the Central Business District; ☎ 504-524-3285) is home to the Louisiana Philharmonic Orchestra. Other productions, and the occasional rock or pop concert, may also play here.

✔ **The Mahalia Jackson Theatre of the Performing Arts** (801 N. Rampart St.; ☎ 504-565-8081) is the favored venue for touring musical shows as well as the home of local opera and ballet performances. It sits inside the 32-acre New Orleans Cultural Center complex in Armstrong Park.

✔ **New Orleans Municipal Auditorium** (1201 St. Peter St.; ☎ 504-565-7490) was once the premier venue for concerts and events. It still hosts the occasional touring show and often plays host to the Jazz and Heritage Festival's nighttime concert series. The auditorium is located inside the New Orleans Cultural Center in Armstrong Park, across a walkway from the Mahalia Jackson Theater of the Performing Arts.

In keeping with its casual vibe, New Orleans is pretty lax about dress codes. Exceptions exist, of course, but generally you can get by with a basic business-casual look. At le chat noir, which aspires to a hip atmosphere where dressing up is half the fun, a semiformal approach is required. But after that, it's fair game.

Symphony

Most people, including the locals, often overlook the **Louisiana Philharmonic Orchestra** (☎ 504-523-6530; www.lpomusic.com) in favor of the city's hopping bar and club scene. It's a shame because the LPO is a delightful way to spend an evening. The most popular program is *Beethoven and Blue Jeans,* which relaxes the formal dress code in a successful attempt to introduce classical music to a wider audience. The season runs from September through May. Tickets range from $13 to $62; prices are higher for special events.

Opera

The **New Orleans Opera Association** (☎ 800-881-4459 or 504-529-2278; www.neworleansopera.org) has been around since 1943, providing local opera buffs with a steady diet of classic performances each season. The company is talented and professional; this isn't the local amateur hour. Often, the association features a star performer from, say, the Metropolitan Opera Company, with local talents in supporting roles. The fare runs from familiar classics to new, edgy works.

Dance

The **Delta Festival Ballet** is comprised primarily of area talent that performs a seasonal schedule, including a popular annual production of *The Nutcracker* at Christmastime. Call ☎ **504-836-7166** for performance calendar, ticket prices, and other information. The **New Orleans Ballet Association,** despite its name, isn't a local company. Instead, it presents a schedule of touring shows. The season generally runs from September to June. Tickets are available through Ticketmaster (☎ **504-522-5555**) or through the Association box office (☎ **504-522-0996**); tickets range from $15 to $70 and can increase for special events.

Chapter 16

Hitting the Clubs and Bars

In This Chapter

▶ Checking out French Quarter nightlife

▶ Finding the best bars and clubs elsewhere in the city

▶ Discovering a spot to suit your style, from hip hangouts to piano bars

Saying that New Orleans is the party capital of the United States is a cliché and a major understatement; however, you can't deny that things are definitely looser here, especially after dark, when the city marches to the beat of a decidedly different drummer than during the weekday 9-to-5 grind. And I don't just mean the slinky, greasy rhythms of funk and R&B or the stately clip of vintage jazz. I'm talking about mood. The city grows livelier; for proof, you need walk no farther than the nearest bar.

What makes for a cool bar? It depends on who you ask. Some people want a nice, dark watering hole, while others want a high-energy dance workout and the chance to discreetly bump into an anonymous member of their preferred sex. This chapter explores all the nooks and crannies of New Orleans's bar scene. It stops in at some rowdy saloons, upscale bars, dance clubs, and your regular hole-in-the-wall dives.

Keep in mind that the selections throughout this chapter aren't all-inclusive. Because New Orleans boasts more bars and music clubs per capita than almost any other city in the United States, you'll doubtless find a host of other happening places on your own. For comprehensive club and bar listings, go online prior to your arrival or pick up a free copy of *Gambit Weekly* (see Chapter 3 or go to www.bestofneworleans.com) or *Offbeat* magazine (see Appendix or go to www.offbeat.com) at your hotel or nearby coffeehouse or retail store. Every Friday, the *Times-Picayune* publishes *Lagniappe*, its pull-out entertainment section (see Chapter 3).

If you're here for **Mardi Gras** (see Chapters 6 and 11 for more information), you may notice that after the last float rolls by, the party simply relocates to another spot, such as a bar. Club owners usually book exciting, party-friendly acts, even on Sunday and Monday nights when many spots would otherwise be dark. If you base your dream image of New Orleans on the constant street-party scenes you've seen in the movies, Mardi Gras is your time.

Playing by the Rules

Some people may be disappointed to discover that the legal drinking age in Louisiana is 21 — for years, it was 18. If you're of drinking age, however, you'll be delighted to know that you can legally walk along any public street with a drink in your hand (though the drink must be in a plastic cup, called a *go-* or *geaux-cup*). Drinking alcohol in a vehicle is illegal, even if you're just a passenger. So if you feel the need to imbibe while getting somewhere, stick to the sidewalks. See Chapter 17 for more information about drinks on the go.

Unless otherwise noted, most places listed in this chapter don't usually charge a cover (though all bets are off during Mardi Gras or Jazz Fest). For locations of nightlife spots inside and outside the French Quarter, refer to the maps later in this chapter.

Entering the Neon Party Zone: French Quarter Nightlife

Tourist nightlife centers around the French Quarter, as you may have guessed. Keep in mind, however, that the key word here is "tourist." Tons of clubs are concentrated here, many solely to cater to the constant influx of visitors (with *some* notable exceptions to this rule). Some are cheap, some are tacky; many are both. Of course, you can find some genuinely good haunts here as well. Where the French Quarter is concerned, the epicenter of nightlife is Bourbon Street.

Drinking in Bourbon Street

Having just cautioned you against relying too much on the Quarter bar scene, I don't want to discourage you from stepping onto world-famous Bourbon Street altogether. (My husband still shakes his head at my insistence that his visiting parents walk at least one block of Bourbon, but I felt it was important that when they returned to their Midwest hometown, they could tell everyone that they had in fact experienced it. That's one of the first questions your family, friends, and coworkers will ask: Did you go to Bourbon Street? Imagine their reaction if you said no! They may make you go back.) But if you stroll down Bourbon and assume that you've experienced all that New Orleans nightlife has to offer, well, you know what they say about people who assume . . . .

Sure, Bourbon Street is a tourist attraction, first and foremost. Like Beale Street in Memphis, it became an attraction because of something genuine and authentic, but almost all vestiges of that elusive something have been replaced by glitter, glitz, and spectacle. Still, seedy as it can be, Bourbon Street can also be a fun barrage of sights, sounds, and smells. With every kind of music, from jazz, blues, and rock-and-roll to rhythm and blues, country, Celtic, and Cajun, it's not the quality so much as the sheer variety that's important here.

Many Bourbon Street establishments are open 24 hours. Others open late in the afternoon, when the area starts to come to life. After 8 p.m. the street is blocked off to traffic, and the streets and sidewalks are filled with people.

You may notice that St. Ann Street, about eight blocks off Canal, marks a division on Bourbon Street — it's the unofficial boundary between the straight and gay sections of the area. Although not every bar or person east of St. Ann is gay, and not every bar or person west is straight, you'll likely notice a marked difference in the feel of the areas.

Be careful when exploring: The farther you get away from the river or the farther you go down Bourbon Street (away from Canal), the fewer people will be around and the less safe the area becomes. If you must explore more-deserted sections, keep alert.

Hitting the quarter notes: Some prime French Quarter spots

Locals widely consider the French Quarter to be one large tourist trap. You need a scorecard to distinguish the authentic, character-filled spots, which *do* exist, from the tourist magnets. Following is my subjective list:

- ✔ Check out the **Funky Pirate** (727 Bourbon St.; ☎ **504-523-1960**) for a true Bourbon Street blues experience. One of the area's biggest (literally and figuratively) blues musicians, Big Al Carson, deals out Chicago-style electric blues most nights. His schedule varies; call to find out when he's playing. No cover, but expect a one-drink minimum.

- ✔ **The Hideout** (1207 Decatur St.; ☎ **504-529-7119**) can best be described as a safe, friendly approximation of a hole-in-the-wall experience. The place used to house a pretty intimidating gay/biker bar, but these days most everyone, from punks to tourists, is welcome.

- ✔ **Molly's at the Market** (1107 Decatur St.; ☎ **504-525-5169**) draws a strange cross-section of locals. Something of a hangout for local media types (especially on Thursday nights), the pub-crawling legions make this a frequent stop as well. That includes Goth types as well as bohemians in tie-dyes who look like they haven't washed in weeks, and even just regular Joes out for a drink.

- ✔ **Ol'Toone's Saloon** (233 Decatur St.; ☎ **504-529-3422**) is a somewhat nondescript bar next to House of Blues on Decatur. A good place to unwind after catching a show next door, it has a pretty good vibe when it fills up. It attracts its fair share of characters and is open 24 hours.

French Quarter Nightlife

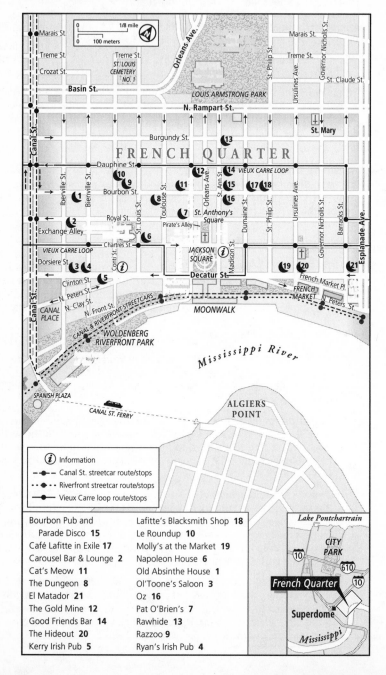

Bourbon Pub and
  Parade Disco **15**

Café Lafitte in Exile **17**

Carousel Bar & Lounge **2**

Cat's Meow **11**

The Dungeon **8**

El Matador **21**

The Gold Mine **12**

Good Friends Bar **14**

The Hideout **20**

Kerry Irish Pub **5**

Lafitte's Blacksmith Shop **18**

Le Roundup **10**

Molly's at the Market **19**

Napoleon House **6**

Old Absinthe House **1**

Ol'Toone's Saloon **3**

Oz **16**

Pat O'Brien's **7**

Rawhide **13**

Razzoo **9**

Ryan's Irish Pub **4**

Getting All Jazzed Up

New Orleans is the birthplace of jazz. Some say the genre was born in the brothels of old Storyville (New Orleans's long-gone, but still-legendary, red-light district), where the city's innovative young musicians entertained the clients, who in turn spread the word about this sexy new music. "Just what is jazz?" you ask. As Louis Armstrong once said, "If you got to ask what it is, you'll never get to know." By the time you've danced your way through these clubs, you'll no longer have to ask.

Preserving the strains of Dixieland jazz

Interested in hearing some old-school jazz? Head to one of these venues for a memorable evening of traditional New Orleans jazz.

✔ For jazz with a little different slant, try **Fritzel's European Jazz Club** (733 Bourbon St.; ☎ 504-561-0432; www.fritzels.info). Fritzel's is known for late-night (or early-morning) jam sessions. Musicians who have finished playing their sets at other jazz clubs often come here to take turns running through old-time traditional jazz. An oasis among the sanitized jazz spots in the French Quarter, this place boasts an agreeable German beer-house decor, with a one-drink minimum per set instead of a cover charge. Come here way after midnight, order a German beer, and watch some talented musicians compare notes. Children aren't allowed. Music starts at 9:30 p.m. and runs late.

✔ The sign outside **Maison Bourbon** (641 Bourbon St.; ☎ 504-522-8818) proclaims that the place is "Dedicated to the Preservation of Jazz," which means that Dixieland jazz is the only item on the musical menu. Despite being located on Bourbon Street, this isn't a tourist trap. No children are allowed, so if you're with kids and want them to get a taste of some Dixieland, simply stand outside the bar — you can hear and see everything just fine. Records and CDs are available for purchase. Show times vary; it's open from 2:30 p.m. to 12:15 a.m. Monday through Thursday, and from 3:30 p.m. to 1:15 a.m. Friday through Sunday. Though you won't face a cover charge, a one-drink minimum is enforced.

✔ The **Palm Court Jazz Café** (1204 Decatur St.; ☎ 504-525-0200; www.palmcourtjazz.com), like Preservation Hall, offers old-style jazz played by old-style musicians — but the Palm Court also has air conditioning, food (which can be a little pricey), and drinks. You may want to make reservations. Music is played from 8 to 11 p.m., Wednesday through Sunday. Cover $5 per person at tables; no cover at bar.

✔ **Preservation Hall** (726 St. Peter St.; ☎ 800-785-5772 or 504-522-2841; www.preservationhall.com) is run by a nonprofit group dedicated to the preservation of jazz. Shows start at 8:30 p.m. and

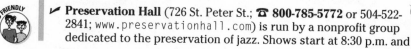

French Quarter Music

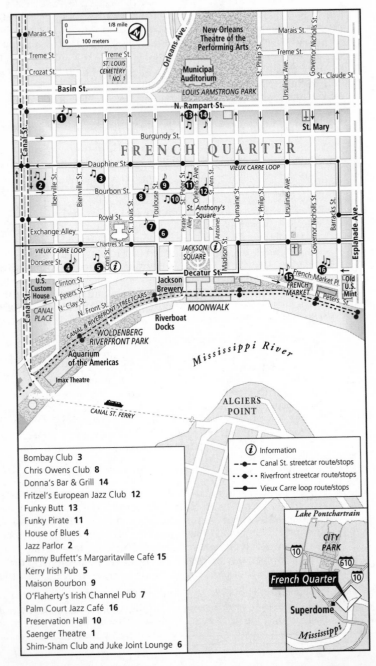

Bombay Club **3**
Chris Owens Club **8**
Donna's Bar & Grill **14**
Fritzel's European Jazz Club **12**
Funky Butt **13**
Funky Pirate **11**
House of Blues **4**
Jazz Parlor **2**
Jimmy Buffett's Margaritaville Café **15**
Kerry Irish Pub **5**
Maison Bourbon **9**
O'Flaherty's Irish Channel Pub **7**
Palm Court Jazz Café **16**
Preservation Hall **10**
Saenger Theatre **1**
Shim-Sham Club and Juke Joint Lounge **6**

end around midnight, with 35-minute sets and about a 10-minute break after each set. The band plays requests if you make a decent offering, but try not to be the fifth person in a row to request "When the Saints Go Marching In." Keep in mind that you'll find minimal seating, no air conditioning, and no food or drinks. Still, you'll almost certainly enjoy yourself, and the kids should love it, too. A selection of tapes and CDs is for sale if you find you can't get enough of the music. Cover $5.

In praise of contemporary jazz

If you have a taste for modern interpretations of jazz, try one of these suggestions.

✔ Jazz Fest–quality music and food from the Brennan family (thanks to the Red Fish Grill right next door) are the twin draws of the **Jazz Parlor** (125 Bourbon St.; ☎ **504-410-1000**), formerly the ambitious Storyville District. Jazz is the order of the day, obviously, and despite the Parlor's prime Bourbon Street real estate, it's the real deal, not watered-down tourist bait. Show times are generally 5, 7:30, and 11 p.m., with a one-drink minimum per person per set.

✔ In comparison with Preservation Hall and the Palm Court, **Snug Harbor** (626 Frenchmen St.; ☎ **504-949-0696**; www.snugjazz.com) is more in line with the times. Located in Faubourg Marigny, just outside the French Quarter, this is one of the prime spots for modern jazz in the city. The place enjoys a very good reputation among local musicians and fans. A show at this small, often-crowded spot is shorthand for class. Drinks, sandwiches, and a full dinner service are available. The cover charge varies according to the performer but is usually between $8 and $20. Shows begin nightly at 9 and 11 p.m.

A lesson in jazz

From the moment the mercurial Buddy Bolden began playing his cornet around town near the end of the 19th century (widely regarded as the starting point of jazz history), New Orleans has enjoyed a reputation as one of the nation's premier music cities. Since then, clubs in the French Quarter have fostered such jazz greats as Louis Armstrong, Jelly Roll Morton, and Sidney Bechet as well as contemporary musicians such as Harry Connick, Jr., several members of the Marsalis family, and other talented folks. More-recent decades have seen the New Orleans music scene broaden well beyond its jazz roots, with musicians such as the Neville Brothers and Dr. John melding unique local sounds and customs together to form rhythm and blues, a direct precursor of rock-and-roll.

- ✔ **The Spotted Cat Cocktail Lounge** (623 Frenchmen St.; ☎ 504-943-3887; www.thespottedcat.com) has been around for a couple years, but it didn't become the slinky hipster place it is now until live music became a regular fixture. Now the sweaty vibe encourages you to quench your thirst with the signature drink, a rum punch chocolate martini. No cover.

- ✔ **Sweet Lorraine's** (1931 St. Claude Ave., ☎ 504-945-9654) aims to be a throwback to the days when jazz clubs lined the streets. This establishment offers a program of modern and traditional jazz. It's not in the safest neighborhood, and parking is a bit chancy, so take a cab. The cover varies from $5 to $15. Show times vary but generally start at 10 p.m. and midnight.

Toe-tapping to the top brass

Try the following venues for some live brass-band music and a basic dive-bar atmosphere.

- ✔ **Donna's Bar & Grill** (800 N. Rampart St.; ☎ 504-596-6914) is known as "Brass Band World Headquarters," the only place in town where you can reliably expect to hear brass-band music (picture a cross between marching-band music and jazz) on a regular basis. Only three blocks from Bourbon Street at North Rampart and St. Ann, Donna's has a funky hole-in-the-wall vibe that's relaxed and unpretentious. The crowds often follow bands onto the street for a second-line parade. Because the neighborhood can be dicey, take a cab if you're concerned about safety. Show times are 10 p.m. Thursday through Monday (closed Tuesday and Wednesday). The average cover is $5.

Takin' it to the streets: Jazz traditions

Jazz in New Orleans has some traditions that may appear odd. For one, you occasionally see musicians marching in a street parade, complete with a brass band — even when it isn't Carnival. Consider it part of the culture. Like the Mardi Gras Indian parades (see Chapter 11), these spontaneous street parties revitalize the community. After you've been here awhile, a brass-band parade in the middle of the afternoon seems as natural as going to the grocery store (or "makin' groceries," as they say here).

Another popular tradition is the jazz funeral. Many respected jazz musicians are sent off to their reward in this fashion, in a procession that can seem inappropriately cheerful. Actually, the mourners are celebrating the deceased's liberation from this world (called *the return*). However, they also show their sorrow while marching in the procession, often signified by shuffling and clapping to a mournful beat while in the *second line*. (Hence, the term "second-line" as it applies to the popular shuffling beat employed by many brass bands and funk and R&B musicians.)

✔ Named after one of the liveliest clubs in the early days of jazz (and for a tune made famous by legendary cornet player Buddy Bolden), the **Funky Butt** (714 N. Rampart St.; ☎ 504-558-0872; www.funky butt.com) performance space is on the second floor, topping a basic dive bar at the ground level. Expect a variety of performers whose styles range from eclectic modern and traditional jazz to rhythm and blues. Like Donna's, it's location is technically on the far edge of the Quarter, but it's worth the walk or taxi ride. If the walk works up your appetite, you can order from a menu featuring Creole and vegetarian cuisine. Shows begin nightly at 10 p.m. and midnight. No cover weekdays; the average cover on Friday or Saturday is between $5 and $10.

Imbibing History

These special spots offer a little bit of history with your liquor; rumor has it that Andrew Jackson patronized one of them. (See Chapter 11 for more on the history of each of these joints.)

✔ Dating from 1772, **Lafitte's Blacksmith Shop** (941 Bourbon St.; ☎ 504-522-9377) is the oldest building in the Quarter and was reportedly the headquarters of the notorious pirate Jean Lafitte. It looks like it hasn't been touched since his heyday. Agreeably dark (barely candlelit at night), all types of characters frequent the popular hangout.

✔ Another dark and historic place that seems full of schemes — or maybe it's just the low-key lighting — is the **Napoleon House** (500 Chartres St.; ☎ 504-524-9752). If you're the imperial type, have a drink and muse over what the place would've been like if Napoleon had moved in here, as certain New Orleanians allegedly hoped he would.

✔ The **Old Absinthe House** (240 Bourbon St.; ☎ 504-523-3181; www.oldabsinthehouse.com) is supposed to be the place where Andrew Jackson and the Lafitte brothers plotted their defense of the city in the Battle of New Orleans. William Makepeace Thackeray, Walt Whitman, and Oscar Wilde are also said to have knocked back a few inside these walls. This place is also said to have been a speakeasy during Prohibition, though when it was closed down in the 1940s, its antique fixtures — including the original marble-topped bar — were regrettably removed.

Keeping Cool: The Hip Spots

The clientele of these spots gives off a certain aura of that indefinable, elusive quality known as "cool." As always, it can be a little difficult to separate the trendsetters from the fashion followers, but they're both here.

✔ **Ampersand** (1100 Tulane Ave.; ☎ 504-587-3737; www.ampersand
nola.com) sits in the shell of the former Oil & Gas Building on the
lip of the Central Business District and serves as one of the city's
premier are-you-cool-enough-to-get-in joints. The split-level club
sports a European-nightspot vibe of the kind more frequently seen
in bigger cities, and stylish dress and superior attitude are required.
A charming space, it has a courtyard and sitting room nestled in a
former bank vault. If aloof sophistication is your cup of Red Bull,
this is your place.

✔ **Café Brasil** (2100 Chartres St.; ☎ 504-949-0851) is the epicenter of
the Frenchmen Street scene; no telling what you may find on any
given night, including R&B, funk, and even jazz. During Mardi Gras
or Jazz Fest it becomes a whirlwind of activity. The scene often
spills out into the street (usually out of sheer necessity when the
crowd becomes too large for the dance floor). Cover ranges from
$5 to $15 when music is playing.

✔ **The Circle Bar** (1032 St. Charles Ave. at Lee Circle; ☎ 504-588-2616)
is an enclave of hipness on the lip of the Warehouse District. It's a
small, comfortable space, with easy bartenders and a clientele of
musicians, workers, and just plain characters. Music runs toward
singer-songwriters and local hard-to-define bands whose followings
make getting around difficult — as I said, it's a tiny place.

✔ **The Dungeon** (738 Toulouse St.; ☎ 504-523-5530) may seem more
imposing than it is, though it's still more of a habitat for fringe characters than college students or button-down tourists. It's a narrow,
two-story hangout with an upstairs dance floor and all sorts of
"spooky" decor. A real late-late-night spot, it doesn't open until
midnight. Cover is around $3.

✔ **d.b.a.** (618 Frenchmen St.; ☎ 504-942-3731; www.drinkgoodstuff.
com) is dedicated to the sale and consumption of quality beer and
liquor, as its Web site address makes clear. An offshoot of a popular
New York hangout, d.b.a. attracts a diverse mix of status-conscious
drinkers to the hot Frenchmen Street restaurant and bar scene. Its
spacious, dark wooden interior and extensive beer list are both
inviting and comforting. Although it's fairly open, crowds can
become hard to navigate during prime weekend hours.

✔ **El Matador** (504 Esplanade Ave.; ☎ 504-586-0790) sits right on
Esplanade Avenue at Decatur Street on the site of a former gay/
drag bar. Its tiny cabaret-style stage sometimes hosts rock bands.
Part of almost every Quarter hipster's nightly itinerary, rock stars
and local celebrities make their way here quite often. Cover is $5 to
$15 when a live band plays.

✔ **F&M Patio Bar** (4841 Tchoupitoulas St.; ☎ 504-895-6784) is a
venerable institution among the college and young working-
professional sets. Late night is prime time here, with service-
industry types, sorority girls, and on-the-prowl yuppies chatting
each other up over a classic rock jukebox. Invariably, some

sloshed individual will jump up on the pool table and start dancing, more because it's expected than because it's funny.

✔ The **Sazerac Bar** (in the Fairmont Hotel, 123 Baronne St.; ☎ 504-529-4733) is frequented by young professionals who come to mingle in the very posh atmosphere. This place was featured in the movie *The Pelican Brief* with Julia Roberts.

✔ **The Shim Sham Club and Juke Joint Lounge** (615 Toulouse St.; ☎ 504-565-5400) is named after an older French Quarter spot run by jazzman Louis Prima's brother back in the jazz/swing heyday. A small bar serves as a kind of anteroom to the performance area in the back, where wingtips, leather jackets, bowling shirts, and retro haircuts are among the fashion accessories. In keeping with its status as an embassy on the fringe, the Shim-Sham hosts bartender/ stripper nights, '80s dance nights, and its own burlesque show, as well as occasional live music. Cover varies from $5 to $20.

✔ The **Whiskey Bar** (201 St. Charles Ave. in the Central Business District/ Warehouse District area; ☎ 504-566-7770) promises a New York–style lounge atmosphere, and the inhabitants delight in dressing up — lots of jackets and short black dresses. The decor is dark and stylish, and the black marble bathrooms are cool. The doormen really give you the New York experience; they look you over before deciding whether to admit you inside.

Hanging Loose: Casual Bars

In their own way, each of these places is fine for just milling around, drinking, talking, and taking in the scenery:

✔ **Le Bon Temps Roule** (4801 Magazine St.; ☎ 504-895-8117) lets the good times roll by being all things to all people: a neighborhood joint, a college hangout, and (on weekends) a popular music destination (thanks in no small part to the lack of a cover charge).

✔ **Live Bait Bar and Grill** (501 River Rd. in Jefferson; ☎ 504-831-3070; www.livebaitbarandgrill.com) is exactly what it says it is — a bait shop and neighborhood bar rolled into one. Bands (from locals to comeback-trail '80s hard-rock acts) regularly play in a large converted-garage area just off to the side, and older regulars coexist peacefully with drunken college types at the bar. It's a loose, friendly place, even given the fleet of Harleys and other motorcycles often found parked in the vicinity.

✔ The **Maple Leaf** (8316 Oak St.; ☎ 504-866-9359) is what a New Orleans club is all about. A small space, it features a hammered tin ceiling, a patio out back, and a good bar. Its reputation is in inverse proportion to its size; the place is almost always packed, with crowds often spilling out into the street. If Beausoleil or the ReBirth Brass Band is playing, you simply have to go. Shows usually begin around 10:30 p.m.; cover varies anywhere from $5 to $20.

New Orleans Nightlife and Music

Ampersand **17**

Circle Bar **2**

Contemporary Arts Center **3**

Ernie K-Doe's
  Mother-in-Law Lounge **19**

Feelings **24**

The Howlin' Wolf **5**

Le chat noir **13**

Le Petit Theatre du Vieux Carre **8**

The Lion's Den **18**

Mahalia Jackson Theatre
  of the Performing Arts **20**

Mermaid Lounge **4**

Michaul's on St. Charles **12**

Mulate's **7**

New Orleans Municipal
  Auditorium **21**

NORD Theater **11**

Old Point Bar **23**

Orpheum Theater **16**

Pete Fountain's **9**

Sazerac Bar **15**

Southern Rep Theatre **22**

True Brew Coffee House
  and Theater **6**

Vic's Kangaroo Café **10**

Whiskey Bar **14**

Zeitgeist Multi-Disciplinary
  Arts Center **1**

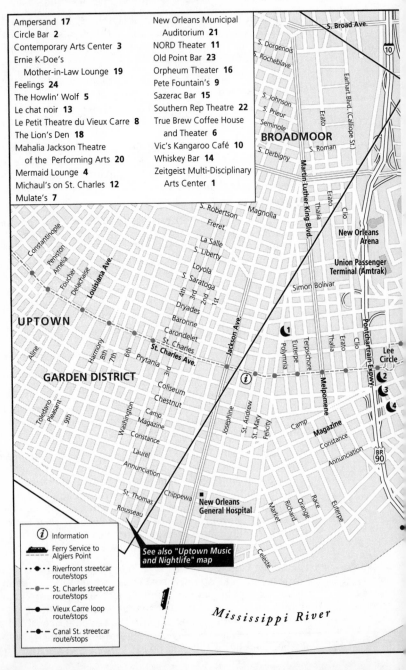

Information

Ferry Service to Algiers Point

Riverfront streetcar route/stops

St. Charles streetcar route/stops

Vieux Carre loop route/stops

Canal St. streetcar route/stops

See also "Uptown Music and Nightlife" map

Mississippi River

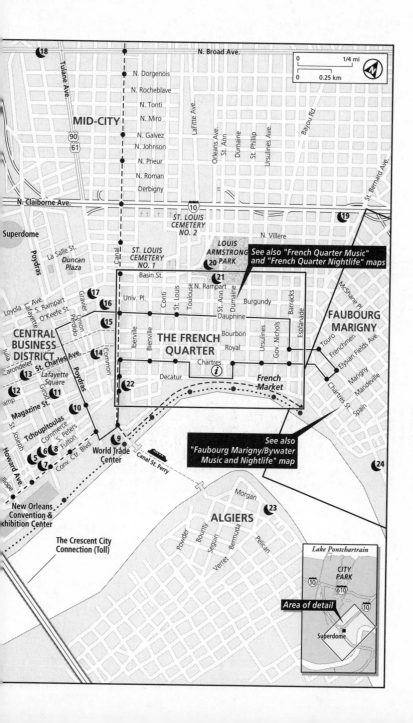

See also "French Quarter Music" and "French Quarter Nightlife" maps

See also "Faubourg Marigny/Bywater Music and Nightlife" map

- **The R Bar** (1431 Royal St. in the Faubourg; ☎ 504-948-7499) attracts a mix of Marigny residents, bohemian types, local musicians, and Frenchmen scene stragglers. This place has one of the best vibes in town: slightly sophisticated, but in a low-key, grungy way. The atmosphere is an odd mish-mash of '50s-style decor and stylish neighborhood charm, with a pool table and a couch or two. An on-site inn (see Chapter 9) rents rooms.

- The **Rivershack Tavern** (3449 River Rd. in Jefferson; ☎ 504-834-4938) is a popular drinking place for a diverse cross-section of locals, from college students to bikers to medical professionals (Ochsner Hospital is just down the road), among others. Located on River Road along the Mississippi River, the Rivershack is renowned as "the home of the tacky ashtrays." You can listen to the jukebox and drink at this unpretentious hangout or enjoy occasional live music (mostly blues and rock). The food is a couple of notches above regular bar food; try the burgers or anything made with alligator.

- A very New Orleans kind of place, **St. Joe's Bar** (5535 Magazine St., Uptown; ☎ 504-899-3744) is a friendly, unpretentious, agreeably dark neighborhood corner bar with intentionally peeled walls and folk-art crosses. Inside, this long, narrow spot has a well-stocked jukebox; outside is a tropical patio that gets crowded on pleasant weekend evenings.

- **Tipitina's** (501 Napoleon Ave.; ☎ 504-895-8477 or 504-897-3943; www.tipitinas.com) was, for a long time, *the* New Orleans music club. Posters advertising shows from the club's long history give the place a tangible sense of legacy and atmosphere. Local bands and touring national alternative rock acts play here, and during Jazz Fest the place is a thriving, visceral center of musical activity. If you can't make it out to Cajun Country, on Sunday afternoons this place holds a "Fais Do Do," complete with free food and dance lessons. The surrounding residential neighborhood has improved considerably, but you still may want to take a cab. (Tipitina's also has a satellite French Quarter location at 233 N. Peters St., open only for private functions and special events.) Shows begin at 10 p.m.; Fais Do Do begins at 5 p.m. Sunday. The cover varies from $5 to $20.

- **Vic's Kangaroo Café** (636 Tchoupitoulas St.; ☎ 504-524-4329) is a friendly Warehouse District spot with an Australian theme (the phone number spells 524-GDAY) that caters to the after-work crowd; have a shepherd's pie and wash it down with something from an impressive beer selection. Regulars and visitors alike can have a good old time playing games of darts or pool. Vic's also offers some better-than-average local blues and R&B acts (not your French Quarter tourist-trap variety).

Chilling to Cajun and Zydeco Music

Because Cajun and zydeco (see the sidebar, "AAIIEEE! Cajun and zydeco in two easy steps" in this chapter) originated not in New Orleans but in the swamps and bayous around Lafayette; the genuine article remains out in the country. Still, on any given night you can find a regional heavy-weight playing somewhere.

- ✔ **Michaul's on St. Charles** (840 St. Charles Ave.; ☎ 504-522-5517) and **Mulate's** (201 Julia St.; ☎ 504-522-1492) present the tourist version of the Cajun experience, with the requisite wood floors and walls, kitsch, and a whole lot of crawfish. However, both clubs offer Cajun dance lessons (Michaul's are free), and you may even catch a really good band that's in town for the day. Shows begin at 7 p.m. in both spots; no covers.

- ✔ Wednesdays and Thursdays are zydeco party time at the celebrity magnet **Mid City Lanes Rock 'n' Bowl** (4133 S. Carrollton Ave.; ☎ 504-482-3133), which also houses a bowling alley. Although the neighborhood is dicey, this is one of the most unique experiences in town. Tom Cruise stopped by when filming *Interview with the Vampire,* and numerous rockers, including Mick Jagger, have been known to sneak in when they're here on tour. Show times vary: Tuesday through Thursday from 8:30 to 9:30 p.m.; Friday and Saturday at 10 p.m. Mid-City is closed both Sunday and Monday. Cover varies from $5 to $20.

Rock-and-Roll All Night

Although New Orleans R&B, as practiced by such legends as Fats Domino, laid the groundwork for what today people call rock-and-roll, the city isn't well known for its contributions to modern-day rock. Still, it *does* boast a good rock scene, including such well-traveled names as the Radiators and modern rockers Better Than Ezra. Following are some of the clubs where you may catch the Next Big Thing or a national touring act:

- ✔ **Checkpoint Charlie's** (501 Esplanade Ave.; ☎ 504-947-0979) tends toward rock and R&B and feels like something between a biker bar and a college hangout. A part of the Frenchmen Street strip in the Faubourg Marigny, it doesn't really fit into the bohemian aesthetic of that hip enclave. This place is good to check out young up-and-coming rock acts. Shows begin at 10:30 p.m.; no cover.

- ✔ From its humble beginnings as a suburban bar and venue for local alternative acts, **The Howlin' Wolf** (828 S. Peters St.; ☎ 504-522-9653; www.howlin-wolf.com) has grown into a Warehouse District

Uptown Nightlife and Music

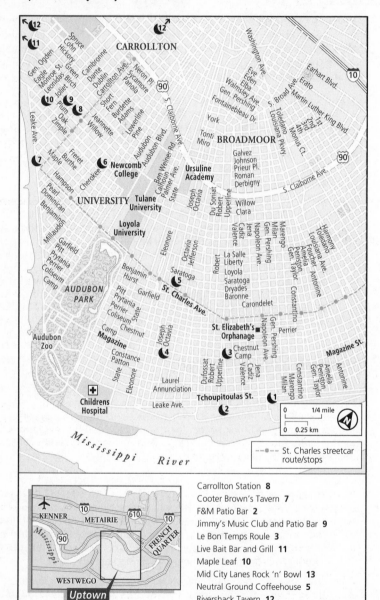

St. Charles streetcar route/stops

Carrollton Station **8**
Cooter Brown's Tavern **7**
F&M Patio Bar **2**
Jimmy's Music Club and Patio Bar **9**
Le Bon Temps Roule **3**
Live Bait Bar and Grill **11**
Maple Leaf **10**
Mid City Lanes Rock 'n' Bowl **13**
Neutral Ground Coffeehouse **5**
Rivershack Tavern **12**
Snake & Jake's Xmas Club Lounge **6**
St. Joe's Bar **4**
Tipitina's **1**

landmark and the main competitor with House of Blues (and, to a lesser extent, Tipitina's) for out-of-town acts. The Wolf's staff is among the friendliest in town, while the overall vibe is among the least pretentious and most agreeable in the city. Shows begin at 10 p.m.; cover varies from $5 to $20.

✔ **Jimmy's Music Club and Patio Bar** (8200 Willow St.; ☎ **504-861-8200**) is right across the street from Carrollton Station, and on weekend nights you're likely to find a good crowd milling about in the street between the two. Jimmy's used to be a prime spot for local rock bands and touring acts, though its smaller capacity precludes it from competing with Tipitina's, the Howlin' Wolf, or House of Blues. Now, obscure local hard-rock acts are featured plus some local and touring reggae, punk, and ska bands. Shows begin at 10 p.m.; cover varies from $5 to $15.

AAIIEEE! Cajun and zydeco in two easy steps

Although jazz was born in the Crescent City, Cajun and zydeco music originated in the wetlands around Lafayette, which was settled by the Acadians (see Chapter 14). Cajun music and zydeco both started out with Acadian folk music and French ballads, evolving into two distinctive new forms of music native to Louisiana and heavily influenced by the cultural diversity of the American Indian, Scotch-Irish, Spanish, Afro-Caribbean, and German folks who also lived in the bayous and swamps near Lafayette. Although both of these native forms rely on the accordion as a core instrument, Cajun music today generally retains a rustic sound and feel, while zydeco has evolved into a more urbanized sound.

A lively style reminiscent of bluegrass and country music, Cajun dance music is traditionally played on button accordions, scratchy fiddles, triangles, and rub-boards (or *frottoir*). Expect to have a great time dancing to it, but don't try to sing along: Many Cajun songs are still sung in the Acadian dialect of French or with such thick accents that you probably can't understand many of the lyrics.

Zydeco began as Cajun dance music but was flavored more than 150 years by the African, blues, and R&B traditions also enjoyed by the rural Creole population. Zydeco has a faster beat than Cajun, especially because funkier rhythms have been mixed in recently. Old-school zydeco performers rely only on the accordion, drums, and trademark rub-board, but over the last few decades some innovative performers have introduced electric guitars and basses, saxophones, and trumpets as well. Some of the genre's elder statesmen good-naturedly compete for the title "King of Zydeco," which comes with a ceremonial crown.

✔ The **Mermaid Lounge** (1100 Constance St. in the Central Business District; ☎ 504-524-4747; www.mermaidlounge.com) has, against all odds, carved a pretty nice niche for itself booking an eclectic mix of acts. The Brigadoon-like club can be hard to find, located on a cul-de-sac under an interstate ramp at the wrong end of a series of one-way streets. On any given night, the club books everything from a legendary Cajun band to the most obscure college or indie-rock group. The mermaid motif, tiny stage, and divelike atmosphere all contribute to one of the coolest vibes in town. Shows begin at 10 p.m.; cover varies from free to $10.

Drafting a Good Time: Prime Places for Beer Nuts

Here are some key spots with some killer brews:

✔ **Carrollton Station** (8140 Willow St.; ☎ 504-865-9190) is a small, folksy spot that's equal parts neighborhood joint, college hangout, and music venue (on the weekends). Order a draft beer (I recommend anything by Abita), strike up a conversation with the person next to you, and enjoy the gristly parade of New Orleans barflies. Occasional cover charge for music on weekends ranges from $5 to $10.

✔ **Cooter Brown's Tavern** (509 S. Carrollton Ave., Uptown at the Riverbend; ☎ 504-866-9104) features a staggering array of domestic and international beers. You can drink your way around the world, and if you follow a beer-a-night itinerary, you'll be in town for a long, long time. This hangout is popular with college students, as well as older professionals, service-industry types, musicians — you name it, they're here. Pretty decent bar food is served until reasonably late.

✔ If you want to kick back in an Irish pub, you have some very good options, such as **Kerry Irish Pub** (331 Decatur St.; ☎ 504-527-5954). This establishment not only boasts a good variety of beers and other spirits but also can show you the proper way to pour pints of Guinness and hard cider. A great spot for throwing darts and shooting pool or for catching some live Irish and alternative folk music.

✔ Similarly, **O'Flaherty's Irish Channel Pub** (514 Toulouse St.; ☎ 504-529-1317) is a popular hangout for those with a palate for stout ale and other such spirits as well as top-notch folk and Celtic music. The supposedly haunted courtyard in the 18th-century building is almost as big a draw as the Irish atmosphere. Together, O'Flaherty's and the Kerry (along with **Ryan's Irish Pub** at 241 Decatur St.; ☎ 504-523-3500) make up what some jokingly refer to as the "Irish Quarter." Cover charge for music is around $5.

Digging for Gold: Hard-to-Find Gems

These bars are all located a good way off the beaten path, in distant sections of town or tucked away in residential neighborhoods.

- ✔ The **Hi-Ho Lounge** (2239 St. Claude Ave., between the Quarter and Bywater; ☎ 504-947-9344) has a particularly haphazard assortment of mismatched furniture that *Gambit Weekly* once called "grunge-dom's living room." The Hi-Ho is completely informal, and you occasionally hear live music from the fringes (including a group that plays on instruments made of old gas tanks). Legend has it that a friendly ghost hangs about the place. Occasional cover charge for music is $5 to $10.

- ✔ The **Neutral Ground Coffeehouse** (5110 Danneel St.; ☎ 504-891-3381; www.neutralground.org) is an amiable throwback to the coffeehouses of the 1960s. Volunteers run it, it has no cover charge (instead, they pass the hat), and it feels kind of like a college-dorm common room. Acoustic and folk performers are on hand most nights, and Sundays feature an open-mike night where anyone can join in.

- ✔ You have to see this place to believe it. The **Saturn Bar** (3067 St. Claude Ave. in Bywater; ☎ 504-949-7532) offers a compelling down-and-dirty experience, populated by veteran barflies and slumming celebrities alike. The crumbling booths and utterly random decor (counters stacked with paper, a life-size mummy, and so on) provide the backdrop for an assortment of characters who come for the renegade ambience and the cheap drinks.

- ✔ **Snake & Jake's Xmas Club Lounge** (7612 Oak St.; ☎ 504-861-2802) appeals to people who like their holiday decor in dark places. Co-owned by local musician Dave Clements and featuring a jukebox heavy on soul and R&B, this is the kind of dive where everybody knows your — and your dog's — name. That's right; pups are welcome, adding to the already unusual mix.

- ✔ **Vaughn's Lounge** (800 Lesseps St.; ☎ 504-947-5562) is a homey little place tucked into the residential Bywater neighborhood. The down-home atmosphere is charming, especially if you're lucky enough to be here when local trumpet player Kermit Ruffins (a modern-day Louis Armstrong) is playing (most Thursday nights, when he's in town); more than likely, he'll be barbecueing on a grill before the show. Be sure to take a cab; parts of this neighborhood are rough. Cover is $10 on Thursday nights.

Faubourg Marigny/Bywater Nightlife and Music

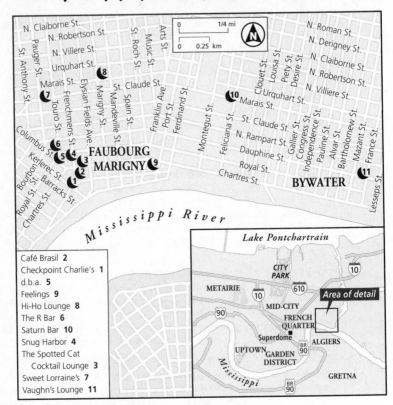

Café Brasil **2**
Checkpoint Charlie's **1**
d.b.a. **5**
Feelings **9**
Hi-Ho Lounge **8**
The R Bar **6**
Saturn Bar **10**
Snug Harbor **4**
The Spotted Cat
Cocktail Lounge **3**
Sweet Lorraine's **7**
Vaughn's Lounge **11**

Playing Your Song: Piano Bars

Piano bars are everywhere in New Orleans, popping up from hotel lobbies to tourist magnets such as Pat O'Brien's. Here are just a few of the choicest establishments:

✔ The **Bombay Club** (830 Conti St., in the Prince Conti Hotel; ☎ 504-586-0972) offers not only live piano jazz Wednesday through Saturday but also world-famous martinis (often voted best in the city by the readers of *Gambit Weekly*).

✔ One of the most popular piano spots in town is the **Carousel Bar & Lounge** (214 Royal St., in the Hotel Montelone; ☎ 504-523-3341). The bar is literally a revolving carousel, so watch your step no matter how little you've had to drink. Catch some great piano music Tuesday through Saturday.

✔ **Feelings** (2600 Chartres St. at Franklin Ave. in the Faubourg; ☎ 504-945-2222; www.feelingscafe.com) is a friendly, funky, low-key neighborhood restaurant in the Faubourg Marigny. People tend to gather in the classic New Orleans courtyard, unless they're inside singing along with the piano player.

✔ **Pat O'Brien's** (718 St. Peter St.; ☎ 504-525-4823; www.patobriens.com) is a popular tourist attraction in the heart of the French Quarter. Despite that (or maybe because of it), it can be a good place to get a look at the teeming masses of humanity. Teeming masses are probably drinking a *Hurricane,* the world-famous gigantic rum drink served in hurricane lamp–style glasses. On weekends, tourists and college types often pack this place with more human flesh per square inch than you can imagine is possible, and sometimes the line outside stretches down the street, which is a bit of a mystery. The popularity of "Pat O's" has more to do with savvy marketing, I think, than anything else (though the high-trafficked location, lush patio/courtyard, and flaming fountain probably have something to do with it).

Shaking Your Groove Thing: The Best Dance Clubs

New Orleans features lots of places to go if you just want to shake your moneymaker.

✔ At the **Cat's Meow** (701 Bourbon St.; ☎ 504-523-1157; www.catsmeow-neworleans.com), you can listen to popular rock songs all night long or sing them yourself — karaoke is available if you have the guts to make a fool out of yourself. Cover charge is $5 for those under 21; free for those older than 21.

✔ **The Gold Mine** (701 Dauphine St.; ☎ 504-586-0745) is a popular spot for college-age kids who congregate here and dance all night long to the latest hits. If that's not your thing, you'd be more comfortable somewhere else. If you stay, try the flaming Dr. Pepper shot. Only open Friday and Saturday nights; $2 cover.

✔ **Razzoo** (511 Bourbon St.; ☎ 504-522-5100) is another popular spot for the young dancing set; high-energy hits and dance mixes are the norm here. Mix it up on the dance floor, and then take a breather out on the patio, where you can watch everyone else dance and delude yourself into thinking that you don't look nearly as foolish on the floor as they do.

Stepping Out: Gay and Lesbian Scene

Are you looking for the best gay and lesbian hangouts? Check out the following:

✔ **Bourbon Pub and Parade Disco** (801 Bourbon St.; ☎ 504-529-2107) is one of the largest gay nightclubs in the United States. Downstairs is the Bourbon Pub, a 24-hour establishment with a video bar. The disco upstairs opens at 9 p.m.; a $5 to $10 cover is charged on weekends.

✔ A legendary spot in the gay community, **Café Lafitte in Exile** (901 Bourbon St.; ☎ 504-522-8397; www.lafittes.com) was opened by Tom Caplinger, who used to run Lafitte's Blacksmith Shop. Reluctant to leave the original place behind, he brought friends and patrons (including Tennessee Williams) with him when he opened this place. Open 24 hours, this bar is usually crowded.

✔ **Good Friends Bar** (740 Dauphine St.; ☎ 504-566-7191; www.goodfriendsbar.com) is a neighborhood type of place with tons of atmosphere and a piano in the corner that invites karaoke-style misuse.

✔ The 24-hour **LeRoundup** (819 St. Louis St.; ☎ 504-561-8340) has a friendly atmosphere, attracting the most diverse crowd around. The bar charges occasional small covers for entertainment/revue-type shows.

✔ The hot dance spot **Oz** (800 Bourbon St.; ☎ 877-599-8200 or 504-592-8200; www.ozneworleans.com) is recognized both locally and nationally as a place to see and be seen. *Gambit Weekly* ranked it as the city's No. 1 dance club, and *Details* magazine ranked it as one of the top 50 clubs in the country. Cover is $3 on Wednesday and Sunday nights; $10, Friday and Saturday nights ($5 discount for gay males).

✔ Don't miss **The Rawhide** (740 Burgundy St.; ☎ 504-525-8106; www.rawhide2010.com) if denim and leather make your scene. During Mardi Gras, this place hosts the best costume contest in town. Cover is $5 Thursday through Sunday nights.

The name game

From Louis Armstrong (whose name graces Armstrong Park) to the ever-expanding Marsalis family, New Orleans is a city of musical names. You can find some on the marquees of the city's most popular (and interesting) nightclubs. Following is the Who's Who of name clubs:

✔ If you're looking for a Vegas-style revue, the **Chris Owens Club** (500 Bourbon St.; ☎ **504-523-6400;** www.chrisowens.com) is it. The ageless, well-proportioned Ms. Owens puts on a high-energy show filled with standards from the worlds of pop, jazz, blues, and country and western. Call for reservations and admission prices. Shows begin at 8:30 p.m. and 10 p.m.

✔ Remember the vintage R&B chestnut "Mother-In-Law"? Before his death in 2001, flamboyant singer Ernie K-Doe turned that song into a career — and later, a nightclub. **Ernie K-Doe's Mother-In-Law Lounge** (1500 N. Claiborne Ave. at Columbus; ☎ **504-947-1078**), is where K-Doe held court for years. If you're interested in New Orleans music history, it's worth a stop. Please take a cab — the neighborhood is rough.

✔ The local **House of Blues** (225 Decatur St.; ☎ **504-529-BLUE [2583];** www.hob.com/venues/clubvenues/neworleans) doesn't *really* fit here, unless you consider celebrity cofounder Dan Aykroyd's alter ego, Elwood Blues, a big name. Most major touring rock, reggae, and hip-hop acts play here. The restaurant is decent if pricey, with some inventive takes on local fare. This national chain has doggedly dedicated itself to the community, and even offers blues scholarships to children. Other chains should be this stylish. Shows usually begin at 9 p.m. Cover varies from $10 to $20.

✔ Parrot heads abound at **Jimmy Buffett's Margaritaville Café** (1104 Decatur St.; ☎ **504-592-2565;** www.margaritaville.com). This chain has contributed to the brand-name takeover of the Quarter. Some touring acts stop here, and Buffett himself sometimes pops by when he's in town, but mostly it's a venue for journeyman local performers, from blues to R&B to reggae and New Orleans roots music. You find music all day long here, with shows generally beginning at 3, 6, and 9 p.m. No cover except for special shows on weekend nights, which start around 10:30 p.m.

✔ If you're in Mid-City, consider a foray into **The Lion's Den** (2655 Gravier St.; ☎ **504-822-4693**). Owned by Irma Thomas, the "Soul Queen of New Orleans," it's especially worth a visit if she's playing, which has been known to happen. A great, sassy performer and a musical treasure, Ms. Thomas is still going strong. Catch a cab, and be aware of your surroundings in this dicey area. Shows begin at 9 p.m. Cover varies; call ahead for price.

✔ Pete Fountain is practically synonymous with New Orleans music. This local boy, once a member of Lawrence Welk's orchestra, plays sweet jazz clarinet Tuesday through Saturday at his club, **Pete Fountain's** (2 Poydras St., in the Hilton Hotel; ☎ **504-523-4374**). The show's at 10 p.m. with a $20 cover charge that includes one drink. Children aren't allowed, and you need reservations.

Part VI
The Part of Tens

The 5th Wave   By Rich Tennant

IN THE ABSENCE OF ANY ALLIGATORS, GRIZZLED CAJUN "SWAMP RAT" LAFITTE WOULD OFTEN WRESTLE AN IBIS FOR CURIOUS TOURISTS

In this part . . .

As complex as its history and culture can be, New Orleans can also be a city of quick answers and easy solutions. At least, that's what these chapters attempt to provide. If you're looking for some authentically decadent New Orleans experiences or want the rundown on tourist spots worth your while, this part is your one-stop answer shop.

Chapter 17

Ten Sinful (But Legal) Experiences

In This Chapter

▶ Downing decadent drinks (and figuring out the drinking laws)

▶ Rolling the dice on the river

▶ Getting down with ghosts, ghouls, and goblins

*N*ew Orleans tends to exaggerate your own vices, which I have found to be all too true. Fortunately, you can get creative and indulge in more than just booze on Bourbon Street. In this chapter, I run down ten experiences that engage one or more of the senses in one wicked way or another, from can't-miss music to sinfully indulgent meals.

Gulping Gin from a "Go-Cup"

Barhopping in New Orleans is a marathon undertaking to begin with, but it'd be much longer and less fun without these handy timesaving measures. The city's permissive liquor laws allow bar patrons to leave the premises with their unfinished drink in hand — provided it's poured into a plastic cup, known as a *go-cup*. Drinking in a go-cup lets drinkers leave at their leisure, without having to worry about finishing their drink in a hurry. Don't be holding a go-cup in your hand if the car you're riding in gets pulled over — and I don't have to tell you to forget about driving with one, right? But if you're walking down Bourbon Street — or any street, for that matter — and want to savor your brew (hopefully one locally made; try a Dixie or an Abita) or just stand still for a while to soak up the atmosphere, these cups rule.

Delighting in Drive-Thru Daiquiris

It makes a perverse kind of sense that the city that lets you walk around with liquor in your hand would let you drive around with it, too. I certainly don't advocate drinking and driving, and the city does have — and enforce — an open-container law that prohibits imbibing while behind the wheel. But that said, ordering a daiquiri from the comfort of your car (as you can do at **New Orleans Original Daiquiris,** 3301 Veterans Blvd. in Metairie, ☎ **504-837-8474**) is a staple of suburban nightlife and quite the "Am I really getting away with this?" experience for first-timers.

You can also grab daiquiris at walk-up windows throughout the city, including New Orleans Original Daiquiris locations in Mid-City (301 N. Carrollton Ave.) and on Bourbon Street (633 Bourbon).

Succumbing to a Liuzza's Po' Boy

New Orleans has countless variations of this popular sandwich. But po' boys from **Liuzza's by the Track** (1518 N. Lopez St.; ☎ **504-943-8667**), a neighborhood hangout within walking distance of the New Orleans Fair Grounds, have extra bite. "Rich" and "buttery" don't begin to describe its bang-fist-on-the-table sensation.

Grooving at the Maple Leaf

Most Tuesday nights when it's not on the road, the ReBirth Brass Band makes the **Maple Leaf** (see Chapter 16) its home for a down-and-dirty whistle-stop tour of modern brass that's become an ingrained local tradition. College students (lots of them), tourists, and all-around music lovers stand shoulder to shoulder in this unassuming nightspot as the band conducts a raucous dance workout. ReBirth is New Orleans's premier purveyor of "modern brass," mixing pop, funk, hip-hop, and gospel elements into the traditional brass-band sound. The band's bawdy grooves and precision swagger are infectious, and a show at the Maple Leaf is nothing short of jubilant musical abandon.

Trying Your Luck with a Lucky Dog

Popularized by John Kennedy Toole's classic novel, *A Confederacy of Dunces,* these high-cholesterol hot dogs are a junk-food staple in the French Quarter. In fact, distinctive hot-dog-shaped Lucky Dog carts (each more than 600 pounds!) are about as common a sight in the Quarter as drunken sailors, even late at night (when they're a godsend for stumbling drunks looking for a quick grease fix). Taste-wise, the mustard-heavy, calorie-laden Dog is far better than your average hot dog. Though each bite brings you closer to cardiac arrest, legions of French Quarter denizens swear that the taste is worth it.

Rolling the Bones

As seen in television and movies, the idea of a riverboat casino holds a certain Mark Twain kind of romance. The reality may not be quite as romantic, but it's an increasingly popular way for locals and tourists to willingly part with large amounts of their cash. Truth be told, you can't see much of the river on a riverboat casino, and not just because it doesn't have windows. Most riverboats are loathe to leave their berths, (which is a sin in itself), for fear of driving away customers who want to be able to come and go at will rather than be stuck, you know, enjoying the sights, sounds, and spray of a riverboat cruise. Still, despite the lack of nautical atmosphere, riverboat casinos (see Chapter 11) combine modern-day avarice with the idyllic sheen of yesteryear — a hard combination to beat.

Having a Hurricane at Pat O'Brien's

Pat O'Brien's (see Chapter 16) is one of New Orleans's most popular bars, due in no small part to its signature drink, the Hurricane. Named for the glass it comes in (its shape resembles a hurricane lamp), this fruity concoction originated during World War II, when rum was so widely available that liquor distributors pushed it heavily and retailers had to find a way to use it all. The Hurricane is a potent cocktail, but its true popularity likely derives as much from the souvenir glass it comes in — which, in case you're interested, has at least one use after you finish your drink: According to the bar's Web site (www.patobriens.com), a Hurricane glass holds exactly $10 in pennies.

Surrendering to Your Slothful Side

New Orleans's signature phrase is "Let the good times roll" for a reason: The city's atmosphere is perfectly suited for indolent lounging, whiling away the hours in as lazy a fashion as you can muster. From a leisurely breakfast of beignets and café au lait at **Café du Monde** (see Chapter 10) to a relaxed **carriage ride** (see Chapter 11) around the Quarter to an unhurried afternoon sipping a Pimm's Cup at **Napoleon House** (see Chapter 11), you can easily make a day out of doing next to nothing. And an evening, too: Idling at **Lafitte's Blacksmith Shop** or nursing an anisette at **Old Absinthe House** (see Chapter 11) is a perfect way to wind down after a hard day of, well, hardly moving. If you're fortunate enough to be staying at a swanky hotel like the **Ritz-Carlton** or the **Windsor Court** (Chapter 9), all the better — spending a whole day lounging and being pampered without ever leaving the premises is possible (if not necessarily advisable).

Meeting Creatures of the Night

New Orleans enjoys a supernatural reputation, and some establishments (such as the **Hi-Ho Lounge** or **Hotel Provincial**) claim to play host to spirits. But spending the night in a particular hotel or bar, waiting for a ghost to come to you, can be a frustrating endeavor, especially when you can be proactive and track down the specters yourself! Outfits such as **Haunted History Tours** and **Magic Walking Tours** (see Chapter 11) offer a variety of walking tours that are themed around ghosts, vampires, and cemeteries. The Cemetery/Voodoo Tour offered by **Historic New Orleans Walking Tours** (see Chapter 11) allows you to take in the tomb of famed voodoo priestess Marie Laveau and an actual voodoo temple.

Speaking of vampires, New Orleans's own Queen of the Damned, vampire novelist **Anne Rice,** used to allow tours of historical landmark **St. Elizabeth's Orphanage** and her Garden District home at **1239 First Street.** But shockingly, in 2004, Rice sold the last of her New Orleans properties and moved to (gasp!) a gated community in the suburbs. Fans can still get their fill of Rice, including autographed books, first editions, and other rarities at the **Garden District Book Shop** (see Chapter 12) and **Stan Rice Gallery** (861 Carondelet St.; ☎ 504-586-9495), which features enigmatic paintings by her late husband. For late-night options, wander Bourbon Street, where you're sure to run into someone (or something) other worldly before long or descend into **The Dungeon** (see Chapters 13 and 16) after midnight.

Suffering Through Saints Games

Yes, Saints games — the way New Orleans's long-suffering football fans have to bear the team's tumultuous ups and downs is indeed a sin. The team once known derisively as "the Aints" perpetually and notoriously fails to capitalize on its momentum; the team's failures are often blamed on the fact that the Superdome is built on a former graveyard (rumors have it that not all the bodies were removed). Still, Saints fans are arguably as tenacious as followers of the Chicago Cubs, and martyrdom is of course alive and well in this predominantly Catholic town.

Chapter 18

Ten (Or So) Tourist Traps That Really Aren't

In This Chapter
▶ Discovering the charms and thrills
▶ Soaking up history in the great indoors and outdoors
▶ Paddling the rivers and swamps

*O*ne of the most charming aspects of New Orleans is that often what appears contrived is authentic and worth your time. The following places and events may seem like tourist traps, but they're actually spots in which to soak up some local lore and character.

The French Quarter

No list of potential tourist traps is complete without mentioning the city's biggest attraction, the French Quarter. Although it's the center of tourist activity, the Quarter is a bona fide historical landmark and a worthwhile attraction. As the city's original settlement, it's the setting for richly detailed stories of grand historical figures, political double-crosses, and events of great significance. It's filled with museums and monuments of fascinating historical import, from the **Cabildo** to **Jackson Square** to the **St. Louis Cathedral** (see Chapter 11). You also find numerous fine restaurants, hotels, and shops here.

What really makes the French Quarter stand out is that it's a functioning neighborhood. Real people live, work, and play within its relatively small confines, acting out the dramas of their own lives among the museums, attractions, historic buildings, and walking tours. Legend and latter-day reality coexist here — you may be sitting in a bar once patronized by a famous figure, next to a self-exiled poet or a pierced and tattooed junior executive with a cellphone and laptop.

Bourbon Street

Some of the places you encounter in New Orleans definitely reek of exploitation, lowest-common-denominator pandering, and opportunism (some also just reek, but that's another story). Bourbon Street — the gaudy, tawdry, and tacky thoroughfare that every visitor knows by name before arriving in New Orleans — is a prime example of this kind of commercialism. Filled with touristy establishments, fleshpots, fast-food joints, and souvenir shops, not to mention street performers, hustlers, and scam artists all competing for your spare change, Bourbon Street is unquestionably a monument to the fine art of separating gullible visitors from their money.

As cheap and plastic as Bourbon Street can be, it can also be oddly exhilarating. Walking along Bourbon Street at night definitely gets the adrenaline going, as you're caught in a current of exploring pedestrians, navigating throngs of tourists, locals, teens, drag queens, scam artists, and performers. Your feet move in sync to a rich soundtrack of jazz, blues, Cajun, Celtic, and rock that blare out of every open doorway. The seedy spectacle — strip clubs, 24-hour bars, and alcohol — can be intoxicating.

Preservation Hall

Finding the appeal of this unassuming hideaway (see Chapter 16) may be difficult at first glance. This nondescript, bombed-out shell of a building is small, crowded, and not air-conditioned, with no seats, no drinks, and no good sight lines. Tourists are herded in, subjected to some traditional Dixieland jazz, and left to their own devices. But you'll likely be too busy enjoying the music to notice, or care about, the lack of creature comforts. Dixieland jazz is often derided as watered-down jazz for tourists, but in the talented hands of the **Preservation Hall Jazz Band,** it becomes so much more. It's a down-and-dirty musical celebration. So pay the cover, shuffle your way inside, and ignore the no-frills surroundings of this quintessential New Orleans experience.

Mardi Gras

For many visitors, Mardi Gras is just an excuse to act rowdy, cavort in the street, and generally make fools of themselves. In this respect, it's no different from spring break at the beach (right down to the frequent exposing of female breasts, but done so here for parade throws).

But if you take the trouble to discover the origins of this legendary street party, you'll find a fascinating tradition, complete with pageantry, spectacle, and history galore that has its roots in the city's large Catholic population. The **Mardi Gras Indians** and the **Zulu** parade are two unique experiences, rich with their own histories and largely unknown to the outside world. Behind the superficial atmosphere, Mardi Gras is a party with a past and a purpose — a bacchanal with tradition.

Lafitte's Blacksmith Shop and Old Absinthe House

The story goes that **Lafitte's** (see Chapter 11), an actual blacksmith shop run by the legendary pirate Jean Lafitte and his brother, was a front for the duo's illegal enterprises (including, allegedly, the movement of slaves). This story may or may not be true, as is the popular rumor that the Lafitte brothers and Andrew Jackson plotted the city's defense during the Battle of New Orleans at the **Old Absinthe House** (see Chapter 11). In any other city, such claims would be dubious at best. But in New Orleans, whether these stories are true is actually beside the point. The beautiful thing is that the rumors very well *could* be true. Lafitte's and Old Absinthe House are legitimate local hangouts independent of the stories attached to them. In what other U.S. city can a resident enjoy a drink while sitting where pirates once smuggled contraband and national historical figures plotted conspiracy?

Congo Square

If you drive by **Armstrong Park** today, you may miss this historical area, where both voodoo and the early rhythms of jazz flourished and grew during the oppressive days of slavery. Congo Square was a meeting and gathering place for local slaves as a result of Napoleonic Law, which mandated that slave owners give their servants Sundays off and provide them with a place to socialize. An uncharacteristically humane impulse in the sordid history of slavery, the law had a completely unintended effect. The congregated slaves used the square for voodoo ceremonies (the religion flourished here as a result) and performed drumming rituals as well, keeping alive the rhythms of their lost homes. Over time, other regional forms, such as work songs, blues, and spirituals, were thrown into the mix.

After the Civil War, some graduates of this early local music "scene" became working musicians, and the city's music absorbed their intuitive blend of European and African rhythms. Legend also states that the madams of nearby Storyville hired some of the square's musicians to entertain their guests, further widening the reach of this burgeoning musical form. In short, both jazz and voodoo made inroads into the United States from this very parcel of land.

Riverboat Cruises and Swamp Tours

Although these two popular draws *are* different, I group them together because of their similarities: They both require water, and they both can seem corny to the casual eye. The very term "riverboat" conjures images of crews in period costumes, hamming up the Mark Twain angle. Cruises do consist of quickie jaunts on a brief section of the Mississippi River, but some riverboat cruises actually are worth taking.

If you're at the **Aquarium of the Americas** (see Chapter 11), for example, a cruise on the stern-wheeler *John James Audubon* can be a fun way to ride over to the aquarium's sister attraction, the **Audubon Zoo** (see Chapter 11). The paddle-wheeler *Creole Queen* is another fun ride, with a stop at **Chalmette Battlefield National Park** for extra educational value (see Chapter 11). Occasionally, musical groups perform at night on a riverboat, providing a unique concert experience (especially during Mardi Gras and Jazz Fest). Finally, don't underestimate the romantic possibilities of a riverboat ride.

Riding the Streetcar

From aprons to postcards, images of the St. Charles Streetcar and the recently reopened Canal Streetcar appear on an array of New Orleans–themed souvenirs (see Chapter 11). Just because it's mainstream doesn't mean it's not cool. Many locals use it every day to get to work and school or to enjoy the ride and remember why they love living here.

Quick Concierge

Fast Facts: New Orleans

AAA

For road service, call ☎ 800-222-4357 or 504-367-4095.

Ambulance

Call ☎ **911** for emergency ambulance service.

American Express

The American Express office (☎ 504-586-8201) is located at 201 St. Charles Ave. in the Central Business District. It's open Monday to Friday from 9 a.m. to 5 p.m. For cardholder services, call ☎ 800-528-4800; for lost or stolen traveler's checks, call ☎ 800-221-7282.

Area Codes

The area code for the greater New Orleans metropolitan area is 504. The North Shore, the region north of the city across Lake Pontchartrain, which includes Slidell, Covington, and Mandeville, is 985.

ATMs

Automatic teller machines are as ubiquitous in New Orleans as they likely are in your hometown. The 800 numbers for the major ATM networks are ☎ 800-424-7787 (800-4CIRRUS) for Cirrus and ☎ 800-843-7587 for Plus.

Among the more convenient ATM locations in the French Quarter are the following: corner of Chartres and St. Ann; 400 block of Chartres near K-Paul's restaurant; corner of Chartres and Toulouse; corner of Royal and Iberville; and 240 Royal St.

Babysitters

Ask your hotel or call one of the following agencies for sitting services: Accents on Children's Arrangements, ☎ 504-524-1227 or Dependable Kid Care, ☎ 504-486-4001.

Business Hours

On the whole, most shops and stores are open from 10 a.m. to 6 p.m. Banks open at 9 a.m. and close between 3 and 5 p.m.

Camera Repair

Try AAA Camera Repair, 1631 St. Charles Ave. (☎ 504-561-5822).

Convention Center

Ernest M. Morial Convention Center, 900 Convention Center Blvd., New Orleans, LA 70130, ☎ 504-582-3000. Convention Center Boulevard sits at the end of the Warehouse District, on the river between Thalia and Water streets; the Canal Streetcar (formerly Riverfront Streetcar) drops you off at the Convention Center.

Credit Cards

Information numbers for American Express are listed earlier in this section (see "American Express"). MasterCard's general information number is ☎ 800-307-7309. For Visa, call ☎ 800-847-2911.

Customs

To reach the New Orleans office of the U.S. Customs Service, call ☎ 504-670-2206.

Dentists

Contact the New Orleans Dental Association (☎ 504-834-6449; www.nodc.org/noda.htm) to find a reliable dentist near you.

Doctors

If you're in need of a doctor, call one of the following: Orleans Parish Medical Society, ☎ 504-523-2474; Tulane Medical Clinic, ☎ 504-588-5800; or Children's Hospital, ☎ 504-899-9511.

Emergencies

For fire, police, and ambulance call ☎ 911.

For the Poison Control Center, call ☎ 800-256-9822.

The Travelers Aid Society (846 Baronne St., ☎ 504-525-8726) also renders emergency aid to travelers in need. For help regarding a missing or lost child, call Child Find at ☎ 800-IAM-LOST (426-5678).

Hospitals

Should you become ill during your visit, most major hospitals have staff doctors on call 24 hours a day. If a doctor isn't available in your hotel or guesthouse, call or go to the emergency room at Ochsner Medical Institutions, 1516 Jefferson Hwy. (☎ 504-842-3460), or the Tulane University Medical Center, 1415 Tulane Ave. (☎ 504-588-5800).

Hot Lines

YWCA Rape Crisis is ☎ 504-483-8888; Travelers Aid Society is ☎ 504-525-8726; Gamblers Anonymous is ☎ 504-431-7867; Narcotics Anonymous is ☎ 504-899-6262; Alcoholics Anonymous is ☎ 504-779-1178.

Information

The local Tourist Information Center is at 529 St. Ann St., ☎ 504-568-5661 or 504-566-5031). Also see "Where to Get More Information" at the end of this appendix.

Internet Access

Three of the most convenient cybercafes are Cybercafe @ the CAC, inside the ground floor of the Contemporary Arts Center (900 Camp St.; ☎ 504-523-0990); Royal Access (621 Royal St.; ☎ 504-525-0401); and The Bastille Computer Cafe (605 Toulouse St.; ☎ 504-581-1150). For a comprehensive list of Internet cafes around the globe, visit www.cybercafes.com.

Liquor Laws

The legal drinking age in New Orleans is 21. You can buy liquor most anywhere 24 hours a day, 7 days a week, 365 days a year. All drinks carried on the street must be in plastic cups; bars often provide one of these plastic *go-cups* so that you can transfer your drink as you leave.

Mail

For U.S. Postal Service information and office hours, call ☎ 800-275-8777.

Maps

You can obtain maps at any of the information centers listed in Chapter 8 or at most hotels; www.mapquest.com is a good online resource for destination-specific

U.S. maps, providing helpful driving information and hotel, restaurant, and attraction information.

Newspapers and Magazines

To find out what's going on around town, pick up a copy of the *Times-Picayune* (www.nola.com) or *Gambit Weekly* (www.bestofneworleans.com). *OffBeat* (www.offbeat.com) is an extensive monthly guide to the city's evening entertainment, art galleries, and special events; it's available in most hotels. Also refer to the "Where to Get More Information" section at the end of this appendix.

Pharmacies

The Walgreens Drug Store at 4400 S. Claiborne Ave. at Napoleon is the closest one to the French Quarter that offers 24-hour pharmacy service; call ☎ 504-891-0976. Take a cab here at night, or have the hotel send a taxi for your prescription.

Police

For nonemergency situations, call ☎ 504-821-2222. For emergencies, dial ☎ **911**.

Radio Stations

Some of the more helpful and/or popular radio stations in the city include WSMB, 1350 AM (sports talk); WWNO, 89.9 FM (National Public Radio, classical); WWOZ, 90.7 FM (New Orleans and Louisiana music; jazz, R&B, and blues); WQUE, 93.3 FM (urban/R&B); and KKND, 106.7 FM (modern rock).

Restrooms

Public restrooms are located at Jax Brewery, Riverwalk Marketplace, Canal Place Shopping Center, Washington Artillery Park, and any of the major hotels.

Safety

Though many areas of New Orleans are perfectly safe, the general rule when visiting any city is to be on your guard all the time. Public transportation is relatively safe, though at night you'd be wise to take a cab if you're traveling to a dimly lit area. The St. Charles and Canal streetcars run 24 hours, but both run through some iffy neighborhoods, which can change from nice to not-so-nice within a couple of blocks; again, take a cab at night. Always use caution when walking through an unlit area at night. Avoid the Iberville Housing Project located between Basin, N. Claiborne, Iberville, and St. Louis streets, just outside of the French Quarter. You should also avoid St. Louis Cemetery No. 2 near Claiborne on the lake side of the Iberville Housing Project unless you're traveling with a large tour group. Also stay away from the area behind Armstrong Park. Remember: The city looks deceptively safe, and neighborhoods change very quickly.

Smoking

In this regard, New Orleans is like most major U.S. cities and more lenient than many. At most attractions and in most business buildings and shops, smokers should be prepared to stand around outside with all the other smokers. Most local restaurants cater to both smokers and nonsmokers; a relative few (in relation to the rest of the country) prohibit smoking altogether. Ask before you sit down.

Taxes

Louisiana's sales tax is very confusing. In addition to the state and federal taxes, each parish (county) may have additional taxes. To make things more confusing, some items such as unprepared food and some types of drugs are partially exempt, while prescriptions are totally exempt. In general, the total sales tax in New Orleans is 9 percent; it's 8.75 percent in Jefferson Parish.

Taxis

In most tourist areas, you can usually hail a taxi or get one at a taxi stand. If you can't find a taxi, call United Cab at ☎ 504-522-9771. If you have any complaints or left something in a taxi, call the Taxicab Bureau at ☎ 504-565-6272.

Time Zone

New Orleans is in the Central time zone. Daylight saving time is in effect from April through October.

Tipping

For most services — including restaurants and taxis — add 15 to 20 percent to your bill (before taxes). Many restaurants automatically add a 15- to 20- percent gratuity for parties of six or more. If you're just drinking at a bar, tipping 10 to 15 percent is typical. You should give bellhops $1 or $2 per bag, maids $1 per day, coat-check people $1 per garment, and automobile valets $1.

Transit Information

For information about streetcars and buses, call the Regional Transit Authority at ☎ 504-248-3900, or check out its Web site at www.norta.org.

Weather Updates

For the date, time, and temperature as well as a prerecorded weather update, including a daily forecast and marine forecast, call ☎ 504-828-4000. On the Web, visit www.intellicast.com for weather updates on all 50 states and most major U.S. cities, including New Orleans. Another handy site is www.weather.com, the online home of The Weather Channel.

Toll-Free Numbers and Web Sites

Major North American carriers

Air Canada
☎ 888-247-2262
www.aircanada.ca

AirTran Airlines
☎ 800-247-8726
www.airtran.com

American Airlines
☎ 800-433-7300
www.aa.com

America West Airlines
☎ 800-235-9292
www.americawest.com

Continental Airlines
☎ 800-525-0280
www.continental.com

Delta Air Lines
☎ 800-221-1212
www.delta.com

Frontier Airlines
☎ 800-432-1359
www.frontierairlines.com

JetBlue Airlines
☎ 800-538-2583
www.jetblue.com

Northwest Airlines
☎ 800-225-2525
www.nwa.com

Southwest Airlines
☎ 800-435-9792
www.southwest.com

United Airlines
☎ 800-241-6522
www.united.com

US Airways
☎ 800-428-4322
www.usairways.com

Car-rental agencies

Alamo
☎ 800-327-9633
www.goalamo.com

Avis
☎ 800-331-1212
www.avis.com

Budget
☎ 800-527-0700
www.budget.com

Dollar
☎ 800-800-4000
www.dollar.com

Enterprise
☎ 800-325-8007
www.enterprise.com

Hertz
☎ 800-654-3131
www.hertz.com

National
☎ 800-CAR-RENT
www.nationalcar.com

Thrifty
☎ 800-367-2277
www.thrifty.com

Major hotel and motel chains

Best Western International
☎ 800-528-1234
www.bestwestern.com

Clarion Hotels
☎ 800-CLARION
www.clarionhotel.com

Comfort Inns
☎ 800-228-5150
www.hotelchoice.com

Courtyard by Marriott
☎ 800-321-2211
www.courtyard.com

Days Inn
☎ 800-325-2525
www.daysinn.com

Doubletree Hotels
☎ 800-222-TREE
www.doubletree.com

Econo Lodges
☎ 800-55-ECONO
www.hotelchoice.com

Fairfield Inn by Marriott
☎ 800-228-2800
www.marriott.com

Hampton Inn
☎ 800-HAMPTON
www.hampton-inn.com

Hilton Hotels
☎ 800-HILTONS
www.hilton.com

Holiday Inn
☎ 800-HOLIDAY
www.basshotels.com

Howard Johnson
☎ 800-654-2000
www.hojo.com

Hyatt Hotels & Resorts
☎ 800-228-9000
www.hyatt.com

ITT Sheraton
☎ 800-325-3535
www.starwood.com

La Quinta Motor Inns
☎ 800-531-5900
www.laquinta.com

Marriott Hotels
☎ 800-228-9290
www.marriott.com

Quality Inns
☎ 800-228-5151
www.hotelchoice.com

Radisson Hotels International
☎ 800-333-3333
www.radisson.com

Ramada Inns
☎ 800-2-RAMADA
www.ramada.com

Red Carpet Inns
☎ 800-251-1962
www.reservahost.com

Renaissance
☎ 800-228-9290
www.renaissancehotels.com

Residence Inn by Marriott
☎ 800-331-3131
www.marriott.com

Ritz-Carlton
☎ 800-241-3333
www.ritzcarlton.com

Sheraton Hotels & Resorts
☎ 800-325-3535
www.sheraton.com

Super 8 Motels
☎ 800-800-8000
www.super8.com

Travelodge
☎ 800-255-3050
www.travelodge.com

Wyndham Hotels and Resorts
☎ 800-822-4200
www.wyndham.com

Where to Get More Information

An excellent source of information is the **New Orleans Metropolitan Convention and Visitors Bureau** (2020 St. Charles Ave., New Orleans, LA 70130; ☎ **800-672-6124** or 504-566-5003; www.nomcvb.com). Staff members are extremely helpful and accessible, and they can give you in depth information on nearly whatever you seek.

Another good resource is the **New Orleans Multicultural Tourism Network** (1520 Sugar Bowl Dr., New Orleans, LA 70112; ☎ **800-725-5652** or 504-523-5652; www.soulofneworleans.com), which can point you to a number of local minority-owned businesses, from convention-related services (such as audio/visual services) to restaurants and hotels.

Tourist offices

The **Tourist Information Center** is located at 529 St. Ann St. (☎ **504-568-5661** or 504-566-5031). It's operated by the State of Louisiana and is located in the French Quarter in the historic Pontalba Buildings next to Jackson Square. Following is a list of other centrally located information centers.

- ✔ **Canal Street and Convention Center Boulevard** (☎ **504-587-0739**), at the beginning of the 300 block of Canal Street on the downtown side of the street

- ✔ Close to the **World Trade Center** (☎ **504-587-0734**) at 2 Canal St.

- ✔ Near the **Hard Rock Cafe** (☎ **504-587-0740**) on the 400 block of North Peters Street

- ✔ **Julia Street and Convention Center Boulevard** (walk-up booth)

- ✔ **Poydras Street and Convention Center Boulevard** (walk-up booth)

- ✔ **Vieux Carre[s1] Police Station** (☎ **504-565-7530**), located at 334 Royal St.

City guides

For a more comprehensive and detail-packed peek at New Orleans than you can find in this book, check out *Frommer's New Orleans* by Mary Herczog (Wiley). Frommers.com is an excellent resource, as well, full of travel tips, online booking options, and a daily e-mail newsletter offering bargains and travel advice.

Some of the most indispensable online city and entertainment guides are the following:

- ✔ *Ambush* (www.ambushmag.com) provides excellent information on what's going on. You can also find a paper copy in most gay-friendly establishments.

- ✔ **Crescent City Connection** (www.satchmo.com) provides a roundup of musical events and resources for wanting information about local musicians. It's especially valuable during Jazz Fest.

- ✔ **New Orleans CitySearch** (http://neworleans.citysearch.com), part of the extensive CitySearch network of city sites, offers staff picks and background information on food, music, entertainment, and the arts.

- ✔ **New Orleans Online** (www.neworleansonline.com) allows you to hone in on exactly what you're looking for; click on "Cuisine" to search for a Cajun restaurant in the French Quarter, for example, and peruse a list of available options.

✔ **New Orleans Travel Guide** (www.neworleans.com) allows you to scan restaurant menus, look inside certain hotels, and order free coupon books online. It also has an extensive list of attractions and links to dozens of useful, informative and/or fun New Orleans resources.

Newspapers and magazines

The *Times-Picayune,* New Orleans's only daily newspaper, offers plenty of dining reviews, music, and entertainment news and information on its Web site, www.nola.com. Check out the BourboCAM, which offers a glimpse of Bourbon Street, or scroll the comments of locals in the 24-hour Yat Chat room.

Gambit Weekly, the city's free alternative weekly paper, offers news, commentary, and staff picks for the best in local dining, music, theater, special events, and more. Its Web site, www.bestofneworleans.com, offers all of the above, as well as a calendar of special events and weekly music club listings.

OffBeat is a local magazine dedicated to the music and musicians of New Orleans and Louisiana, from Cajun to jazz to R&B, and beyond. Its Web site, www.offbeat.com, reproduces many of the columns and features of the magazine, which boasts a dedicated readership of loyal music fans from all over the world.

Transit information

The **Regional Transit Authority** (☎ 504-248-3900; www.norta.org) runs the city's public transportation. Its Web site offers a comprehensive look at bus routes, the St. Charles and Canal streetcar routes, and information on **VisiTour** passes.

Index

Accommodations Index

Restaurant Index

BUSINESS, CAREERS & PERSONAL FINANCE

0-7645-5307-0   0-7645-5331-3 *†

Also available:

- Accounting For Dummies †
  0-7645-5314-3
- Business Plans Kit For Dummies †
  0-7645-5365-8
- Cover Letters For Dummies
  0-7645-5224-4
- Frugal Living For Dummies
  0-7645-5403-4
- Leadership For Dummies
  0-7645-5176-0
- Managing For Dummies
  0-7645-1771-6

- Marketing For Dummies
  0-7645-5600-2
- Personal Finance For Dummies *
  0-7645-2590-5
- Project Management
  For Dummies
  0-7645-5283-X
- Resumes For Dummies †
  0-7645-5471-9
- Selling For Dummies
  0-7645-5363-1
- Small Business Kit For Dummies *†
  0-7645-5093-4

HOME & BUSINESS COMPUTER BASICS

0-7645-4074-2   0-7645-3758-X

Also available:

- ACT! 6 For Dummies
  0-7645-2645-6
- iLife '04 All-in-One Desk Reference
  For Dummies
  0-7645-7347-0
- iPAQ For Dummies
  0-7645-6769-1
- Mac OS X Panther Timesaving
  Techniques For Dummies
  0-7645-5812-9
- Macs For Dummies
  0-7645-5656-8
- Microsoft Money 2004 For Dummies
  0-7645-4195-1

- Office 2003 All-in-One Desk
  Reference For Dummies
  0-7645-3883-7
- Outlook 2003 For Dummies
  0-7645-3759-8
- PCs For Dummies
  0-7645-4074-2
- TiVo For Dummies
  0-7645-6923-6
- Upgrading and Fixing PCs
  For Dummies
  0-7645-1665-5
- Windows XP Timesaving
  Techniques For Dummies
  0-7645-3748-2

FOOD, HOME, GARDEN, HOBBIES, MUSIC & PETS

0-7645-5295-3   0-7645-5232-5

Also available:

- Bass Guitar For Dummies
  0-7645-2487-9
- Diabetes Cookbook For Dummies
  0-7645-5230-9
- Gardening For Dummies *
  0-7645-5130-2
- Guitar For Dummies
  0-7645-5106-X
- Holiday Decorating For Dummies
  0-7645-2570-0
- Home Improvement All-in-One
  For Dummies
  0-7645-5680-0

- Knitting For Dummies
  0-7645-5395-X
- Piano For Dummies
  0-7645-5105-1
- Puppies For Dummies
  0-7645-5255-4
- Scrapbooking For Dummies
  0-7645-7208-3
- Senior Dogs For Dummies
  0-7645-5818-8
- Singing For Dummies
  0-7645-2475-5
- 30-Minute Meals For Dummies
  0-7645-2589-1

INTERNET & DIGITAL MEDIA

0-7645-1664-7   0-7645-6924-4

Also available:

- 2005 Online Shopping Directory
  For Dummies
  0-7645-7495-7
- CD & DVD Recording For Dummies
  0-7645-5956-7
- eBay For Dummies
  0-7645-5654-1
- Fighting Spam For Dummies
  0-7645-5965-6
- Genealogy Online For Dummies
  0-7645-5964-8
- Google For Dummies
  0-7645-4420-9

- Home Recording For Musicians
  For Dummies
  0-7645-1634-5
- The Internet For Dummies
  0-7645-4173-0
- iPod & iTunes For Dummies
  0-7645-7772-7
- Preventing Identity Theft
  For Dummies
  0-7645-7336-5
- Pro Tools All-in-One Desk
  Reference For Dummies
  0-7645-5714-9
- Roxio Easy Media Creator
  For Dummies
  0-7645-7131-1

* Separate Canadian edition also available
† Separate U.K. edition also available

Available wherever books are sold. For more information or to order direct: U.S. customers
visit www.dummies.com or call 1-877-762-2974.
U.K. customers visit www.wileyeurope.com or call 0800 243407. Canadian customers visit
www.wiley.ca or call 1-800-567-4797.

SPORTS, FITNESS, PARENTING, RELIGION & SPIRITUALITY

0-7645-5146-9

0-7645-5418-2

Also available:

- Adoption For Dummies
  0-7645-5488-3
- Basketball For Dummies
  0-7645-5248-1
- The Bible For Dummies
  0-7645-5296-1
- Buddhism For Dummies
  0-7645-5359-3
- Catholicism For Dummies
  0-7645-5391-7
- Hockey For Dummies
  0-7645-5228-7

- Judaism For Dummies
  0-7645-5299-6
- Martial Arts For Dummies
  0-7645-5358-5
- Pilates For Dummies
  0-7645-5397-6
- Religion For Dummies
  0-7645-5264-3
- Teaching Kids to Read
  For Dummies
  0-7645-4043-2
- Weight Training For Dummies
  0-7645-5168-X
- Yoga For Dummies
  0-7645-5117-5

TRAVEL

0-7645-5438-7

0-7645-5453-0

Also available:

- Alaska For Dummies
  0-7645-1761-9
- Arizona For Dummies
  0-7645-6938-4
- Cancún and the Yucatán
  For Dummies
  0-7645-2437-2
- Cruise Vacations For Dummies
  0-7645-6941-4
- Europe For Dummies
  0-7645-5456-5
- Ireland For Dummies
  0-7645-5455-7

- Las Vegas For Dummies
  0-7645-5448-4
- London For Dummies
  0-7645-4277-X
- New York City For Dummies
  0-7645-6945-7
- Paris For Dummies
  0-7645-5494-8
- RV Vacations For Dummies
  0-7645-5443-3
- Walt Disney World & Orlando
  For Dummies
  0-7645-6943-0

GRAPHICS, DESIGN & WEB DEVELOPMENT

0-7645-4345-8

0-7645-5589-8

Also available:

- Adobe Acrobat 6 PDF
  For Dummies
  0-7645-3760-1
- Building a Web Site For Dummies
  0-7645-7144-3
- Dreamweaver MX 2004
  For Dummies
  0-7645-4342-3
- FrontPage 2003 For Dummies
  0-7645-3882-9
- HTML 4 For Dummies
  0-7645-1995-6
- Illustrator CS For Dummies
  0-7645-4084-X

- Macromedia Flash MX 2004
  For Dummies
  0-7645-4358-X
- Photoshop 7 All-in-One Desk
  Reference For Dummies
  0-7645-1667-1
- Photoshop CS Timesaving
  Techniques For Dummies
  0-7645-6782-9
- PHP 5 For Dummies
  0-7645-4166-8
- PowerPoint 2003 For Dummies
  0-7645-3908-6
- QuarkXPress 6 For Dummies
  0-7645-2593-X

NETWORKING, SECURITY, PROGRAMMING & DATABASES

0-7645-6852-3

0-7645-5784-X

Also available:

- A+ Certification For Dummies
  0-7645-4187-0
- Access 2003 All-in-One Desk
  Reference For Dummies
  0-7645-3988-4
- Beginning Programming
  For Dummies
  0-7645-4997-9
- C For Dummies
  0-7645-7068-4
- Firewalls For Dummies
  0-7645-4048-3
- Home Networking For Dummies
  0-7645-42796

- Network Security For Dummies
  0-7645-1679-5
- Networking For Dummies
  0-7645-1677-9
- TCP/IP For Dummies
  0-7645-1760-0
- VBA For Dummies
  0-7645-3989-2
- Wireless All In-One Desk Referen
  For Dummies
  0-7645-7496-5
- Wireless Home Networking
  For Dummies
  0-7645-3910-8

HEALTH & SELF-HELP

0-7645-6820-5 *†   0-7645-2566-2

Also available:

Alzheimer's For Dummies
0-7645-3899-3

Asthma For Dummies
0-7645-4233-8

Controlling Cholesterol For Dummies
0-7645-5440-9

Depression For Dummies
0-7645-3900-0

Dieting For Dummies
0-7645-4149-8

Fertility For Dummies
0-7645-2549-2

Fibromyalgia For Dummies
0-7645-5441-7

Improving Your Memory For Dummies
0-7645-5435-2

Pregnancy For Dummies †
0-7645-4483-7

Quitting Smoking For Dummies
0-7645-2629-4

Relationships For Dummies
0-7645-5384-4

Thyroid For Dummies
0-7645-5385-2

EDUCATION, HISTORY, REFERENCE & TEST PREPARATION

0-7645-5194-9   0-7645-4186-2

Also available:

Algebra For Dummies
0-7645-5325-9

British History For Dummies
0-7645-7021-8

Calculus For Dummies
0-7645-2498-4

English Grammar For Dummies
0-7645-5322-4

Forensics For Dummies
0-7645-5580-4

The GMAT for Dummies
0-7645-5251-1

Inglés Para Dummies
0-7645-5427-1

Italian For Dummies
0-7645-5196-5

Latin For Dummies
0-7645-5431-X

Lewis & Clark For Dummies
0-7645-2545-X

Research Papers For Dummies
0-7645-5426-3

The SAT I For Dummies
0-7645-7193-1

Science Fair Projects For Dummies
0-7645-5460-3

U.S. History For Dummies
0-7645-5249-X

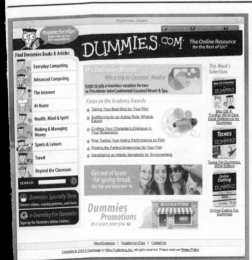

Get smart @ dummies.com®

- Find a full list of Dummies titles
- Look into loads of FREE on-site articles
- Sign up for FREE eTips e-mailed to you weekly
- See what other products carry the Dummies name
- Shop directly from the Dummies bookstore
- Enter to win new prizes every month!

* Separate Canadian edition also available
† Separate U.K. edition also available

Available wherever books are sold. For more information or to order direct: U.S. customers visit www.dummies.com or call 1-877-762-2974.
U.K. customers visit www.wileyeurope.com or call 0800 243407. Canadian customers visit www.wiley.ca or call 1-800-567-4797.